Music Theory Essentials

Music Theory Essentials offers an antidote to music theory textbooks that are overly long and dense. Focusing on the essentials, this text provides a clear-cut guide to the key concepts of music theory. Beginning with no assumptions about music theory knowledge, the book covers the core elements of music fundamentals, diatonic and chromatic harmony, post-tonal theory, and popular music in a single concise volume. Emphasizing critical thinking skills, this book guides students through conceptualizing musical concepts and mastering analytic techniques.

Each chapter concludes with a selection of applications designed to enhance engagement:

- **Exercises** allow students to apply and practice the skills and techniques addressed in the chapter.
- **Brain Teasers** challenge students to expand their musical understanding by thinking outside the box.
- **Exploring Music** offers strategies for students to apply learned concepts to the music they are currently learning or listening to.
- **Thinking Critically** encourages students to think more deeply about music by solving problems and identifying and challenging assumptions.

A companion website provides answers to book exercises, additional downloadable exercises, and audio examples.

Straightforward and streamlined, *Music Theory Essentials* is a truly concise yet comprehensive introduction to music theory that is accessible to students of all backgrounds.

Jason W. Solomon is Associate Professor of Music at Agnes Scott College, Georgia, USA.

Music Theory Essentials

A Streamlined Approach to Fundamentals, Tonal Harmony, and Post-Tonal Materials

JASON W. SOLOMON

NEW YORK AND LONDON

First published 2019
by Routledge
52 Vanderbilt Avenue, New York, NY 10017

and by Routledge
2 Park Square, Milton Park, Abingdon, Oxon, OX14 4RN

Routledge is an imprint of the Taylor & Francis Group, an informa business

© 2019 Taylor & Francis

The right of Jason W. Solomon to be identified as author of this work has been asserted by him in accordance with sections 77 and 78 of the Copyright, Designs and Patents Act 1988.

All rights reserved. No part of this book may be reprinted or reproduced or utilised in any form or by any electronic, mechanical, or other means, now known or hereafter invented, including photocopying and recording, or in any information storage or retrieval system, without permission in writing from the publishers.

Trademark notice: Product or corporate names may be trademarks or registered trademarks, and are used only for identification and explanation without intent to infringe.

Library of Congress Cataloging-in-Publication Data
CIP data has been applied for.

ISBN: 978-1-138-05250-5 (hbk)
ISBN: 978-1-138-05253-6 (pbk)
ISBN: 978-1-315-16774-9 (ebk)

Typeset in Caslon
by codeMantra

Visit the companion website: www.routledge.com/cw/solomon

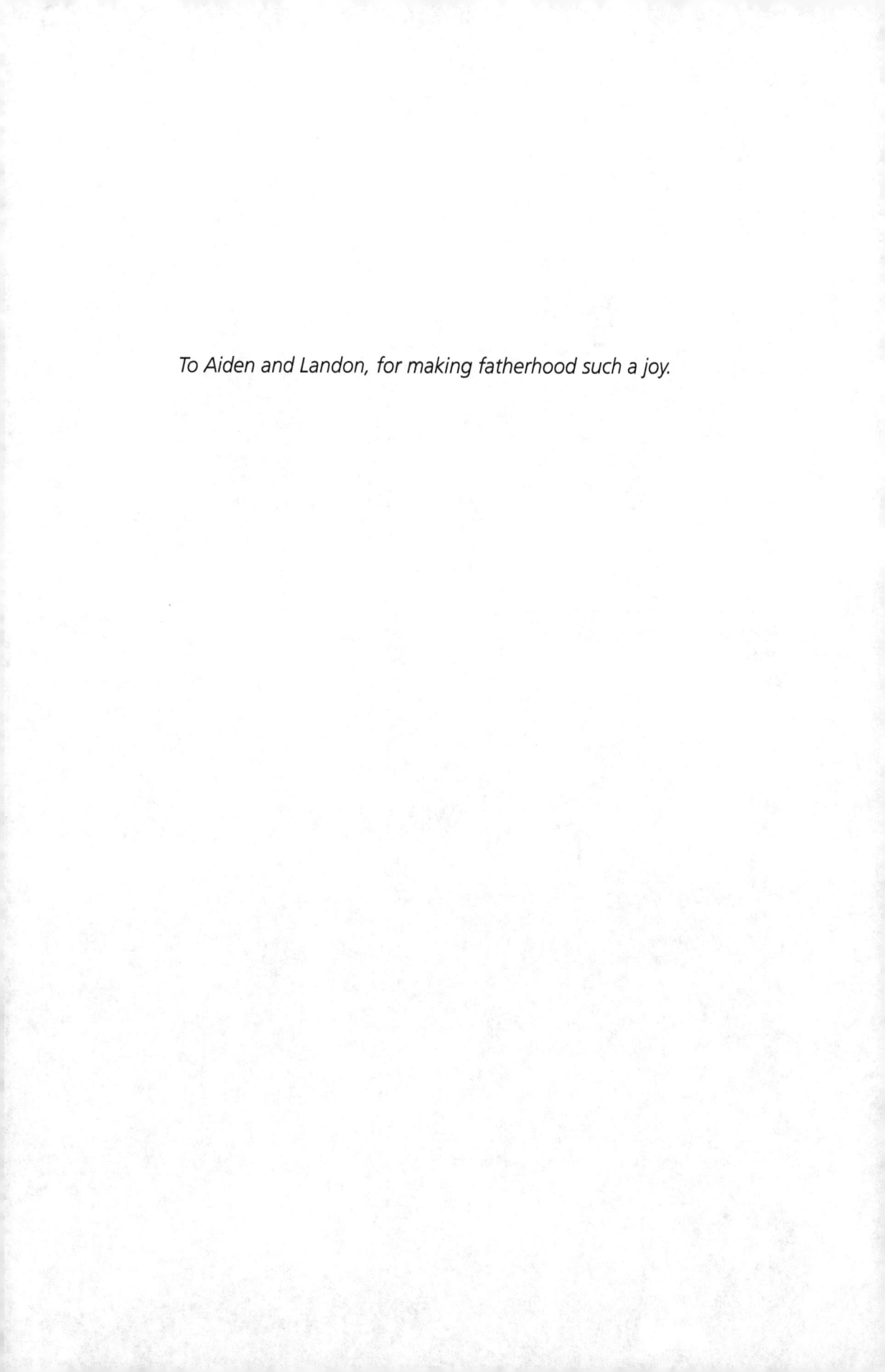

To Aiden and Landon, for making fatherhood such a joy.

Contents

Preface		xiii
Acknowledgements		xviii
PART I	**FUNDAMENTALS**	**1**
Chapter 1	**Pitch and Notation**	**3**
	Pitch	3
	The Notation of Pitch	4
	Accidentals	6
	Applications	8
Chapter 2	**Intervals**	**11**
	Classifying Intervals	11
	Recognizing and Labeling Intervals	12
	Enharmonic Intervals	16
	Compound Intervals	16
	Applications	17
Chapter 3	**Scales and Melody**	**20**
	Scales	20
	The Major Scale	20
	The Minor Scale	21
	Scale Degree Names	23
	Melody	24
	Applications	26

Chapter 4 Keys — 29
- Major Keys — 30
- Minor Keys — 33
- Determining the Key of a Musical Work — 34
- Parallel Keys — 34
- The Circle of Fifths — 35
- Applications — 36

Chapter 5 Chords — 39
- Triads — 39
- Seventh Chords — 40
- Diatonic Chords and Roman Numerals — 41
- Chord Position and Inversion Symbols — 43
- Labeling Diatonic Chords — 44
- Spelling Diatonic Chords — 46
- Chord Symbols — 47
- Applications — 48

Chapter 6 Musical Time — 51
- Beat — 51
- Tempo — 51
- Duration — 51
- Guidelines for Notating Durations and Rhythms — 54
- Meter — 55
- Time Signatures — 56
- Irregular Meters — 58
- Rhythm — 60
- Applications — 63

Chapter 7 Introduction to Voice Leading and Counterpoint — 66
- Motion Between Two Voices — 66
- Counterpoint — 67
- Applications — 71

PART II DIATONIC HARMONY — 75

Chapter 8 Four-Part Voice Leading — 77
- Four Voices in the Grand Staff (SATB) — 77
- Chord Voicing — 78

	Four-Part Voice Leading	80
	Labeling Chords in SATB Voicing	84
	The Fundamental Progression: I–V–I	85
	Applications	86
Chapter 9	**Nonchord Tones**	**89**
	Nonchord Tones Involving Two Steps	89
	Nonchord Tones Involving One Step and One Unison	90
	Incomplete Neighbors: Nonchord Tones Involving One Step and One Leap	91
	Other Nonchord Tones	92
	Identifying Nonchord Tones	93
	Applications	94
Chapter 10	**Tonal Function, Syntax, and Prolongation**	**96**
	Tonal Function	96
	Tonal Syntax: T–PD–D–T	98
	Prolongation	99
	Techniques of Prolongation	99
	Applications	101
Chapter 11	**Triad Inversions**	**105**
	First Inversion	105
	Second Inversion	109
	Applications	114
Chapter 12	**Seventh Chords**	**118**
	The Dominant Seventh Chord (V^7)	118
	The Leading-Tone Seventh Chord ($vii^{\varnothing 7}$ and vii^{o7})	122
	The Supertonic Seventh Chord (ii^7 and $ii^{\varnothing 7}$)	125
	Other Seventh Chords	126
	Applications	127
Chapter 13	**Motive, Phrase, Cadence, and Period Structure**	**130**
	Motive	130
	Phrase	132
	Cadence	132
	Period Structure	134
	Phrase Group	136
	Applications	137

Chapter 14 Harmonic Sequences — 140
- Fifths Sequences — 140
- Descending Thirds Sequence — 142
- Parallel $^6_3$ Chords — 143
- Applications — 145

PART III CHROMATIC HARMONY — 147

Chapter 15 Secondary Dominants and Tonicization — 149
- Secondary Dominant Seventh Chords — 150
- Secondary Leading-Tone Seventh Chords — 154
- Applications — 157

Chapter 16 Modulation I: Phrase Modulation and Diatonic Pivot Chords — 160
- Closely and Distantly Related Keys — 160
- Phrase Modulation — 161
- Diatonic Pivot Chord Modulation — 162
- Recognizing and Analyzing a Modulation — 164
- Applications — 165

Chapter 17 Modal Mixture — 168
- Modal Borrowing — 168
- Quality Conversion — 171
- Spelling Mixture Chords — 172
- Chromatic Mediants — 172
- Applications — 174

Chapter 18 The Neapolitan and Augmented Sixth Chords — 177
- The Neapolitan Chord ($\flat$II^6) — 177
- Augmented Sixth Chords (+6) — 179
- Chromatic Predominant Chords and Prolongation — 182
- Applications — 183

Chapter 19 Modulation II: Chromatic Pivot Chords, Enharmonic Reinterpretation, and Common-Tone Modulation — 188
- Chromatic Pivot Chords — 188
- Enharmonic Reinterpretation — 190
- Common-Tone Modulation — 195
- Applications — 197

Chapter 20	**Dominant Ninth Chords, Altered Dominants, and Embellishing Chords**	**199**
	Dominant Ninth Chords (V^9)	199
	Altered Dominant Chords ($V+$, V^7_+, V^{O7})	200
	Embellishing Chords (CT^O7 and $CT+6$)	202
	Applications	206
PART IV	**POST-TONAL AND POPULAR MATERIALS**	**209**
Chapter 21	**The Dissolution of the Tonal System**	**211**
	Progressive Tonality	211
	Ambiguity	211
	Unresolved Dissonance and Implied Tonality	212
	Dissonant Prolongation	214
	Suspended Tonality	215
	Applications	220
Chapter 22	**New Pitch Collections**	**223**
	The Diatonic Collection	223
	The Pentatonic Collection	226
	The Octatonic Collection	228
	The Whole-Tone Collection	231
	The Hexatonic Collection	232
	Applications	234
Chapter 23	**Centricity and Harmony**	**238**
	Centricity	238
	Harmony	240
	Applications	244
Chapter 24	**Set Theory**	**247**
	Pitch-Class Sets	247
	Transposition and Inversion of Pitch-Class Sets	249
	Set Class and Prime Form	250
	Segmentation	252
	Analysis	253
	Applications	257

Chapter 25 Serialism — 260
- Twelve-Tone Rows — 260
- Row Transformations — 261
- The Twelve-Tone Matrix — 262
- Analysis — 265
- Serialism: Beyond Pitch — 266
- Advanced Topics for Further Exploration — 267
- Applications — 267

Chapter 26 Introduction to Jazz and Pop Harmony — 270
- Sus Chords — 270
- Sixth Chords — 271
- Seventh Chords — 271
- Extensions: Ninths, Elevenths, and Thirteenths — 272
- ii–V–I — 275
- Chord Substitution — 276
- Form and Progression in Pop and Jazz — 279
- Applications — 282

Appendix: List of Set Classes — 285
Credits — 289
Notes on the Text — 291
Index of Musical Examples — 293
Index of Terms and Concepts — 295

Preface

Simplicity boils down to two steps: Identify the essential. Eliminate the rest.
—Leo Babauta

A number of music theorists recently lamented the current state of music theory textbooks in an online forum operated by the Society for Music Theory.[1] Most of the discussion centered on the mammoth size of recent texts. One observer stated, "Theory textbooks are too long—I think an optimal introductory textbook would be much shorter and more focused on the core information that students really need to remember." Another participant echoed this sentiment: "Beginning music theory students need a kind of Michelin Guide that is compendious rather than encyclopedic." Several theorists described abandoning textbooks altogether in favor of more concise, in-house materials. While these views are not universal among theory instructors, they reflect a palpable and growing dissatisfaction with the sheer length, thick text, and high cost of textbooks currently used in music programs throughout the United States.

In an attempt to account for every musical possibility, many theory texts include too many exceptional examples and occlude the *essential*. These books can be cluttered, wordy, and at times confusing for the student. When using an expansive and overly inclusive textbook, it can be challenging for the instructor—particularly one who is not a music theorist per se—to determine which topics are essential and which ones are not. Some might feel pressured to get through every section in a chapter, but doing so would require racing through the material or treating it in a superficial manner unbeneficial to the student. With a narrowed scope addressing the core aspects of music in a clear and concise way, *Music Theory Essentials* seeks to facilitate learning on the part of the student as well as teaching on the part of the instructor.

Music Theory Essentials presents a straightforward and streamlined approach to music theory instruction. To this end, lengthy paragraphs and dense prose are avoided in favor of short, explanatory passages and lists. Clear-cut illustrations of musical phenomena are paired with examples from the common-practice and popular-music repertoires. Musical examples have been carefully scrutinized and selected for their transparency, and the number of examples is limited for two reasons: first, to economize on space and cost; and second, to provide instructors with flexibility so that they might incorporate additional examples of their choosing. An extensive list of supplemental musical examples is available on the companion website, and instructors might couple this text with an anthology of complete musical works, a collection of short examples (e.g., *Anthology of Music for Analysis* by Timothy Cutler or *Music for Analysis* by Benjamin, Horvit, and Nelson), or the ever-growing number of online resources like the *Internet Music Theory Database* (www.musictheoryexamples.com) or *Music Theory Examples by Women* (www.musictheoryexamplesbywomen.com).

Music Theory Essentials is designed for the standard music theory sequence and is tailored to the liberal arts curriculum, where many students enter with little-to-no knowledge of music theory but a comprehensive and critical investigation of topics is expected. With roughly equal space devoted to fundamentals, diatonic harmony, chromatic harmony, and post-tonal/popular materials, this book's contents divide nicely into three or four semesters of study. However, music curricula vary widely in terms of content emphasis, pacing, and integration of areas of study (sometimes combining theory, history, and keyboard skills), and the flexibility of this textbook makes it well suited to a broad range of curricular approaches.

The study of fundamentals in Part I begins from ground zero, assuming no prior experience with music theory on the part of the student. The book proceeds with a logical ordering of topics, emphasizing tonal harmony in its central parts and concluding with an examination of post-tonal and popular materials. *Music Theory Essentials* covers a wide range of material in a succinct manner to eliminate the need for students to acquire separate textbooks for the study of fundamentals or post-tonal music. Although the sequence of topics is necessarily cumulative, instructors will find it relatively easy to reorder the presentation of chapter contents. For example, some instructors might want to teach musical time (Chapter 6) earlier in the term—perhaps to break up the discussion of pitch fundamentals. In addition, some instructors might find that Part I of the book can be used either sparingly, for review, or for student reference, particularly for sequences in which the first semester of theory presumes or requires considerable knowledge of fundamentals on the part of the student.

Rather than simply presenting musical concepts and analytic techniques, *Music Theory Essentials* guides the reader in conceptualizing its contents by suggesting specific strategies for learning and mastering skills. Step-by-step procedures are clear and easy to follow, and guided scenarios model the application of these steps. Memorization tips for recognizing notes on the staff in various clefs as well as processes for labeling diatonic chords and constructing twelve-tone matrices are just some of the strategies and techniques offered throughout the text. The particular tactics offered here are by no means the only ones available, and the instructor might offer their own strategies as supplements in an effort to equip each student with a set of different procedures from which to choose.

Selected Features of This Textbook:

- Comprehensive but concise coverage of the *essential* components of music theory, from fundamentals through post-tonal and popular music.
- Emphasis on harmonic function, so students learn not only what chords *are*, but also what they *mean* and *do* in the context of a chord progression.
- Novel, succinct chapter organization:
  - A single chapter (Chapter 10) introduces the concepts of tonal function and prolongation.
    - Closer examination of these topics permeates subsequent chapters.
  - Nonchord tones are discussed before chord inversions, as the latter are understood in terms of the former (e.g., the *passing* and *neighbor* six-four chords).
  - First and second inversions of triads are discussed in a single chapter (Chapter 11).
  - Chromatic Predominant chords ($\flat II^6$ and +6) are treated in the same chapter (Chapter 18).
  - Chapter 21 describes the systematic dissolution of the tonal system in an effort to contextualize the post-tonal trends and sounds that follow.
  - Individual chapters explore the basics of set theory (Chapter 24) and serialism (Chapter 25).
- Throughout the book, popular music is treated as an extension of the tonal system—not as a separate system or distinct musical language.
  - Chapter 26 explores unique features of popular music, with a particular focus on jazz harmony.
- Musical examples are limited and clear.
- Many chapters feature the *quick peek*, a single-staff summary of a chord's spelling, doubling, and resolution that precedes diagrams in four voices and examples from the literature.
- *Pitch-class wheels* (aka, clockface diagrams) are employed to model musical structures, relationships, and processes in pitch-class space—helping the reader to grasp abstract concepts through visual diagrams.
- Each chapter concludes with a set of four *Applications* to be used for practice, homework, group work, or class discussion:
  - *Exercises* allow the student to apply and practice the skills and techniques addressed in the chapter.

- - *Brain Teasers* challenge students to expand their musical understanding by thinking outside the box.
  - *Exploring Music* offers strategies for students to apply theory concepts to the music they are currently learning or listening to.
  - *Thinking Critically* encourages students to think more deeply about music by solving problems and identifying and challenging assumptions.
    - This section might be used for short writing assignments—an activity that is challenging to incorporate into the music theory classroom.
- Answers and discussion prompts for the Applications are provided in the *online component* to this textbook; the website also contains supplemental exercises corresponding to those in the book (answer keys to the supplemental exercises are available only to instructors).
- The website hosts the audio for musical examples as well as a robust list of supplemental musical examples.

Visit the companion website: www.routledge.com/cw/solomon

To the Student

What is Music Theory?

Music is the art of harnessing sound for expressive purposes, and theory is the science of music. At its core, music theory seeks to explain how music is put together, and how it *works*. Theory explains the workings of large-scale musical systems, such as the tonal system underlying more than four centuries of classical and popular musical practice, as well as the inner-workings and idiosyncrasies of specific musical works. In other words, theory can teach us what Beethoven and the Beatles have in common, but also what sets them apart.

So, what comes first: the music or the theory? In most cases, theory follows musical practice. Just as scientists continue to discover new facts about life and the world around us, theorists continue to find new ways to describe the structures and meanings of music. This is not to say that composers never use theory or devise their own theories to create music. However, most of our analytic techniques have been developed by music theorists who examine a large body of music to try and understand it, and explain it, better.

Why Do We Study Music Theory?

We study music theory in order to better understand music. As we improve our understanding of music, we enhance our ability to create music through performing, conducting, composing, or arranging. It helps to be fluent in the language of music in order to communicate effectively with other musicians. People sometimes draw a distinction between feeling and thinking about music. Perhaps these two modes of musical experience are somewhat distinct, but I believe they are intimately connected and that they inform and reinforce one another. Have you ever wanted to know why a certain song evokes certain emotions? Feelings might prompt you to analyze certain aspects of the song to answer such questions. Conversely, thinking about the elements and structures of the song might open up deeper levels of emotional interaction with the music. And that is perhaps the main benefit to studying music theory: better *understanding* leads to deeper *appreciation*, which enhances the *experience* of music.

Studying music theory also promotes critical thinking. Yes, there are terms to memorize and strategies to practice. Yes, some things are simply right or wrong. For example, there is only one way to correctly spell the key signature for E major. Part I of this book explores such fundamental musical concepts. However, beginning in Part II, some matters will require analysis and informed interpretation. For instance, a specific chord could be playing one of two different musical "roles" depending upon the harmonic context surrounding it. The study of music theory will not only train you to determine what a chord *is*, but also to interpret what that chord is *doing* in the music. And of course, exercising critical thinking reaches beyond the study of music and into many aspects of your life.

Note

1 The forum, *Smt-talk*, has since been replaced by *SMT Discuss*. The discussion thread referenced here can be found in the Smt-talk Archives: http://lists.societymusictheory.org/pipermail/smt-talk-societymusictheory.org/2012-April/thread.html#start

Acknowledgements

I would like to thank my wife, Qiao, and my sons, Aiden and Landon, for their patience and support during the writing process.

Thank you to my parents, Larry and Becky, who never flinched when I told them years ago I wanted to go to college to study music.

Thank you to my current and former students at Agnes Scott College, Western Carolina University, and Georgia Southern University. Your passion for music and eagerness to engage with it critically has inspired the conceiving, writing, and refining of this textbook, and has also shaped my thinking about music in general.

Thank you to the wonderful colleagues I have had the privilege of knowing and working with over the years. I especially want to thank my current colleagues at Agnes Scott College: Qiao Solomon, Tracey Laird, David D'Ambrosio, and Dawn-Marie James.

Many thanks to the anonymous readers who provided invaluable feedback during the early stages of this project, and also to the many friends, colleagues, and students who offered suggestions and corrections along the way.

Thank you to my friends and partners in the Georgia Guitar Quartet: Kyle Dawkins, Brian Smith, and Phil Snyder. We have been making music together for over two decades, and you have taught me much about music.

A big thank you to Adrian Childs for his friendship and expert mentorship.

Thank you to the following incredibly talented performers who recorded the musical examples (available on the companion website):

Amy Chang, Viola
Hyunjung Rachel Chung, Piano[1]
Barney Culver, Cello
David D'Ambrosio, Piano[2]
Adelaide Federici, Violin

Sungbae Kim, Tenor
Qiao Solomon, Violin
Tiffany Uzoije, Soprano

The majority of musical examples are performed by pianist David D'Ambrosio. David is one of the most thoughtful and sensitive musicians I have ever had the pleasure of knowing, working with, and listening to. David, thank you for your friendship and musicianship.

All musical examples were recorded and produced by Sungbae Kim at Studio Jeeb (Roswell, GA) and Maclean Recital Hall, Agnes Scott College (Decatur, GA). I thank Sungbae for the many hats he wore during the recording process, and for wearing each of them so very well.

Funding for the recording of musical examples was provided by the Holder Fund, an internal grant from Agnes Scott College. I am extremely grateful to the college, selection committee, and grant administrators for this award.

Finally, thank you to Genevieve Aoki, music editor at Routledge, for believing in this project, and also for her guidance and assistance during the writing process.

Notes

1 Examples 11.15, 12.4, 17.11, 19.8, 20.7, 21.1, 24.10.
2 All piano tracks *except* Examples 11.15, 12.4, 17.11, 19.8, 20.7, 21.1, 24.10.

Part I

Fundamentals

Part I introduces the fundamental elements of music. Chapter 1 explains the basics of pitch notation, including the staff, note names in various clefs, and accidentals. Chapter 2 examines intervals (two notes combined together) and offers strategies for their identification and spelling. The study of intervals is critical to subsequent chapters of this textbook and to musical understanding as a whole, as intervals are the building blocks of larger musical structures like scales and melodies (Chapter 3), keys (Chapter 4) and chords (Chapter 5). Chapter 6 explores various aspects of musical time, including tempo, meter, rhythm, and rhythmic notation. Chapter 7 begins to integrate elements of pitch and time and introduces important voice-leading concepts and procedures to be built upon throughout the remainder of this book.

1

Pitch and Notation

Pitch

Pitch refers to the perceived highness or lowness of a sound. Musical sound sources like vocal cords and guitar strings vibrate at various frequencies. The brain interprets frequency as pitch—the faster the rate of vibration, the higher the perceived pitch. Pitches combine to form structures such as melodies and chords.

A musical pitch is often referred to as a *note*. Notes are named with the first seven letters of the alphabet: A–B–C–D–E–F–G. This series of letters repeats throughout the pitch continuum; the pitch above G is another A. The pitches A through G, without any sharps (#) or flats (♭) attached to them, are the *natural notes*. The natural notes are the white keys of the piano.

The pitch continuum is divided into *octaves*. Each octave begins on C and contains the seven pitches ordered C–D–E–F–G–A–B. A numeric suffix indicates the octave designation of a pitch. Example 1.1 shows where each octave begins on the piano keyboard, extending from just below C1 to C8 (notes get higher from left to right on the keyboard). C4 is known as *middle C* and is located toward the center of the keyboard. The D above middle C is D4 (belonging to the same octave as C4), and the B below middle C is B3 (belonging to the octave below).

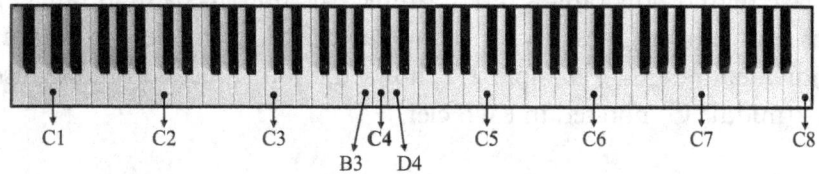

EXAMPLE 1.1 Octave and pitch locations on the keyboard.

All pitches with the same letter name sound similar because their frequencies are multiples of one another. For example, A4 vibrates at 440 Hz (hertz = cycles per second). A3 vibrates at half the frequency (220 Hz), while A5 vibrates twice as fast (880 Hz). All pitches with the same letter name belong to the same general *pitch class*. A3, A4, and A5 all belong to pitch-class A. However, because we hear A5 to be higher than A4, these are different specific pitches.

The Notation of Pitch

Music is notated on the musical *staff*. The staff contains five *lines* and four *spaces*. Pitches are represented as *noteheads* placed either on a line or in a space, as shown in Example 1.2. Higher sounding pitches are placed higher on the staff: the second pitch in Example 1.2 sounds higher than the first one.

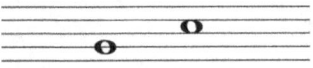

EXAMPLE 1.2   Two noteheads placed on the staff.

We can see from Example 1.1 that the musical pitch continuum is vast—the keyboard alone spans over seven octaves and contains eighty-eight pitches. The staff, however, has only five lines and four spaces—enough to accommodate only nine different noteheads. This limitation is overcome with ledger lines and a variety of different clefs. As shown in Example 1.3, *ledger lines* are short lines that extend the staff in either direction. In theory, ledger lines can be added indefinitely, but in practice, multiple ledger lines make reading notes extremely difficult.

EXAMPLE 1.3   Two noteheads placed on ledger lines above and below the staff.

Clefs are symbols appearing at the beginning of the staff that assign specific pitches to the lines and spaces (and ledger lines, by extension). Different instruments have high or low ranges. For example, the flute has a high range, and the tuba has a low range. These two instruments use different clefs to accommodate their individual ranges. Example 1.4 shows the four most commonly used clefs with C4 (middle C) notated in each clef.

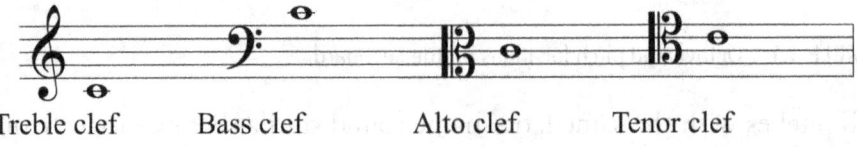

Treble clef   Bass clef   Alto clef   Tenor clef

EXAMPLE 1.4   The four common clefs with C4 notated.

The ***treble clef***, used for instruments with high ranges like the flute, is also known as the "G clef" because it loops around the line where G4 is located (see Example 1.5). The ***bass clef***, used by low instruments like the tuba, has two dots surrounding F3 and is often referred to as the "F clef." The ***alto*** and ***tenor clefs*** are identical symbols with different vertical orientations. These are referred to as "C clefs" because their central crooks pinpoint the location of C4.

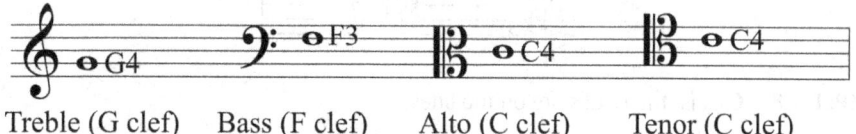

Treble (G clef)   Bass (F clef)   Alto (C clef)   Tenor (C clef)

EXAMPLE 1.5   The four clefs with reference pitches.

The letter names for pitches ascend on the staff, alternating lines and spaces. Example 1.6 places the natural notes of the C4 octave on a staff with the treble clef. The natural notes spanning from C to C form the ***natural scale***, which you might recognize as the C-major scale. Notice how G4 (identified by the clef's loop) can be used as a reference pitch: since G is on a line, the note in the space just below it is F and just above it is A. Now refer to the alto clef in Example 1.4, where C4 is notated on the middle line. What pitch is found on the next *line* up?[1]

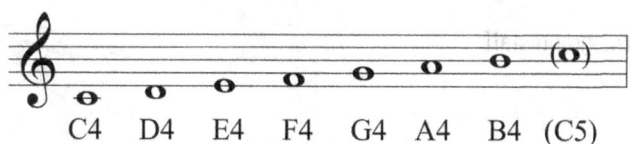

C4   D4   E4   F4   G4   A4   B4   (C5)

EXAMPLE 1.6   The natural scale: pitches of the C4 octave in the treble clef.

To identify pitches in the treble and bass clefs, remember: "the FACEs are in the spaces." As shown in Example 1.7, the pitches located in the spaces of the treble clef spell "FACE" going up. In bass clef, the entire FACE is shifted one space lower than in treble clef. Remember the location of FACE in each clef and you can easily determine the notes on the lines. For example, the note on the line between F and A is G.

EXAMPLE 1.7   Identifying treble and bass clef pitches: the FACEs are in the spaces.

Example 1.7 also labels the line notes in both clefs. While these sequences do not form an acronym like FACE, you can use a mnemonic such as "Every Good

Band Deserves Fans" for the line notes ascending in treble clef and "Good Bands Deserve Fans Always" for those in bass clef.

In both C clefs, FACE is located on the lines, as shown in Example 1.8.[2] The specific pitch C identified by FACE differs in each clef: in bass clef it is C3; in both C clefs, C4; in treble clef, C5.

EXAMPLE 1.8   C clefs: the FACEs are on the lines.

Keyboard instruments like the piano have wide ranges, so they use the grand staff. The *grand staff*, shown in Example 1.9, consists of two staves, each with a different clef. The right hand performs the music in the upper treble staff while the left hand plays the notes in the lower bass staff.

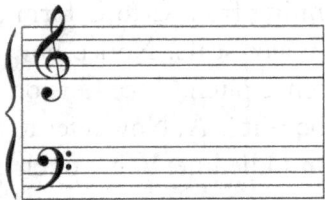

EXAMPLE 1.9   The grand staff.

Accidentals

Only seven letters (A through G) are used to name pitches, but there are a total of twelve pitches in every octave. The white keys of the piano account for the seven natural notes, and the black keys represent the other five pitches. Naming these five notes requires an accidental to be added to one of the seven letter names. ***Accidentals*** are symbols that raise or lower a pitch in half-step increments *without* changing the letter name of that pitch. A *half step* is the distance from one key on the piano to the next adjacent key, often going from a white key to a black key, or vice versa. The symbol, name, and effect of the five accidentals are listed in Example 1.10.

Symbol	Name	Effect on Note
♯	Sharp	Raises 1 half step
♭	Flat	Lowers 1 half step
♮	Natural	Cancels an accidental
×	Double Sharp	Raises 2 half steps
♭♭	Double Flat	Lowers 2 half steps

EXAMPLE 1.10   Accidentals.

The white keys C and D are labeled on the keyboard in Example 1.11. The black key situated between them is one half step *above* C and one half step *below* D. It can therefore be notated as either C♯ or D♭. The pitches C, C♯, D♭, and D♮ are projected from the keyboard and notated in the treble staff. The natural sign (♮) on the last note cancels the flat previously affecting D, returning D♭ to D♮. In musical notation, an accidental applied to a note remains in effect unless canceled out by another accidental (especially a ♮), or until a measure line is crossed.

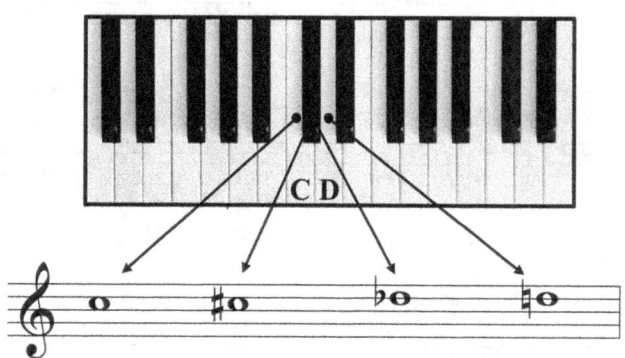

EXAMPLE 1.11 The black key between C and D spelled as both C♯ and D♭.

C♯ and D♭ are **enharmonic pitches**: they are spelled differently but sound exactly the same. This is similar to certain words in the English language. For example, "there" and "their" sound the same when spoken, but their spellings—and *meanings*—differ. In the context of a spoken sentence, we understand the intended meaning, but in writing, spelling matters. We shall soon discover how the musical context determines which enharmonic spelling of a pitch is most appropriate.

Double sharps (×) and double flats (♭♭) raise or lower a pitch by a total of *two* half steps, which equals one *whole step*.[3] Adding × to C raises the note one half step to the next black key (C♯) *plus* an additional half step to the next white key. Therefore, C× is enharmonic with D. What pitch is enharmonic with D♭♭?[4]

We can see in Example 1.1 that no black key lies between B and C or between E and F. These two pairs of natural notes are already one half step apart. This means that B♯ is enharmonic with C. What note is enharmonic with F♭?[5]

Finally, notice that we write "C♯" and say "C sharp," but when we notate pitches in the staff we always place the accidental *in front of* the notehead. It is important to place the accidental neatly on the exact same line or space as the notehead it precedes.

Applications

Exercises

1. Identify the following pitches with letter name and numerical octave designation. Identify the clefs at the beginning of each line.

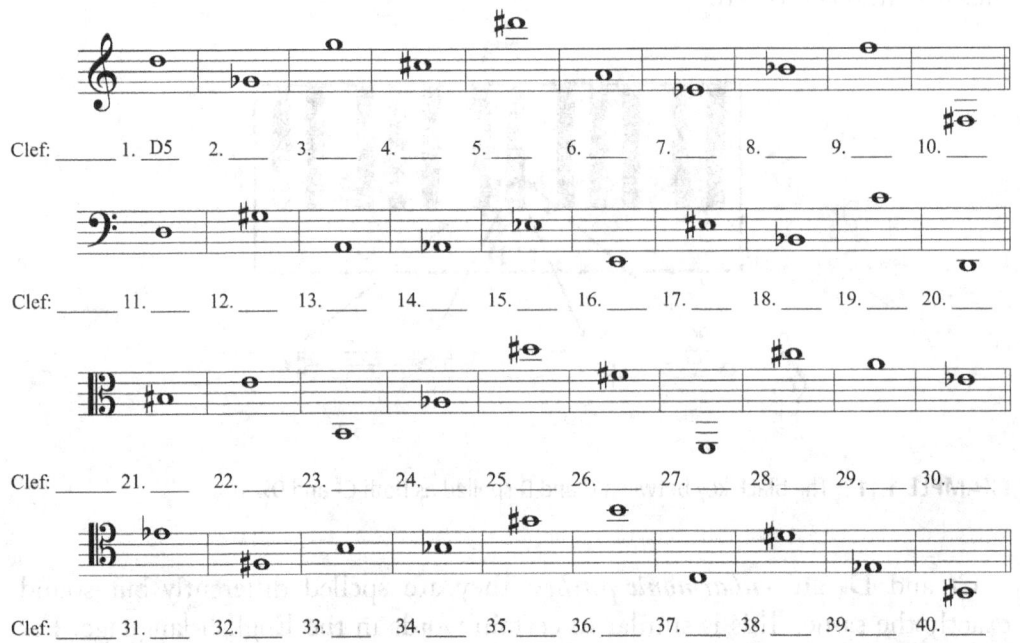

2. Notate the pitches. Use ledger lines as necessary.

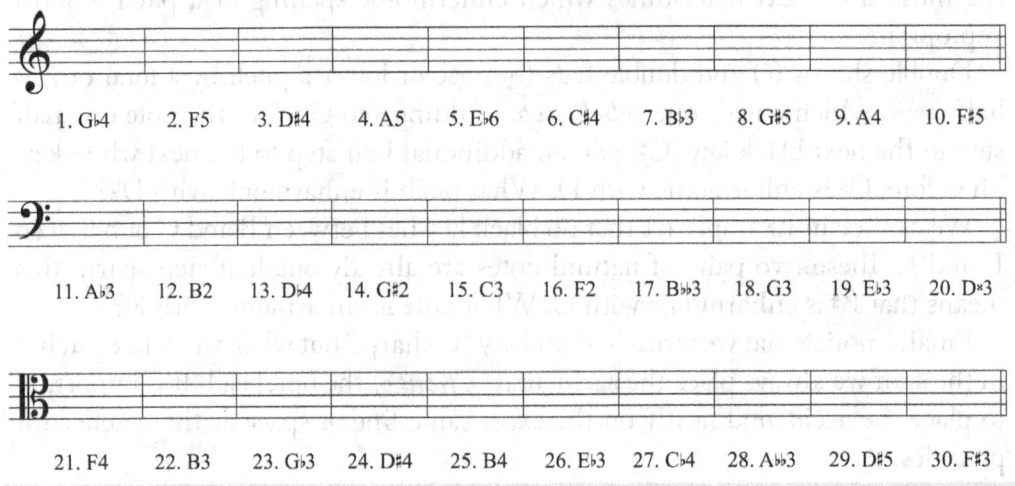

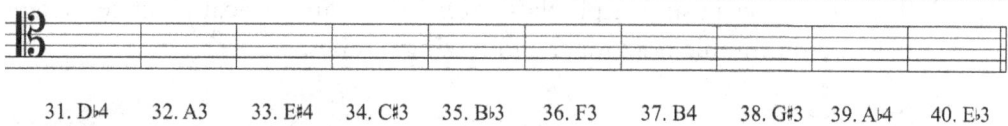

3. Determine the two enharmonic spellings for each of the five black keys in the C4 octave. Notate the two pitches in the staff and then write the names of the pitches below each note.

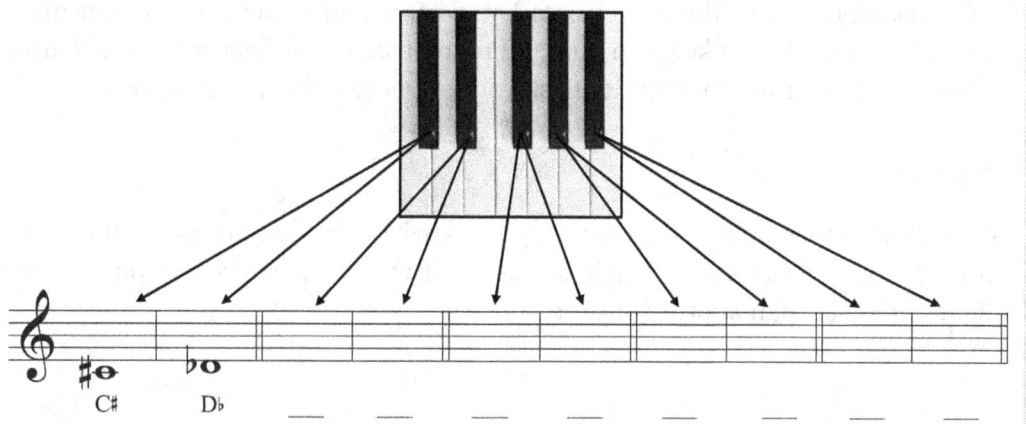

Brain Teasers

1. Label the pitch notated in the bass clef with the correct letter name and octave designation. Then re-notate the exact same pitch in the treble clef to the right.

2. Refer to Example 1.1. How would you label the pitch immediately below C1? Provide a letter name *and* numerical octave designation.

_____

3. While triple sharps and triple flats do *not* occur in musical practice, determine an enharmonic note for the following pitches:

   a. C♭♭♭ = _____
   b. A♭♭♭ = _____
   c. G𝄪♯ = _____

Exploring Music

Isolate a passage from a piece you are learning or one provided by your instructor. Label each pitch with the appropriate letter name and numeric octave designation. If the music has a key signature (a group of sharps or flats at the beginning of each line), your instructor might ask you to ignore it for this exercise.

Thinking Critically

Why do we experience pitches to be high or low? Pitches are not physical objects in space that we can see or touch, so how is it that we perceive one pitch to be higher or lower than another one?

Notes

1. The note in the space above C4 is D4, so the note on the next line up is E4.
2. Many musicians are fluent in either treble or bass clef (or both), but fewer play instruments that use a C clef. However, every musician should be able to read notes in all clefs. Fortunately, you can use your knowledge of the treble clef to quickly read notes in either C clef. When reading in the alto clef, determine what the note would be in treble clef and then think *up* one letter name. For example, in the treble clef the note on the middle line is B. Think *up* one letter name—this note is C in alto clef. When reading in tenor clef, think *down* one letter from what the pitch would be in treble clef—the note on the middle line is A in the tenor clef.
3. Half steps and whole steps are *intervals*, to be discussed in the next chapter.
4. D♭♭ is enharmonic with C.
5. F♭ is enharmonic with E.

2
Intervals

Combining two pitches together forms an *interval*. Intervals are the elemental building blocks of scales, melodies, and chords. The notes of a ***harmonic interval*** occur at the same time (Example 2.1a), while those of a ***melodic interval*** sound consecutively (Example 2.1b).

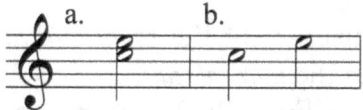

EXAMPLE 2.1 Harmonic interval (a) and melodic interval (b).

Classifying Intervals

Intervals are either ***consonant*** (stable) or ***dissonant*** (unstable). Dissonant intervals sound harsh and tend to resolve to consonant ones. An interval is labeled based on its *size* and *quality*.

Size

- The numeric name, indicated by ordinal numbers (second, third, fourth, etc.).
- Determined by counting the total number of lines and spaces between the two notes, *including* the lines and spaces the noteheads are on.
  - The intervals in Example 2.1 are both thirds: count the space for the lower note (C) as *1*, the D line above it as *2*, and the space for the upper note (E) as *3*.

Quality

- Specifies the *kind* of second, third, fourth, etc.
- Perfect (P), major (M), minor (m), augmented (+), or diminished (°).

Example 2.2 shows that consonant intervals are either perfect or imperfect. ***Perfect consonances***, the most stable class of intervals, include the perfect unison (P1), perfect fourth (P4), perfect fifth (P5), and perfect octave (P8). ***Imperfect consonances*** include thirds and sixths, which can be major or minor. ***Dissonances*** include seconds (m2, M2), sevenths (m7, M7), and all augmented or diminished intervals, including the tritone (+4, °5).

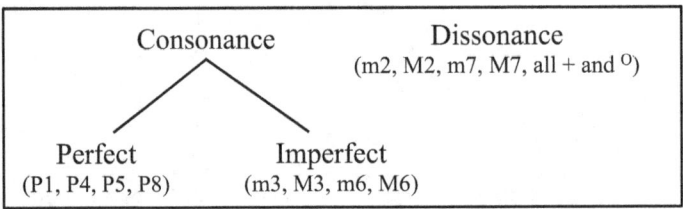

EXAMPLE 2.2   Interval categories.

Recognizing and Labeling Intervals

The three-step process outlined below is one of many approaches to learning and mastering intervals.

Step 1: Memorize the qualities of the *small natural intervals*—the seconds, thirds, and fourths found in the *natural scale*.

- *Seconds*: As depicted in Example 2.3, there are only two natural minor seconds (m2): E–F and B–C. The five remaining natural seconds are all major (M2): C–D, D–E, F–G, G–A, A–B.[1]
- *Thirds*: Example 2.3 highlights the three natural M3s: C–E, F–A, G–B. The remaining thirds are m3s: D–F, E–G, A–C, B–D.
- *Fourths*: F–B is an +4. All other natural fourths are perfect (P4): C–F, D–G, E–A, G–C, A–D, B–E.

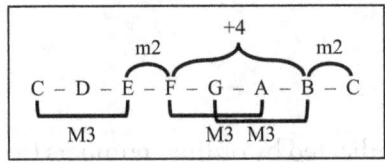

EXAMPLE 2.3   m2, M3, and +4 in the natural scale.

By memorizing the six intervals labeled in Example 2.3, you will know the remaining small natural intervals by default. For example: "G–A is a second and is *not* one of the two m2s, so it *must* be a M2."

Step 2: Apply knowledge of **interval inversion** to determine the *large natural intervals*: fifths, sixths, and sevenths.

To invert an interval, swap the position of its notes, either by moving the upper note down one octave or by shifting the lower note up an octave. In Example 2.4, the top note (E) of a M3 has been shifted down an octave to become the lower note of a m6. The same two notes, C and E, form each interval—the difference is which note is on bottom and which one is on top.

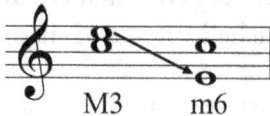

EXAMPLE 2.4 M3 inverted as m6.

Inverting Size: The size, or numeric name, of two intervals related by inversion will sum to 9. Above we inverted a *third* to form a *sixth* (3 + 6 = 9). Seconds invert into sevenths (2 + 7 = 9), and fourths invert into fifths (4 + 5 = 9). Example 2.5 summarizes the inversion of interval size.[2]

> Seconds ↔ Sevenths
> Thirds ↔ Sixths
> Fourths ↔ Fifths

EXAMPLE 2.5 The inversion of interval size.

Inverting Quality: Example 2.6 shows how inversion affects interval quality. Inverting a perfect interval results in another perfect interval. Inverting a major interval forms a minor interval, and vice versa, as we discovered above in Example 2.4. Inverting an augmented interval (+) yields a diminished interval (°), and vice versa. Above we learned that the only natural fourth that is *not* perfect is F–B, which is an +4. What is the inversion of this interval?[3]

> P ↔ P
> M ↔ m
> + ↔ °

EXAMPLE 2.6 The inversion of interval quality.

When you encounter a natural interval larger than a fourth, consider its inversion. Example 2.7 presents the interval F–E. Imagine or sketch its inversion, E–F (shown in parentheses). If you have memorized that E–F is a m2, and you understand that *any* m2 inverts as a M7, you will recognize F–E as a M7.

EXAMPLE 2.7 Calculating a large natural interval.

Inverting an interval may result in a change of *quality* but never in a change of *class*: the M3 and m6 in Example 2.4 are both classified as imperfect consonances; the M7 and m2 in Example 2.7 are both dissonances. Example 2.8

orders the intervals P1 through P8 from smallest to largest. The intervals expand by one half step (or m2) from left to right. The curved lines show how the intervals invert into one another: perfect consonances are connected with solid lines, imperfect consonances with dashed lines, and dissonances with dotted lines.

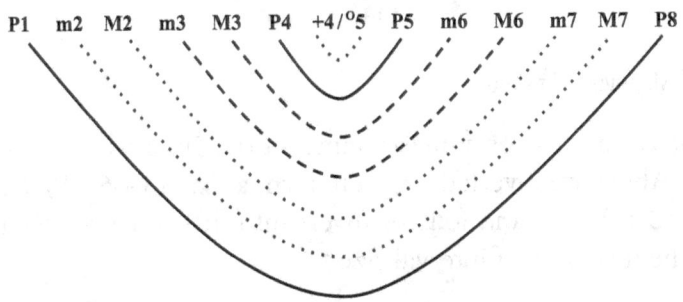

EXAMPLE 2.8 Inverting simple intervals.

Step 3: Understand how ***accidentals*** transform interval quality.

A ♯ raises a note by half step, and a ♭ lowers a note by half step. How do these accidentals affect interval quality? Example 2.9a shows the natural m3 B–D. Adding a ♯ to the top note *expands* the interval by one half step, so the m3 becomes a M3 (Example 2.9b). But adding a ♯ to the lower note draws it closer to the upper note, which *compresses* the interval by one half step, turning the m3 into a °3 (Example 2.9c). Adding a ♭ to the top note of the original m3 compresses it by half step to a °3 (Example 2.9d). Adding a ♭ to the lower note expands the interval, creating the M3 B♭–D (Example 2.9e).

EXAMPLE 2.9 Expanding and compressing a third with accidentals.

The intervals in Example 2.9 are different qualities of third. Adding accidentals to an interval transforms its quality but *does not change its size*. (In order to change size, the noteheads themselves must be moved.) Example 2.10 reveals how interval quality changes as an interval is expanded or compressed by half step.

$$\text{o} \leftrightarrow \text{P} \leftrightarrow +$$
$$\text{o} \leftrightarrow \text{m} \leftrightarrow \text{M} \leftrightarrow +$$

EXAMPLE 2.10 Transforming interval quality.

Example 2.11 shows the systematic expansion of a third as it transforms from °3 to +3. The natural sign (♮) added to the second interval cancels out the previous ♭, thereby raising the top note and expanding the interval.

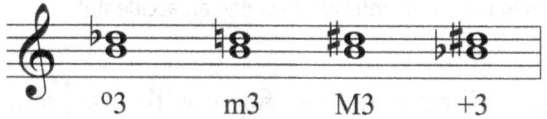

EXAMPLE 2.11 The gradual expansion of a third.

The last interval in Example 2.11 involves different accidentals added to each note: the ♯ on top and the ♭ on bottom pull the notes apart to augment the interval. What happens when the *same* accidental is added to both notes? Example 2.12 demonstrates that interval quality is *not* affected when either sharps or flats are added to both notes—the entire interval is simply boosted up or down by half step.

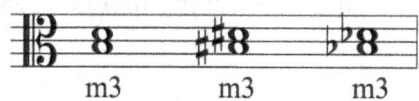

EXAMPLE 2.12 Adding the same accidental to both notes of an interval.

Putting It All Together

By combining knowledge of the small natural intervals, inversion, and how accidentals affect interval quality, we can identify any interval. Consider the second given in Example 2.13.[4] What is its quality? To begin, temporarily ignore the accidental and consider the interval in its "natural" form. B–C is a m2. Now factor the ♯ back in: since ♯ on the top note expands the interval, B–C♯ is a M2.

EXAMPLE 2.13 Determining a small interval containing an accidental.

Example 2.14 provides a large interval involving one accidental. To identify it, begin by inverting the interval and temporarily ignoring the accidental. (Sketch or imagine this process.) Doing so reveals E(♮)–G, which is a natural m3. Next, consider how small intervals invert: m3 inverts as M6, so G–E(♮) is a M6. Finally, factor the accidental back in: the ♭ on top compresses the interval to a m6. The original interval, G–E♭, is a m6.

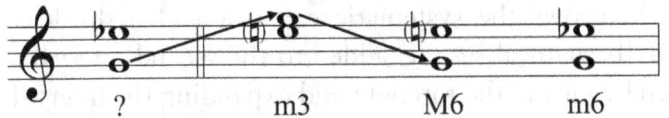

EXAMPLE 2.14 Determining a large interval involving an accidental.

With practice you will become more fluent with this process, and with experience you will eventually be able to recognize intervals without going through all the steps.

Enharmonic Intervals

In Chapter 1 we learned about enharmonic pitches—those that sound the same but are spelled differently, like C♯ and D♭. Consider the two intervals in Example 2.15, a m3 and an +2. These *enharmonic intervals* sound the same but have different spellings, and they will serve different musical functions.

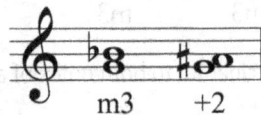

EXAMPLE 2.15 Enharmonic intervals.

Compound Intervals

So far we have been working with *simple intervals*—those smaller than an octave. *Compound intervals* are larger than an octave and may be thought of as a simple interval plus an octave.[5] The major ninth (M9) shown in Example 2.16 is a M2 plus an octave, or a "compound M2." A compound interval is classified based on its simple counterpart, so the M9 is a dissonance. A m10, which is a m3 plus an octave, is an imperfect consonance.

EXAMPLE 2.16 M9.

Applications

Exercises

1. Label each interval by its size and quality.

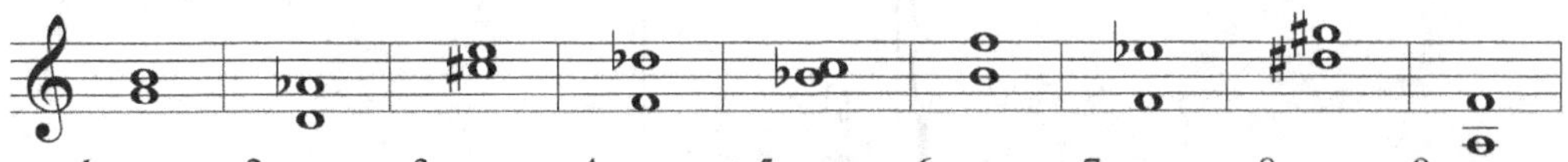

1. ___ 2. ___ 3. ___ 4. ___ 5. ___ 6. ___ 7. ___ 8. ___ 9. ___

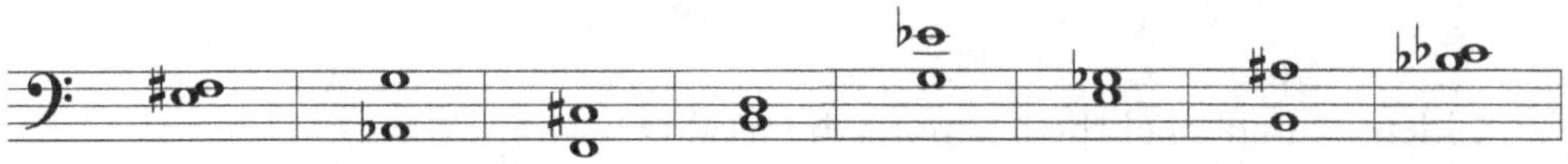

10. ___ 11. ___ 12. ___ 13. ___ 14. ___ 15. ___ 16. ___ 17. ___

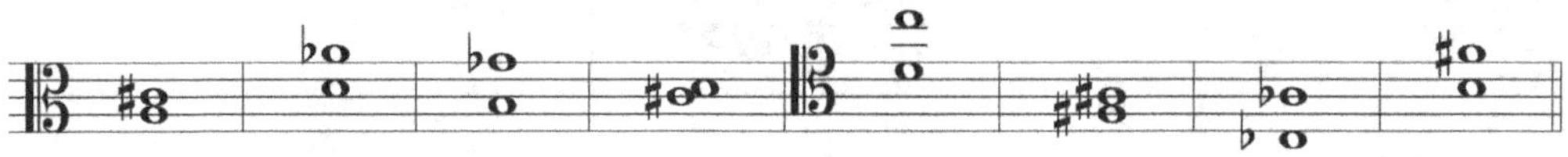

18. ___ 19. ___ 20. ___ 21. ___ 22. ___ 23. ___ 24. ___ 25. ___

2. Form the requested interval by adding the correct note *above* the given note.

1. M3 2. P4 3. m6 4. M2 5. M7 6. M6 7. °5 8. m3 9. m7 10. m2

3. Form the requested interval by adding the correct note *below* the given note.

1. M6 2. +4 3. m3 4. m7 5. m2 6. M3 7. P4 8. m6 9. M2 10. M7

Brain Teasers

1. If an interval and its inversion complete a perfect octave (P8), why do their sizes add up to 9? In other words, why do the sizes of complementary intervals (such as the M3 and m6 in Example 2.4) add up to 9 instead of 8?

2. Identify and label the harmonic interval below. Is there more than one option for classifying this interval?

3. Identify and label the harmonic interval below.

Exploring Music

1. Examine the score of a work of music that you play regularly or that you are currently learning. Of the *melodic* intervals present, are most of them small (seconds and thirds) or large (fourths and larger)? Select a passage and label a series of melodic intervals by their size and quality.
2. Practice listening to music and gauging the general size of the melodic intervals you hear. Do you hear more small or large intervals? What happens melodically after a large leap? As you learn to identify specific intervals, practice identifying them in everyday songs that you hear. For example, "Somewhere Over the Rainbow" begins with an ascending perfect octave.

Thinking Critically

1. Why is an +4 or °5 called the "tritone?"
2. Perfect consonances sound stable because the frequencies of their two pitches are in a simple ratio. For instance, the ratio for a P8 is 2:1, so if the upper note is vibrating at 440 Hz, the lower note is at 220 Hz. The ratio for the P5 is 3:2. At what frequency will the lower note of a P5 be vibrating if the upper note vibrates at 780 Hz?

Notes

1 A m2 is equivalent to a *half step*; a M2 is the same as a *whole step*.
2 All natural unisons are perfect, and a unison inverts as an octave (1 + 8 = 9).
3 A diminished fifth (°5).
4 Although the sharp is out in front of the entire interval, it is in the same space as the notehead C, so the notes involved are B(♮) and C♯. It is necessary for the noteheads to be touching one another to indicate that this is a harmonic interval (both notes sounding simultaneously).
5 The "small" and "large" intervals discussed previously are all simple intervals.

3
Scales and Melody

Scales

A scale is a linear ordering of notes in a pattern of whole steps and half steps. Scales are used to generate melodies and harmonies. Although there are many different kinds of scales, the diatonic major and minor scales form the basis of tonal music.

The Major Scale

In the previous two chapters we discussed the *natural scale*—the ordering of natural notes from C to C. Owing to its particular sequence of whole steps and half steps, the natural scale is a major scale; because it begins and ends on C, it is the C-major scale. Example 3.1 shows the C-major scale with each pitch numbered as a ***scale degree***.[1] Scale-degree numbers indicate a note's position within a scale.

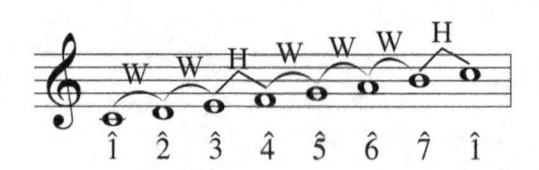

EXAMPLE 3.1 The C-major (natural) scale.

In the C-major scale, the natural half steps (m2) E–F and B–C fall between scale degrees $\hat{3}$–$\hat{4}$ and $\hat{7}$–$\hat{1}$. The distance between all other scale degrees is a whole step (M2). This pattern of whole steps and half steps, *W–W–H–W–W–W–H*, is what defines the major scale—it is the underlying structure shared by *all* major scales. When we apply this pattern beginning on a note other than C, one or more accidentals are needed. Example 3.2 shows a major scale beginning on D. Two sharps are applied to preserve the pattern of whole and half steps.

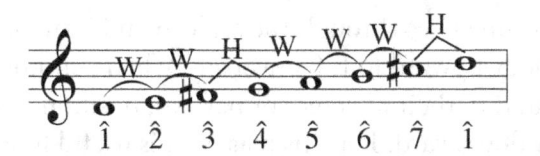

EXAMPLE 3.2 The D-major scale.

Compare the notes of the C-major scale in Example 3.1 with those of the D-major scale in Example 3.2. Although they feature five of the same notes (D, E, G, A, and B), these pitches are contextualized differently in each scale. In Example 3.1, D is $\hat{2}$; in Example 3.2, it is $\hat{1}$. The same pitch therefore has a different *meaning* in each scale, as reflected by the different scale-degree numbers assigned to it.

When a major scale requires more than one accidental, they will be all of the same kind—either all ♯s or all ♭s. Example 3.3 shows the A♭-major scale, which requires multiple flats to preserve the *W–W–H–W–W–W–H* pattern.

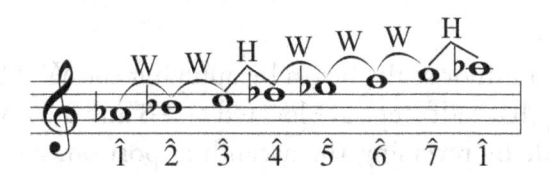

EXAMPLE 3.3 The A♭-major scale.

The Minor Scale

The minor scale involves a different pattern of whole and half steps: *W–H–W–W–H–W–W*. Example 3.4 applies this pattern beginning on the pitch A. Half steps are located between $\hat{2}$–$\hat{3}$ and $\hat{5}$–$\hat{6}$.[2]

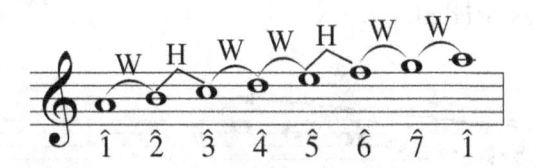

EXAMPLE 3.4 The A-minor scale.

The minor scale is more complicated than major because two of its scale degrees are variable. In many musical situations, accidentals are applied to raise $\hat{6}$ and $\hat{7}$ by one half step. In Example 3.5, the A-minor scale is shown with these variable scale degrees.

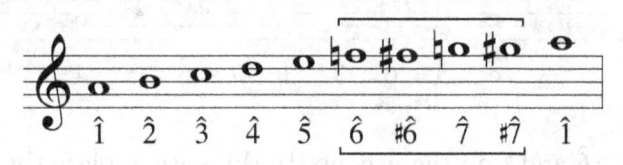

EXAMPLE 3.5 The A-minor scale with variable $\hat{6}$ and $\hat{7}$.

When a melodic line rises through the scale, $\hat{6}$ and $\hat{7}$ are often raised, as if they are lifting the melody upward to $\hat{1}$. Conversely, when a minor melody descends, $\hat{6}$ and $\hat{7}$ are often found in their lowered, or natural, positions, as if they are sinking to pull the melody downward. For this reason, it is useful to write the minor scale both ascending and descending, as shown in Example 3.6. The ascending leg of the scale features raised $\hat{6}$ and $\hat{7}$, and the descending form features the lowered $\hat{6}$ and $\hat{7}$ (the ♮s cancel out the previous sharps and return the scale degrees to their "natural" positions).[3]

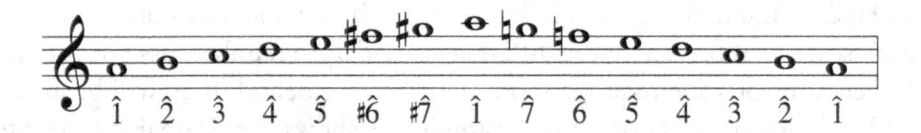

EXAMPLE 3.6 The A-minor scale ascending and descending.

When writing a minor scale, begin by applying the W–H–W–W–H–W–W pattern, ensuring that half steps are located at $\hat{2}$–$\hat{3}$ and $\hat{5}$–$\hat{6}$. Write the descending leg of the scale by reversing the ascending portion. Next, raise $\hat{6}$ and $\hat{7}$ by one half step in the ascending portion of the scale. This might involve adding ♯s to these notes or removing a ♭ and replacing it with a ♮. Finally, in the descending portion of the scale, ensure that $\hat{6}$ and $\hat{7}$ are in their natural positions—each a half step lower than in the ascending part of the scale. This might entail leaving a flat in place and/or adding a ♮ to cancel out a previous ♯. Example 3.7 demonstrates this step-by-step process with the G-minor scale.

Step 1: Apply the W–H–W–W–H–W–W pattern ascending from G. Use accidentals as needed.

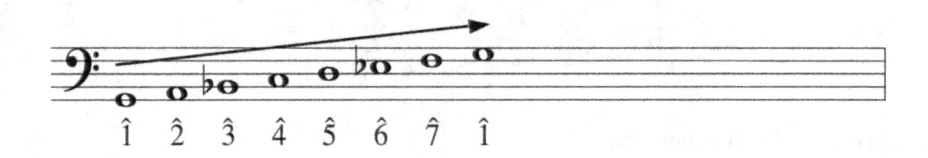

Step 2: Add the descending portion of the scale.

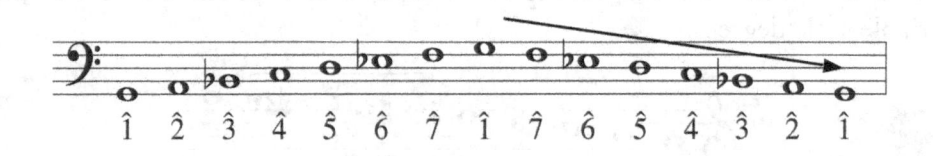

Step 3: Raise $\hat{6}$ and $\hat{7}$ on the way up. In this case, replace the ♭ on E with a ♮, then add a ♯ to F.

Step 4: Return $\hat{6}$ and $\hat{7}$ to their natural positions on the way down. In this case, place a ♮ on F (to indicate that it is no longer F♯), and leave the ♭ on E (in Step 3 it was raised in the ascending leg, so it is still in its natural position in the descending leg).

EXAMPLE 3.7 Spelling the G-minor scale.

Scale Degree Names

The names of the scale degrees are given in Example 3.8. The ***tonic*** ($\hat{1}$), which functions as the musical focal point, or "center of gravity," is placed in the middle of the diagram. The other scale degrees "orbit" the tonic and are named based on their location relative to $\hat{1}$. The ***dominant*** ($\hat{5}$) is a P5 *above* $\hat{1}$, and the ***subdominant*** ($\hat{4}$) is a P5 *below* the tonic.[4] The ***mediant*** ($\hat{3}$) is a third above the tonic, the ***submediant*** ($\hat{6}$) a third below. The ***supertonic*** ($\hat{2}$) is a step above $\hat{1}$.[5] Finally, $\hat{7}$ is called the ***leading tone*** ($\hat{7}$) when it is a m2 below tonic. When it is a M2 below $\hat{1}$, as in the descending portion of the minor scale, $\hat{7}$ is referred to as the ***subtonic***.

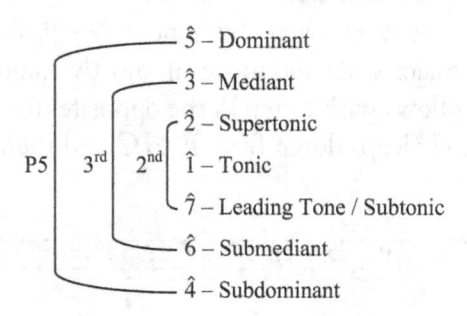

$\hat{5}$ – Dominant
$\hat{3}$ – Mediant
$\hat{2}$ – Supertonic
$\hat{1}$ – Tonic
$\hat{7}$ – Leading Tone / Subtonic
$\hat{6}$ – Submediant
$\hat{4}$ – Subdominant

EXAMPLE 3.8 Scale degree names.

As demonstrated in previous examples, scales are typically written from $\hat{1}$ to $\hat{1}$ spanning one octave. In Example 3.9, the C-major and C-minor scales are shown with scale degrees arrayed around the central tonic and their exact intervallic distances from $\hat{1}$ labeled. When $\hat{6}$ and $\hat{7}$ are raised in minor, their names and distances below $\hat{1}$ match $\hat{6}$ and $\hat{7}$ in major. For example, raising $\hat{7}$ in minor changes the subtonic to the leading tone (B♭ ↗ B♮ in C minor).

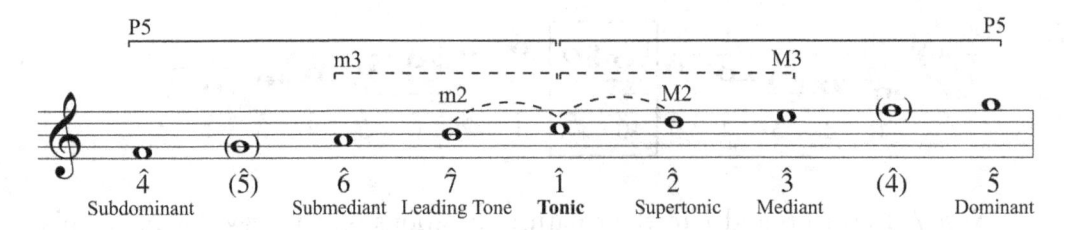

EXAMPLE 3.9A The C-major scale with $\hat{1}$ at the center.

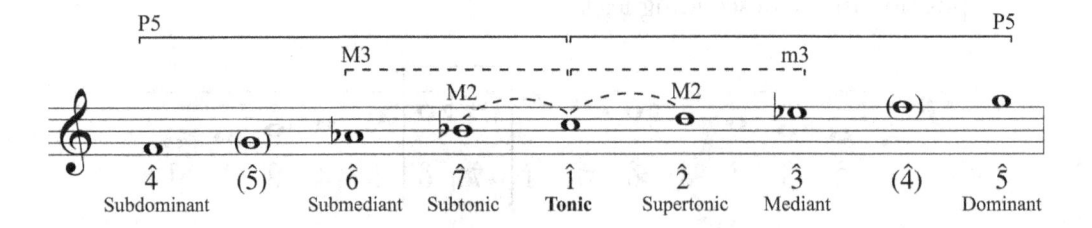

EXAMPLE 3.9B The C-minor scale with $\hat{1}$ at the center.

Melody

A *melody* is a unique ordering of notes from a specific scale. Melodies involve various kinds of motion and typically feature a distinctive rhythm (a topic addressed in Chapter 6).

When a melody note moves to an adjacent scale degree, as when $\hat{4}$ moves either down to $\hat{3}$ or up to $\hat{5}$, the melodic motion is **conjunct**, or *stepwise*. When a melody *leaps*—skipping over one or more scale degrees—the motion is **disjunct**. Most melodies involve a combination of conjunct and disjunct motion, but conjunct motion typically predominates.

The familiar theme from Beethoven's Symphony No. 9, shown in Example 3.10, uses notes from the C-major scale and moves in mostly conjunct motion.[6] When a melody leaps, it often follows with a step in the opposite direction. In measure 9 of Example 3.10, the melody leaps down from E to C and then steps up to D.

EXAMPLE 3.10 Theme from Beethoven's Symphony No. 9, IV.

Some scale degrees have melodic *tendencies*—they tend to move in a certain direction to a specific scale degree. All scale degrees are drawn to $\hat{1}$, which explains why melodies frequently end on $\hat{1}$. We might imagine that $\hat{1}$ exerts a strong gravitational pull or magnetic attraction on the other scale degrees. In particular, $\hat{7}$ has a strong tendency to *lead* to $\hat{1}$—hence its name, the *leading* tone. Because they are separated by only a m2, the attraction between $\hat{1}$ and $\hat{7}$ is particularly strong.

Melodies often end in a stepwise, descending manner, as if gravity pulls the melody down to rest on $\hat{1}$. Many melodies begin on $\hat{3}$ or $\hat{5}$, move among various scale degrees, and ultimately settle on $\hat{1}$. As $\hat{1}$ can be thought of as a melodic goal, melodies sound complete, or finished, when they reach this goal. So, although a melody might exhibit some local ascents, the global, long-range melodic motion is a broad descent from either $\hat{3}$ or $\hat{5}$ to $\hat{1}$. This is the case in Example 3.10, where the melody begins on $\hat{3}$, rises quickly to $\hat{5}$, weaves its way up and down the scale, and eventually closes with a stepwise descent from $\hat{2}$ to $\hat{1}$.

Minor Melodies

Minor melodies involve the variable $\hat{6}$ and $\hat{7}$. When a minor melody rises by step from $\hat{5}$ to $\hat{1}$, $\hat{6}$ and $\hat{7}$ are usually raised. Raising $\hat{7}$ in minor draws it nearer to $\hat{1}$, increasing the attraction between these scale degrees as well as the likelihood that $\hat{7}$ will move to $\hat{1}$.[7] Raising $\hat{6}$ along with $\hat{7}$ avoids an +2 between $\hat{6}$ and the leading tone. If the melody rises from $\hat{5}$ but only makes it to $\hat{6}$ or $\hat{7}$ before returning to $\hat{5}$, $\hat{6}$ and $\hat{7}$ might remain in their natural positions. Conversely, when a melody descends by step from $\hat{1}$ down to $\hat{5}$, $\hat{7}$ and $\hat{6}$ are likely to remain natural. But if the line falls from $\hat{1}$ to either $\hat{7}$ or $\hat{6}$ and then rises back to $\hat{1}$, $\sharp\hat{6}$ and $\sharp\hat{7}$ are likely to be found.

Expanding on the analogy to gravity might clarify these melodic tendencies. For a line to ascend from $\hat{5}$ to $\hat{1}$, a certain *force* must be applied to raise $\sharp\hat{6}$ and $\sharp\hat{7}$ and propel the melody upward to $\hat{1}$. If the melody rises from $\hat{5}$ to $\natural\hat{6}$ or $\natural\hat{7}$, then the line lacks the momentum to attain $\hat{1}$ and drops back down to $\hat{5}$. Similarly, when a line descends from $\hat{1}$ and travels through $\natural\hat{7}$ and $\natural\hat{6}$, the *weight* of these naturally low scale degrees sinks the melody down to $\hat{5}$. But if it tries to descend through $\sharp\hat{7}$ and $\sharp\hat{6}$, the melody meets the counterforce that was necessary to raise those degrees in the first place and is driven back up to $\hat{1}$. The melody in Example 3.11 is created from the A-minor scale and demonstrates these melodic tendencies.

EXAMPLE 3.11 Minor melody.

Applications

Exercises

1. Spell the following major scales ascending from $\hat{1}$ to $\hat{1}$ and spanning one octave. Apply accidentals to notes as needed (do not use a key signature).

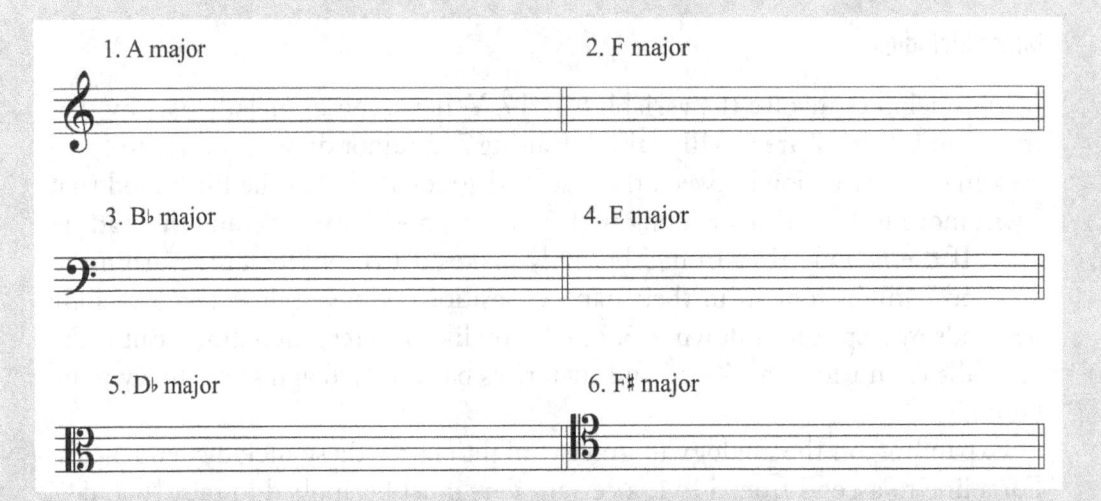

   1. A major
   2. F major
   3. B♭ major
   4. E major
   5. D♭ major
   6. F♯ major

2. Spell the following minor scales ascending and descending within one octave. Raise $\hat{6}$ and $\hat{7}$ when ascending from $\hat{1}$ to $\hat{1}$, and use the lowered (or natural) $\hat{6}$ and $\hat{7}$ when descending back to $\hat{1}$. Apply accidentals to notes as needed (do not use a key signature). Remember that accidentals remain in effect unless canceled by another accidental (such as ♮) or until a measure line is crossed.

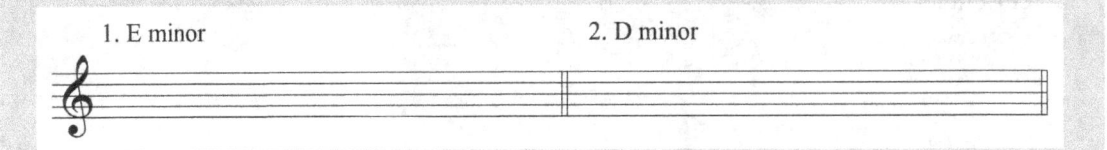

   1. E minor
   2. D minor

3. F♯ minor   4. G♯ minor

5. C minor   6. F minor

Brain Teasers

1. Spell an F♭ major scale. Apply accidentals to notes as needed (do not use a key signature).

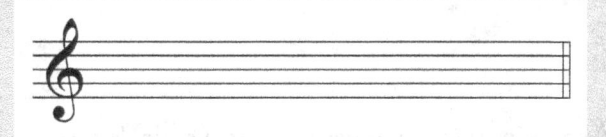

2. Spell an E♯ minor scale. Raise $\hat{6}$ and $\hat{7}$ when ascending and use the lowered (or natural) $\hat{6}$ and $\hat{7}$ when descending. Apply accidentals to notes as needed (do not use a key signature).

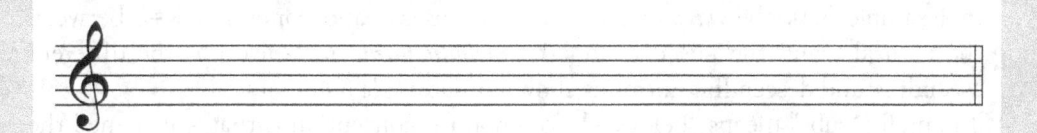

Exploring Music

1. Analyze minor-mode melodies provided by your instructor. Circle $\hat{1}$ each time it occurs (in any octave). Make a note of other scale degrees that receive emphasis through repetition. Identify and mark the variable $\hat{6}$ and $\hat{7}$. Describe the specific musical situations in which these scale degrees are raised, as well as those in which they remain in their natural positions.
2. Compose a melody using the C-major scale. Apply the melodic tendencies discussed throughout this chapter. As you are composing, play or sing the notes of your melody. The process of composing a melody involves trial and error, so use your ears to evaluate and edit your progress. Try ending the melody on $\hat{7}$ and see (or hear) what you think!

Thinking Critically

Throughout this chapter, metaphors of musical *forces* are evoked to describe melodic motion and the tendencies of scale degrees: "*gravity* pulls the melody down to rest on $\hat{1}$"; "$\hat{1}$ exerts a strong *gravitational pull* or *magnetic attraction* on the other scale degrees"; "raising $\hat{7}$ in minor draws it nearer to $\hat{1}$, increasing the *attraction* between these scale degrees as well as the likelihood that $\hat{7}$ will move to $\hat{1}$." Do these metaphors accurately describe our experience of music? When you listen to music, do you feel or sense these musical forces at work? Can you think of other forces besides gravity and magnetism that might account for musical processes and our experience of those processes?

Notes

1 The caret (^) specifies that a number refers to a scale degree.
2 The minor scale beginning on A is a rotation of the C-major (natural) scale: it is the natural notes ordered A–A.
3 Music theory traditionally describes three different forms of the minor scale: the **natural minor scale** (not to be confused with the *natural scale* discussed throughout this book) is the W–H–W–W–H–W–W pattern beginning on any pitch (as shown in Example 3.4); the **harmonic minor scale** raises $\hat{7}$ and contains an +2 between the natural $\hat{6}$ and the raised $\hat{7}$; and the **melodic minor scale** features the different ascending and descending forms as shown in Example 3.6.
4 The prefix "sub-" means "below." A common misconception is that $\hat{4}$ is named the subdominant because it is the scale degree immediately below $\hat{5}$.
5 The prefix "super-" means "above."
6 The original melody is in D major. This tune is also known as the "Ode to Joy."
7 As two oppositely charged magnets are brought closer together, the magnetic attraction between them grows stronger.

4

Keys

A *key* designates a pitch as the tonal center ($\hat{1}$) and contextualizes other pitches as scale degrees around that center. Keys correspond to the major and minor scales. A musical work in the key of E major, for example, fixes E as tonic and derives its melodic and harmonic material primarily from the E-major scale.

To simplify notation, the accidentals necessary to spell the scale associated with a key are placed at the beginning of the staff as a *key signature*. Example 4.1 shows the E-major scale.

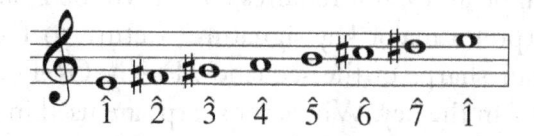

EXAMPLE 4.1 The E-major scale.

In Example 4.2, the four sharps used to spell the E-major scale are arranged in a specific order. This is the key signature for E major. With this key signature in place, performers know that *every* F, C, G, and D encountered in the staff should be raised—performed as F♯, C♯, G♯, and D♯.

EXAMPLE 4.2 The key signature for E major.

The E-major scale in Example 4.3 is notated with a key signature and sounds identical to the scale in Example 4.1.

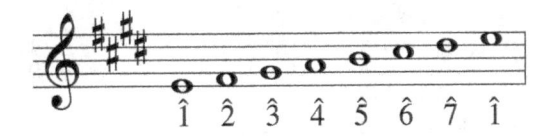

EXAMPLE 4.3 The E-major scale with key signature.

Major Keys

In Chapter 3 we learned that some major scales require ♯s and others require ♭s. A key signature, then, involves a grouping of either ♯s or ♭s. Those requiring ♯s are referred to as *sharp keys*, and those using ♭s are *flat keys*. The complete ordering of sharps, ***F♯–C♯–G♯–D♯–A♯–E♯–B♯***, is notated in Example 4.4. The sharps begin with F♯ and ascend by P5.

EXAMPLE 4.4 The ordering of sharps.

Any grouping of ♯s in a key signature proceeds in this order. If a key signature requires one ♯, it will be an F♯; if it requires two, it will be F♯ and C♯; and so on.

How do we interpret a major key signature? Return to Example 4.2, which contains the first four sharps of the sequence: F♯–C♯–G♯–D♯. The last sharp in the signature, D♯, is $\hat{7}$ in the key. Whenever sharps are used in a major key signature, the last sharp is *always* $\hat{7}$. Simply think up a m2 from this sharp to determine the major key: a m2 up from D♯ is E.

Memorize the sequence of sharps (you might devise a mnemonic to help you remember it). In addition, practice writing the sharps in the various clefs, as shown in Example 4.5. Pay careful attention to the exact octave placement of each sharp in the different clefs. The overall shape of the sequence is the same in the treble, bass, and alto clefs, but it differs in the tenor clef.

EXAMPLE 4.5 The sequence of sharps in the four clefs.

Flat keys use the following sequence of flats: ***B♭–E♭–A♭–D♭–G♭–C♭–F♭***. The ordering of flats is the sequence of sharps *reversed*, as shown in Example 4.6. Whereas the sharps progress by *ascending* P5, the flats are ordered by *descending* P5.

Sharps →
F – C – G – D – A – E – B
← Flats

EXAMPLE 4.6 The sequence of sharps (left to right) and flats (right to left).

Example 4.7 shows the sequence of ♭s in all four clefs. The overall shape of this sequence is the same across the clefs. Memorize the sequence of flats and practice writing it in each clef.

EXAMPLE 4.7 The sequence of flats in the four clefs.

For major keys involving flats, the second-to-last flat in the signature indicates $\hat{1}$. Example 4.8 shows a signature with four ♭s: B♭–E♭–A♭–D♭. Since the second-to-last flat is A♭, this is the key signature for A♭ major.

EXAMPLE 4.8 The key signature for A♭ major.

The key signature for F major involves only one flat (B♭) and is shown in Example 4.9. Since there is no second-to-last flat in this case, it is best to memorize this signature.[1] F major is the *only* major key involving flats that does not have a flat note as $\hat{1}$.

EXAMPLE 4.9 The key signature for F major.

Spelling Major Key Signatures

We will now explore how to write signatures for major keys. The key signature for C major is blank—it requires no ♯s or ♭s. Sharps are needed for a signature whenever $\hat{1}$ of the key is either a natural note other than C or F (e.g., G major), *or* a sharp note (F♯ major). To spell the signature for any sharp key, begin writing the sequence of sharps and stop once the ♯ representing $\hat{7}$ in the key has been listed. The following two scenarios model this process.

Scenario 1: **Spell the key signature for A major.**

Step 1: $\hat{1}$ is a natural note (A) other than C or F, so this is a sharp key.
Step 2: A m2 below A is G♯; G♯ is $\hat{7}$ in the key of A major.
Step 3: Begin writing the sequence of ♯s and proceed until G♯ is reached. Only the first three ♯s are needed, as shown in Example 4.10.

EXAMPLE 4.10   The key signature for A major.

Scenario 2: **Spell the key signature for F♯ major.**

Step 1: $\hat{1}$ is a sharp note (F♯), so this is a sharp key.
Step 2: A m2 below F♯ is E♯; E♯ is $\hat{7}$ in the key of F♯ major.
Step 3: Start writing the sequence of ♯s and proceed until E♯ is in place. The first six ♯s are needed, as shown in Example 4.11.

EXAMPLE 4.11   The key signature for F♯ major.

With the exception of F major, $\hat{1}$ in flat keys is a flat note (B♭ major, G♭ major). To spell the signature for a flat key, begin writing the series of ♭s. Once the flat representing $\hat{1}$ is in place, write the next flat in the sequence. The following scenario models this process.

Scenario 3: **Spell the key signature for D♭ major.**

Step 1: $\hat{1}$ is a flat note (D♭), so this is a flat key.
Step 2: Begin writing the sequence of flats and continue until D♭ ($\hat{1}$) is reached.
Step 3: Add the next flat in the sequence (G♭). The first five ♭s are needed, as shown in Example 4.12.

EXAMPLE 4.12   The key signature for D♭ major.

Minor Keys

Minor key signatures correspond to the minor scale and do *not* reflect the raised forms of $\hat{6}$ and $\hat{7}$ (these scale degrees will often be raised with accidentals applied to notes). Minor key signatures use the same sequences of ♯s and ♭s explored above. Every minor key has a "partner" major key, meaning that the two keys have identical key signatures. A major key and a minor key that share the same key signature are called *relative keys*. Relative keys have different tonic notes.

One approach to interpreting and writing minor key signatures is to think in terms of the relative major key. The tonics of relative major and minor keys are a m3 apart; specifically, $\hat{1}$ of the minor key is a m3 *below* $\hat{1}$ of its relative major key. Example 4.13 notates $\hat{1}$ of the relative major and minor keys sharing a key signature of three flats. These tonic notes are a m3 apart, with the major tonic forming the *top* note of the m3 (open notehead) and the minor tonic the *bottom* note (filled-in notehead).

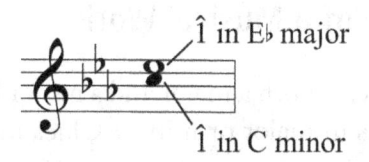

EXAMPLE 4.13 $\hat{1}$ of relative keys E♭ major and C minor.

When asked to identify a minor key signature, first determine the major key that it indicates. A key signature of two sharps is provided as Example 4.14. The last sharp, C♯, is $\hat{7}$ in the key of D major. A m3 below D is B, so this signature also represents the key of B minor. D major and B minor are *relative keys*.

EXAMPLE 4.14   Key signature with two sharps.

Spelling Minor Key Signatures

Think in terms of the relative major key when spelling a minor key signature. The following scenario models this process.

Scenario 4: **Spell the key signature for G♯ minor.**

Step 1: A m3 *above* G♯ is B, so G♯ minor and B major are relative keys sharing the same key signature.

Step 2: Write the signature for B major. This is a sharp key, so begin writing the sequence of ♯s until A♯ is in place (A♯ is $\hat{7}$ in the key of B major). See Example 4.15.

EXAMPLE 4.15   The key signature for G♯ minor.

The procedures outlined above provide reliable means for determining keys and spelling key signatures. With repetition and experience, you will soon be able to recognize or write a key signature without needing to follow these steps. For example, you will see a key signature with three sharps and know that the key is either A major or F♯ minor.

Determining the Key of a Musical Work

If a key signature can indicate both a major and a minor key, how do we determine whether a musical work is in major or minor? Clues in the music itself can help pinpoint the exact key.

Tonal melodies often emphasize $\hat{1}$ by repeating, beginning on, and/or ending on this scale degree. Other scale degrees that might receive emphasis include $\hat{3}$ and $\hat{5}$. If the key signature features three sharps and the pitch A is continually stressed, the music is likely in A major. If F♯ is more prominent, then the work is probably in F♯ minor. Minor works often involve numerous accidentals due to the variable $\hat{6}$ and $\hat{7}$.[2] If you spot recurring accidentals, determine if they are raising $\hat{6}$ and $\hat{7}$. An abundance of D♯s and E♯s, for example, would clarify that a signature of three sharps indicates the key of F♯ minor.

Music often begins and ends on the *tonic chord*, which is formed by combining the prominent scale degrees $\hat{1}$, $\hat{3}$, and $\hat{5}$. In the key of A major, these three scale degrees would form an A-major chord. (We will learn about chords in the next chapter.)

Parallel Keys

We learned above about relative keys, a pair of keys—one major, one minor—that share a key signature but have different tonics. A♭ major and F minor are relative keys: they both have a key signature of four ♭s but different tonal centers ($\hat{1}$ is A♭ in A♭ major; $\hat{1}$ is F in F minor).

Parallels keys are a pair of keys—again, one major, one minor—that have the same tonic note but different key signatures. The total number of accidentals in their respective key signatures differs by three. Consider C major and C minor. C is $\hat{1}$ in both keys. The key signature for C major is empty, and that for C minor contains three ♭s. E major and E minor are parallel keys: E major has four ♯s, and E minor has one ♯ (4 − 1 = 3).

Parallel keys and scales differ by three scale degrees: $\hat{3}$, $\hat{6}$, and $\hat{7}$ are one half step *lower* in the minor key compared to the parallel major key. Any major scale can be converted to the parallel minor scale by applying accidentals to lower $\hat{3}$, $\hat{6}$, and $\hat{7}$. In Example 4.16, the F major and F minor scales are spelled without key signatures. Both scales contain B♭ as $\hat{4}$, but F minor also includes A♭ ($\hat{3}$), D♭ ($\hat{6}$), and E♭ ($\hat{7}$). Remember that $\hat{6}$ and $\hat{7}$ will often be raised in minor—making these scale degrees look and sound just like they do in the parallel major.

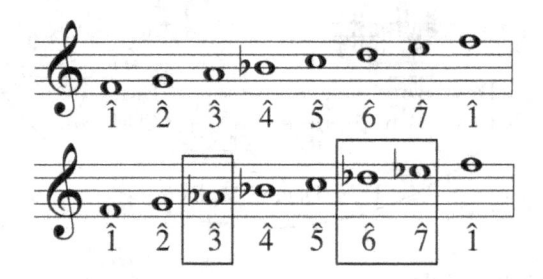

EXAMPLE 4.16 Comparing the F-major and F-minor scales.

Example 4.17 compares the key signatures for F major and F minor, which differ by four flats.

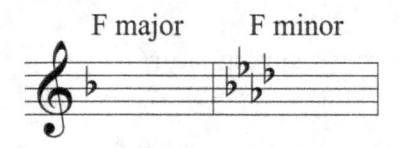

EXAMPLE 4.17 Comparing the F-major and F-minor key signatures.

The Circle of Fifths

The *circle of fifths* in Example 4.18 shows all major and minor key signatures. Moving clockwise from C major, a ♯ is added to each new key and the keys *ascend* by P5. Going counterclockwise, a ♭ is added and the keys *descend* by P5. Relative major and minor keys sharing a key signature are grouped together. Parallel minor keys are located three positions counterclockwise from each major key (because parallel keys differ by *three* accidentals).[3] Three pairs of enharmonic keys are located at the bottom of the circle.

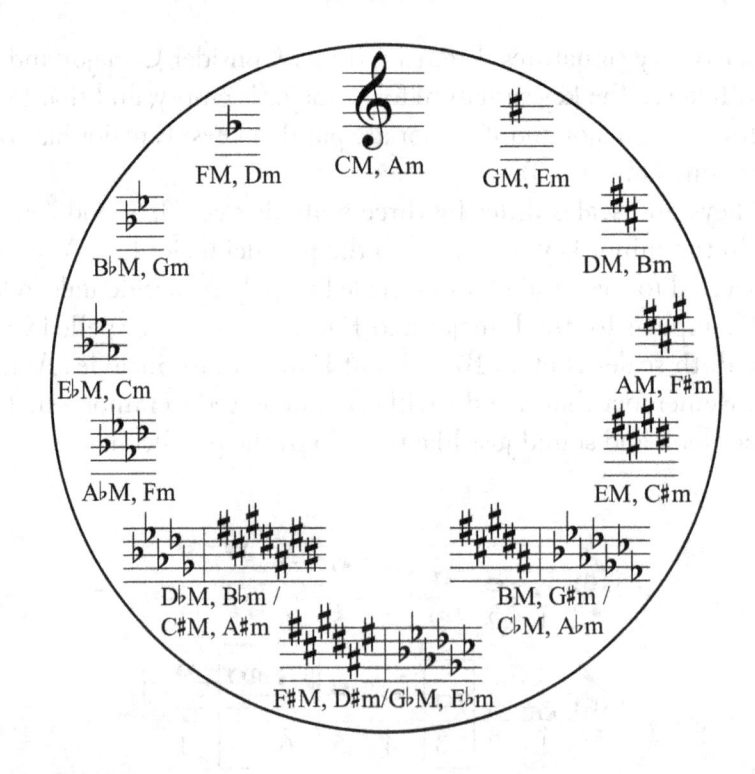

EXAMPLE 4.18 The circle of fifths.

Applications

Exercises

1. Label the following *major* key signatures.

2. Label the following *minor* key signatures.

1. ___ 2. ___ 3. ___ 4. ___ 5. ___ 6. ___ 7. ___ 8. ___

9. ___ 10. ___ 11. ___ 12. ___ 13. ___ 14. ___ 15. ___ 16. ___

3. Write the following *major* key signatures.

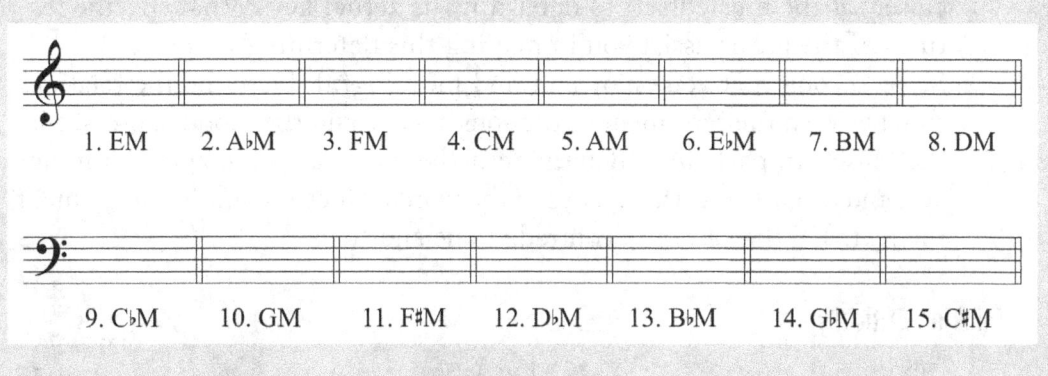

1. EM   2. A♭M   3. FM   4. CM   5. AM   6. E♭M   7. BM   8. DM

9. C♭M   10. GM   11. F♯M   12. D♭M   13. B♭M   14. G♭M   15. C♯M

4. Write the following *minor* key signatures.

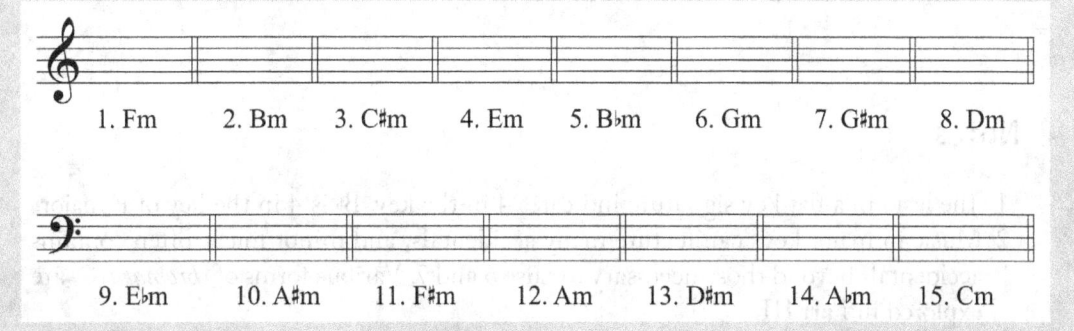

1. Fm   2. Bm   3. C♯m   4. Em   5. B♭m   6. Gm   7. G♯m   8. Dm

9. E♭m   10. A♯m   11. F♯m   12. Am   13. D♯m   14. A♭m   15. Cm

Brain Teasers

1. Write the key signature for B♭♭ major in the treble staff below. This key exists in theory, but not in practice. What more practical key is enharmonic with B♭♭ major?

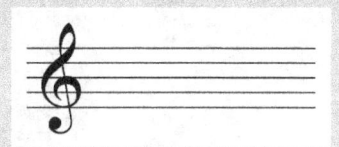

2. In the bass staff below, write the key signature for E♯ minor. Like B♭♭ major, E♯ minor is a theoretical key not found in practice. What more practical key is enharmonic with E♯ minor?

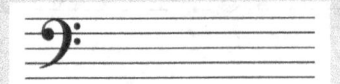

Exploring Music

1. Using music that you are currently learning or performing, or music selected from an anthology or online resource, determine the two potential keys for the work—the major key and its relative minor. Then, look closely at the music itself to determine its actual key. What specific features of the music assist you in making this determination?
2. Select a song that you enjoy and find meaningful. Describe the relationship between the sentiment of the song's lyrics and the mood expressed by the music. In particular, determine if the music is in a major or a minor key, and discuss how this relates to the words. Does the music complement the text? Do they seem to contradict one another?

Thinking Critically

Consider the key signatures for the parallel keys D major and D minor. How do these signatures display a difference of three accidentals?

Notes

1 The last ♭ in a flat key signature indicates $\hat{4}$ in the key. B♭ is $\hat{4}$ in the key of F major.
2 Music in major keys can feature many accidentals, and minor music often contains accidentals beyond those necessary to raise $\hat{6}$ and $\hat{7}$. Various forms of *chromaticism* are explored in Part III.
3 Thinking of the circle of fifths as a clock face, C major lies at the 12:00 position. The parallel minor key, C minor, is three positions counterclockwise, at the 9:00 position (12 − 9 = 3). E major is at 4:00; E minor is at 1:00 (4 − 1 = 3).

5

Chords

Two or more pitches sounding at the same time produce *harmony*. We learned in Chapter 2 that two notes form an interval. Three or more notes sounding together create a *chord*. The most common chords are *triads*, consisting of three notes, and *seventh chords*, comprising four notes. Chords are built by stacking thirds.

Triads

A triad contains three **chord members**. The lowest note of the triad is the **root**. The middle note is the **third**, which lies a third above the root. The top note, the **fifth**, is a fifth above the root. Example 5.1 shows a triad with its chord members labeled.

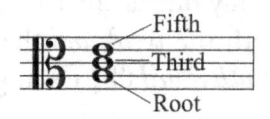

EXAMPLE 5.1   The chord members of a triad.

Triads have a *lower third*, from root to third, and an *upper third*, from third to fifth. The qualities of these two thirds determine the overall quality of the triad. There are four qualities of triad: major (M), minor (m), augmented (+), and diminished (°). M and m triads are *consonant*; + and ° are *dissonant*.

Example 5.2 shows all four triad qualities built on C. A *major triad* (Example 5.2a) has a M3 for its lower third and a m3 for its upper third. The *framing interval*, from root to fifth, is a P5. Because the root of this major triad is C, it is a C-major triad (CM). In a *minor triad* (Example 5.2b), the m3 is on bottom and the M3 is on top. The framing interval is a P5. A *diminished triad* (Example 5.2c) involves two m3s and the framing interval of a °5. An *augmented triad* (Example 5.2d) contains two M3s and is framed by an +5.

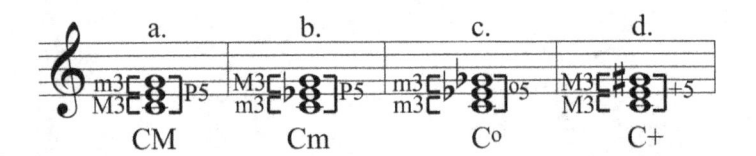

[Musical example showing four triad qualities on C: CM, Cm, C°, C+]

EXAMPLE 5.2 The four triad qualities built on C.

How would you label the triad in Example 5.1? First, determine the root of the chord. Then, determine the triad's quality by assessing the quality of its two thirds.[1]

Seventh Chords

A seventh chord contains four pitches; it is a triad with an additional third stacked on top, resulting in the interval of a seventh up from the root. The quality of a seventh chord is determined by the quality of its underlying triad as well as the quality of its seventh. Because the seventh is a dissonant interval, *all* seventh chords are dissonant.

The five qualities of seventh chord are given in Example 5.3, all built on the root C. The quality of the underlying triad is shown to the left of each chord, and the quality of seventh is shown to the right. The ***major–major seventh chord*** (MM7; Example 5.3a) is a major triad with a M7: both the underlying triad *and* the seventh are major. The ***major–minor seventh chord*** (Mm7; Example 5.3b) is a major triad with a m7. A minor triad with a m7 forms a ***minor–minor seventh chord*** (mm7; Example 5.3c). The ***half-diminished seventh chord*** (⌀7; Example 5.3d) involves a ° triad with a m7—only one of the two components of the chord, the triad, is diminished. When both the triad *and* the seventh are diminished, the result is a ***fully diminished seventh chord*** (°7; Example 5.3e).[2]

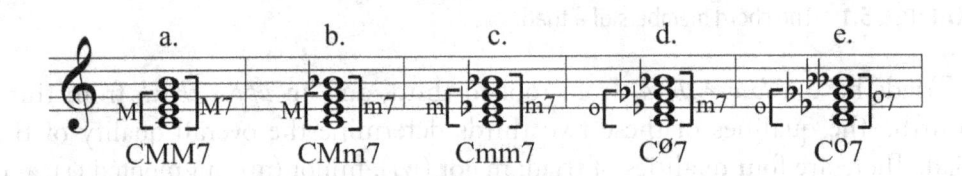

[Musical example showing five seventh chord qualities: CMM7, CMm7, Cmm7, C⌀7, C°7]

EXAMPLE 5.3 The five seventh chord qualities built on C.

To spell the various qualities of triad and seventh chord, stack the proper thirds on top of the root, using accidentals as necessary. For example, to spell E♭Mm7, build a major triad on E♭ by stacking a major third and then a minor third: E♭–G–B♭. Then add a m7 up from the root: E♭–G–B♭–D♭.

Diatonic Chords and Roman Numerals

Diatonic chords are built by stacking notes found in a single key. Each scale degree may serve as the root of a triad or seventh chord. Example 5.4 demonstrates the process of building a ***diatonic triad*** on $\hat{1}$ in the key of F major. Beginning with $\hat{1}$ as the root, skip $\hat{2}$ and select $\hat{3}$ to serve as the third of the chord. Then, skip $\hat{4}$ and select $\hat{5}$ to serve as the fifth of the chord.

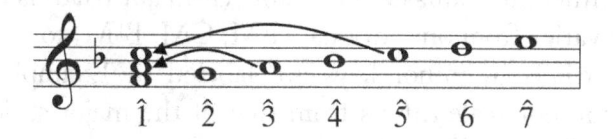

EXAMPLE 5.4   Building a diatonic triad on $\hat{1}$.

Example 5.5 shows the chord qualities that arise from stacking diatonic thirds on each scale degree in a major key.[3] The triads built on $\hat{1}$, $\hat{4}$, and $\hat{5}$ are major; those on $\hat{2}$, $\hat{3}$, and $\hat{6}$, are minor; and the triad on $\hat{7}$ is diminished. Example 5.5 is in F major, but the *same* chord qualities are found in *any* major key.

EXAMPLE 5.5   Diatonic triad qualities in major keys (F major shown).

Roman numerals are applied to label the root and quality of a diatonic chord. The scale degree number of a chord's root determines the Roman numeral ($\hat{1}$ is the root of I). Uppercase Roman numerals indicate a major chord, and lowercase indicate minor. A lowercase Roman numeral with a ° specifies a diminished triad. Example 5.6 shows the diatonic triads in F major labeled with Roman numerals.

EXAMPLE 5.6   Diatonic triads in major keys (F major shown).

The name of a diatonic chord is derived from the name of the scale degree serving as the root: I is the tonic chord, ii is the supertonic chord, iii is the mediant chord, and so on.[4]

Roman numerals give chords a *context*—they provide insight into how a chord will function in relation to the other chords in a key. In the key of F major, an F-major triad is I. However, in the key of C major, an F-major triad is IV, and in the key of B♭ major, it is V. In each key, the F-major chord is the same structure—a major triad spelled F–A–C. However, the chord will play a different musical *role* in each key, and the Roman numerals help to identify the chord's specific role. In this sense, an F-major triad is like a versatile actor who can play various roles in different dramas—the "actor" (F-major triad) is the same, but its "role" (I, IV, V) varies from one "drama" (FM, CM, B♭M) to another.[5]

The diatonic triads in minor keys are labeled in Example 5.7. Since the structure of the minor scale differs from that of the major scale, the emergent chord qualities differ as well.

Fm: i   ii°   III   iv   v   VI   VII
Root: 1̂   2̂   3̂   4̂   5̂   6̂   7̂

EXAMPLE 5.7   Diatonic triads in minor (F minor shown).

We learned in Chapter 3 that 6̂ and 7̂ are often raised in minor. These variable scale degrees not only impact melody but also harmony. Typically, 7̂ is raised when it appears as the third of the dominant chord, which converts the "natural" v to V. As 7̂ is also frequently raised when it serves as a root, it converts VII to vii°. Although these two chords require accidentals, they are so common that they are considered diatonic in minor keys. The most common diatonic chords in minor are shown in Example 5.8.[6]

Fm: i   ii°   III   iv   V   VI   vii°
Root: 1̂   2̂   3̂   4̂   5̂   6̂   ♯7̂

EXAMPLE 5.8   Most common diatonic triads in minor.

Diatonic seventh chords may be built on any scale degree. In Classical music, only a few appear regularly: those built on 2̂, 5̂, and 7̂. Example 5.9 shows these diatonic seventh chords in both major and minor keys. An uppercase Roman numeral with a ^{7} attached (V^7) indicates a Mm7 chord, lowercase with ^{7} (ii^7) means mm7, and lowercase with ^{ø7} or ^{o7} means half- or fully diminished seventh. The dominant seventh chord is Mm7 in both major and minor keys, but the qualities of the supertonic and leading-tone seventh chords differ between major and minor.

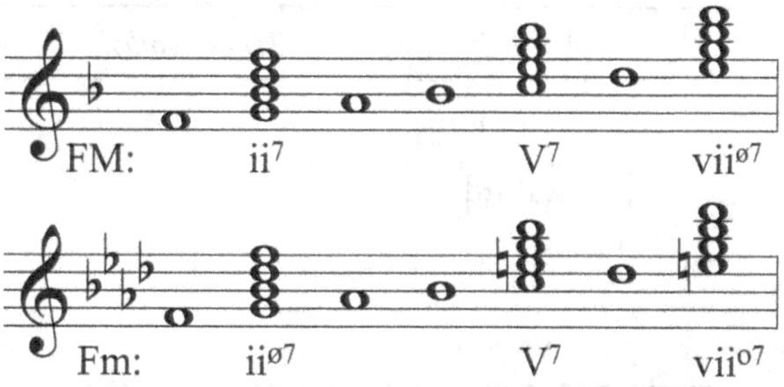
FM:
ii7
V7
viiø7
Fm:
iiø7
V7
viio7

EXAMPLE 5.9 Common diatonic seventh chords in major and minor (F major and F minor shown).

Chord Position and Inversion Symbols

Chords often appear with some member other than the root as the lowest note. Such chords are ***inverted***. Although inverted chords look like they are constructed from intervals other than thirds, it is possible to rearrange the notes in stacked thirds in order to locate the actual root. The first chord in Example 5.10 seems to feature a stacked third and then a stacked fourth. However, we can rearrange the three notes of the chord so that it is stacked in thirds—in this case by moving the highest note G down one octave. Doing so reveals G as the root. Since G is $\hat{4}$ in the key of D major, this G-major triad is the IV chord. But how do we account for the fact that the *third* of the chord, B, is the lowest note in the original positioning of the chord?

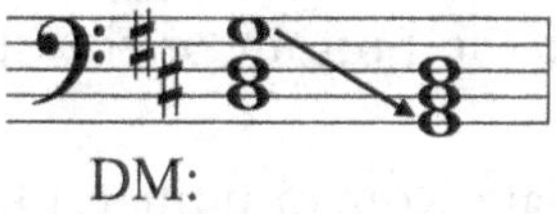
DM:

EXAMPLE 5.10 Rearranging an inverted triad.

The chord member that is the lowest note determines the ***position*** of a chord. When the root is the lowest note, the chord is in ***root position***. When the third is lowest, it is in ***first inversion***, and when the fifth is lowest, it is in ***second inversion***. If the seventh of a seventh chord is the lowest note, it is in ***third inversion***. The initial IV chord in Example 5.10 is in first inversion.

Inversion symbols are small Arabic numerals placed to the right of a Roman numeral to identify the position of the chord. The chart in Example 5.11 shows the inversion symbols for the different positions of triads and seventh chords.[7]

Position	Member in Bass	Triad Symbol	7th Chord Symbol
Root Position	Root	—	7
First Inversion	Third	6	6/5
Second Inversion	Fifth	6/4	4/3
Third Inversion	Seventh	—	2

EXAMPLE 5.11   Inversion symbols for triads and seventh chords.

Labeling Diatonic Chords

A complete Roman-numeral label indicates:

1. The root of the chord
2. The quality of the chord
3. Whether the chord is a triad or seventh chord
4. The position of the chord

Above we determined that the chord in Example 5.10 is IV in the key of D major. Since the third is lowest in its initial positioning, it is in first inversion, and the complete label for the chord is IV^6. The process for labeling a diatonic chord involves a few simple steps:

Step 1: If the chord is inverted, rearrange it to view it in neatly stacked thirds. Use scratch paper or make this a mental process. Be careful to preserve the original three notes of the chord.

Step 2: Locate the root at the bottom of the stack and determine its scale degree in the key.

Step 3: Apply the appropriate Roman numeral to the triad or seventh chord, making sure it accurately reflects the quality of the chord.

Step 4: Look back at the original positioning of the chord. Determine which chord member is lowest and apply any necessary inversion symbol to the right of the Roman numeral.

Examples 5.12 and 5.13 demonstrate the process of applying Roman numeral labels to chords.

E♭M:

EXAMPLE 5.12   Labeling a triad.

Step 1: Observe that the chord is inverted since it is not stacked in thirds. Rearrange the chord to view it in root position. In this case, the simplest way to rearrange the chord is to shift the F up one octave.

E♭M:

Step 2: Now that the chord is in root position, determine the scale degree number of its root. The root, B♭, is $\hat{5}$ in the key of E♭ major.

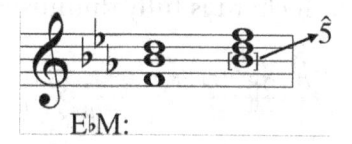

E♭M:

Step 3: Label the chord with the appropriate Roman numeral. In major keys, the diatonic triad built on $\hat{5}$ is major: V.

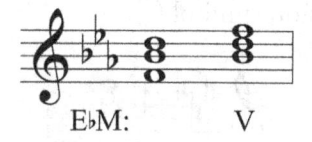

E♭M: V

Step 4: Return to the original positioning of the chord. Since the fifth, F, is the lowest note, the triad is in second inversion. Apply the proper inversion symbol to the right of the Roman numeral.

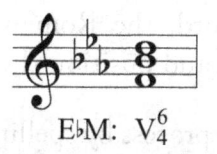

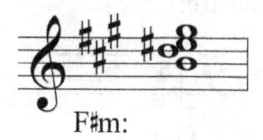

E♭M: V^6_4

F♯m:

EXAMPLE 5.13 Labeling a seventh chord.

Step 1: This four-note chord is an inverted seventh chord. To rearrange it in stacked thirds, either move the two bottom notes up one octave or move the two upper notes down one octave. Here, the two top notes are moved down to keep the notes in the staff and avoid ledger lines.

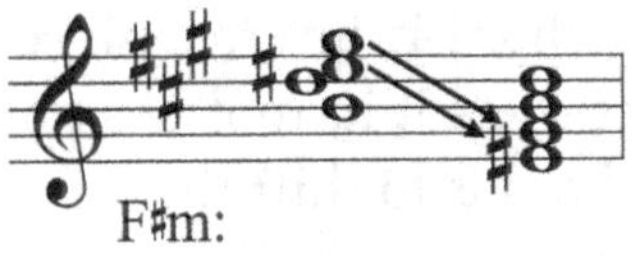
F♯m:

Step 2: The root, E♯, is ♯$\hat{7}$ (the leading tone) in the key of F-sharp minor.

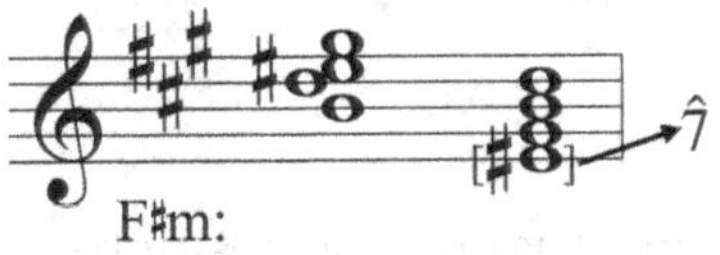
F♯m:
7̂

Step 3: Label the chord with the appropriate Roman numeral. In minor keys, the leading-tone seventh chord is fully diminished: vii^{o7}.

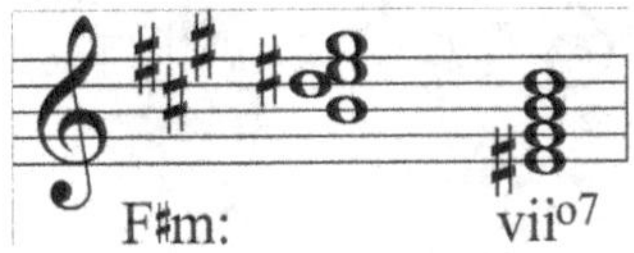
F♯m:
vii°7

Step 4: Look back at the original positioning of the chord. Since the fifth, B, is the lowest note, the seventh chord is in second inversion. Exchange the ^{7} with the proper inversion symbol ($^4_3$).

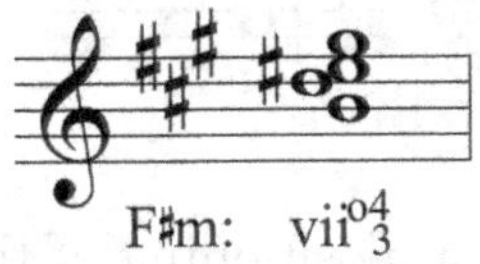
F♯m: vii°4/3

Spelling Diatonic Chords

When spelling a diatonic chord, the Roman numeral will specify all the information necessary to spell and position the chord properly.

Example 5.14 demonstrates the process by spelling V$^6_5$ in the key of G minor.

Step 1: Draw a clef and add the key signature for G minor.[8] Label the key directly beneath the signature.

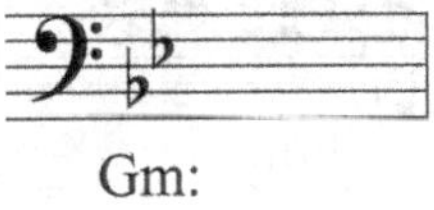
Gm:

EXAMPLE 5.14 Spelling V$^6_5$ in G minor.

Step 2: Spell V^7 in root position by determining $\hat{5}$ in G minor (D) and stacking three notes, in thirds, on top of this note (sketch this lightly or spell it on scratch staff paper). Because this V^7 is built in a minor key, remember to *raise the third* of the chord to establish the leading tone (F → F♯). Confirm that the chord quality is Mm7.

Gm: (V⁷)

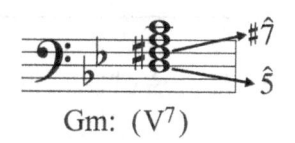

Step 3: Rearrange the chord in first inversion, with its third as the lowest note. In this case, simply transfer the root (D) up one octave.

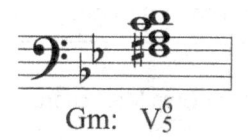

Gm: V$^6_5$

Chord Symbols

In popular music, chords are represented by chord symbols, or lead-sheet symbols. **Chord symbols** show the root, quality, and lowest note of a triad or seventh chord. They might also show added notes or altered chord members. Example 5.15 shows the symbols for common chord types.

Symbol	Description
C	Major triad
Cm	Minor triad
C/E	Major triad, first inversion
C/G	Major triad, second inversion
Cm6	Minor triad with sixth added above root
C7	Mm7
Cm7	mm7
Cmaj7	MM7
C°7	°7
Cm7♭5	ø7

EXAMPLE 5.15 Common chord symbols (with C as the chord root).

The letter following a slash (/) specifies the lowest note of an inverted chord: C/E means a C-major triad with E in the bass. A "6" indicates that a sixth above the root is added to the chord: Cm6 means the pitch A is added to a C-minor chord. The "♭5" in Cm7♭5 means the fifth of a minor–minor seventh chord has been lowered by one half step (this chord is equivalent to a half-diminished seventh chord). Additional chord types and chord symbols are explored in Chapter 26.

Roman numerals can be inferred from chord symbols. Example 5.16 provides lyrics from the chorus of "You Don't Own Me" with chord symbols placed at approximate points where the chords occur. Each chord is diatonic in the key of G major—what Roman numerals would apply to them?[9]

> G
> And don't tell me what to do
>
> Em
> And don't tell me what to say
>
> C
> And please, when I go out with you
>
> D7
> Don't put me on display

EXAMPLE 5.16 Lesley Gore, "You Don't Own Me," chorus.

Popular music is often notated in the form of a ***lead sheet***, which provides the essential elements of a song: key, melody, lyrics, and chords represented by chord symbols. Lead-sheet notation appears throughout this book.

Applications

Exercises

1. Spell triads and seventh chords, using accidentals as needed.

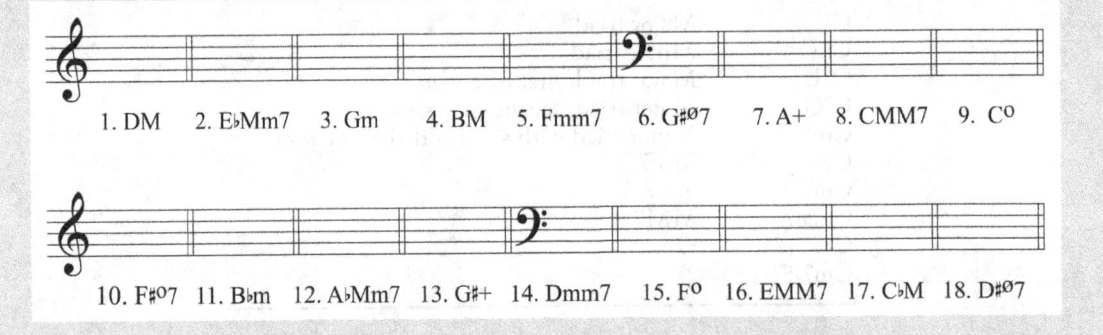

   1. DM   2. E♭Mm7   3. Gm   4. BM   5. Fmm7   6. G#ø7   7. A+   8. CMM7   9. C°

   10. F#°7   11. B♭m   12. A♭Mm7   13. G#+   14. Dmm7   15. F°   16. EMM7   17. C♭M   18. D#ø7

2. Provide labels for triads and seventh chords indicating chord root and quality. (Labels should look like those in Exercise 1 above.)

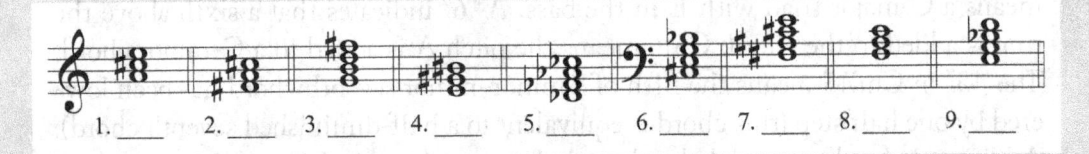

   1. _____   2. _____   3. _____   4. _____   5. _____   6. _____   7. _____   8. _____   9. _____

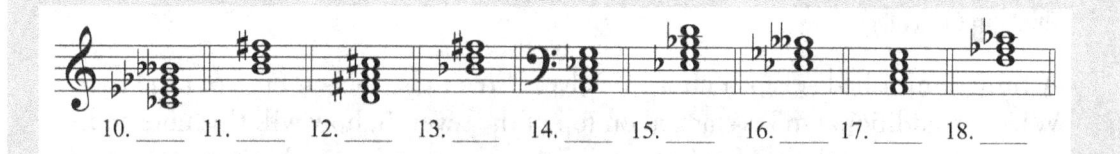

3. Spell diatonic triads and seventh chords in the keys indicated. Arrange chords in the correct position as specified by inversion symbols.

1. GM: IV   V^7 vi   ii^6 2. Dm: i$^6_4$ III   V$^6_5$ ii^{ø7}

3. B♭M: vi   iii   ii$^4_3$ vii$^{ø6}_5$ 4. C♯m: iv^6 vii^{o7} VI   V^2

4. Label diatonic triads and seventh chords with the proper Roman numeral and any necessary inversion symbol.

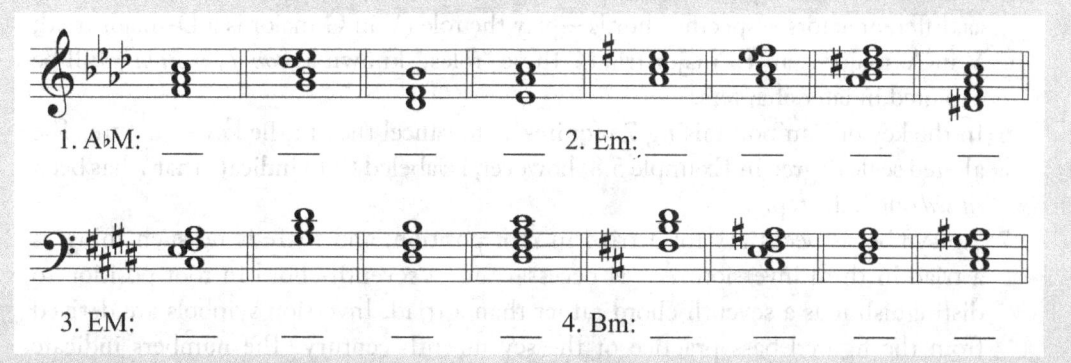

1. A♭M: _____ _____ _____ _____   2. Em: _____ _____ _____ _____

3. EM: _____ _____ _____ _____   4. Bm: _____ _____ _____ _____

Brain Teasers

1. What Roman numeral would be applied to Am6 in the key of E minor?
2. What Roman numeral would be applied to C♯m7♭5 in the key of D major? Or to the same chord in B minor?

Exploring Music

Listen to musical works and songs in a variety of styles. Identify the qualities of the chords that you hear. In a given song, do you hear more major or minor chords?

Thinking Critically

A fully diminished seventh chord involves three m3s stacked up from the root. When an additional m3 is stacked on top of the seventh, how will this note compare to the root of the chord? What does this observation say about the structure of the °7 sonority?

Notes

1 The root of the chord is A. The lower third, A–C, is a m3, and the upper third, C–G, is a M3. This is an A-minor triad, labeled Am.
2 The fully diminished seventh chord consists exclusively of stacked m3s.
3 Recall that the B♭ in the key signature applies to *all* B noteheads appearing in any octave.
4 At this point, numbers are being used to refer to three different elements: scale degree, chord member, and chord. It is important to use the appropriate symbols and terminology to distinguish among these elements: "$\hat{4}$ is the third of ii" clearly indicates that the fourth scale degree is the third of the supertonic triad.
5 To extend this analogy, Roman numerals are like set dramatic roles. For example, V is always the same role regardless of key. The role does not change from key to key as different actors—specific chords—play the role (V in G major is a D-major triad; V in A♭ major is an E♭-major triad). These "roles," known as *tonal functions*, will be explored in later chapters.
6 In the key of F minor, raising $\hat{7}$ requires a ♮ to cancel the ♭ in the key signature. The altered scale degree in Example 5.8, however, is labeled ♯$\hat{7}$ to indicate that $\hat{7}$ has been *raised* one half step.
7 No symbol is necessary for a triad in root position, and there is no such thing as a triad in third inversion. A ^{7} is necessary for a seventh chord in root position to distinguish it as a seventh chord rather than a triad. Inversion symbols are derived from the figured-bass practice of the seventeenth century. The numbers indicate the generic intervals above the lowest note. For example, a triad in second inversion features a *sixth* and a *fourth* above the lowest note (the fifth of the chord), hence the symbol $^6_4$. The inversion symbols shown here and used throughout this text are the common abbreviated symbols. For example, the complete inversion symbol for a first-inversion triad is $^6_3$, but it is usually abbreviated as ^{6}. Many texts use $^4_2$ as the symbol for a third-inversion seventh chord, but ^{2} suffices since no other symbols contain a 2.
8 Using a key signature limits the number of accidentals needed to apply to chord members. When spelling diatonic chords using a key signature, the only chords that require an extra accidental are V, V^7, vii°, and vii°^{7}—*in minor keys only*.
9 G–Em–C–D7 = I–vi–IV–V^7.

6
Musical Time

Music is a dynamic art that unfolds over time. Composers organize and shape different aspects of musical time, including the overall speed of the music, the way that beats cluster into recurring groups, and rhythmic patterns involving activity both on and between beats.

Beat

The ***beat*** is the recurring *pulse* of the music to which you might tap your foot, nod your head, or coordinate complex dance moves. The beat is typically periodic and steady but can also be irregular.

Tempo

Tempo refers to the *speed* of the music. The faster the tempo, the closer the beats are to one another in time. Terms such as Lento, Andante, and Allegro prescribe a narrow range of acceptable tempos, allowing performers some flexibility. Tempo is precisely measured in *beats per minute* (bpm)—for example, 60 bpm is one beat per second.[1]

The tempo of music often changes either suddenly or gradually. An ***abrupt shift*** is a sudden increase or decrease in tempo. An ***accelerando*** is a gradual increase in tempo, and a ***ritardando*** is a gradual decrease in tempo. When a ritardando occurs at the end of a work, the music slows to a stop. ***Rubato*** refers to a subtle fluctuation in tempo—a "give and take" of musical time—to lend expressivity to the music.

Duration

Duration refers to the length, or value, of a note. Values can be divided into smaller values, and they can be summed to create larger values. A value is either ***simple***, dividing evenly into two smaller, equal parts, or ***dotted***, dividing into three equal parts. Example 6.1 shows simple values from the whole note through the thirty-second note.

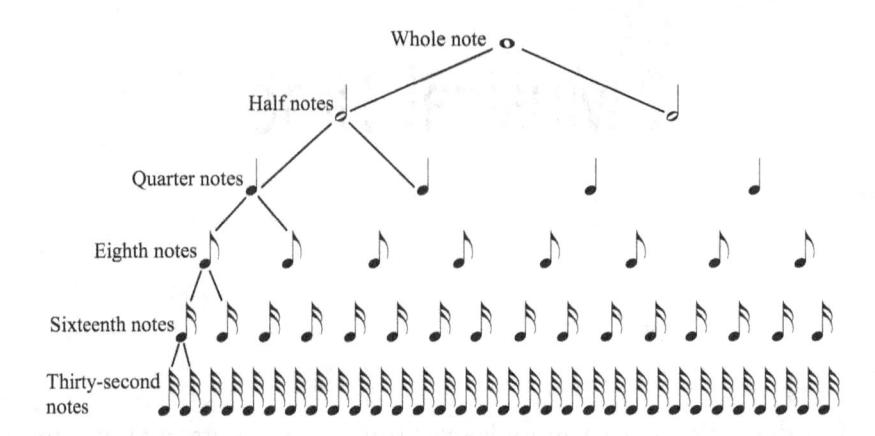

EXAMPLE 6.1 Simple values.

The names of the values derive from how many units of that value can fit into a single whole note. For example, one whole note divides into two half notes, four quarter notes, eight eighth notes, sixteen sixteenth notes, and so on.[2] Values are differentiated by open and solid noteheads, *stems* (the vertical line extending from the notehead), and either *flags* (the wavy lines extending from stems) or *beams* (horizontal lines connecting values smaller than the quarter note). The notation of durations shall be discussed further below.

Adding a ***dot*** to a note increases its value by half. A dotted quarter note is essentially one-and-a-half quarter notes, or the equivalent of one quarter + one eighth. A simple quarter note divides into two eighth notes, and a dotted quarter note divides into three eighth notes. Example 6.2 shows two different divisions of the dotted quarter value.

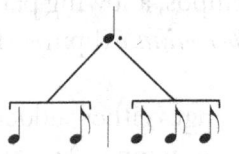

EXAMPLE 6.2 Two different divisions of the dotted quarter note.

A ***double dot*** increases the value of a note by three-fourths of itself. A double-dotted quarter note equals one quarter + one eighth + one sixteenth (or one quarter + three sixteenths).

A ***tie*** is used to sum two values together to create a single, longer value. A quarter note tied to another quarter note equals one half note. The second quarter note—the value that the tie stretches into—is not rearticulated, so the tied quarter notes in Example 6.3 sound *exactly* like a single half note.

EXAMPLE 6.3 Two tied quarter notes = one half note.

Dots and ties can be used to express the same duration. In Example 6.4, the dotted quarter and the quarter tied to an eighth sound identical.

EXAMPLE 6.4 Dots and ties expressing the same duration.

Ties, however, can express durations that dots cannot, such as the half note tied to an eighth note shown in Example 6.5.

EXAMPLE 6.5 Creating a unique duration with a tie.

Rests indicate durations of silence. Example 6.6 shows rest symbols through the thirty-second rest and their exact placement in the staff. The whole rest suspends from the second staff line from the top, and the half rest sits on the middle line—regardless of clef. Rests smaller than the quarter rest are differentiated by the number of mini flags coming off the *left* side of the rest; just as the sixteenth note has two flags, the sixteenth rest has two mini flags.

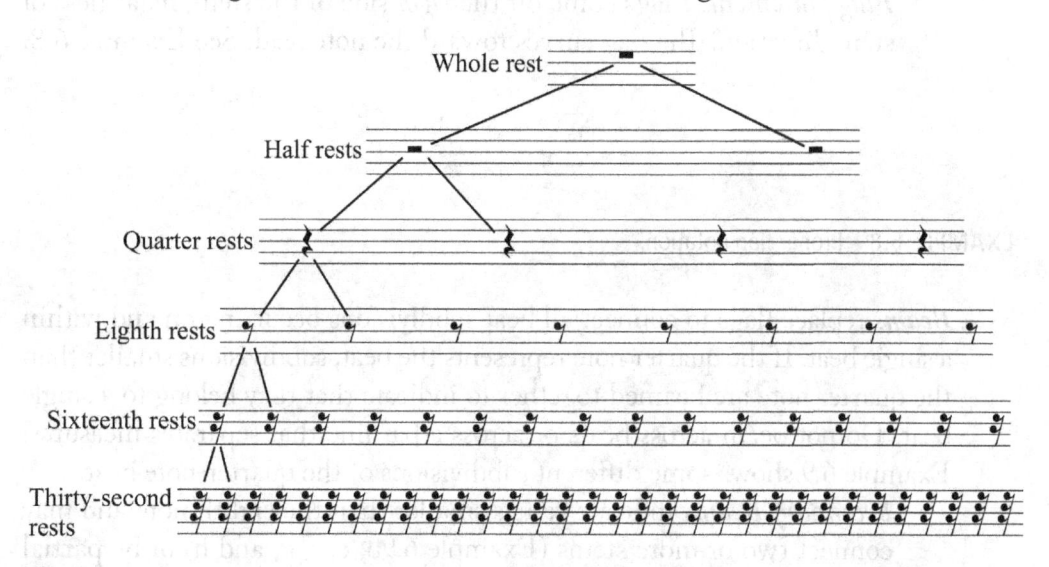

EXAMPLE 6.6 Rests.

Any rest can be dotted. Rests are never beamed together, and ties are not used with rests.

Guidelines for Notating Durations and Rhythms

1. **Stems** are vertical lines that extend from noteheads. They are used for all durations shorter than the whole note.
   - **Stem direction**: Stems go *up* when the notehead is *below* the middle line of the staff and *down* when the notehead is *above* the middle line. If the notehead is *on* the middle line, the stem can go either direction.
     - If two different voices are present in a single staff, the upper voice always uses upward stems and the lower voice uses downward stems.
   - **Stem placement**: *Upward* stems extend from the *right* side of the notehead; *downward* stems extend from the *left* side of the notehead.
   - **Stem length**: Stems extend exactly one octave from the notehead. If the notehead is on C5, the downward stem should extend to C4. See Example 6.7.

EXAMPLE 6.7 Proper stem notation.

2. **Flags** are curved lines placed at the end of stems. They are used for all durations shorter than the quarter note. The more flags, the shorter the duration.
   - **Flag placement**: Flags come off the *right* side of the stem, regardless of stem direction. The flag curves toward the notehead. See Example 6.8.

EXAMPLE 6.8 Proper flag notation.

3. **Beams** replace flags to connect all beat subdivisions occurring on and within a single beat. If the quarter note represents the beat, subdivisions smaller than the quarter note are beamed together to indicate that they belong to a single beat. Do not beam across beats or across a bar line that separates measures. Example 6.9 shows some different subdivisions of the quarter-note beat.
   - **Secondary Beams** indicate values smaller than the eighth note and may connect two or more stems (Example 6.9b, c, f, g, and h) or be partial "stubs" branching off a single stem (Example 6.9d, e, and g). The stubs are necessary to avoid creating two sixteenth notes when the desired rhythm is an eighth beamed to a sixteenth. Partial secondary beams are the width of a notehead and are placed inside the primary beam.

EXAMPLE 6.9 Beams grouping various subdivisions of the quarter-note beat.

4. **Beam placement and stem direction**: Beams are placed at the end of the stems they connect. They may be straight (Example 6.9a–e; g–h) or slanted (Example 6.9f). When multiple notes that should be beamed together occur both above and below the middle line of the staff, then all stems must go in the same direction. The general rule is that the notehead *farthest* from the middle line determines the direction of all stems to be beamed together. Example 6.9h contains three notes below the middle line and a fourth note above the line. Since this fourth note is farther from the middle line than the three notes preceding it, every stem goes *down*.
5. **Dots** are placed to the *right* of a notehead. When the note is on a line, the dot is placed just above the line. See the two dotted notes at the beginning of Example 6.10.
6. **Ties** connect from one notehead to another. Ties can extend the value of a note across a bar line (but dots cannot). Example 6.10 shows examples of dots and ties.

EXAMPLE 6.10 Dots and ties.

Meter

Meter refers to the grouping of beats, typically into recurring patterns. The most common meters in classical and popular music are groupings of two beats (***duple meter***), three beats (***triple meter***), and four beats (***quadruple meter***). These are known as ***regular meters***. Each grouping occupies a ***measure***, or ***bar***, of music. Measures are separated by ***bar lines***—vertical lines spanning the staff. In a triple meter, each measure contains exactly three beats. The first beat of each measure is called the ***downbeat***, and the last beat is the ***upbeat***.

Meters have a natural ***metric accent***, which is a pattern of strong (accented) and weak (unaccented) beats. In any meter, the downbeat receives the strongest emphasis. Various musical events might mark the downbeat, including a change of harmony, the start of a new section (such as the chorus), or the entrance of a vocal line or instrumental solo. Metric accents for the three common types of meter are shown in Example 6.11.

> **Duple**: | Strong – Weak | Strong – Weak |
> **Triple**: | Strong – Weak – Weak | Strong – Weak – Weak |
> **Quadruple**: | Strong – Weak – Less Strong – Weak | Strong – Weak – Less Strong – Weak |

EXAMPLE 6.11 Metric accents.

In each meter, the downbeat is strong and the upbeat is weak. Weak beats are often called *offbeats*. Quadruple meters have two strong beats (beats 1 and 3), with beat 3 typically less strong than beat 1 (but stronger than beats 2 and 4).

Meters are classified as either simple or compound. In a *simple meter*, each beat divides into two equal parts, and the duration of the beat is a simple, non-dotted value. In a *compound meter*, each beat divides into three equal parts, and the beat is a dotted value.

Time Signatures

In notated music, the meter is indicated at the beginning of the score with a *time signature*. The time signature provides three important pieces of information:

1. The number of beats in each measure
2. The value of the beat
3. Whether the meter is simple or compound

The time signature involves two numbers aligned vertically. It appears on the first line of music following the clef and key signature (see Example 6.12) and is not repeated on subsequent lines.

EXAMPLE 6.12 Time signature placement.

The meaning of the two numbers in the signature depends on whether the meter is simple or compound.

In *simple time signatures*:

- The top number shows the *number* of beats in each measure.
  - Will be 2 (duple), 3 (triple), or 4 (quadruple).
- The bottom number reveals the *value* of the beat.
  - 2 = half note, 4 = quarter note, 8 = eighth note, and so on.

The $\frac{4}{4}$ time signature in Example 6.12 indicates a simple quadruple meter, with the quarter note serving as the beat. The time signature $\frac{4}{8}$ is also classified as a simple quadruple meter, but with the eighth note serving as the beat.

In *compound time signatures*:

- The top number shows the total number of beat *subdivisions* in each measure.
  - Will be 6, 9, or 12.
  - Divide this number by three to determine the number of beats in each measure.
- The bottom number indicates the value of each beat *subdivision*.
  - These values will cluster together in groups of three to form each beat.
  - If the bottom number is 8, indicating an eighth note, identify the single duration that is equivalent to three eighth notes: the dotted quarter note is the value of the beat.

Compound time signatures require a bit of interpretation and math. The time signature $\frac{6}{8}$ indicates that there are six eighth notes in each measure. But how many *beats* are in each measure? (The answer is *not* six.) Whenever the top number of the signature is 6, 9, or 12, divide this number by three to determine the number of beats in each measure: 6 ÷ 3 = 2, so $\frac{6}{8}$ is a compound *duple* meter. What is the value of each beat? (*Not* the eighth note.) The eighth notes cluster together into groups of three; the six eighth notes in each bar cluster into two groups of three. The equivalent of three eighth notes can be expressed as a single dotted quarter note, and this is the value of each beat.

To summarize, the top number of the time signature classifies the meter (simple triple, compound quadruple, etc.), and the bottom number indicates the value of the beat (simple meters) or beat subdivisions (compound meters).

The six types of regular meter are given in Example 6.13, with the *top* number of the time signature in parentheses. (The bottom number varies based on the value of the beat: $\frac{3}{4}$, $\frac{3}{8}$, and $\frac{3}{16}$ are all classified as compound triple meters.)

Simple Duple (2)	Compound Duple (6)
Simple Triple (3)	Compound Triple (9)
Simple Quadruple (4)	Compound Quadruple (12)

EXAMPLE 6.13   The six types of regular meter.

While many musical works remain in the same meter, some change meter either permanently or temporarily. In notated music, a meter change is indicated by a new time signature.

The time signature $\frac{4}{4}$ occurs so commonly in music that it is referred to as **common time** and is often identified by a ℂ in the time signature. The time signature $\frac{2}{2}$, known as **cut time** or ***alla breve***, is often designated with the symbol ₵ and is typically associated with a fast tempo. These two alternative time signatures are shown in Example 6.14.

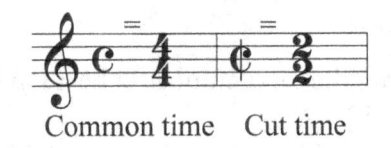

EXAMPLE 6.14 Symbols for common time and cut time.

Irregular Meters

The meters discussed above are regular meters, meaning the top number of the time signature is divisible by either two or three. *Irregular meters*, also known as *composite, additive,* and *asymmetrical meters*, have a top number that is *not* divisible by two or three, such as five or seven.

Irregular meters sound like a combination of two different meters. For example, $\frac{5}{8}$ sounds like alternating measures of $\frac{3}{8}$ and $\frac{2}{8}$. The splitting of an irregular meter like $\frac{5}{8}$ into either a 3+2 or 2+3 pattern might emerge from the durations of longer notes, the grouping of smaller notes, or the placement of accents. Example 6.15 shows a measure of $\frac{5}{8}$, with both longer durations (dotted quarter + quarter) and the beaming of eighth notes reflecting a 3+2 grouping.

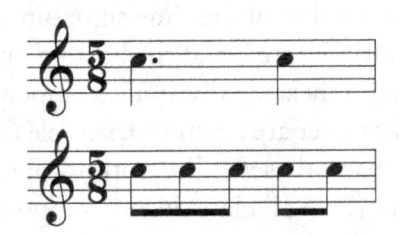

EXAMPLE 6.15 $\frac{5}{8}$ subdivided as 3+2.

Example 6.16 shows $\frac{5}{8}$ divided as 2+3.

EXAMPLE 6.16 $\frac{5}{8}$ subdivided as 2+3.

Example 6.17 shows how $\frac{7}{8}$ (or $\frac{7}{4}$) is often divided as 2+2+3 or 3+2+2.

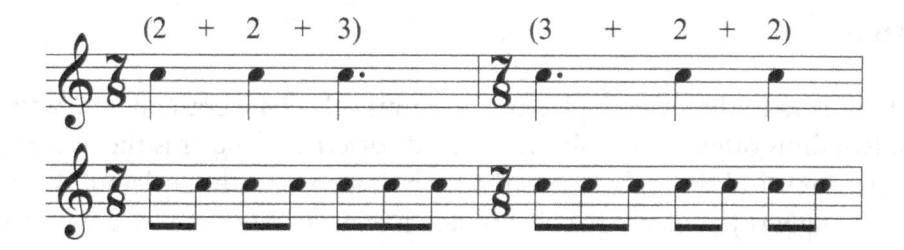

EXAMPLE 6.17 Subdivisions of $\frac{7}{8}$.

Irregular meters can also be heard as regular meters with either an extra or a missing beat unit. For example, $\frac{5}{8}$ can sound like $\frac{6}{8}$ minus an eighth note in each bar. In other words, we might expect to hear 3+3—the regular subdivision of $\frac{6}{8}$—but instead hear 3+2. We might hear $\frac{7}{8}$ (especially 2+2+3) as $\frac{3}{4}$ with an extra eighth note added to one of the beats. Accordingly, the lengths of the actual beats in each measure differ (quarter notes versus dotted quarter notes), which contributes to the "lopsided" sound of irregular meters.

A regular meter can be subdivided in an irregular manner—$\frac{4}{4}$ can be broken down as 3+3+2 eighths, which could sound like $\frac{9}{8}$ with an eighth note missing from the last beat. On the top level of Example 6.18, this irregular subdivision is achieved by duration; on the bottom level, by the grouping and beaming of eighth notes as well as accent marks.

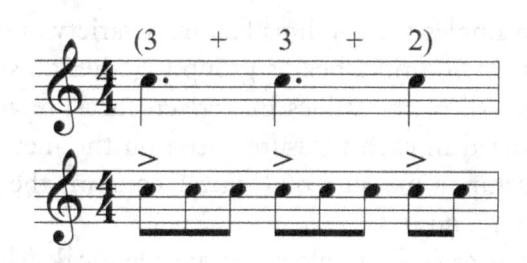

EXAMPLE 6.18 Irregular subdivision of $\frac{4}{4}$.

The Aural Identification of Meter

These steps assist in determining the meter of a musical work aurally:

1. Locate the recurring pulse. Decide if the meter is regular or irregular (it will usually be regular).
2. Identify the downbeat—a periodically accented beat. Count this beat as "1" each time it occurs.
3. Count the number of beats between each downbeat. If you count "1, 2, 3" the meter is triple; "1, 2, 3, 4" indicates a quadruple meter; and so on.
4. Listen to the subdivisions of beats to decide if the meter is simple or compound.

Rhythm

Rhythm refers to the specific placement of musical events both on and between beats. Rhythms often involve short, repeated patterns. If meter is the underlying skeleton of musical time, rhythm is the flesh draped over the skeleton. A multitude of unique rhythms are possible in any meter. Some examples are provided in Example 6.19.

EXAMPLE 6.19 Examples of rhythms in different meters.

In each of these examples the rhythms feature a variety of durations and subdivisions of the beat. In addition, beams group together all subdivisions falling within a single beat. All of the values in a given measure add up to the total number of beats allowed in each measure based on the meter. In other words, regardless of the rhythm, a measure of $\frac{4}{4}$ *always* contains the equivalent of four quarter notes—no more, no less.

The first two measures of Example 6.19c are identical. Music often features short rhythmic *motives* that are repeated. The repeating rhythm might occur with a repeating pitch pattern, as heard in many catchy guitar riffs. Such repetition helps to unify a musical work and make it memorable.

Grouplets

A *grouplet* creates subdivisions of the beat that do not occur naturally in a given meter. The most common grouplet is the ***triplet*** in a simple meter. In $\frac{4}{4}$, the quarter-note beat normally breaks down into an even number of parts: two eighths, four sixteenths, eight thirty-seconds, and so on. A triplet imposes a compound beat subdivision and allows the beat to break down into three equal parts. A triplet means "three eighths in the space of two eights." A ***sextuplet*** divides the quarter-note beat into six equal parts. See the triplet and sextuplet in Example 6.20.

EXAMPLE 6.20 A triplet and sextuplet in a simple meter.

Grouplets also allow a dotted value in a compound meter to divide into an even number of parts. The dotted quarter beat in ⁶⁄₈ normally breaks down into three eighth notes, but a *duplet* divides it evenly into two eighths ("two eighths in the space of three eighths"). A *quadruplet* divides a beat into four equal parts. A duplet and quadruplet are notated in Example 6.21.

EXAMPLE 6.21 A duplet and quadruplet in a compound meter.

A beat can be divided by any number, as shown by the grouplets in Example 6.22. A grouplet is necessary whenever the desired subdivision does not occur naturally in the given meter.

EXAMPLE 6.22 Other grouplets.

Notating Grouplets

Grouplets occurring *within* the span of a quarter note can be beamed together, as is the case for all the grouplets above (Examples 6.20–6.22). A small Arabic numeral representing the type of grouplet (3 for triplet, 5 for quintuplet, and so on) is placed on or under the beam.

For grouplets spanning any duration *longer* than a quarter note, such as the quarter-note triplet in Example 6.23, a bracket is used since the notes cannot be beamed together. A number representing the type of grouplet occurs with the bracket. The triplet in Example 6.23 occurs in the space of two quarter notes (one half note).

EXAMPLE 6.23 A bracket with quarter-note triplets.

Syncopation

Syncopation obscures the underlying metric accent by shifting attack points to the normally weak beats or locating them off (or between) the beats.

As discussed above, the natural metric accent for a quadruple meter falls on beats 1 and 3. In Example 6.24, accents are placed on beats 2 and 4. This specific type of syncopation is known as the ***backbeat***, and it occurs in numerous popular songs. One source refers to the backbeat as the "heartbeat of rock 'n' roll."[3] The accents on the offbeats might be provided by handclaps, a snare drum, or a strumming pattern on the guitar. Syncopation does not negate the natural metric accent—the downbeat is still marked by events like chord changes, section changes, or instrumental entrances. Syncopation adds a layer of rhythmic complexity.

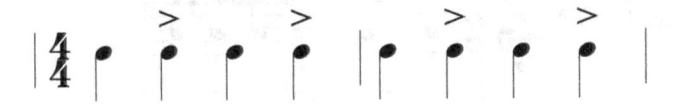

EXAMPLE 6.24   The backbeat (accents on beats 2 and 4).

Other types of syncopation are more complex, like the rhythm shown in Example 6.25. Here, ties are used to displace attack points such that they occur between beats.

EXAMPLE 6.25   Highly syncopated rhythm.

Polyrhythm

A *polyrhythm* occurs when two or more different rhythms occur simultaneously. The rhythms might sound unrelated or in conflict with one another. Polyrhythms are common in music for more than one instrument (or part), and they typically involve different kinds of beat subdivision, such as the "two-against-three" pattern formed by layering a triplet beat subdivision on top of an even (duple) beat subdivision, as shown in Example 6.26.

EXAMPLE 6.26   The "two-against-three" polyrhythm.

Applications

Exercises

1. Classify regular meters as simple or compound, and as duple, triple, or quadruple.

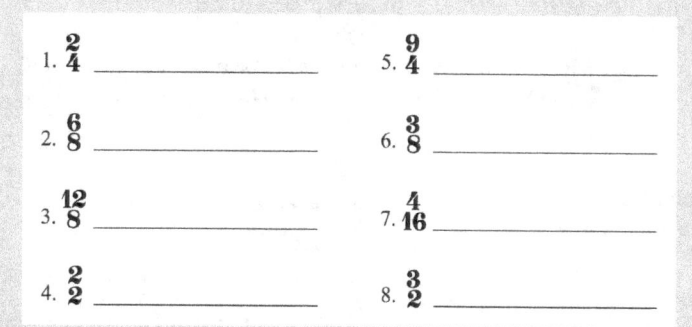

   1. $\frac{2}{4}$ _____   5. $\frac{9}{4}$ _____

   2. $\frac{6}{8}$ _____   6. $\frac{3}{8}$ _____

   3. $\frac{12}{8}$ _____   7. $\frac{4}{16}$ _____

   4. $\frac{2}{2}$ _____   8. $\frac{3}{2}$ _____

2. Beam the rhythms below to reflect the given meter (do not alter the series of durations).

a.

b.

3. Express the total duration of each rhythmic pattern below as a single note value, using dots as needed.

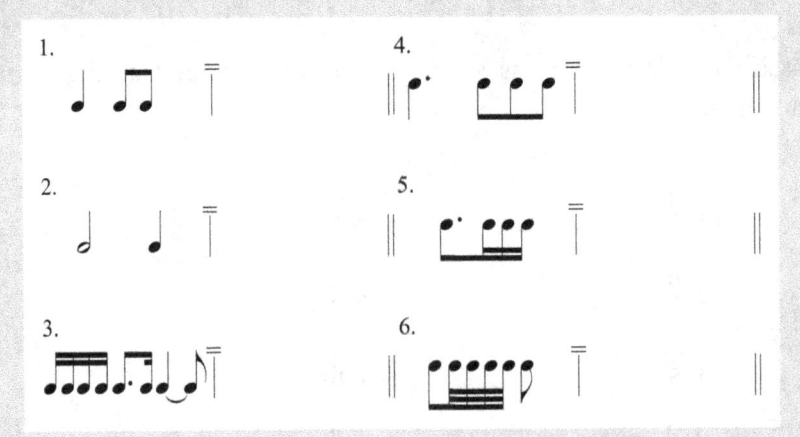

4. Answer conceptual questions about musical time.

   a. What is the essential difference between a simple and a compound meter?
   b. In $\frac{3}{4}$, there are _____ beats per measure, and the value of each beat is _____.
   c. In $\frac{12}{8}$, there are _____ beats per measure, and the value of each beat is _____.
   d. In any simple meter, how would one divide a beat into three equal parts?

Brain Teasers

1. What do common time and cut time have in common?
2. What do $\frac{2}{4}$ and $\frac{6}{8}$ have in common? What is different about them?
3. What do $\frac{3}{4}$ and $\frac{6}{8}$ have in common? What is different about them?

Exploring Music

1. Listen to musical works in various styles and practice identifying the meter. Refer to "The Aural Identification of Meter," above.
2. Listen to "Rock Island Line," a 1955 novelty song performed by Johnny Cash. What kind of tempo change occurs in this song? How does this change in tempo complement the narrative of the lyrics?

Thinking Critically

Why does the time signature for a compound meter indicate the total number and value of the beat *subdivisions* rather than the beat itself?

Notes

1 Tempos can be accurately measured and set with a *metronome*.
2 Four quarter notes occupy the same amount of time as two half notes or one whole note. Whereas we would hear the onset, or attack, of each quarter note, the whole note would sustain over the same amount of time.
3 Steven Valdez, *A History of Rock Music*, 5th ed. (Dubuque, IA: Kendall Hunt Publishing, 2014), 48.

7

Introduction to Voice Leading and Counterpoint

Voice Leading is the manner in which two or more melodic lines, or voices, move together through time. Voice-leading processes promote the independence of separate lines while at the same time helping them flow together in a harmonious fashion.

Motion Between Two Voices

Two voices can display five types of motion relative to one another.

1. *Static motion*: Neither voice changes pitch. The notes are either sustained (Example 7.1a) or repeated (Example 7.1b).

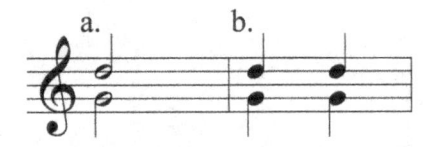

EXAMPLE 7.1 Static motion.

2. *Oblique motion*: One voice stays the same while the other voice changes pitch. The voice in motion might step or leap in either direction.

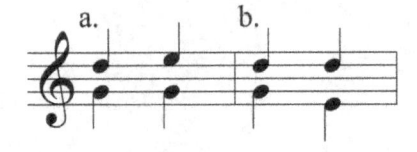

EXAMPLE 7.2 Oblique motion.

3. *Contrary motion*: Both voices move in opposite directions, either converging (Example 7.3a) or diverging (Example 7.3b).

EXAMPLE 7.3 Contrary motion.

4. *Similar motion*: Voices move in the same direction, but by different intervals.

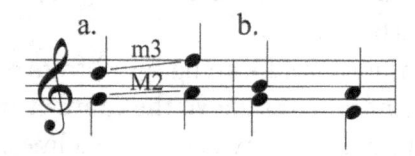

EXAMPLE 7.4 Similar motion.

5. *Parallel motion*: Voices move in the same direction and by the same *size*—but not necessarily *quality*—of interval. The size of successive intervals formed by the two voices remains the same. In Example 7.5a, both voices step down by M2, causing one M3 to move to another M3. In Example 7.5b, both voices step up, but one moves by m2 while the other moves by M2, resulting in parallel sixths of different qualities (M6 → m6).

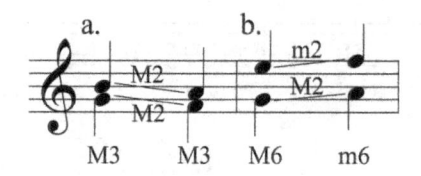

EXAMPLE 7.5 Parallel motion.

The parallel *imperfect* consonances (thirds and sixths) in Example 7.5 are very common. However, parallel *perfect* consonances (fifths and octaves) destroy voice independence and were typically avoided during the common practice.

Counterpoint

Counterpoint is the technique of combining a new melodic line with an existing line. **Species counterpoint** explores this process in four increasingly complex stages, or *species*.[1]

In species counterpoint, the existing melody consists of whole notes and is known as the **cantus firmus**. In the examples of species 1–3 that follow, the new melodic line (or, counterpoint) is added above the same cantus firmus.[2]

First Species

- The new line added above the cantus firmus is in whole notes, creating a note-to-note (1:1) counterpoint.
    - Follow the general melodic principles discussed in Chapter 3.
    - Use only diatonic pitches, raising $\hat{6}$ and $\hat{7}$ as appropriate in minor.
    - Use mostly stepwise motion.
        - A leap should be followed by a step in the opposite direction.
        - Do not leap by seventh, or by any + or ° interval.
            - Be mindful of the tritone between $\hat{4}$ and $\hat{7}$, and also between $\hat{2}$ and $\hat{6}$ in minor.
            - In minor, avoid leaping by +2 from $\hat{6}$ to #$\hat{7}$.
    - The counterpoint remains above the cantus firmus at all times.
- Use *only* consonant intervals between the two lines.
    - Begin with P5 or P8.
    - End with P8.[3]
    - Use mostly imperfect consonances (thirds and sixths) in the middle.
        - Approach P5 and P8 with either contrary or oblique motion—*never* with parallel or similar motion.
        - The final two intervals are a sixth opening to an octave, with $\hat{2}$–$\hat{1}$ in the cantus firmus and $\hat{7}$–$\hat{1}$ in the counterpoint (remember to raise $\hat{7}$ in minor, as shown in Example 7.6b).
    - Avoid P4, which is an unstable dissonance in a two-voice context.

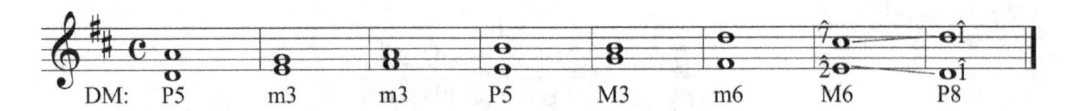

EXAMPLE 7.6A First species.

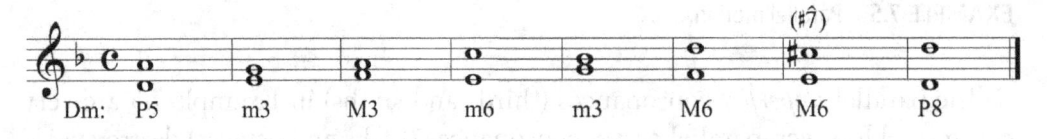

EXAMPLE 7.6B First species (minor key).

Second Species

Most of the rules of first species apply to second species, with the following changes:

- The counterpoint is composed in half notes.
    - The last measure is a whole note.
    - The second-to-last measure may be a whole note.
    - Notes are *not* immediately repeated in the counterpoint.
    - The counterpoint may leap from one consonant note to another.

- Consonant intervals appear on all downbeats.
  - Avoid placing the same kind of perfect interval (P5 or P8) on consecutive downbeats.
- Dissonant intervals may be used, but *only* on the second half note of each measure.
  - Remember that P4 is a dissonance in a two-voice context.
  - The dissonant note in the counterpoint must be approached *and* resolved by step.
    - A *passing tone* (pt) is approached and resolved by step in the *same* direction. Three passing tones are circled and labeled in Example 7.7.
    - A *neighbor tone* (nt) is approached and resolved by step in *opposite* directions. One neighbor tone is circled and labeled in Example 7.7.[4]

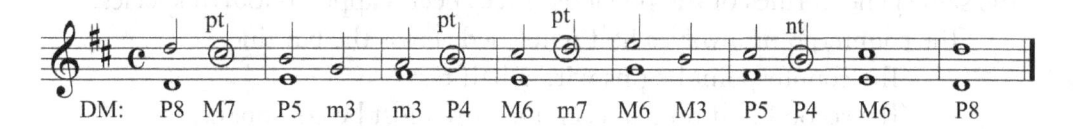

DM: P8 M7 P5 m3 m3 P4 M6 m7 M6 M3 P5 P4 M6 P8

EXAMPLE 7.7 Second species.

Third Species

Most of the rules of first and second species apply to third species, with the following changes:

- The counterpoint is composed in quarter notes.
  - The last measure is a whole note.
- Consonant intervals appear on all downbeats.
  - Avoid placing perfect consonances (P5 or P8) on consecutive downbeats and also on consecutive strong beats (beats 1 and 3 in a single measure).
- Dissonant intervals may be used on beats 2–4 of each measure.
  - The dissonant note is either a passing tone or a neighbor tone.
- In minor (Example 7.8b), $\hat{6}$ and $\hat{7}$ are raised *only* in the final ascent of the counterpoint.

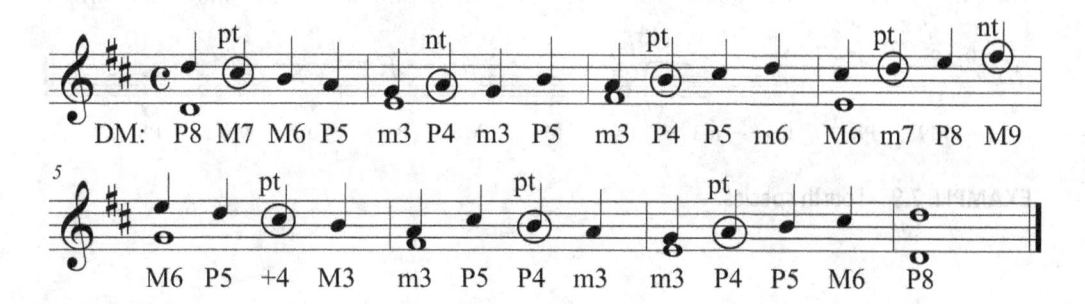

DM: P8 M7 M6 P5 m3 P4 m3 P5 m3 P4 P5 m6 M6 m7 P8 M9

M6 P5 +4 M3 m3 P5 P4 m3 m3 P4 P5 M6 P8

EXAMPLE 7.8A Third species.

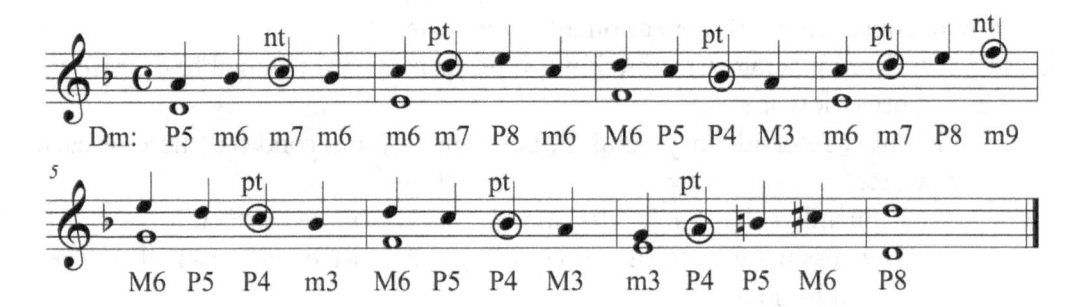

EXAMPLE 7.8B Third species (minor key).

Fourth Species

The same general rules of the previous three species apply to fourth species.
- The counterpoint involves half notes tied across the bar line.
  - The counterpoint begins with a half rest.
  - The second half note in each measure must be consonant.
  - The first half note in each measure may be consonant or dissonant.
    - The second half note of a measure may step or leap to the first note of the next measure (rather than tie into it) *only* if the downbeat is consonant. See Example 7.9, measures 6–7, 10–11, and 12–13.
    - The only dissonance allowed on a downbeat is a suspension. A *suspension* (sus) is a strong-beat dissonance that follows a consonance and resolves *down by step* to another consonance.
      - Suspension labels specify the size of the dissonant interval and the consonant interval of resolution: "7-6 sus" indicates a dissonant seventh resolving to a consonant sixth. The three types of suspension occur throughout Example 7.9, which sets fourth species counterpoint above a new cantus firmus.

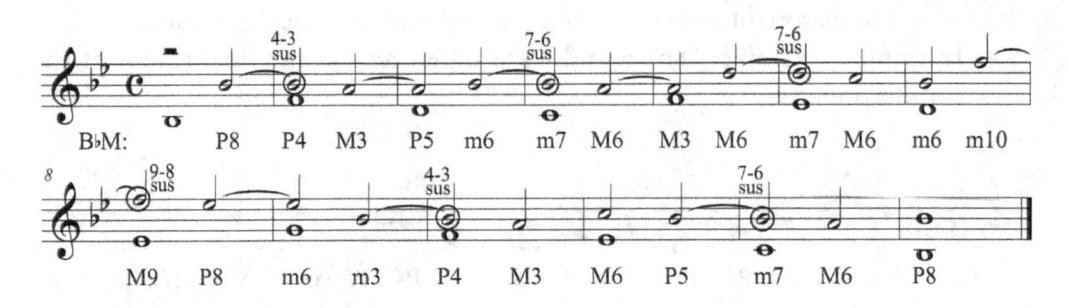

EXAMPLE 7.9 Fourth species.

Applications

Exercises

1. Provide a counterpoint in *first* species above each cantus firmus. Label all intervals beneath the staff.

   a. Fux

   CM:

   b. Fux

   Am:

2. Provide a counterpoint in *second* species above each cantus firmus. Label all intervals beneath the staff.

   a. Fux

   CM:

   b. Fux

   Am:

3. Provide a counterpoint in *third* species above each cantus firmus. Label all intervals beneath the staff.

   a. Fux

   CM:

   b. Fux

   Am:

4. Provide a counterpoint in *fourth* species above each cantus firmus. Label all intervals beneath the staff.

   a. Fux

   CM:

   b. Fux

   Am:

Brain Teasers

1. How is *static motion* a type of motion if neither voice changes pitch?
2. In *fifth species* counterpoint, also known as free counterpoint, the counterpoint alternates among species 1–4, exhibiting whole notes, half notes, quarter notes, and half notes tied across the bar line. Compose a counterpoint in fifth species to the cantus firmus below.

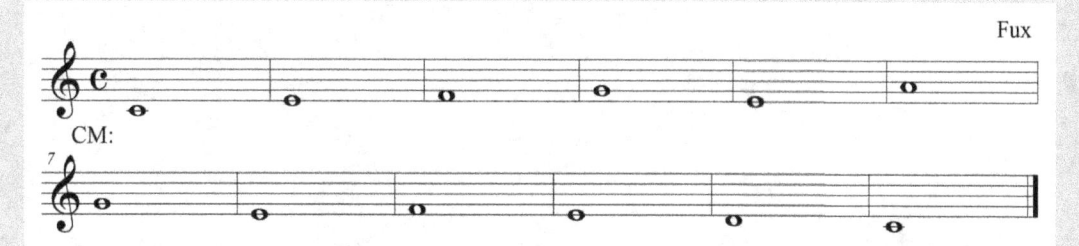

Thinking Critically

Which types of motion between two voices best promote voice independence, and why? What other factors impact the independence among voices?

Notes

1 The first systematic (and most well-known) presentation of species counterpoint appears in Johann Joseph Fux's 1725 Latin treatise *Gradus ad Parnassum* ("Steps to Parnassus"). See also *The Study of Counterpoint from Johann Joseph Fux's Gradus ad Parnassum*, trans. and ed. Alfred Mann (New York: W. W. Norton, 1971).
2 The counterpoint may be added below the cantus firmus, and the cantus firmus and counterpoint may be written in separate staves. The minor-mode version of this cantus firmus appears in Examples 7.6b and 7.8b.
3 P1 may be used as the starting or ending interval, but not within the phrase. In second, third, and fourth species, the unison is not used on downbeats. For simplicity, P1 is avoided altogether in this chapter.
4 Some sources do not permit neighbor tones in second species.

Part II

Diatonic Harmony

Diatonic harmony refers to the triads and seventh chords that are found in a given key as well as the behavior of these chords. Building on the voice-leading principles introduced in Chapter 7, Chapter 8 explores the manner in which chords connect, or *lead*, to other chords. Chapter 9 describes the various types of nonchord tones that ornament musical lines. Chapter 10 introduces the critical concept of *tonal function*—the musical role that a given chord plays relative to other diatonic chords. In this chapter, we begin to understand the *meaning* of chords as well as the logic behind the ordering of chords in chord progressions. Chapter 11 addresses inverted triads and how they operate in a musical context—often prolonging, or expanding, a certain tonal function. After examining seventh chords and their inversions in Chapter 12, Chapter 13 explores small musical units known as motives and phrases, cadences (musical punctuation ending a phrase), and period structures (two or more phrases combined). The final chapter of Part II, Chapter 14, considers patterns of chordal motion known as harmonic sequences.

8
Four-Part Voice Leading

Tonal activity can be effectively modeled in four parts, or voices. The voice-leading tendencies and harmonic processes examined in this particular musical texture occur in other kinds of textures and across many musical styles. This chapter builds on principles explored in Chapter 7.

Four Voices in the Grand Staff (SATB)

From high to low, the four voices are: *soprano* (S), *alto* (A), *tenor* (T), and *bass* (B). When notated in the grand staff, soprano and alto share the upper (treble) staff, and tenor and bass occupy the lower (bass) staff. Example 8.1 shows the relative location and practical range of each voice.

EXAMPLE 8.1 SATB ranges in the grand staff.

Although their ranges overlap, voices are kept distinct in strict voice leading. For example, the alto voice remains below the soprano and above the tenor. Stem direction differentiates the voices sharing a staff: stems go up for the higher voice in each staff (S and T) and down for the lower voice (A and B). The soprano voice typically carries the primary melody.

Chord Voicing

Chord voicing refers to the manner in which chord members are arranged in the various voices. There are numerous ways to voice any given chord.

Doubling

When voicing a seventh chord, each chord member may be assigned to a separate voice. When setting a triad, however, one of the chord members (root, third, or fifth) must be *doubled*, meaning it appears in two different voices. In Example 8.2, a C-major triad is voiced with three different doublings—each of which varies the sonority of the chord.

EXAMPLE 8.2 Doublings for a C-major triad.

How do we determine which chord member to double? While doubling is ultimately governed by voice-leading principles (outlined below), observe the following general guidelines:

- When possible, double the *root* of major and minor triads.
- Double the *third* of diminished triads (vii°).
- Do not double *tendency tones*, which include the leading tone ($\hat{7}$) and chord sevenths.

Additional doubling conventions shall be explored later.

Close and Open Spacing

Chords may be narrowly or widely spaced in the staff. Avoid more than one octave between adjacent upper voices—between soprano and alto, and between alto and tenor. More than an octave between adjacent voices creates a gap in the musical texture that disrupts the harmonious blending of voices.[1] More than an octave between tenor and bass is permissible.

In *close spacing* there is *less than one octave* between the soprano and tenor voices (Example 8.3a). In *open spacing* there is *one octave or more* between soprano and tenor (Example 8.3b). Which spacing options do the voicings in Example 8.2 exhibit?[2]

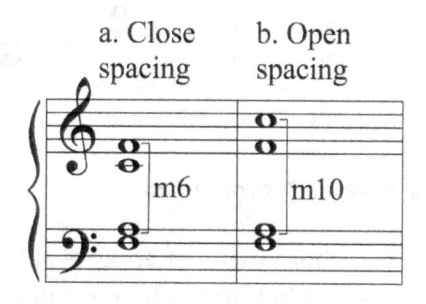

EXAMPLE 8.3 Close and open spacing.

Procedure for Voicing a Chord

Step 1: Spell the chord in a single staff, and in root position.
Step 2: Project the chord into the grand staff in SATB voicing.
- Place the correct chord member in the bass voice based on the required position of chord.
  - Is the chord in root position or inverted?
- Choose a chord member to double.
- Choose a close or open spacing.

Step 3: Make sure all chord members are accounted for and that there is not more than one octave between adjacent upper voices (S and A; A and T).

Example 8.4 demonstrates the process of voicing ii⁶ in A major.

Step 1: Spell ii in root position in a single staff (Example 8.4a). (This procedure is outlined in Chapter 5.)

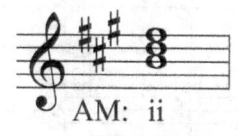

EXAMPLE 8.4A Voicing ii⁶ in A major: root position.

Step 2: Project the chord into the grand staff. Since the chord should be in first inversion, place the third (D) in the bass. Determine a chord member to double, and choose an open or close spacing. Six viable voicing options are shown in Example 8.4b.

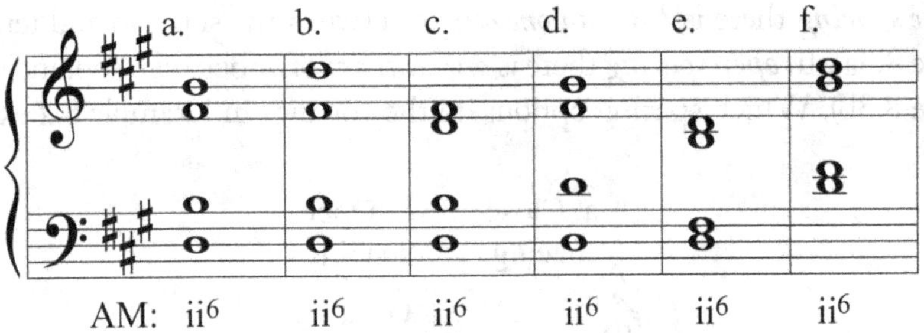

EXAMPLE 8.4B Voicing ii^6 in A major: chord projected.

Step 3: Confirm that each chord member appears at least once, and that there is no more than one octave between adjacent upper voices.

As discussed in Chapter 5, Roman-numeral labels provide important information about chords (root, quality, type, and position). However, they do *not* provide details pertaining to voicing, such as doubling or spacing.

Changing the Voicing or Position of a Chord

A chord may be rearranged in the staff to vary its sonority or allow a different chord member to assume the melody in the soprano voice. This might alter the spacing, doubling, or position of the chord.

A ***change of voicing*** occurs when the bass remains the same and some or all of the upper voices are redistributed, as in Example 8.5a. A ***change of position*** involves motion in the bass from one chord member to another, resulting in a new position that is reflected in the Roman numeral. With a change of position, at least one upper voice should remain static. See Example 8.5b.

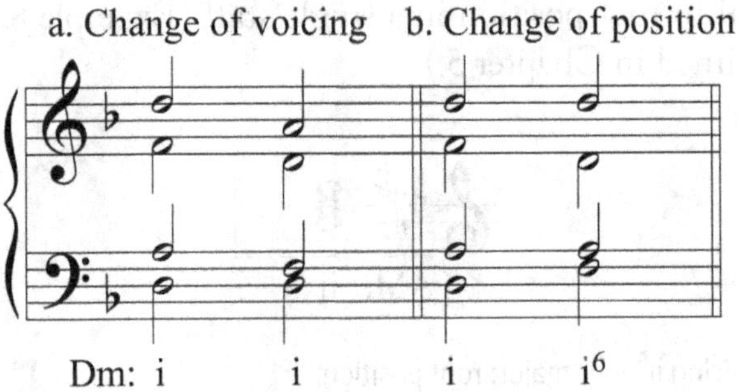

EXAMPLE 8.5 Changing the voicing and position of a chord.

Four-Part Voice Leading

Voice leading is the manner in which multiple voices move together through time. Voice-leading procedures preserve the independence of melodic layers while at the same time allowing them to fuse into chords that *progress* from one to another. In this sense, voice leading is the process of connecting chords to form *chord progressions*.

Economy of Motion

When changing the voicing or position of a chord, voices are essentially arpeggiating a single chord, so leaps in those voices are acceptable. However, when progressing from one chord to a *different* chord, each voice should move the shortest distance possible to form the new chord.

When connecting two chords, apply *economy of motion*: maintain any *common tones* shared by the chords, and strive for *conjunct motion* in the voices that move—but avoid parallel perfect fifths and octaves. While economy of motion is an important goal in voice leading, the smoothest option is never the only correct way to connect two chords.

Guidelines for Voice Leading

Common Tones
- Two chords often share one or more common tones. For example, I and V both contain 5̂. This scale degree can be retained *in the same voice* when progressing from I to V. In Example 8.6, 5̂ is held in the tenor voice.

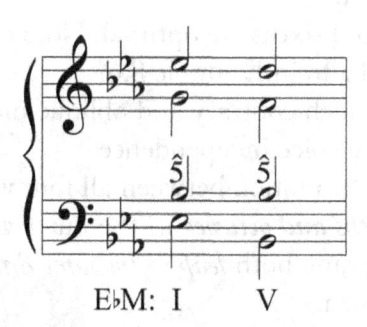

E♭M: I   V

EXAMPLE 8.6   Common tone (5̂) maintained in the tenor voice.

Conjunct and Disjunct Motion
- The bass tends to leap more than other voices, as the position of chords being connected more or less determines the motion of the bass line. In Example 8.6, I and V are both in root position, so the bass *must* leap from 1̂ to 5̂, either *up* a P5 or *down* a P4.
- The soprano, alto, and tenor voices are often able to step to the nearest member of the next chord. In Example 8.6, the soprano and alto both move down by step.
  - The three upper voices rarely need to leap by more than a third.

Types of Motion[3]
- Avoid **parallel fifths and octaves** between *any* two voices.[4] A parallel fifth (//P5) occurs when two voices forming a P5 both move to form a different P5. Although it appears economical, the poor voice leading of Example 8.7 contains //P5 *and* //P8. (A proper way to connect IV to V is detailed below.)
  - Avoid moving in contrary motion from P5 to P5, or from P8 to P8.

EXAMPLE 8.7 Parallel P5 and P8 (poor voice leading).

- **Unequal fifths** occur when P5 moves to °5 (or vice versa). These are permissible.
- Parallel thirds and sixths are optimal. Note the parallel sixths between the soprano and alto in Example 8.6.
- Incorporate as much contrary and oblique motion as possible, as these motions promote voice independence.
  - Avoid similar motion between all four voices.
- Avoid **direct fifths and octaves** in the outer voices.[5] These occur when the bass and soprano both *leap in the same direction* to form a P5 or P8, as in Example 8.8a.
- Avoid **voice crossing**—when a voice crosses an adjacent voice. In the V chord of Example 8.8b, the alto voice is above the soprano voice.
- Avoid **voice overlap**—when a voice moves below the previous note of the voice immediately below it, or moves above the previous note of the voice just above it. In Example 8.8c, the alto F♯ leaps up to B, overlapping A in the soprano.[6] What other problem occurs in Example 8.8c?[7]
- A **unison** doubling between adjacent voices is *not* a voice crossing. Unisons must only be approached and left by contrary or oblique motion. Parallel perfect unisons are avoided, and approaching a unison with similar motion causes voice overlap. Example 8.8d shows the

correct treatment of a unison doubling between bass and tenor: the unison is approached by contrary motion and left by oblique motion.

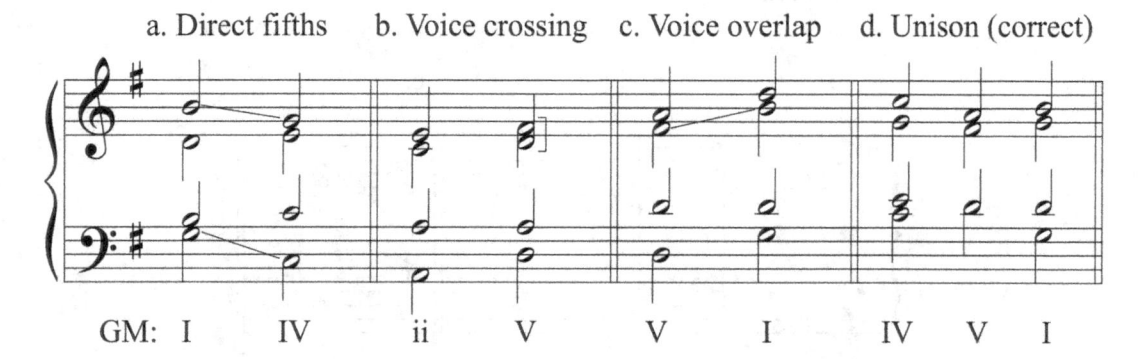

a. Direct fifths   b. Voice crossing   c. Voice overlap   d. Unison (correct)

GM: I   IV   ii   V   V   I   IV   V   I

EXAMPLE 8.8 Problematic voice leading (a–c) and proper unison treatment (d).

Root-Position Progressions

The general voice-leading guidelines explored above underlie more specific procedures for connecting root-position chords. The following examples demonstrate the most economical voice leading for connecting diatonic root-position *triads* with roots separated by third, fifth, and second.[8] Each example contains several chord-to-chord connections in the key of C major, with the root doubled in every chord.

Root Motion by Third (Example 8.9)
- The bass leaps up or down by third.
- Two common tones are maintained.
- One upper voice moves by step, contrary to the bass.

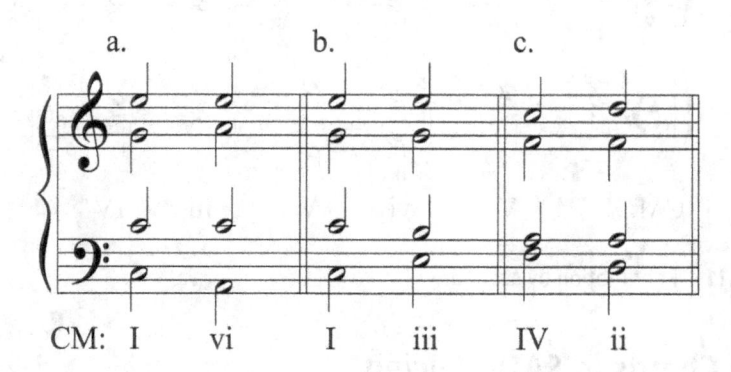

a.   b.   c.

CM: I   vi   I   iii   IV   ii

EXAMPLE 8.9 Root motion by third.

Root Motion by Fifth (Example 8.10)
- The bass leaps up or down by fifth or fourth.
- One common tone is maintained.

- Two upper voices move by step in the same direction.
  - The direction of motion depends on the specific chords being connected.

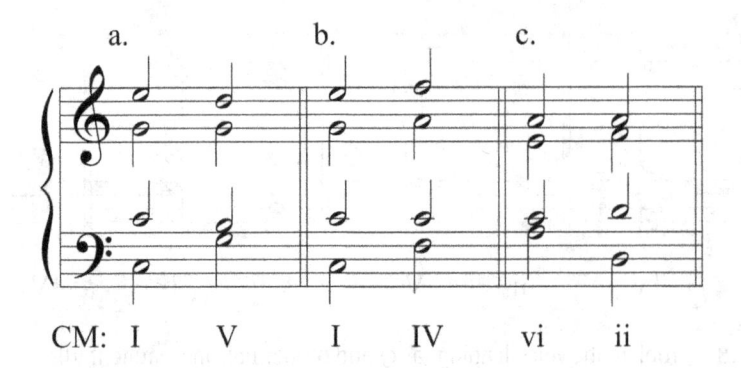

CM: I   V   I   IV   vi   ii

EXAMPLE 8.10 Root motion by fifth.

Root Motion by Second (Example 8.11)
- The bass steps up or down.
- No common tones.
- Two upper voices move by step, one leaps by third—all in the same direction, but contrary to the bass.

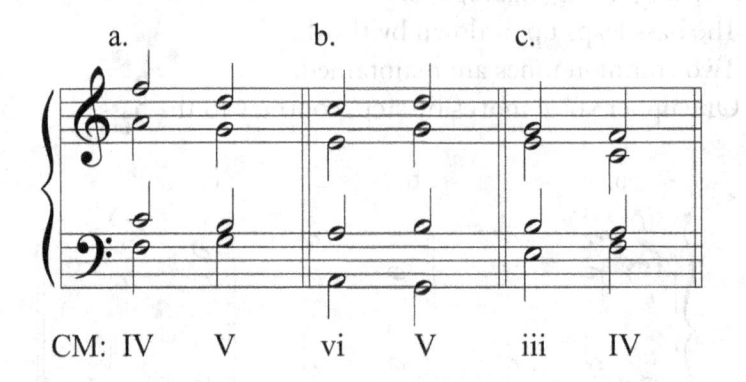

CM: IV   V   vi   V   iii   IV

EXAMPLE 8.11 Root motion by second.

Labeling Chords in SATB Voicing

In Chapter 5 we learned how to apply Roman numerals to triads and seventh chords stacked neatly in a single staff. When chords are voiced in four parts, we encounter numerous options for spacing and doubling. A process for labeling chords in SATB voicing is outlined below and modeled in Example 8.12.

Step 1: Transfer all notes in the chord to a *single staff* and arrange them in *stacked thirds*.
- Use any clef, and stack in any octave.
- Be careful to account for every pitch.
- Any note doubled in SATB voicing need only be represented *once* in the single staff.
  - In Example 8.12, the B♭ doubled in the soprano and tenor appears only once in the transfer (as the root of the chord).

Step 2: Locate the root at the bottom of the stack and determine its scale degree in the key. Apply the appropriate Roman numeral to the chord.

Step 3: View the original voicing of the chord. Determine which chord member is lowest and apply the necessary inversion symbol to the right of the Roman numeral.

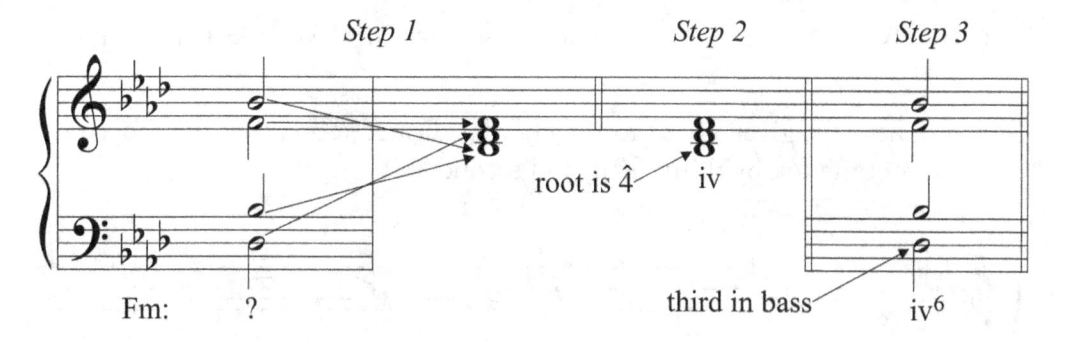

EXAMPLE 8.12 Labeling a chord in SATB voicing.

The Fundamental Progression: I–V–I

The chord progression I–V–I is the essence of tonal harmony. The framing tonic chords serve as stable points of departure and return. The dominant destabilizes the tonic to set up its eventual return.

This fundamental progression is often elaborated with other chords. The progressions I–IV–V–I and I–ii–V–I contain chords (IV and ii) expanding the motion from I to V. These progressions involve root motion by fifth (I–IV, ii–V, V–I) and by second (IV–V, I–ii). An elaboration combining these two progressions, I–IV–ii–V–I, incorporates root motion by third (IV–ii). In subsequent chapters we will learn more about the fundamental progression and various means of elaborating it.

Applications

Exercises

1. Voice chords (SATB) with the requested *spacing* (<u>O</u>pen or <u>C</u>lose) and *doubling* (<u>R</u>oot, 3rd, or 5th).

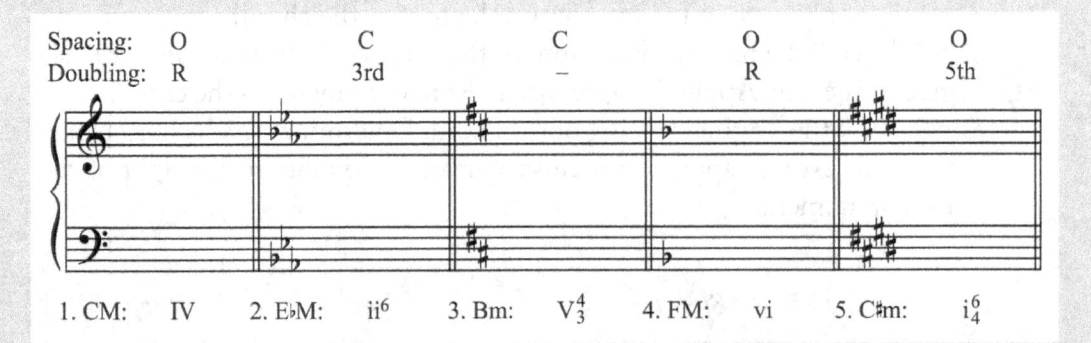

Spacing: O   C   C   O   O
Doubling: R   3rd   –   R   5th

1. CM: IV   2. E♭M: ii⁶   3. Bm: V$^4_3$ 4. FM: vi   5. C♯m: i$^6_4$

2. Connect the given chord to the chord indicated, observing the procedures for root motion by third, fifth, and second.

1. A♭M: I vi   2. Bm: i III   3. AM: vi IV   4. FM: I V   5. DM: IV I

6. C♯m: V i   7. E♭M: IV V   8. GM: vi V   9. Gm: III iv

3. Label triads and seventh chords with the proper Roman numeral and any necessary inversion symbol.

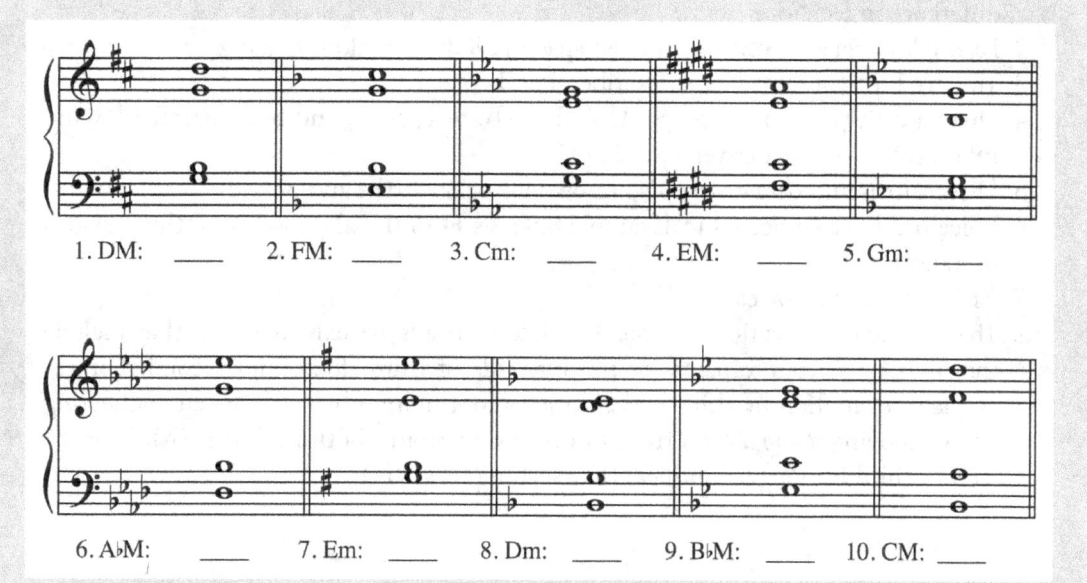

1. DM: ____   2. FM: ____   3. Cm: ____   4. EM: ____   5. Gm: ____

6. A♭M: ____   7. Em: ____   8. Dm: ____   9. B♭M: ____   10. CM: ____

Brain Teaser

What is problematic about the voicing of this chord?

Exploring Music

Listen to any musical work titled a fugue (you can easily find many examples by J. S. Bach). Focus on hearing the three or four individual lines as separate, independent melodies. Then, listen to any of Bach's many chorales, applying the same listening strategy. While chorales typically sound more chordal than fugues, it is still possible to perceive four distinct melodic lines.

Thinking Critically

Why are parallel perfect fifths (//P5) and parallel perfect octaves (//P8) considered faulty?

Notes

1 The gap between the alto and tenor voices can be difficult to spot because of the difference in clef.
2 Examples 8.2a and 8.2c are in open spacing; 8.2b is in close spacing.
3 The five types of motion are described in Chapter 7.
4 There are *six* pairs of voices: S–A, A–T, T–B, S–T, A–B, and S–B. Parallel P5 and P8 must be avoided between all six pairs.
5 Direct fifths and octaves are also known as *hidden* fifths and octaves.
6 Voice overlap also occurs in Example 8.8b, as F♯ in the alto lies above the previous soprano E.
7 //P5 in the outer voices.
8 These three root-position motions for diatonic triads are exhaustive, as they include the inversional counterparts for the intervals of third, fifth, and second. For example, root motion by third is the same as root motion by sixth: when connecting I to vi, moving *down a third* from $\hat{1}$ or *up a sixth* from $\hat{1}$ both lead to $\hat{6}$. (Moving the bass by third is more economical than leaping by sixth.)

9
Nonchord Tones

Nonchord tones:
- Are melodic embellishments that do not belong to the prevailing chord
- Sound dissonant against chord members
- May occur in any voice (SATB) but are most common to the main melody
- May be diatonic or chromatic
- Are classified by how they are approached and resolved—by the *interval* (unison, step, or leap) and the *direction* (same, different, down, or up) of the approach and resolution
- Are *accented* if occurring on a beat or with a chord change, and *unaccented* if falling between beats and chords
- Are circled and labeled in analysis

Nonchord Tones Involving Two Steps

Passing tone (pt)
- Approached by step
- Resolved by step in *same* direction as approach
- Usually unaccented
- The interval of a third between two notes in the melody can be filled in with a passing tone: the nonchord tone *passes* from one chord member to another (see Example 9.1a–b).

Neighbor tone (nt)
- Approached by step
- Resolved by step in the *opposite* direction
- Usually unaccented
- A voice steps away from a chord member and then returns:
  - Upper neighbor: voice steps up and then down (Example 9.1c)
  - Lower neighbor: voice steps down and then up (Example 9.1d)

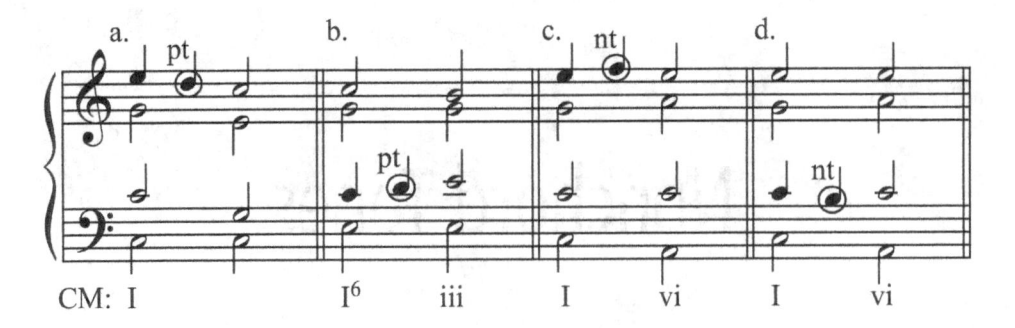

EXAMPLE 9.1 Passing tones (a–b) and neighbor tones (c–d).

Nonchord Tones Involving One Step and One Unison

Suspension (sus)
- Approached by unison (the same note)
- Resolved by step, usually *down*
- Accented
- As most voices move to form a new chord, one voice sustains a pitch from the previous chord. The *suspended* nonchord tone eventually steps down to a chord tone.
- Specific types: ***4-3 sus, 9-8 sus, 7-6 sus*** (Example 9.2a–c)
  - The first number indicates the dissonant interval formed between the bass and the suspension. The second number indicates the consonant interval formed when the suspended note steps down to a chord tone.
    - *4-3 sus* identifies the suspension is a *fourth* above the bass that resolves down to form a *third* with the bass.
  - The intervals are often compound.[1]
  - The suspended note might be sustained with a tie or rearticulated.
- The ***2-3 sus*** is the only suspension that occurs *in* the bass voice (Example 9.2d).[2]
- Upward resolving suspensions are less common. These are sometimes referred to as *retardations* (Example 9.2e).

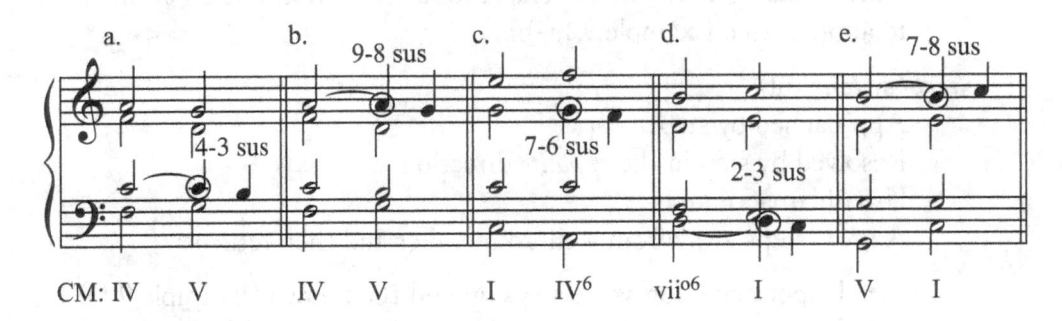

EXAMPLE 9.2 Suspensions.

Anticipation (ant)
- Approached by step in either direction
- Resolved by unison
- Unaccented
- One voice *anticipates* the next chord and moves to a member of that chord before the other voices move (see Example 9.3).

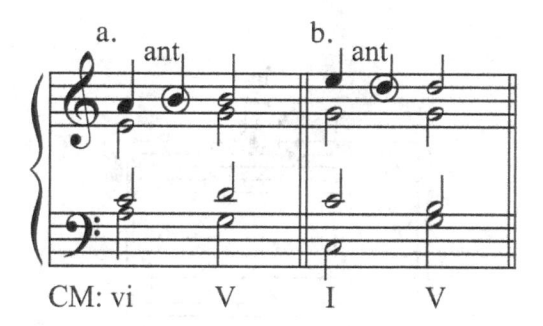

EXAMPLE 9.3 Anticipations.

Incomplete Neighbors: Nonchord Tones Involving One Step and One Leap

Appoggiatura (app)
- Approached by leap
- Resolved by step in the opposite direction
- May be accented or unaccented
- Considered an *incomplete* neighbor because its resolution resembles that of the neighbor tone (Example 9.4a–b)

Escape tone (et)
- Approached by step
- Resolved by leap in the opposite direction
- Unaccented
- Approach resembles the neighbor tone (Example 9.4c)

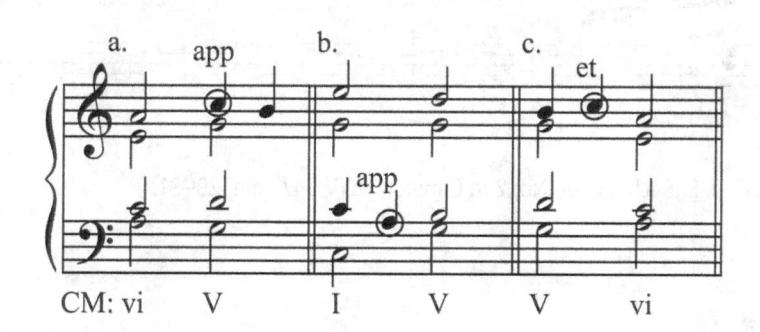

EXAMPLE 9.4 Appoggiaturas (a–b) and escape tone (c).

Other Nonchord Tones

Neighbor group (ng)[3]
- The upper and lower neighbor tones occur consecutively
- Involves a leap from upper to lower neighbor, or from lower to upper neighbor (Example 9.5)

EXAMPLE 9.5 Neighbor group.

Pedal tone[4]
- A tone is sustained while harmonies shift around it
- Occurs most often in the bass and is typically a prominent scale degree like $\hat{1}$ or $\hat{5}$
  - In Example 9.6, a tonic pedal ($\hat{1}$) is sustained in the bass at the close of the piece.

EXAMPLE 9.6 J. S. Bach, Fugue No. 2 in C minor, BWV 847, mm. 29–31.

Identifying Nonchord Tones

When analyzing music, how do we distinguish nonchord tones from actual chord members? Consider the following two principles:

1. Relatively shorter note values in a voice often indicate the presence of a nonchord tone.
   - In Examples 9.1 through 9.4, nonchord tones occur in the voice moving in quarter notes against other voices moving in half notes.
2. When determining the Roman numeral for a chord, a note that does not stack neatly (in thirds) with other notes is a nonchord tone.

A procedure for locating and labeling nonchord tones is as follows:

Step 1: Determine the Roman numeral for a chord by stacking the notes occurring together in thirds in a single staff (this process is outlined in Chapters 5 and 8). A note that does not stack neatly—or that forms a chord that is stylistically uncharacteristic—is a nonchord tone.[5]
   - In Example 9.7, eighth notes in the soprano voice suggest the presence of a nonchord tone. The notes occurring on and within the second beat (enclosed in a square) are stacked in a single staff. The pitch B does not fit into the stack—it is a nonchord tone.

Step 2: Determine the type of nonchord tone based on its approach and resolution. Circle and label the nonchord tone.
   - The nonchord tone in Example 9.7 is approached by unison and resolved by downward step, so it is a suspension.[6] Since it forms a dissonant (compound) fourth above the bass that resolves to a consonant third, it is circled and labeled a "4-3 sus."

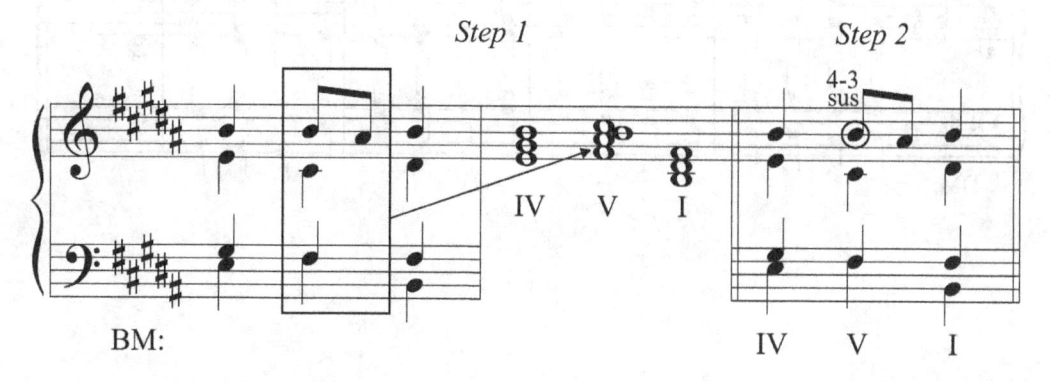

EXAMPLE 9.7 Labeling a chord and a nonchord tone.

Applications

Exercises

1. Analyze the following chorale by J. S. Bach. Label each chord with a Roman numeral and any necessary inversion symbol. Circle and label all nonchord tones. (In m. 5, consider the A♭ in the tenor voice to be a chord tone.)

EXAMPLE 9.8 J. S. Bach, Chorale 22, "Schmücke dich, o liebe Seele," mm. 1–5.

2. Analyze the progression below by labeling each chord with a Roman numeral and any necessary inversion symbol. Then, add nonchord tones to the progression. (You might consider copying the progression onto staff paper). Strive to incorporate a variety of nonchord tones in different voices (however, do not add too many simultaneous nonchord tones in multiple voices).

Brain Teaser

Label the chords below. Is it possible to add a passing tone in the soprano voice? Why or why not?

Fm: ____ ____

Exploring Music

Listen to the chorale in Example 9.8 (Exercise 1). How does the presence of nonchord tones—and the eighth-note activity occurring with the nonchord tones—in multiple voices impact your experience of the music?

Thinking Critically

In Example 9.6, how should the final chord be labeled? How do we account for its presence—where does it come from? What effect does this chord have on the end of this Fugue in C *minor*? (This type of chord will be examined in Chapter 17.)

Notes

1. With the 9–8 sus, the ninth is almost always a compound second (second + octave). It is rarely a simple second resolving to a unison doubling between bass and tenor (a 2–1 sus).
2. This suspension might form a ninth with either the alto or the soprano; it would still be labeled 2–3 sus.
3. Also known as a *double neighbor*.
4. Also known as *pedal point*.
5. A nonchord tone might stack as the seventh of a chord. Recall that only V^7, $vii^{ø7}$ (vii^{o7}), and ii^7 ($ii^{ø7}$) are typical seventh chords in music of the common practice.
6. At first glance, we might assume that the A in the soprano voice is a lower neighbor tone to B. However, the process of stacking all notes occurring on and within the beat reveals that A is in fact a chord tone. Most importantly, when listening to the short progression, the B stands out to the ear as the dissonant nonchord tone.

10

Tonal Function, Syntax, and Prolongation

We have learned to label diatonic triads and seventh chords with Roman numerals and inversion symbols. These labels specify what chords *are*. In this chapter, we begin to explore what chords *do*.

Tonal Function

Tonal function refers to the *behavior* of chords. The function of a chord is the *role* that it plays in a musical context.[1] There are three tonal functions: ***Tonic*** (T), ***Predominant*** (PD), and ***Dominant*** (D). In short, T provides stability, D destabilizes T, and PD transitions from T to D. Example 10.1 arranges the diatonic triads in a chart of tonal functions.

Function:	T	PD	D
Third ↑	iii	vi	vii°
Prototype:	I	IV	V
Third ↓	vi	ii	iii

EXAMPLE 10.1 Chart of tonal functions (major keys).

Each vertical column contains three different chords capable of serving a function. The primary triads (I, IV, and V) appear in the middle row of the chart as the ***prototype chords***—those that *best* fulfill each function. The top row features triads with roots a diatonic third *above* the roots of the prototype chords, and the bottom row contains chords a third *below* the prototypes.

Observe the following features of the chart:

1. Every diatonic triad appears *at least* once.
2. Each prototype chord (I, IV, and V) appears *only* once.
3. Two triads (iii and vi) appear twice in separate categories.

Think of chords as actors and each tonal function as a role in a script. There are more chords than there are functions, just as there are more actors in Hollywood than there are available movie roles. Different chords can serve each function, just as different actors can play a given role. However, some actors can play a role better than others, just as certain chords are better at serving a particular function. For instance, the prototype chords are so good at serving their respective functions that they are essentially "typecast" into playing those musical roles all the time.

The minor mode does not have a separate set of rules for tonal function. Although chord qualities differ, the Roman numerals for minor keys occupy the same locations in the chart as those for major keys, as shown in Example 10.2. In the Dominant category, V and vii° appear in place of the natural v and VII. V and vii° are *stronger* Dominant-functioning chords because they contain the leading tone, but v and VII can serve a weak Dominant function.

Function:	T	PD	D
Third ↑	III	VI	vii°
Prototype:	i	iv	V
Third ↓	VI	ii°	III

EXAMPLE 10.2 Chart of tonal functions (minor keys).

Adding the seventh to V, ii (ii°), or vii° enhances the function of these chords. For example, V^7 is a stronger Dominant-functioning chord than V.

Tonal Function and Scale-Degree Content

The triads lying a third above and below a prototype chord share two out of three tones with the prototype, which explains in part why they can serve the same function. However, it is ultimately the scale-degree contents of a chord that determine its functional potential. For example, $\hat{1}$ is the root of I, the prototype chord for the Tonic function. Considering the other two chords in the T category, vi contains $\hat{1}$ (as its third), but iii does not. For this simple reason, vi is a better T-functioning chord than iii. Similarly, $\hat{4}$ is the root of IV, the PD prototype. The ii chord also contains $\hat{4}$ and is therefore a stronger PD chord than vi.[2] Although vi appears in both the T and PD categories, it functions better as a Tonic chord owing to the scale degrees it contains.

In the Dominant category, vii° is a dissonant and unstable triad. Its leading-tone root and instability make it a better D chord than iii.

Although iii appears in two categories, its scale-degree contents leave it with a bit of an identity crisis. It *can* function as either T or D, but it does neither very convincingly because $\hat{3}$ has a strong Tonic association and $\hat{7}$ has a strong

Dominant association. Perhaps this "functional confusion" explains why iii is the least encountered diatonic triad in common practice music.

Tonal Syntax: T–PD–D–T

In the previous section, we learned that its scale-degree contents make vi a better Tonic than Predominant chord. However, since vi is capable of serving either function, how do we distinguish its function when we encounter it in analysis? We must examine the surrounding musical context to determine where it occurs in the tonal syntax.

The *tonal syntax* is a specific ordering of the tonal functions over time: **T–PD–D–T**. The fundamental component of the syntax is T–D–T: the harmony departs from T, arrives at D, and ultimately returns to T. The PD function is very often present but is not essential to tonal structure.

Understanding how the functions are ordered in time provides deeper insight into the nature of each function. T bookends the syntax, serving as a stable point of departure and return. The role of D is to destabilize T and set up its return. In large part because they contain $\hat{7}$, D-functioning chords have a strong attraction to T and typically resolve to a T-functioning chord. When present, PD *expands* the motion from T to D by pivoting between these two critical functions.

The T–PD–D–T syntax is the framework underlying all tonal music. This skeletal structure lurking beneath the musical surface is "fleshed-out" in a multitude of ways. In a sense, the syntax is a simple depiction of the rules governing harmonic structure—explaining how chords progress and why we sense harmonic motion, or direction, in music.

Example 10.3 shows three unique expressions of the tonal syntax. A *syntactic analysis* showing the functions of chords appears below the Roman numerals. In Example 10.3a, the prototype chords fulfill each function. This I–IV–V–I progression is a common elaboration of the *fundamental progression* (I–V–I) discussed at the end of Chapter 8.

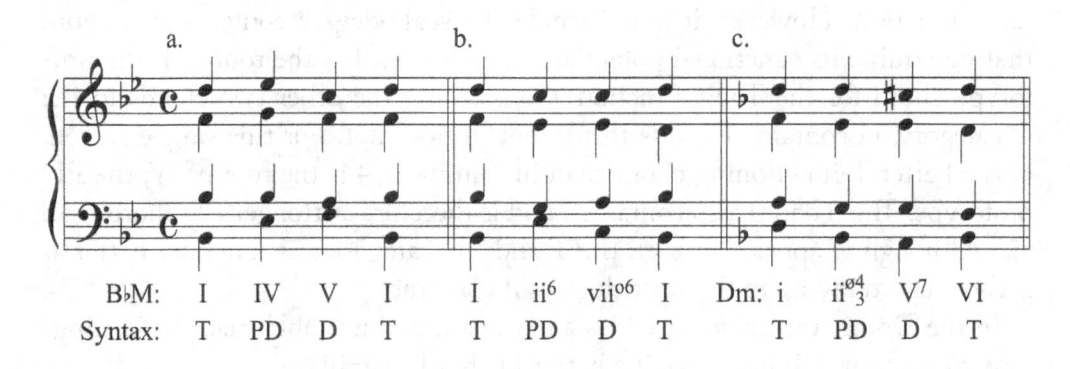

B♭M: I IV V I   I ii⁶ vii°⁶ I   Dm: i ii$^{ø4}_{3}$ V⁷ VI

Syntax: T PD D T   T PD D T   T PD D T

EXAMPLE 10.3 Three expressions of tonal syntax.

Substitution

Substitution is when a chord from the same function category appears in place of a prototype chord, as occurs in Examples 10.3b and 10.3c. In 10.3c, VI is clearly serving a Tonic function; VI cannot be a PD chord in this case because it follows D. It is the musical *context*—the positioning of chords relative to one another—that disambiguates the chord's function.

The motion from V to VI (or vi) is a ***deceptive resolution***. When music arrives on V, the listener anticipates a resolution to I, and V does lead to I most of the time. But when vi substitutes for I in this context, it serves a weak Tonic function, so the expectation for a strong and stable T is not met. Following a deceptive resolution, music typically returns to V and then resolves to I.

V–IV–I

While rarely found in classical music, the harmonic motion V–IV–I is common in popular music. This progression challenges a syntactic analysis because the PD prototype appears *after* D. IV might be viewed as an interpolation between V and I that delays the resolution of D to T. Since IV contains $\hat{1}$, we might hear it anticipating T in this context. The effect of IV anticipating I is particularly noticeable in passages where the melody concludes on $\hat{1}$ as the harmony reaches IV on a downbeat, as occurs at the end of each verse in "Let It Be" by The Beatles.

Prolongation

In the three progressions of Example 10.3, a single chord fulfills each function. Often, however, two or more chords will serve a given function. ***Prolongation*** occurs when a tonal function is expanded over time, often with more than one chord. The various techniques of prolongation help to account for the tremendous variety of harmonic activity encountered on the surface of music—activity that ultimately boils down to the same skeletal syntax: T–(PD)–D–T.

Techniques of Prolongation

Duration and Repetition

The simplest way to prolong a function over time is to sustain or repeat the same chord.

Series

Different chords capable of serving the same function often appear back to back, in a series. In Example 10.4, the T and PD functions are both initiated by their prototype chord and then prolonged with another chord from the same function category. The lines drawn between functions in the syntactic analysis indicate prolongational spans.[3]

EXAMPLE 10.4 Prolongation by series.

Chord Inversions

As evident in Example 10.3 (b and c), inverted chords can be functional. However, inverted chords are often prolongational. **Bass arpeggiation** occurs when a single chord changes position as the bass voice moves from one chord member to another. In Example 10.5a, T and PD are both prolonged through bass arpeggiation with the motions I–I^6 and IV–IV^6. In Example 10.5b, iii substitutes for I^6 in the bass arpeggiation to harmonize $\hat{7}$ in the soprano. In this context, the rare mediant triad prolongs T.

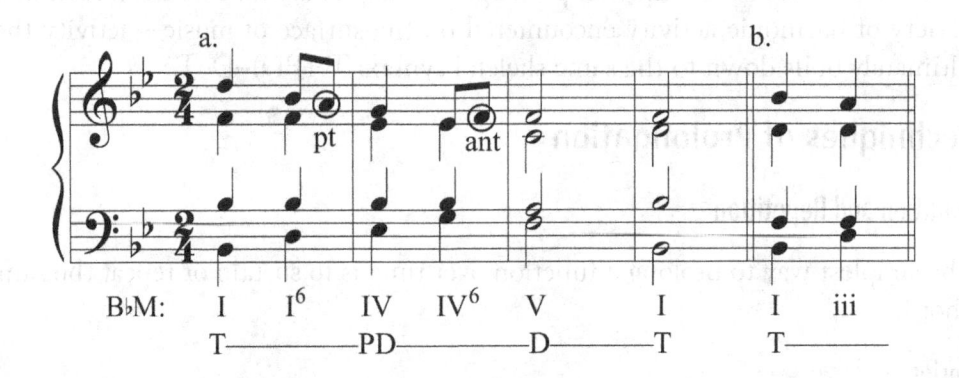

EXAMPLE 10.5 Prolongation by bass arpeggiation.

A *neighbor motion in the bass* can support an inverted chord that is prolongational rather than functional. In Example 10.6, the bass neighbors down from $\hat{1}$ to $\hat{7}$ and back up to $\hat{1}$. The lower neighbor $\hat{7}$ supports a V⁶ chord.[4] Such activity often occurs early in a musical passage—too soon to have reached the structural D. Therefore, this *neighbor V⁶* simply prolongs the initial T of the syntax.

DM: I   V⁶   I
     T————————

EXAMPLE 10.6 Neighbor motion in the bass (neighbor V⁶ chord).

We have briefly examined some first-inversion chords to gain a sense of how they contribute to the prolongation of tonal function. Our understanding of prolongation will expand in the next chapter as we take a closer look at inversions in general and at second-inversion triads in particular. A triad in second inversion is inherently nonfunctional and therefore prolongational.

Applications

Exercises

1. Practice drawing the chart of tonal functions for both major and minor keys. Begin by listing the prototype chords in the middle row. Then provide the diatonic triads a third above and below the prototypes. (For minor, use the more common V and vii° rather than the natural v and VII.)

Major

Function:	T	PD	D
Third ↑			
Prototype:			
Third ↓			

Minor

Function:	T	PD	D
Third ↑			
Prototype:			
Third ↓			

2. Analyze two chorales by J. S. Bach. After determining the key, label each chord with the proper Roman numeral and inversion symbol (if needed). Circle and label nonchord tones. Below the Roman numerals, provide a syntactic analysis that includes labels for the tonal functions and lines drawn between functions to indicate prolongational spans.

EXAMPLE 10.7 J. S. Bach, Chorale 14, "O Herre Gott, dein göttlich Wort" (mm. 1–2).

EXAMPLE 10.8 J. S. Bach, Chorale 146, "Werr nur den lieben Gott läßt walten" (mm. 1–3).

Brain Teaser

One of the chorales in Exercise 2 contains two instances of voice overlap. Can you locate them?

Exploring Music

When listening to the musical examples in this textbook, the music you are currently learning or performing, and the music you listen to on a daily basis, challenge yourself to hear the shifts of tonal function underlying surface-level chord changes. In other words, listen *into* the music. Consider Example 10.4 above. After opening on I (T), the progression contains five chord changes but only three shifts of function. The chord changes on the surface provide effective contrasts of mode and color, but the deeper shifts of tonal function create harmonic motion.

Thinking Critically

1. Analyze this short excerpt from a chorale by J. S. Bach. How do you explain the harmonic motion on the first two beats of m. 1? Does it relate to the deceptive resolution of Example 10.3c or the V–IV motion described in this chapter? How does the tonal syntax unfold in the passage as a whole?

EXAMPLE 10.9 J. S. Bach, Chorale 58, "Herzlich lieb hab' ich dich, o Herr" (m. 1).

2. How might adding a seventh to V, ii, or vii° enhance the function of these chords?
3. Look up "prototype" and "syntax" in a dictionary. How do the general meanings of these words support their application in tonal function theory?

Notes

1. Tonal function theory was first developed and promoted by music theorist Hugo Riemann (1849–1919). See, in particular, Hugo Riemann, *Vereinfachte Harmonielehre, odor die Lehre von den tonalen Funktionen der Akkorde* (London: Augener, 1893), trans. Henry Bewerung as *Harmony Simplified, or The Theory of Tonal Functions of Chords* (London: Augener, 1896). See also Daniel Harrison, *Harmonic Function in Chromatic Music: A Renewed Dualist Theory and an Account of Its Precedents* (Chicago: University of Chicago Press, 1994).
2. IV and ii are roughly equivalent in terms of functional strength, and they occur in near equal frequency as PD chords in music of the common practice. In many popular styles, including folk, rock, and country, IV is the more prevalent PD chord. In jazz, however, ii predominates.
3. In the syntactic analyses appearing throughout this book, lines connect one function label to the next even when a function is not being prolonged.
4. In fact, *three* voices (S, A, and B) neighbor away from and back to tonic chord members to produce this prolongational V^6. This economical voice leading results in a doubled fifth in the V^6.

11

Triad Inversions

We have learned that the functional *potential* of a chord derives from its scale-degree contents, but that a chord's function is ultimately determined by the *context* in which it occurs—its location relative to other chords within the tonal syntax. The bass position of a chord also influences its functionality, in part because inverted chords are less stable than those in root-position. Inverted chords may be functional or prolongational—at times, they prolong a function other than that implied by their Roman numeral.

First Inversion

Primary Triads in First Inversion: I^6, IV^6, and V^6

A first-inversion primary triad may initiate or prolong the function for which it serves as prototype. For example, I^6 may initiate or prolong T; IV^6 may begin or expand PD, and V^6 may fall anywhere in a Dominant span (see the discussion of *bass arpeggiation* in Chapter 10). In Example 11.1, iv^6 is the sole chord serving the PD function.

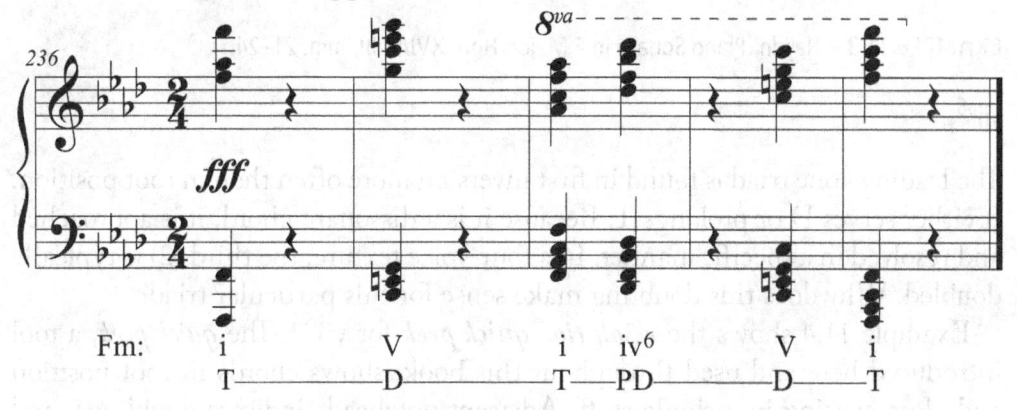

EXAMPLE 11.1 Liszt, Grand Étude No. 10 in F Minor, S. 137, mm. 236–40.

In addition to serving or prolonging D, V⁶ often prolongs Tonic function. In Example 11.2, a *neighbor V⁶* prolongs the initial T of the tonal syntax (see also Example 10.6).

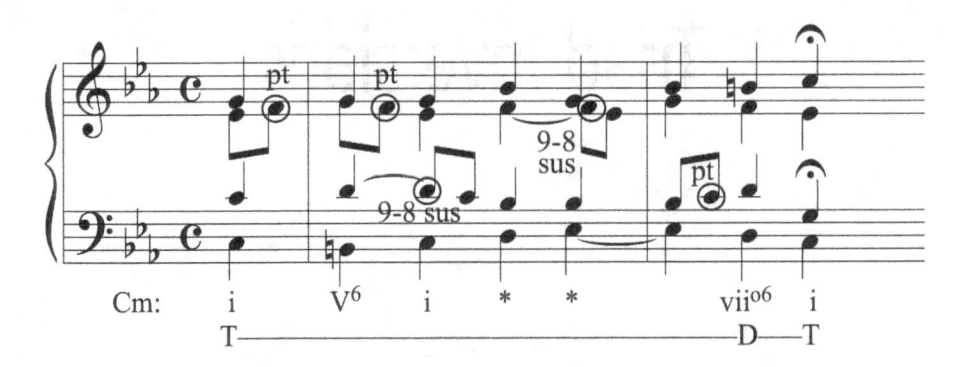

[Musical notation: Cm: i V⁶ i * * vii°⁶ i
T————————————————D——T]

EXAMPLE 11.2   J. S. Bach, Chorale 196, "Da der Herr Christ zu Tische sass," mm. 1–2.[1]

ii⁶

ii, a strong PD chord, is frequently found in first inversion. This position emphasizes $\hat{4}$ in the bass, which steps up to $\hat{5}$ as the syntax shifts from PD to D. In Example 11.3, ii⁶ substitutes for IV.

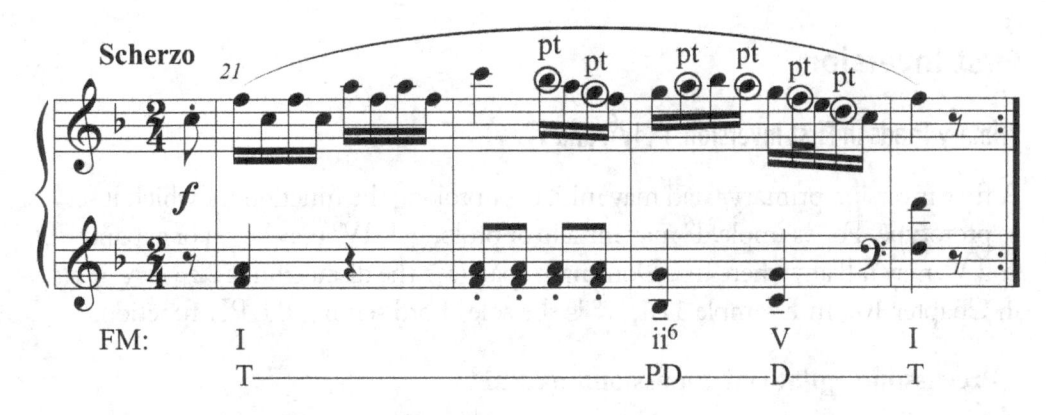

[Musical notation: Scherzo, FM: I ii⁶ V I
T————————PD——D——T]

EXAMPLE 11.3   Haydn, Piano Sonata in F Major, Hob. XVI/9, III, mm. 21–24.

vii°⁶

The leading-tone triad is found in first inversion more often than in root position. It either serves D or prolongs T. Because it is a dissonant chord, it is approached and resolved in a specific manner. In a four-voice texture, the third ($\hat{2}$) is typically doubled. Why does this doubling make sense for this particular triad?[2]

Example 11.4 shows the **resolution quick peek** for vii°⁶. The *quick peek*, a tool introduced here and used throughout this book, shows chords in root position and close spacing in a single staff. Adjacent noteheads indicate doublings, and lines trace the paths that chord tones take as the chord resolves. These same doublings and resolutions play out when the chords are projected into a four-voice texture, where voicing and spacing options are many and one or both chords might be inverted (see Example 11.5).

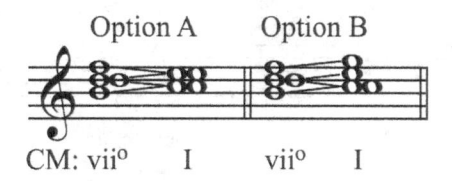

EXAMPLE 11.4 Resolution quick peek for vii^{o6}.

When resolving vii^{o6} to I:
- All chord members resolve by step.
- The root ($\hat{7}$) resolves up by step ($\hat{7}$–$\hat{1}$).
  - $\hat{7}$ is raised in minor.
- The doubled third ($\hat{2}$) moves by step in contrary motion ($\hat{2}$–$\hat{1}$ and $\hat{2}$–$\hat{3}$).[3]
  - If $\hat{2}$–$\hat{1}$ occurs in the bass, the tonic chord is in root position (Example 11.5a).
  - If $\hat{2}$–$\hat{3}$ occurs in the bass, the tonic is in first inversion (Example 11.5b).
- Two options for resolving the fifth:
  - *Option A* (Examples 11.5a and b)
    - The fifth ($\hat{4}$) resolves *down* by step ($\hat{4}$–$\hat{3}$).
      - The unstable °5 frame collapses to form the lower third of the tonic chord.
    - The tonic chord contains a doubled root, doubled third, and *no fifth*.
      - A chord missing its fifth is an ***incomplete chord***.
  - *Option B* (Example 11.5c)
    - The fifth ($\hat{4}$) resolves *up* by step ($\hat{4}$–$\hat{5}$).
      - The °5 frame moves to a P5, resulting in *unequal fifths*.
    - The tonic chord is complete, with a doubled root, one third, and one fifth.

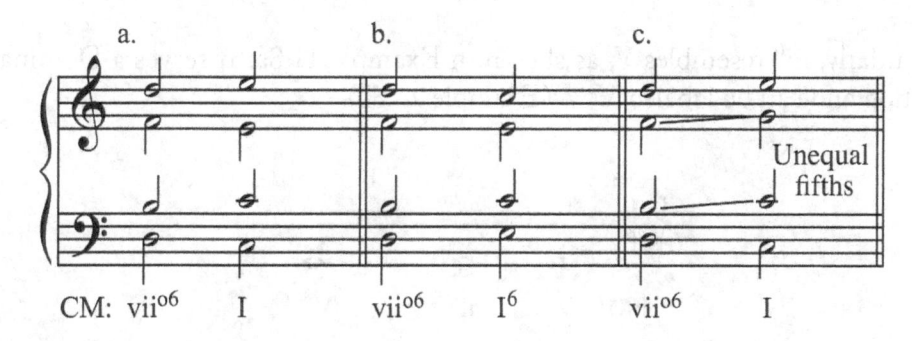

EXAMPLE 11.5 Resolving vii^{o6} to I in four voices.

In Example 11.6, a *passing vii⁰⁶* connects I to I⁶, prolonging Tonic function. How does Schumann resolve the fifth of vii⁰⁶?[4]

AM: I vii⁰⁶ I⁶ ii
T—————————PD

EXAMPLE 11.6 Robert Schumann, Nord oder Süd from *Vier Gesänge*, Op. 59, No. 1, mm. 1–2.

5–6 Technique (vi⁶ and iii⁶)

We learned in Chapter 10 that vi and iii are capable of serving two different functions: vi as either T or PD; iii as T or D. When vi or iii appear in first inversion, the scale degree in the bass sways the chord's function. Example 11.7a compares vi⁶ to I, the Tonic prototype. Like I, vi⁶ includes $\hat{1}$ in the bass and will therefore serve or prolong T. vi⁶ can also be labeled I⁵⁻⁶ (Example 11.7b), which identifies it as I with its *fifth* displaced up a step to form a *sixth* above the bass. This elaboration of a triad is referred to as *5–6 technique*.

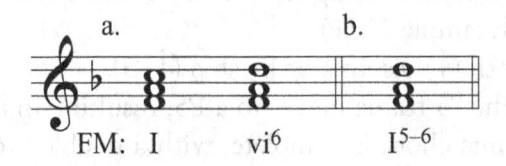

FM: I vi⁶ I⁵⁻⁶

EXAMPLE 11.7 vi⁶ as I⁵⁻⁶.

Similarly, iii⁶ resembles V, as shown in Example 11.8a. It serves a Dominant function and can be labeled V⁵⁻⁶ (Example 11.8b).

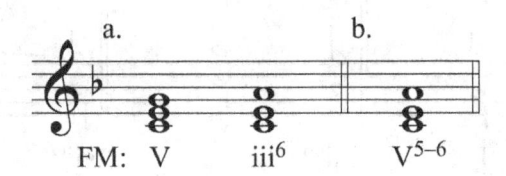

FM: V iii⁶ V⁵⁻⁶

EXAMPLE 11.8 iii⁶ as V⁵⁻⁶.

V^{5-6} appears at the end of Example 11.9. This apparent III+^{6} is augmented because the passage is in minor and $\hat{7}$ is raised in the D-functioning chord.

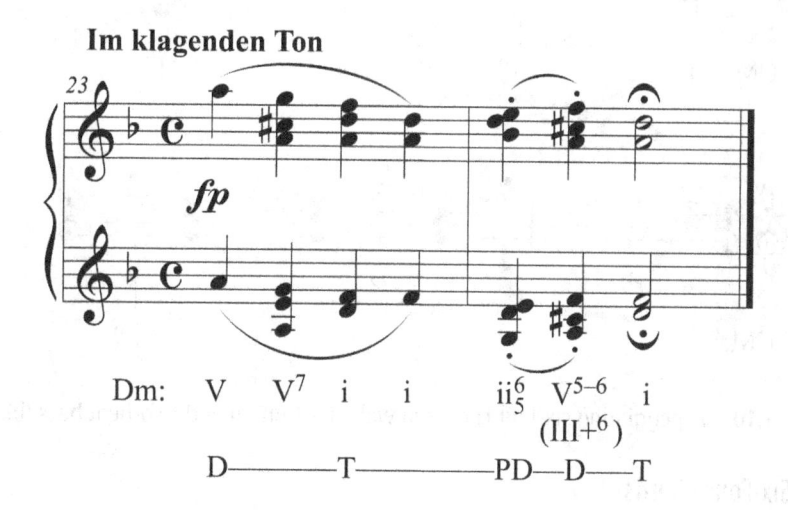

EXAMPLE 11.9 Robert Schumann, "Little Folk Song" from *Album for the Young*, Op. 68, No. 9, mm. 23–24.

Second Inversion

Triads in second inversion are *nonfunctional*—and thereby prolongational—by nature. Positioning a triad in second inversion destabilizes it to the point that it loses its functional potential, so its Roman numeral will not accurately reflect its role in the musical context. There are four varieties of six-four chord: arpeggiating, neighbor, passing, and cadential.

Arpeggiating Six-Four Chords

Arpeggiating six-four chords occur when a bass voice leaping among members of a static chord reaches the fifth. In a progression such as I–I^6–I$^6_4$–I^6–I, T is expanded as I changes position. The bass may exhibit any pattern of arpeggiation. In the familiar waltz formula of Example 11.10a, the bass oscillates between the root and fifth of a tonic triad. A similar oscillating pattern is often heard in country music (and related styles), where it is referred to as the *two-beat bass* (see Example 11.10b).[5]

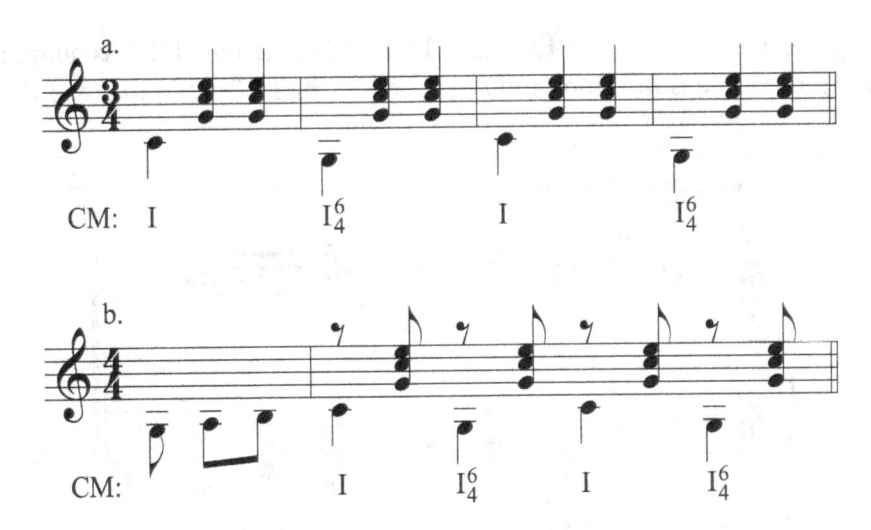

EXAMPLE 11.10 Arpeggiating six-four chords in waltz pattern (a) and two-beat bass (b).

Neighbor Six-Four Chords

In Example 11.11a, a *neighbor six-four chord* results from a stationary bass and simultaneous neighbor activity in two upper voices.[6] Although the six-four chord *looks like* IV$_4^6$, this entire passage is simply an elaboration of I. Since labeling it "IV$_4^6$" would be misleading in terms of the chord's function, we apply the label N$_4^6$. Besides the fact that it is a second-inversion triad, why else does this "IV$_4^6$" *not* serve a Predominant function?[7]

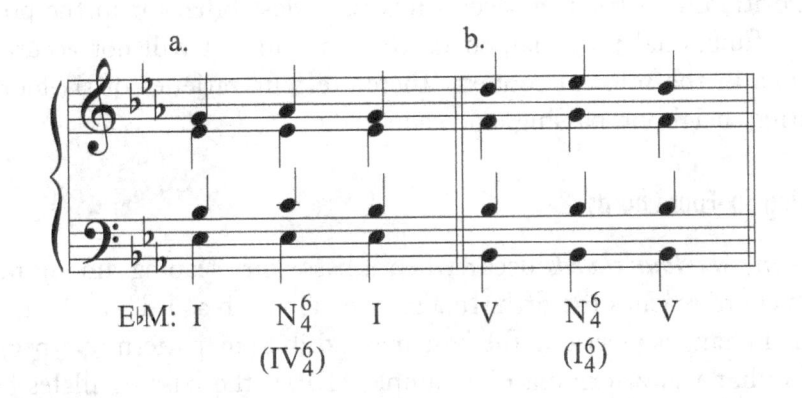

EXAMPLE 11.11 Neighbor six-four chords.

A N$_4^6$ chord can also embellish V, as shown in Example 11.11b. This N$_4^6$ *looks like* I$_4^6$ but does not *sound*, or *function*, like a tonic chord.

Voice Leading with N$_4^6$

Step 1: Begin with a root-position I or V, and double the root in an upper voice.

Step 2: Hold the two roots as common tones for the duration of the embellishment.

Step 3: Neighbor the third and the fifth *up* a step, and then back down.

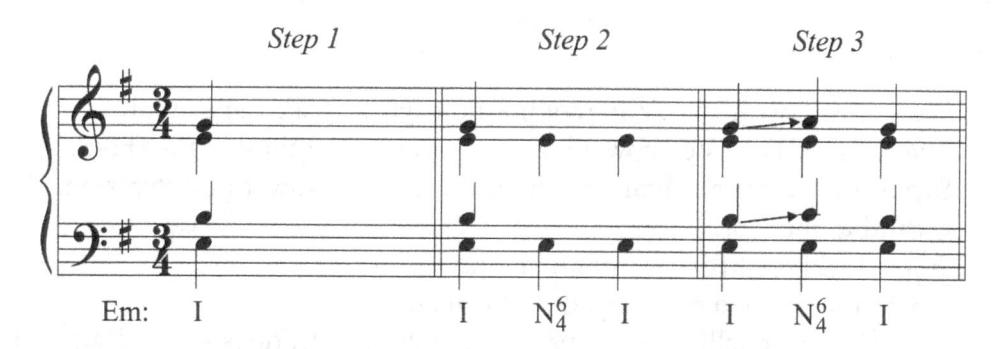

EXAMPLE 11.12 Writing a neighbor six-four chord.

Passing Six-Four Chords and Filled-in Bass Arpeggiation

In Example 11.13, the progression from Example 10.5a is recomposed with a ***passing six-four chord*** (P_4^6) connecting I to I^6 to further expand T. The P_4^6 results in a ***filled-in bass arpeggiation***, as the bass motion from the root to the third of I is *filled in* with stepwise motion: $\hat{1}$ *passes* through $\hat{2}$ on its way to $\hat{3}$. The same process then occurs at the Predominant level as the motion from IV to IV^6 is smoothed out with a passing six-four. The original bass arpeggiations are still present, but they are now elaborated with nonfunctional, passing six-four chords.

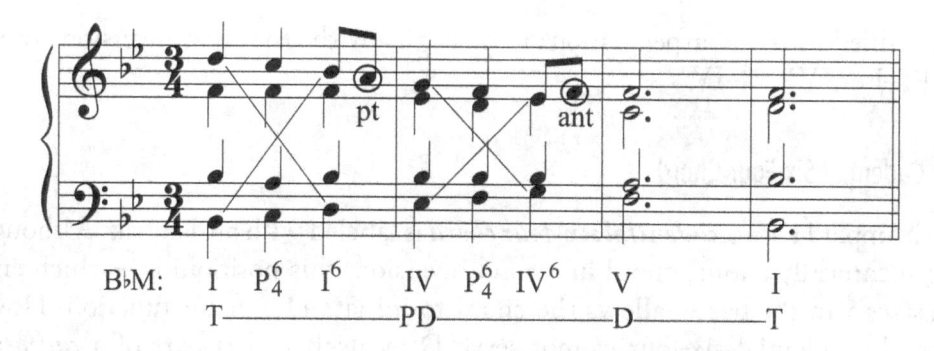

EXAMPLE 11.13 Filled-in bass arpeggiation with passing six-four chords.

Each X in Example 11.13 highlights a ***voice exchange***, where two voices trade chord members through stepwise, contrary motion. In the first filled-in bass arpeggiation of Example 11.13, the bass moves stepwise from the root *up* to the third of I; at the same time, the soprano steps *down* from the third to the root. This strong contrapuntal gesture recurs in m. 2 at the Predominant level. A voice exchange may involve any two voices but often occurs between the outer voices.

Voice Leading with P$^6_4$:

Step 1: Begin with I or IV in root position and with a doubled root.
Step 2: In the bass, step upward from the root to the third of the chord.
Step 3: In the voice containing the third, pass downward by step from the third to the root.
Step 4: Hold the fifth as a common tone.
Step 5: The doubled root neighbors down and back up.
  ◦ When embellishing I, this neighbor activity features $\hat{1}$–$\hat{7}$–$\hat{1}$. Raise $\hat{7}$ in minor. (This passing six-four chord should *look like* V$^6_4$.)

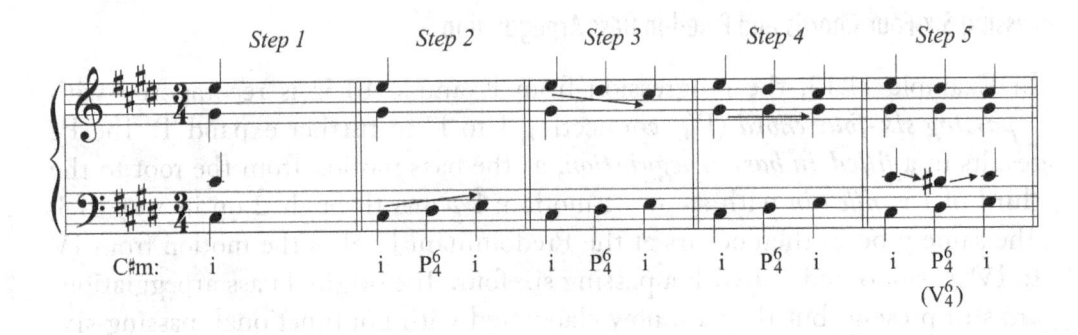

EXAMPLE 11.14 Writing a passing six-four chord.

A filled-in bass arpeggiation may begin with the first-inversion triad: I^6–P$^6_4$–I or IV^6–P$^6_4$–IV.

The Cadential Six-Four Chord

In Example 11.15, a ***cadential six-four chord*** is labeled with an asterisk. Although it is technically a tonic chord in second inversion, this positioning—which emphasizes $\hat{5}$ in the bass—allows the chord to initiate Dominant function. However, the cadential six-four cannot serve D by itself and is part of a *cadential formula*: it is preceded by PD and leads smoothly to a root-position V (or V^7). The cadential six-four expands D by delaying the arrival of the literal V chord. This cadential formula often appears at the end of a musical phrase, and the cadential six-four typically receives more metric accent than the V that follows. In Example 11.15, the cadential six-four falls *on* beat 2 and moves to V on the "and" of that beat.

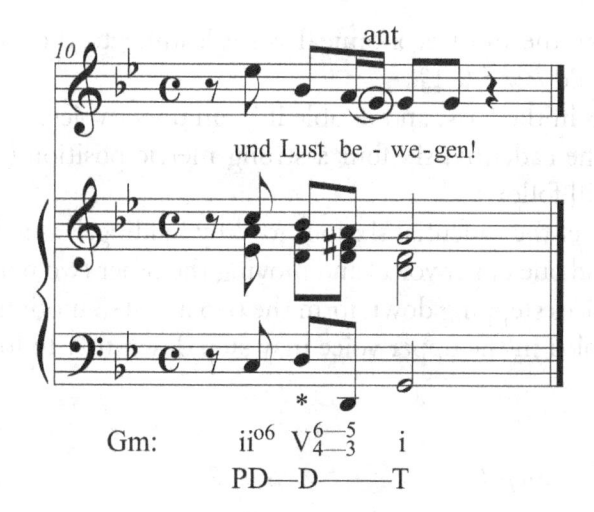

EXAMPLE 11.15 J. S. Bach, "Soll den der Pales Opfer" (Recitative) from Cantata No. 208, m. 10.

The label for the cadential six-four requires explanation. "V$_4^6$" does *not* specify a dominant chord in second inversion. Rather, the complete label V$_{4-3}^{6-5}$ indicates a dominant chord in root-position with nonchord tones in the upper voices. The nonchord tones form a *sixth* and *fourth* above the bass (5̂) and resolve down by step to form a *fifth* and *third* above the bass, respectively.

The cadential six-four in Example 11.16a occurs in an arpeggiated piano texture. Example 11.16b simplifies this texture by *verticalizing* the notes within each beat (in this case, every note is a chord tone). This procedure is useful when analyzing complex textures.

EXAMPLE 11.16 Mozart, Piano Sonata in G Major, K. 283, I, mm. 117–118 (a), textural simplification (b).

Voice Leading with the Cadential Six-Four:

Step 1: Begin with a Predominant chord like IV or ii^6.
  ◦ With ii^6 (in a major key), voice the root (2̂) *above* the fifth (6̂) to avoid //P5 when leading to the cadential six-four.

Step 2: Follow the most economical voice leading to the cadential six-four, which should *look like* I$^6_4$.
- Place $\hat{5}$ in the bass, and double it in an upper voice.
- Give the cadential six-four a strong metric position (relative to the V that will follow).

Step 3: Connect the cadential six-four to V by holding $\hat{5}$ as a common tone (in the bass and one upper voice) and moving the other two notes down by step.
- The voices stepping down form the 6–5 and 4–3 motions above the bass.
- $\hat{5}$ doubled in the upper voice may step down to $\hat{4}$ to form V^7.

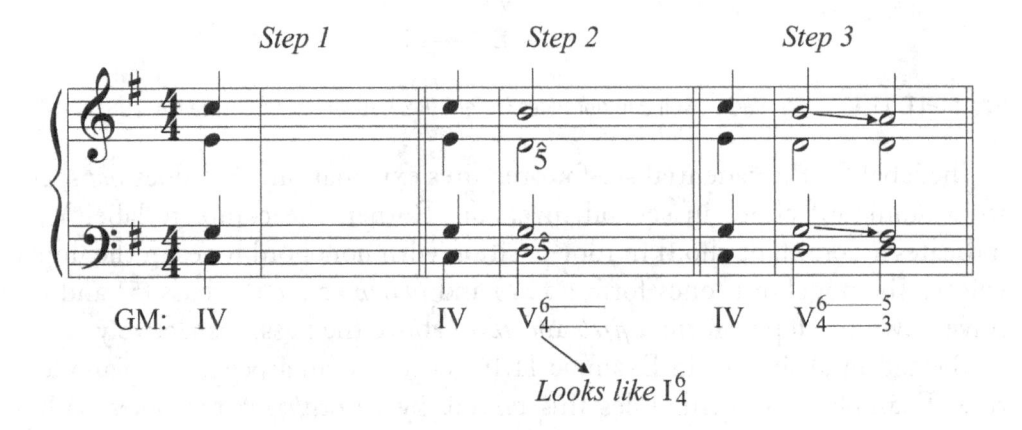

EXAMPLE 11.17 Writing a cadential six-four chord.

Applications

Exercises

1. Spell and resolve vii^{o6} chords in four voices. Observe the doubling and resolution tendencies described in this chapter (choose option A or B for resolving the fifth). The first vii^{o6} chord is voiced.

1. FM: vii^{o6} I   2. Bm: vii^{o6} i   3. EM: vii^{o6} I^6 4. Gm: vii^{o6} i^6

2. Complete short progressions involving neighbor six-four chords.

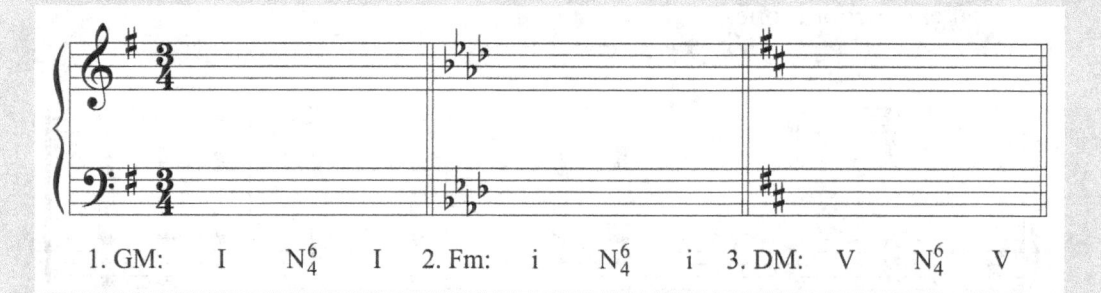

1. GM: I   N$_4^6$ I   2. Fm: i   N$_4^6$ i   3. DM: V   N$_4^6$ V

3. Complete short progressions involving passing six-four chords. Mark voice exchanges with an "X."

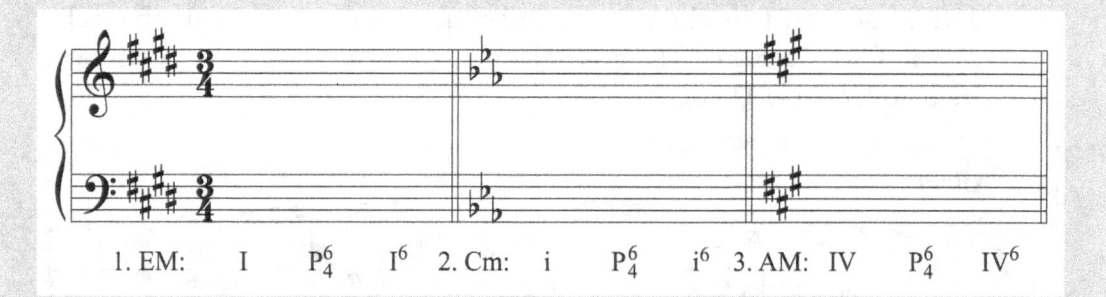

1. EM: I   P$_4^6$ I^6 2. Cm: i   P$_4^6$ i^6 3. AM: IV   P$_4^6$ IV^6

4. Complete short progressions involving cadential six-four chords.

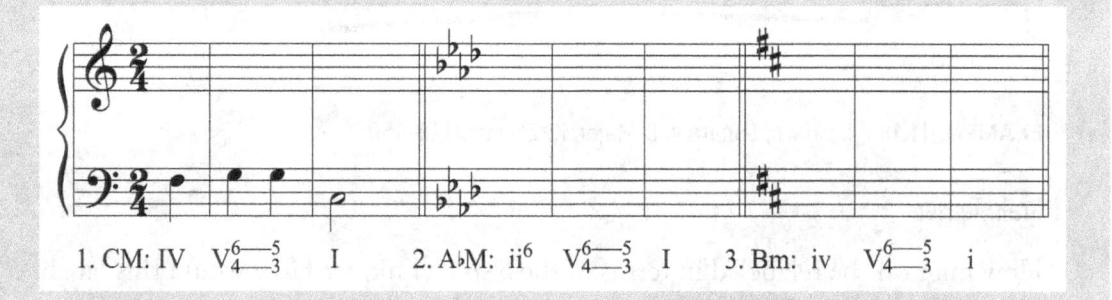

1. CM: IV   V$_{4\ -\ 3}^{6\ -\ 5}$ I   2. A♭M: ii^6 V$_{4\ -\ 3}^{6\ -\ 5}$ I   3. Bm: iv   V$_{4\ -\ 3}^{6\ -\ 5}$ i

5. Provide a Roman-numeral and syntactic analysis of the following chord progression. Label six-four chords as described in this chapter. Circle and label nonchord tones.

A♭M:

6. Provide a Roman-numeral and syntactic analysis of the passage in Example 11.18. Label six-four chords as described in this chapter. Apply the technique of "verticalizing" the arpeggiated notes occurring within each beat (refer to Example 11.16).

DM:

EXAMPLE 11.18   Scarlatti, Sonata in D Major, K. 21, mm. 148–150.

Brain Teaser

How might ii^6 be relabeled in terms of the 5–6 technique? How would this label mesh with the function of ii^6?

Thinking Critically

Refer to the passing vii^{o6} in Example 11.6. How could one voice be altered to convert this chord into a passing six-four?

Notes

1. The two chords marked with an asterisk will be addressed in Chapter 15.
2. The root is the leading tone ($\hat{7}$), and the fifth ($\hat{4}$) is the upper note of the diminished fifth frame. Both of these scale degrees are tendency tones that resolve in a particular manner. If either of them were doubled, //P8 would result during the resolution (e.g., $\hat{7}-\hat{1}$ occurring in two voices).
3. In Example 11.2, vii^{o6} resolves to I in m. 2, where it substitutes for V to serve a Dominant function. $\hat{2}-\hat{1}$ plays out in the bass. Instead of resolving D in the tenor (doubled $\hat{2}$) up to E♭ ($\hat{3}$), Bach leaps down by P5 to G, the fifth of i. Although this voice leading is not the most economical, it allows for the fifth to be included in the tonic chord.
4. The fifth resolves *up* by step (option B).
5. Steven Valdez, *A History of Rock Music*, 5th ed. (Dubuque, IA: Kendall Hunt Publishing, 2014), 37.
6. Owing to the stationary bass, the neighbor six-four is also known as the *pedal six-four*.
7. PD should *precede* D in the tonal syntax. This IV$^6_4$ does not lead to a D-functioning chord.

12

Seventh Chords

Seventh chords are dissonant harmonies that tend to resolve in a particular manner. Sevenths are freely added to chords in various styles of popular music, especially jazz. However, in Classical music, only three diatonic seventh chords are common: V^7, $vii^{ø7}$ (vii^{o7} in minor), and ii^7 ($ii^{ø7}$).

Chord sevenths are dissonant tendency tones that usually resolve *down* by step. Sevenths are *function enhancers*: adding the seventh to V, vii°, and ii improves the function of these chords. V^7, for example, is a stronger Dominant-functioning chord than V.

The Dominant Seventh Chord (V^7)

Because it so sharply defines the tonic, V^7 is among the most important chords in tonal music.

V^7 Basics

- Strong Dominant function
- Mm7 quality
    - In minor keys, the third is raised to produce the leading tone.
- Scale degrees as chord members:
    Seventh = $\hat{4}$
    Fifth = $\hat{2}$
    Third = $\hat{7}$
    Root = $\hat{5}$
- Contains two dissonant intervals: a seventh (between $\hat{5}$ and $\hat{4}$) and a tritone (between $\hat{7}$ and $\hat{4}$)

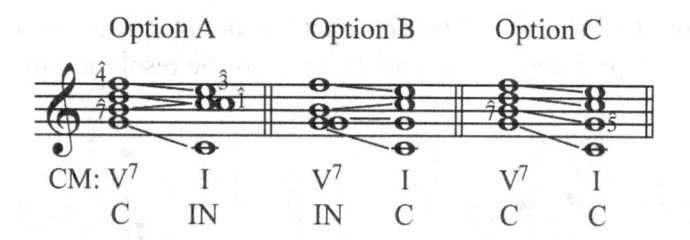

EXAMPLE 12.1 Resolution quick peek for V^7.

Resolving V^7 to I in Root Position

- Bass leaps from $\hat{5}$ to $\hat{1}$.
- The leading tone ($\hat{7}$) and chord seventh ($\hat{4}$) are **tendency tones**: they resolve by step in specific directions when V^7 resolves to I.
  - $\hat{7}$ resolves *up* to $\hat{1}$.
  - $\hat{4}$ resolves *down* to $\hat{3}$.
- $\hat{2}$ resolves down to $\hat{1}$, or up to $\hat{3}$.
- *Option A*: A *complete* (C) V^7 resolves to an *incomplete* (IN) I (Example 12.2a).
  - The incomplete I has a tripled root, one third, and no fifth.
- *Option B*: An *incomplete* V^7 resolves to a *complete* I (Example 12.2b).
  - When voicing an incomplete V^7, double the root and omit the fifth.
    - Do not omit or double either tendency tone ($\hat{7}$ or $\hat{4}$).
- *Option C*: Both V^7 and I are *complete* by "frustrating" the leading tone.
  - If $\hat{7}$ is located in an inner voice (alto or tenor), it may leap down by a third to $\hat{5}$, the fifth of I (Example 12.2c).

EXAMPLE 12.2 Resolving V^7 to I.

The Passing Seventh

The seventh of V^7 often appears as a passing tone. Example 12.3 shows several different options for labeling the *passing seventh*. In Example 12.3a, B♭ is circled and labeled as a passing tone. In Example 12.3b, all notes occurring on the first half of the measure are considered chord tones of V^7. Example 12.3c finds the middle ground: the label V^{8-7} reflects that the doubled root forming an octave above the bass steps down to the seventh prior to the resolution to i.

Fm: V i V^7 i V^{8-7} i

EXAMPLE 12.3 Three ways to label the passing seventh.

In Example 12.4, upper voices stagger down by step from the cadential six-four to a complete V^7. The 4–3 descent in the tenor is ornamented with an appoggiatura. V^7 resolves to an incomplete I to close the verse of this Lied.

A♭M: ii^7 $V^{8-7}_{6-5}_{4-3}$ I
       PD—D————————————T
                        V^7
                        (C)

EXAMPLE 12.4 Clara Schumann, "Ich Hab' In Deinem Auge," Op. 13, No. 5, mm. 27–28.

V^7 Inversions

- Inverted V^7 chords may serve D but often prolong T.
- When V^7 is inverted, both V^7 and I are *complete*.
- Resolving an inverted V^7 to I (regardless of position and voicing):
  - Tendency tones resolve: $\hat{7} \nearrow \hat{1}$ and $\hat{4} \searrow \hat{3}$.
  - $\hat{5}$ holds as a common tone.

- - $\hat{2}$ resolves down to $\hat{1}$, or up to $\hat{3}$.
- Position specifics:
  - V_5^6 resolves to I (Example 12.5a).
    - Bass: $\hat{7} \nearrow \hat{1}$
  - V_3^4 resolves to I (Example 12.5b) *or* I^6 (Example 12.5c).
    - Bass: $\hat{2} \searrow \hat{1}$ *or* $\hat{2} \nearrow \hat{3}$
  - V^2 resolves to I^6 (Example 12.5d).
    - Bass: $\hat{4} \searrow \hat{3}$

GM: V_5^6 I V_3^4 I V_3^4 I^6 V^2 I^6

All chords are complete

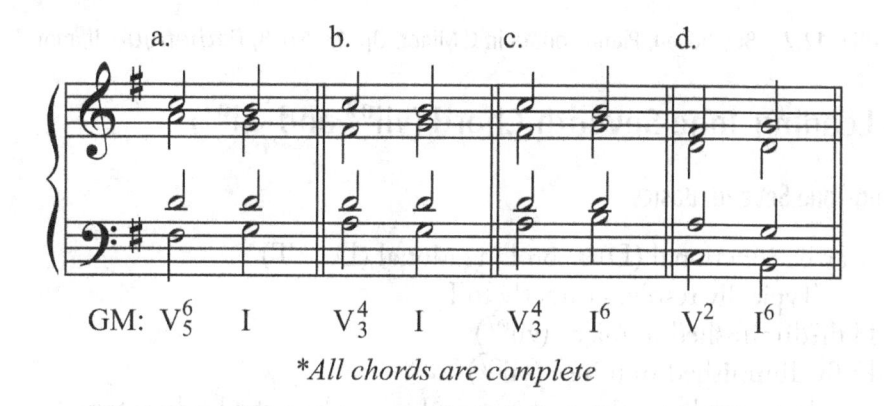

EXAMPLE 12.5 Resolving inversions of V^7.

In Example 12.6, V_3^4 prolongs T. The bass note of this chord (D) acts like an upper neighbor tone to $\hat{1}$ (C). V_5^6 functions as D at the end of the phrase.

CM: I V_3^4 I N_4^6 I V_5^6 I
T————————————————D—T

EXAMPLE 12.6 Mozart, Piano Sonata in C Major, K. 545, I, mm. 1–4.

Example 12.7 features several inverted dominant chords prolonging T. The first two of these are inverted dominant sevenths: V^2 and V_5^6.[1]

A♭M: I   V² I⁶ V⁶₅   I   V⁶ vi *   V
      T―――――――――――――――――――――――――――D

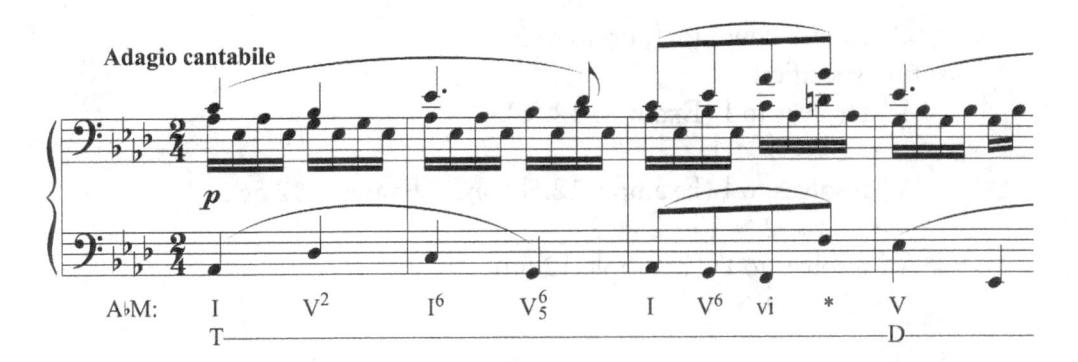

EXAMPLE 12.7   Beethoven, Piano Sonata in C Minor, Op. 13, No. 8, *Pathétique*, II, mm. 1–4.

The Leading-Tone Seventh Chord (vii^{ø7} and vii^{o7})

Leading-Tone Seventh Basics

- May be functional (D) *or* prolongational (D or T)
  - Typically resolves directly to I
- Half-diminished in major (vii^{ø7})
- Fully diminished in minor (vii^{o7})
  - In minor keys, the root is raised to produce the leading tone.
  - vii^{o7} contains two interlocked tritones: one between the root and fifth, and the other between the third and seventh.²
- Scale degrees as chord members:
  - Seventh = $\hat{6}$
  - Fifth = $\hat{4}$
  - Third = $\hat{2}$
  - Root = $\hat{7}$

Cm: vii^{o7}   i   vii^{o7}   i

EXAMPLE 12.8   Resolution quick peek for vii^{o7}.

Resolving vii^{ø7} and vii^{o7} in Any Position

- All voices resolve by step.
  - Root steps *up*: $\hat{7} \nearrow \hat{1}$.
  - Fifth and seventh step *down*: $\hat{4} \searrow \hat{3}$ and $\hat{6} \searrow \hat{5}$.
  - Two options for resolving the third:

- *Option A*: Third steps *up* ($\hat{2} \nearrow \hat{3}$).
    - The tonic chord has a doubled third (Example 12.9a and c).
- *Option B*: Third steps *down* ($\hat{2} \searrow \hat{1}$).
    - The tonic has a doubled root (Example 12.9b, d–e).
    - With vii^{o7}, this creates acceptable unequal fifths (^{o}5–P5) as the third and seventh step down (Example 12.9b).
    - With vii^{ø7}, this results in faulty //P5 if the seventh is voiced *above* the third (Example 12.9d).
        - If the seventh is voiced *below* the third, the //P4 that occur are acceptable (Example 12.9e).

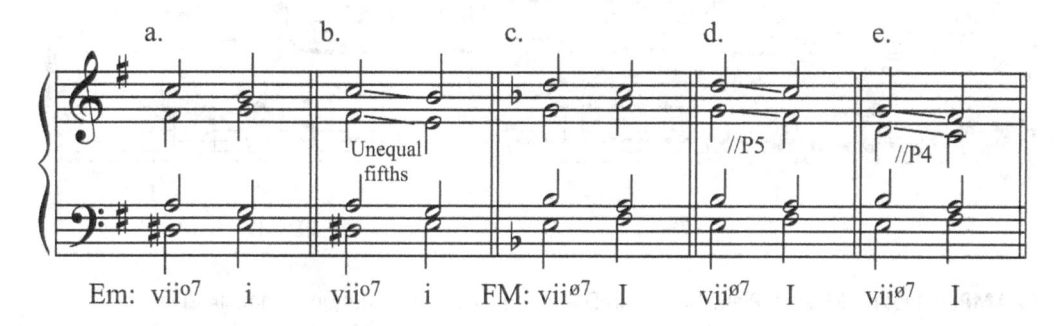

EXAMPLE 12.9 Resolving the leading-tone seventh chord.

- Position specifics:
    - vii^{o7} resolves to i (Examples 12.9a–e).
        - Bass: $\hat{7} \nearrow \hat{1}$
    - vii$^{o6}_5$ resolves to i (Example 12.10a) *or* i^6 (Example 12.10b).
        - Bass: $\hat{2} \searrow \hat{1}$ *or* $\hat{2} \nearrow \hat{3}$
        - vii$^{ø6}_5$ should resolve to I^6 to avoid //P5 (Example 12.10e and f).
    - vii$^{o4}_3$ resolves to i^6 (Example 12.10c).
        - Bass: $\hat{4} \searrow \hat{3}$
    - vii^{o2} resolves to i$^6_4$ (Example 12.10d).
        - Bass: $\hat{6} \searrow \hat{5}$

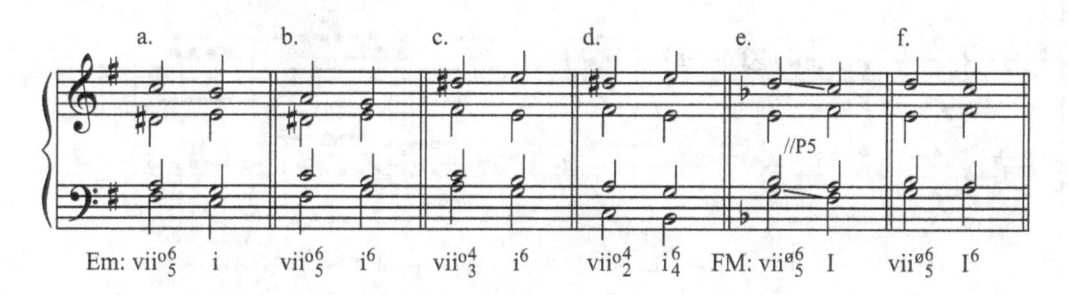

EXAMPLE 12.10 Resolving inversions of the leading-tone seventh chord.

The tonal syntax unfolds twice in Example 12.11, with vii^{ø7} serving the initial D. On a deeper level of tonal structure, the first statement of the syntax is embedded in the opening Tonic span, as indicated by the parentheses enclosing function labels in the syntactic analysis (PD–D–T). In m. 15, the bass arpeggiates chord members of IV and vii^{ø7}, and the root is the structural bass note of each chord, even though it arrives *after* the fifth. How does Mozart resolve the third of vii^{ø7}?[3]

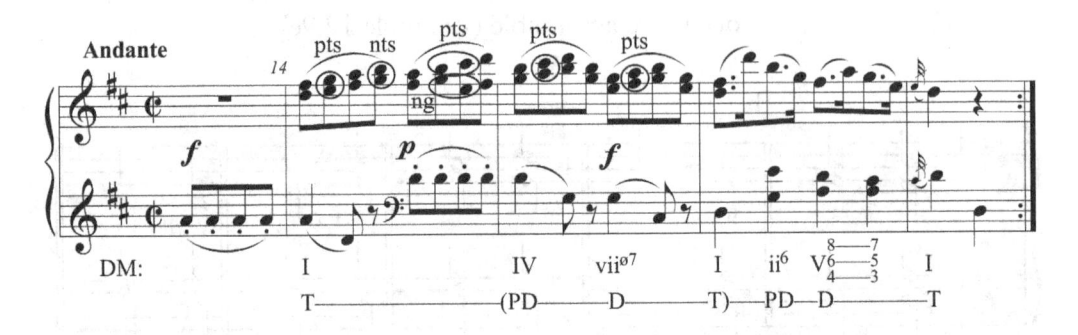

EXAMPLE 12.11 Mozart, Piano Sonata in D Major, K. 284, III, Variation V, mm. 14–17.

Two leading-tone seventh chords occur in the first half of Example 12.12. The syntactic analysis reveals that two surface-level D–T motions are embedded in the opening Tonic span. How does Haydn resolve the third of vii^{o7} and vii$^{o6}_{5}$?[4]

EXAMPLE 12.12 Haydn, String Quartet in G Major, Op. 17, No. 5, III, mm. 1–8.

The Supertonic Seventh Chord (ii^7 and ii^{ø7})

The seventh is frequently added to ii (or ii°) to enhance its Predominant function. Any position is possible, but ii^7 and ii$^6_5$ are the most common. Regardless of position, the voice leading to V, V^7, or the cadential six-four is highly economical.

Resolving ii^7 and ii^{ø7}

- The seventh, $\hat{1}$, resolves *down* to $\hat{7}$ (Example 12.13a–b, d, and f).
  - The seventh sustains on $\hat{1}$ if ii^7 moves through the cadential six-four on its way to V (Example 12.13c and e).
- When the third, $\hat{4}$, appears in an upper voice, it may sustain as a common tone to become the seventh of V^7 (Example 12.13b and d).
- ii^7 in root position may be complete or incomplete, and may resolve to a Dominant-functioning chord that is complete or incomplete. Various resolution options are given in Example 12.13.
  - In Example 12.13a, a complete ii^7 resolves to an incomplete V. The soprano may also leap down (C ↘ A), allowing V to be complete.
  - ii^{ø7} in minor is typically complete. Its fifth, $\hat{6}$, has a strong tendency to resolve down by half step to $\hat{5}$.
- When ii^7 is inverted, all chords may be complete.
  - Like ii^6, ii$^6_5$ places $\hat{4}$ in the bass, which steps up to $\hat{5}$ with the tonal shift to D (Example 12.13f).

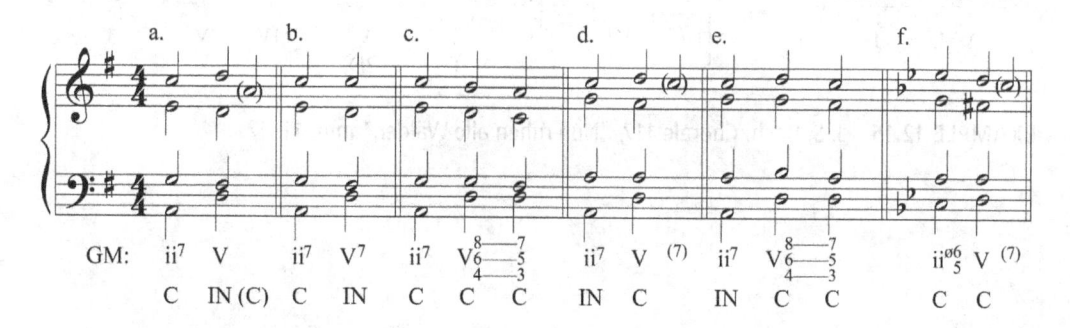

EXAMPLE 12.13 Resolving ii^7.

In Example 12.14, ii$^{ø6}_5$ substitutes for iv at the end of a filled-in bass arpeggiation prolonging PD. How does the leading tone of V^7 resolve?[5]

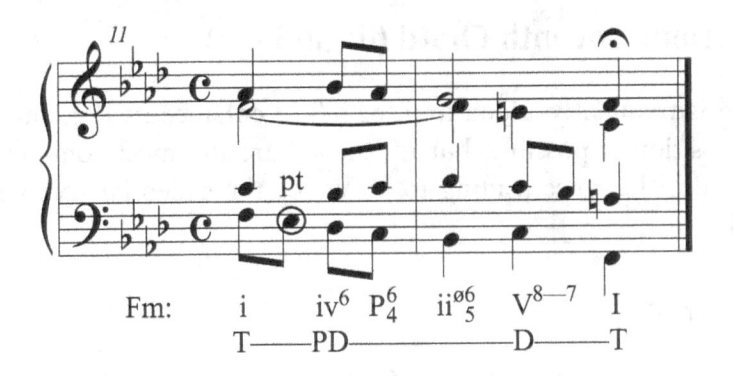

EXAMPLE 12.14 J. S. Bach, Chorale 25, "Wo soll lich fliehen hin," mm. 11–12.

Other Seventh Chords

Diatonic seventh chords other than V^7, $vii^{ø7}$, and ii^7 are less typical of common practice music. Many times, the pitch that *seems* to form the seventh of a chord like I^7, iii^7, IV^7, or vi^7 can be considered a nonchord tone. In Example 12.15a, the soprano-note C appears to form a IV^7 chord on the downbeat of m. 12. This tone is labeled an (accented) passing tone in Example 12.15b.[6]

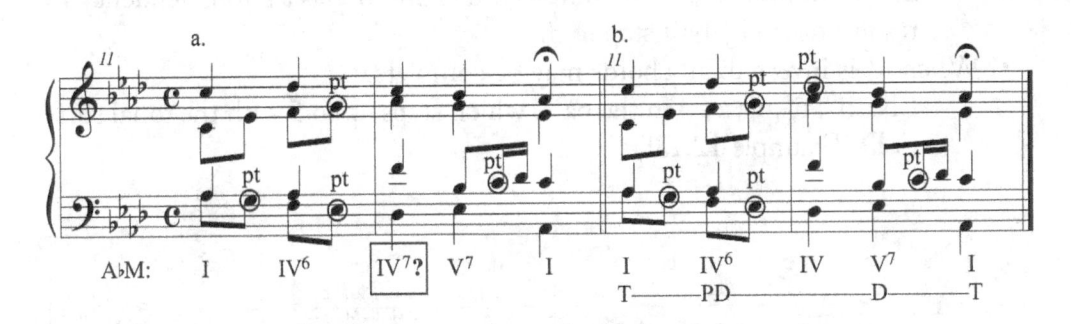

EXAMPLE 12.15 J. S. Bach, Chorale 117, "Nun ruhen alle Wälder," mm. 11–12.

Applications

Exercises

1. Spell and resolve dominant seventh chords in root position. Chord voicings should be either *complete* (C) or *incomplete* (IN), as indicated below the Roman numerals.

1. A♭M:	V⁷	I	2. DM:	V⁷	I	3. F♯m:	V⁷	i	4. B♭M:	V⁷	I
	C	IN		IN	C		C	IN		C	C

5. C♯m:	V⁷	i	6. E♭M:	V⁷	I	7. Em:	V⁷	i	8. Fm:	V⁷	i
	IN	C		C	IN		C	C		IN	C

2. Spell and resolve inverted dominant seventh chords. All chords should be complete. Add any necessary inversion symbol to the tonic chord.

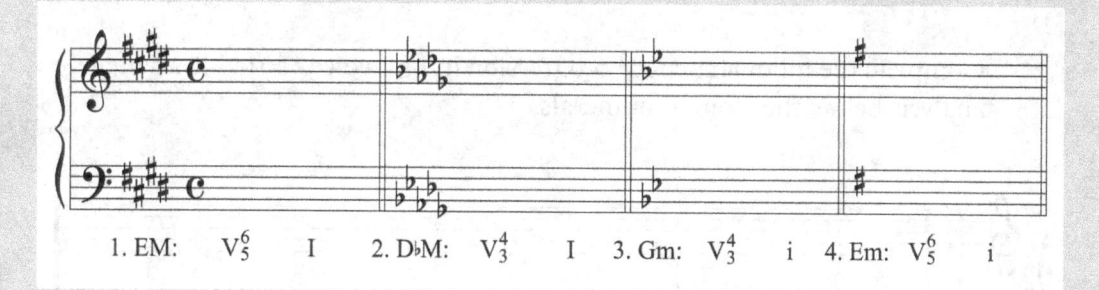

1. EM:	V$^6_5$	I	2. D♭M:	V$^4_3$	I	3. Gm:	V$^4_3$	i	4. Em:	V$^6_5$	i

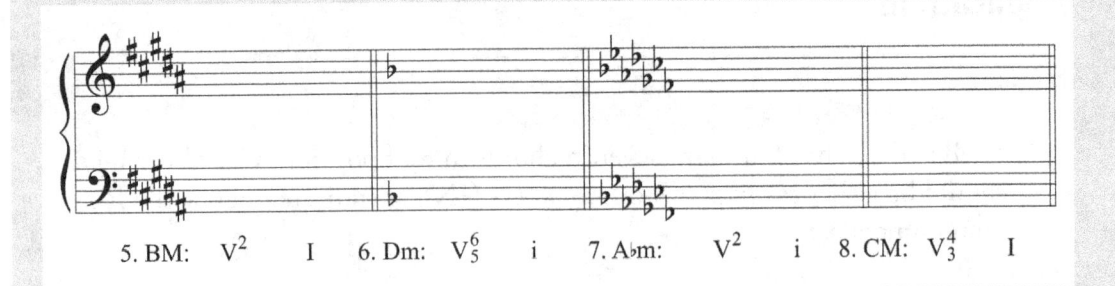

5. BM: V² I   6. Dm: V⁶₅ i   7. A♭m: V² i   8. CM: V⁴₃ I

3. Spell and resolve leading-tone seventh chords in root position and inversion. Add any necessary inversion symbol to the tonic chord.

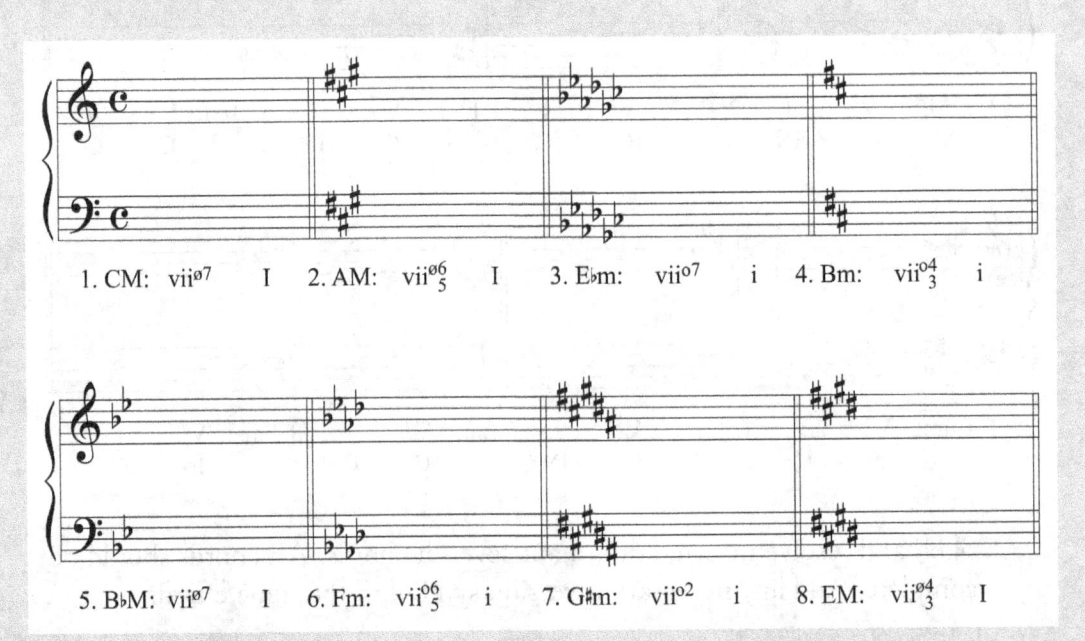

1. CM: vii⌀⁷ I   2. AM: vii⌀⁶₅ I   3. E♭m: vii°⁷ i   4. Bm: vii°⁴₃ i

5. B♭M: vii⌀⁷ I   6. Fm: vii°⁶₅ i   7. G♯m: vii°² i   8. EM: vii°⁴₃ I

4. Complete the following chord progression in four voices. Provide a syntactic analysis below the Roman numerals.

B♭M: I V⁶ I I⁶ IV P⁶₄ IV⁶ ii⁶₅ V⁶₄—⁷₅₃ I

Brain Teaser

What triad is shared by V^7 and $vii^{ø7}$? How do these two seventh chords differ in terms of their scale-degree contents?

Thinking Critically

An incomplete triad or seventh chord is missing its fifth. Compared with other chord members (root, third, and seventh), why is it possible to omit the fifth (i.e., why is *this* particular chord member nonessential)?

Notes

1 The bass notes of these two chords (D♭ and G) function as incomplete neighbors to tonic chord members. We will study the chord marked with an asterisk in Chapter 15.
2 The lower tritone of vii^{o7} is the same one found in V^7. These tendency tones resolve the same: $\hat{7} \nearrow \hat{1}$ and $\hat{4} \searrow \hat{3}$.
3 The third (E) resolves *down* (option B). It is voiced below the seventh (B), but the seventh does not resolve down by step in this texture, so there are no //P5.
4 The third (A) resolves *up* (option A) in both chords.
5 The leading tone of this complete V^7 is frustrated, resolving down by leap.
6 Although it is prevalent in jazz and other popular styles, the major-major seventh sonority (diatonic I^7 and IV^7 in major keys) is not characteristic of Classical music.

13

Motive, Phrase, Cadence, and Period Structure

Composers apply principles of repetition, contrast, variation, and development to organize their musical ideas and craft coherent musical structures. *Musical form* is the study of these principles and structures. This chapter examines some small units of musical form.

Motive

A **motive** is a short musical idea that repeats to unify a musical passage or entire work. Motives typically combine a characteristic melodic shape with a particular rhythm. The guitar riff in "The Wanton Song" by Led Zeppelin (Example 13.1) is built from a repeated four-note motive.[1]

EXAMPLE 13.1   Led Zeppelin, "The Wanton Song," opening guitar riff.

Example 13.2 shows the unison opening of Beethoven's fifth symphony. A four-note motive is presented in mm. 1–2, and a varied form of the motive follows in mm. 3–5. How would you describe the relation between the initial and varied forms of the motive?[2]

EXAMPLE 13.2   Beethoven, Symphony No. 5 in C Minor, Op. 67, I, mm. 1–5.

Developmental Procedures

As Example 13.2 demonstrates, a motive that repeats is often varied in some way. The principle of *varied repetition* allows musical ideas to recur without becoming monotonous. It also enables composers to *develop* their musical ideas.

The initial version of a motive is referred to as the ***prime form***. The prime form given in Example 13.3a is treated to the following developmental procedures:

- ***Sequence*** (Example 13.3b): The motive is shifted to a different region of the scale while its shape, or contour, is preserved.
  - Interval *size*—but not *quality*—is preserved.
- ***Transposition*** (Example 13.3c): The motive is shifted and accidentals are added to it, transferring it to a different scale or key.
  - Intervallic size *and* quality are preserved.
- ***Retrograde*** (Example 13.3d): The order of notes is reversed; the motive is "turned around backwards."
  - The original rhythm is preserved in Example 13.3d, but it could also be reversed.
- ***Inversion*** (Example 13.3e): The motive is "flipped upside down" as the direction of intervals is changed.
  - The initial *ascending* third of the motive in Example 13.3a becomes a *descending* third in Example 13.3e, and so on.
- ***Retrograde-Inversion*** (Example 13.3f): A combination of retrograde and inversion.
- ***Augmentation*** (Example 13.3g): The motive is "stretched out" over time as note values are increased.
- ***Diminution*** (Example 13.3h): The motive is compressed in time as note values are decreased.

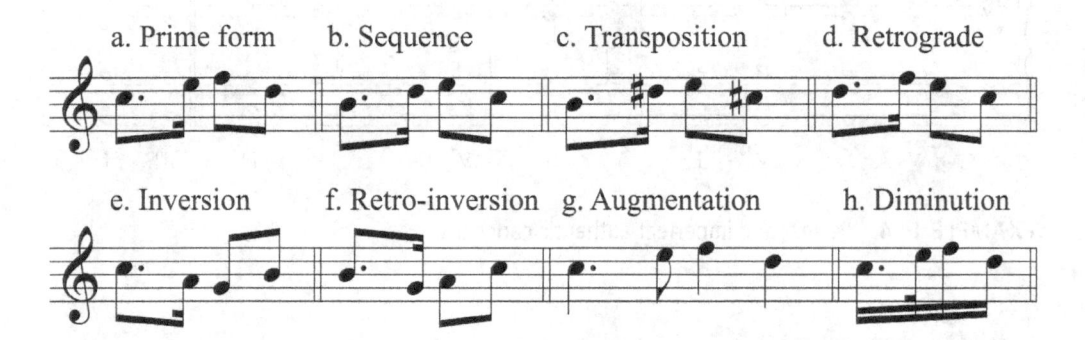

EXAMPLE 13.3 Developmental procedures applied to a motive.

These developmental procedures are often applied in combination. For example, a motive may be sequenced, retrograded, and augmented at the same time.

Phrase

A musical *phrase* exhibits tonal motion, or progress through the tonal syntax. Sufficient tonal progress occurs in one of three ways: T–D, D–T, or T–D–T. (Recall that the Predominant function is nonessential and may or may not be present in the transition from T to D.) A phrase is typically four measures long, but any length is possible.[3] Several of the musical examples in the previous chapter are complete phrases (see Examples 12.6, 12.7, 12.11, and 12.12). A phrase closes with a cadence.

Cadence

A *cadence* is a type of musical punctuation ending a phrase. Cadences provide a degree of closure or repose, allowing the music to breathe.

Authentic Cadence (PAC and IAC)

An *authentic cadence* occurs when V–I (or V^7–I) closes the phrase. In a *perfect authentic cadence (PAC)*, both chords are in root position, and the melody concludes on $\hat{1}$ over I, so the music finds complete harmonic and melodic closure (see Example 13.4a and b). In an *imperfect authentic cadence (IAC)*, one or both chords are inverted, or the melody ends on a note other than $\hat{1}$, such as $\hat{3}$ or $\hat{5}$. Complete closure is not obtained with an IAC. Example 13.4 (c–f) shows several IACs. In Example 13.4f, vii^{o6} substitutes for V.

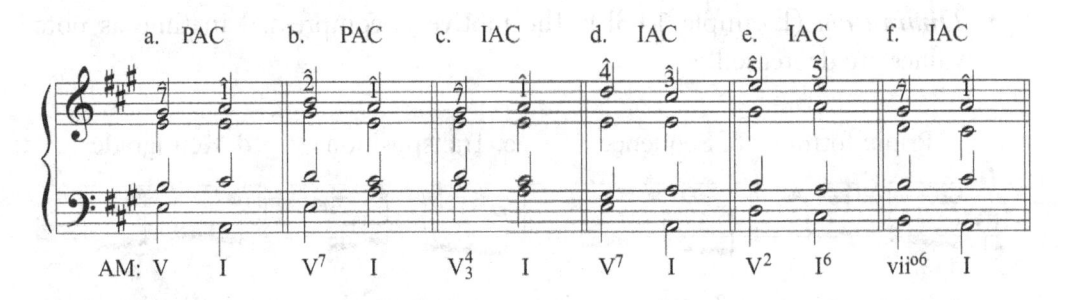

EXAMPLE 13.4 Perfect and imperfect authentic cadences.

Half Cadence (HC)

A *half cadence (HC)* occurs when a phrase ends on V. As the anticipated return to T is denied or postponed, the phrase sounds unfinished and open-ended. See Example 13.5a. In a *Phrygian half cadence*, V is approached by iv^6 in a minor key. (Example 13.5b).

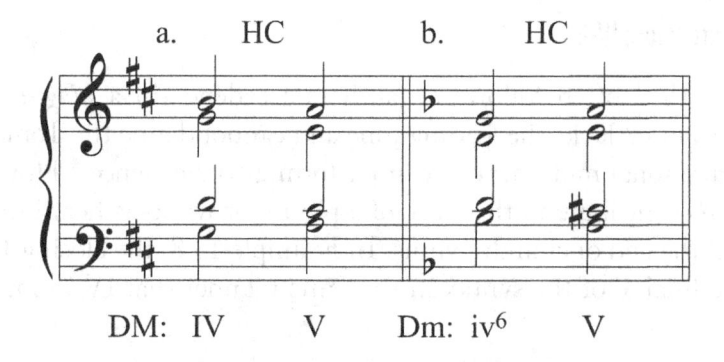

EXAMPLE 13.5 Half cadence (a) and Phrygian half cadence (b).

Deceptive Cadence (DC)

V–vi closes the phrase. The music returns to Tonic function, but with vi substituting for I. See Example 13.6.

EXAMPLE 13.6 Deceptive cadences.

Not every V–vi motion is a cadence. In Example 13.7, a *deceptive resolution* occurs toward the end of a phrase, where a cadence is expected (m. 4). The music, however, continues to the PAC that closes the phrase. This deceptive resolution extends the phrase beyond the 4-measure norm.

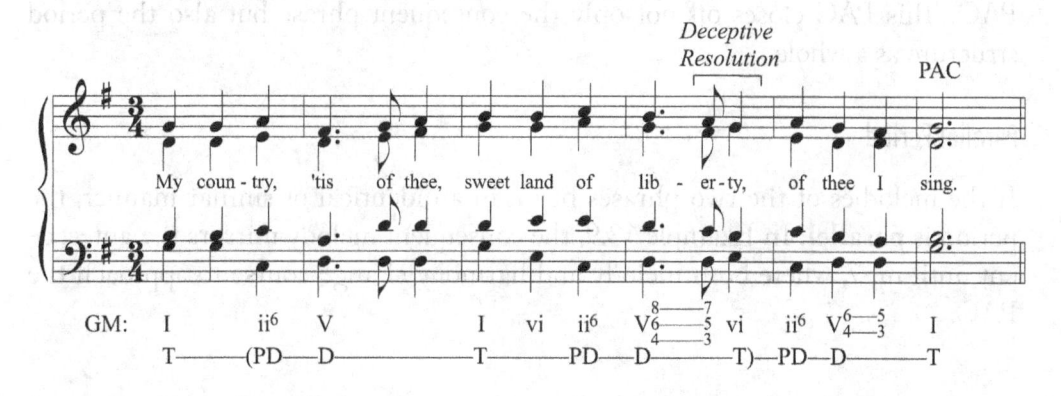

EXAMPLE 13.7 "My Country, 'Tis of Thee," mm. 1–6.

The Plagal Extension: IV–I

The motion IV–I often follows an authentic cadence in a *plagal extension* of Tonic function. IV lacks the leading tone and cannot define the Tonic. IV–I does not constitute tonal motion, so it cannot form a true cadence.[4] However, plagal extensions *do* contribute to the close of a phrase or work, as heard in the "Amen tag" sung at the end of church hymns. In Example 13.8, the closing IV–I motion extends the final T of the syntax in the same manner that IV in m. 15 expands the initial T.

EXAMPLE 13.8 Hymn, "Come, Thou Fount of Every Blessing," mm. 13–18 (last line).

Period Structure

Two phrases might group into a larger structure called a *period*. The phrases forming a period exhibit an *antecedent–consequent* relationship.

Antecedent and Consequent

The first phrase of a period, the *antecedent*, ends with any cadence *other than* a PAC. By ending with a HC, IAC, or DC, the antecedent is open-ended, and musical continuation is expected. The *consequent* that follows ends *only* with a PAC. This PAC closes off not only the consequent phrase but also the period structure as a whole.

Parallel Period

If the melodies of the two phrases begin in an identical or similar manner, the period is **parallel**. In Example 13.9, the consequent melody mirrors the antecedent until m. 7, where both melody and harmony change course to approach the PAC.

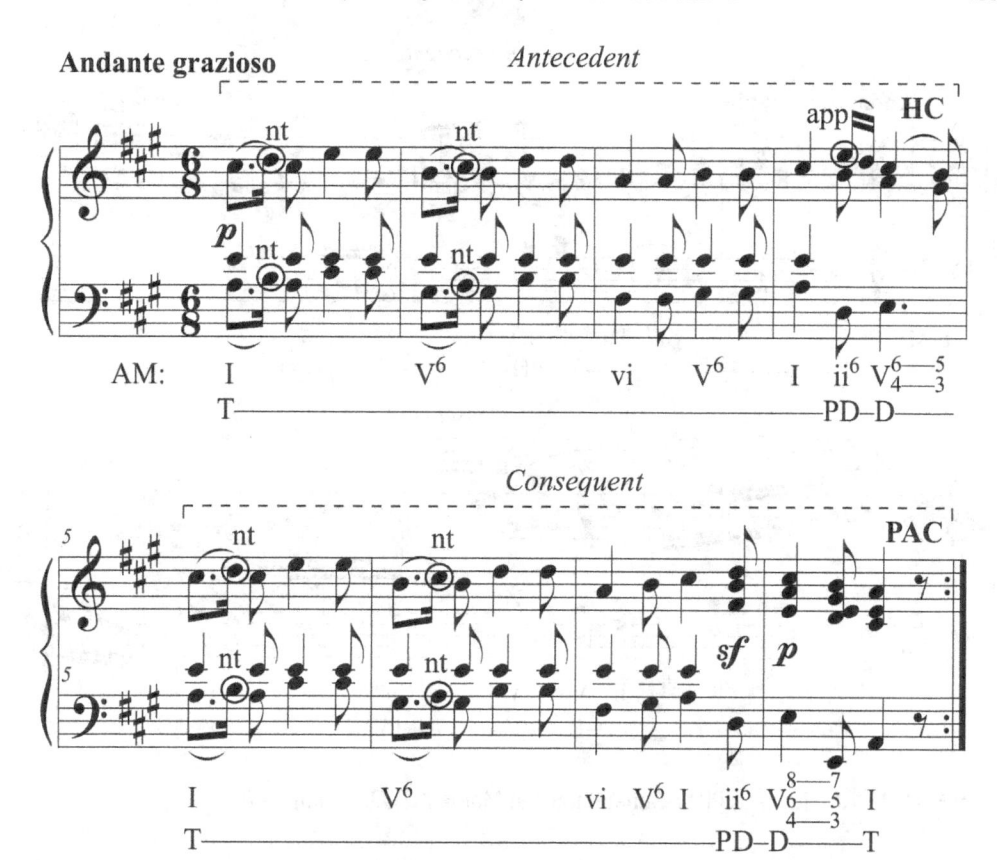

EXAMPLE 13.9 Mozart, Piano Sonata in A Major, K. 331, I, mm. 1–8.

Contrasting Period

In a ***contrasting*** period, the melodic beginnings of the two phrases are not similar, as in Example 13.10. After V is reached in m. 4, a melodic **link** connects the end of the antecedent to the beginning of the consequent. In this analysis, only one nonchord tone—a chromatic passing tone—is circled and labeled (m. 4). *Why* is this nonchord tone classified as a passing tone?[5] Can you identify the remaining nonchord tones in this passage?

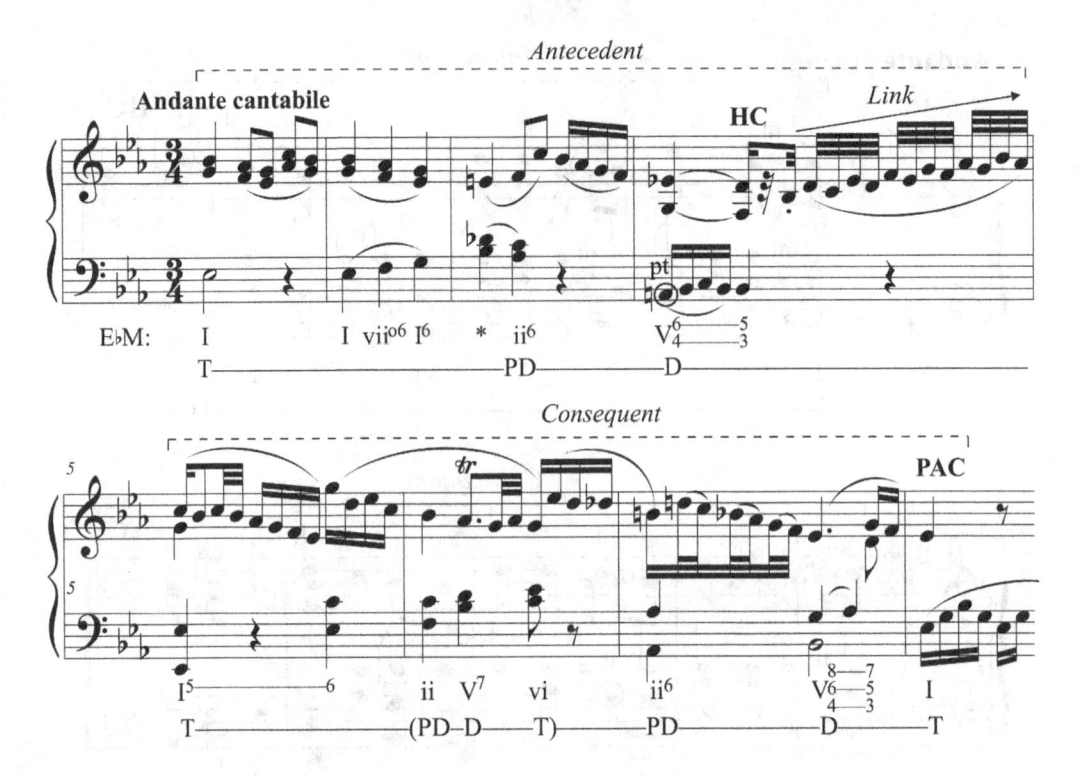

EXAMPLE 13.10   Mozart, Piano Sonata in B-flat Major, K. 333, II, mm. 1–8.

Three- and four-phrase periods are possible. In a three-phrase period, the first two phrases are antecedents ending with weak cadences, and the third phrase, the consequent, closes with a PAC.

Phrase Group

Two or more phrases that group together to form a section or part of a work, but that lack an antecedent–consequent design, constitute a ***phrase group***. Like periods, phrase groups may be parallel or contrasting.

Motive, Phrase, Cadence, and Period Structure

Applications

Exercises

1. Develop the given motive by applying the procedures indicated. (For retrograde and retrograde-inversion, reverse the series of pitches but preserve the original rhythm.)

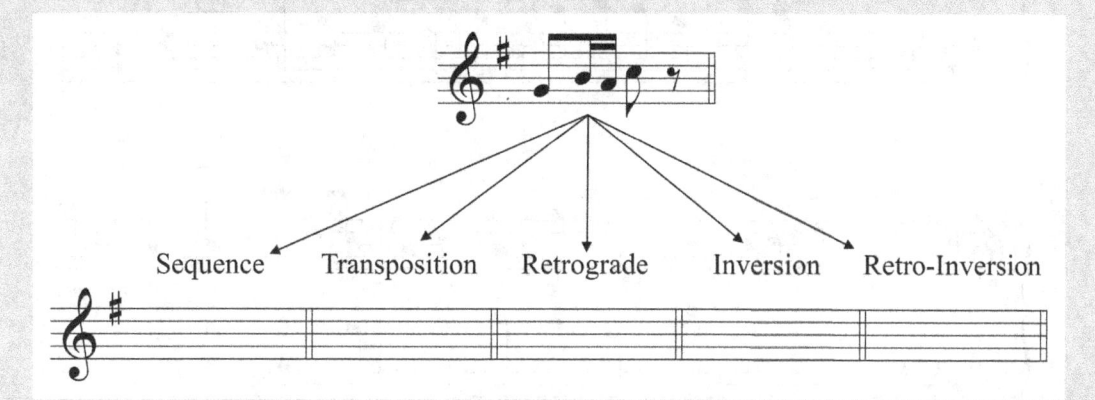

   Sequence   Transposition   Retrograde   Inversion   Retro-Inversion

2. Each short example represents a cadence ending a phrase. In the blanks provided, label chords with Roman numerals and inversion symbols, and label cadences as PAC, IAC, HC, or DC.

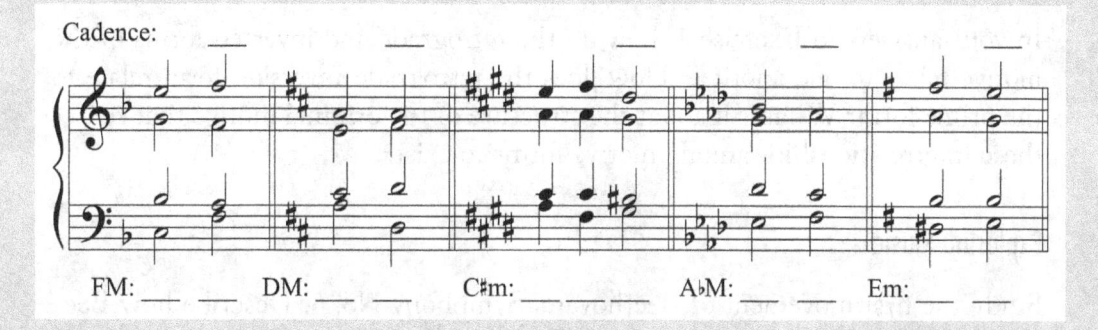

   Cadence: ___   ___   ___   ___   ___

   FM: ___ ___   DM: ___ ___   C♯m: ___ ___   A♭M: ___ ___   Em: ___ ___

3. Locate and label cadences in the example below. Do the two phrases form a period structure? If so, determine whether the period is parallel or contrasting.

EXAMPLE 13.11 Mozart, Piano Sonata in B-flat Major, K. 333, III, mm. 1–8.

Brain Teaser

In your answers to Exercise 1, how do the retrograde and inverted forms of the motive relate to one another? How does the retrograde-inversion form relate to the prime form? What is it about the structure of the original motive that causes these interrelationships among motive forms to exist?

Exploring Music

Study the first movement of Beethoven's Symphony No. 5. Describe how Beethoven develops the motive introduced in Example 13.2.

Thinking Critically

The developmental procedures outlined in this chapter (refer to Example 13.3) are not exhaustive. How else might a motive be altered or developed? Of the procedures discussed in this chapter, as well as those you come up with, identify which developmental procedures: 1) alter the orientation of a motive (without changing its shape); 2) change the dimensions or proportions of a motive; and 3) modify the actual shape or structure of a motive.

Notes

1 In many rock songs, such as "You Really Got Me" by the Kinks, riffs are constructed from short chord sequences.
2 The varied form (mm. 3–5) is one step lower than the initial form. The motive forms are related by *sequence*.
3 Meter and tempo influence phrase length. 8-measure phrases are common. A 5-measure phrase can often be explained as an expanded version of a "normalized" 4-measure phrase.
4 Many sources refer to this IV–I motion as a *plagal cadence*.
5 The bass leaps down by M7 from A♭ to A(♮), as the bass line is displaced down an octave in the middle of the passing gesture A♭–A(♮)–B♭.

14

Harmonic Sequences

Chapter 13 described the melodic *sequence*—a pattern of notes that repeats at a different pitch level. A ***harmonic sequence*** is a repeating pattern of root motion in a succession of chords. In sequences, tonal function is often suspended temporarily as the recurring root and bass motion assumes priority. Accordingly, certain voice-leading norms, like $\hat{7}$ resolving to $\hat{1}$, might be absent. Harmonic sequences that do not conform to tonal syntax typically prolong a function or connect one function to another.

Fifths Sequences

In a *fifths sequence*, the root motion either descends or ascends by a fifth. Example 14.1 presents a complete ***descending fifths sequence*** in both major and minor.[1] While a clear PD–D–T emerges at the end of each sequence, the interior portion is functionally ambiguous and serves to expand the motion from T to PD. In addition, observe the following features:

- As the *roots* descend by fifth, the *bass* alternates between descending fifths and ascending fourths.
    - All fifths and fourths in the bass are perfect, except +4 as IV moves to vii° (Example 14.1a), and °5 as VI moves to ii° (Example 14.1b).
- The diminished triads vii° and ii°, which typically appear in first inversion, are in root position to preserve the root/bass pattern.
    - The leading-tone root of vii° is doubled and does *not* resolve up to $\hat{1}$.
- In Example 14.1b, VII appears instead of vii°.

Harmonic Sequences 141

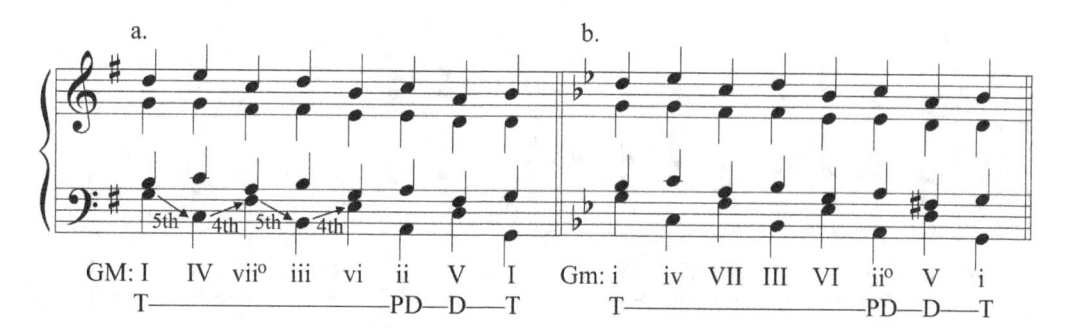

EXAMPLE 14.1 Descending fifths sequence in major (a) and minor (b).

In Example 14.2, an ***ascending fifths sequence*** governs the harmonic motion from I to iii. The sequence is broken when iii moves to IV to initiate PD. The V–ii motion, which contradicts the norms of the tonal syntax, occurs in this context because the root pattern of the sequence briefly takes precedence over the usual function of chords. Ascending fifths sequences are less common in minor keys.

EXAMPLE 14.2 Ascending fifths sequence.

Any or all of the root-position triads in a fifths sequence may be replaced with inverted chords, seventh chords, or both. In Example 14.3a, every other chord in the ascending fifths sequence is in first inversion. In Example 14.3b, a seventh is added to the chords of a descending fifths sequence in minor, and the seventh chords alternate between complete and incomplete voicings. Diatonic seventh chords that are otherwise uncommon in Classical music often appear in sequences.

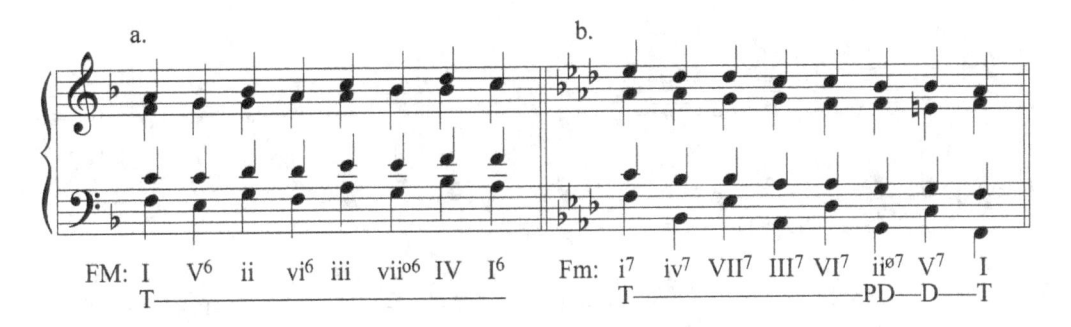

EXAMPLE 14.3 Ascending fifths with inversions (a); descending fifths with seventh chords (b).

Descending Thirds Sequence

Example 14.4 involves a partial *descending thirds sequence*: I–vi–IV–ii–vii°. This sequence conforms to tonal syntax—it prolongs both T and PD with two chords per function and leads to a weak Dominant—unison $\hat{7}$, which implies vii° or perhaps V^6. This weak D gives way to fully fleshed-out chords that quickly culminate in an emphatic PAC.

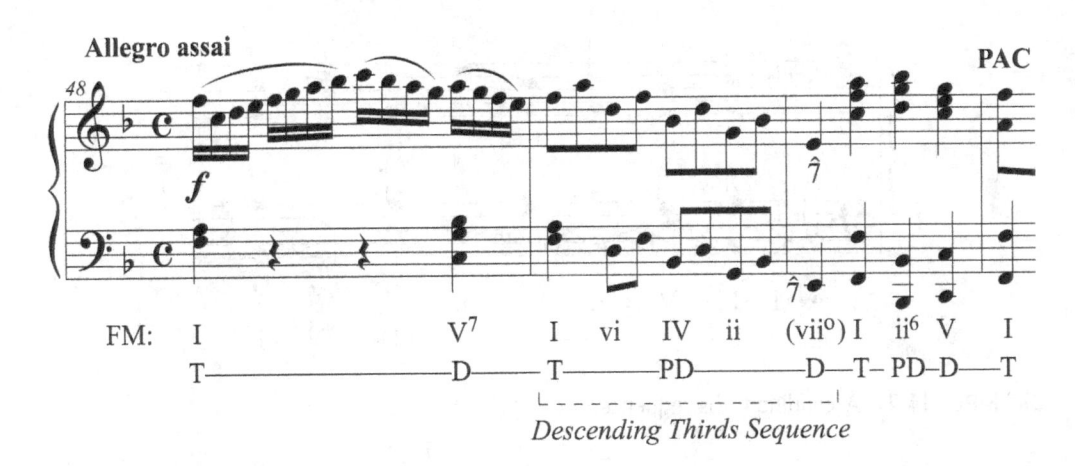

EXAMPLE 14.4 Mozart, "Der Hölle Rache kocht in meinem Herzen" from *The Magic Flute*, K. 620, mm. 48–51 (orchestral reduction).

The descending thirds sequence most often includes "connector chords" inserted between the regular chords of the pattern. In Example 14.5, the connector chords are first-inversion triads allowing for a stepwise descent in the bass. The chords forming the descending thirds sequence are underlined.

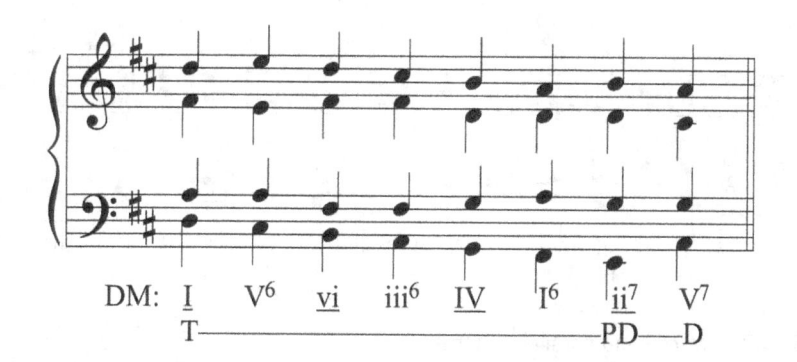

EXAMPLE 14.5 The descending thirds sequence with first-inversion connector chords.

The "Pachelbel" Sequence

Repositioning the connector chords in Example 14.5 in root position forms the "Pachelbel" sequence found in numerous tonal works, including Pachelbel's Canon in D. See Example 14.6.

EXAMPLE 14.6 The "Pachelbel" sequence.

Parallel $^6_3$ Chords

Unlike root-position and second-inversion chords, first-inversion chords may move by step in parallel motion. Example 14.7 presents a sequence of *descending parallel $^6_3$ chords*. To avoid //P5, chord roots are voiced *above* fifths in the upper voices. When parallel $^6_3$ chords occur in a four-voice texture, one upper voice leaps to alternate doublings from chord to chord and avoid faulty parallels (observe the tenor in Example 14.7a). This sequence is found most often in a three-voice texture, which eliminates the disjunct voice (Example 14.7b). Descending parallel $^6_3$ chords are often ornamented with a chain of 7-6 suspensions (Example 14.7c).

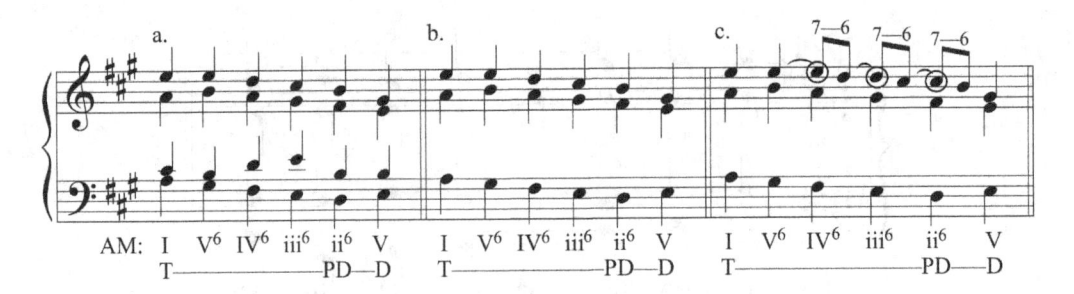

EXAMPLE 14.7 Descending parallel $^6_3$ chords.

The series of $^6_3$ chords in Example 14.7 is nonfunctional until ii^6, which breaks the sequence to function as PD.

A sequence of ***ascending parallel $^6_3$ chords*** is shown in Example 14.8a.[2] In Example 14.8b, the sequence is ornamented by the *5–6 technique*, as root-position and first-inversion triads alternate. The Roman numerals in parentheses highlight the apparent first-inversion chords that result from the linear 5–6 motion in the soprano.

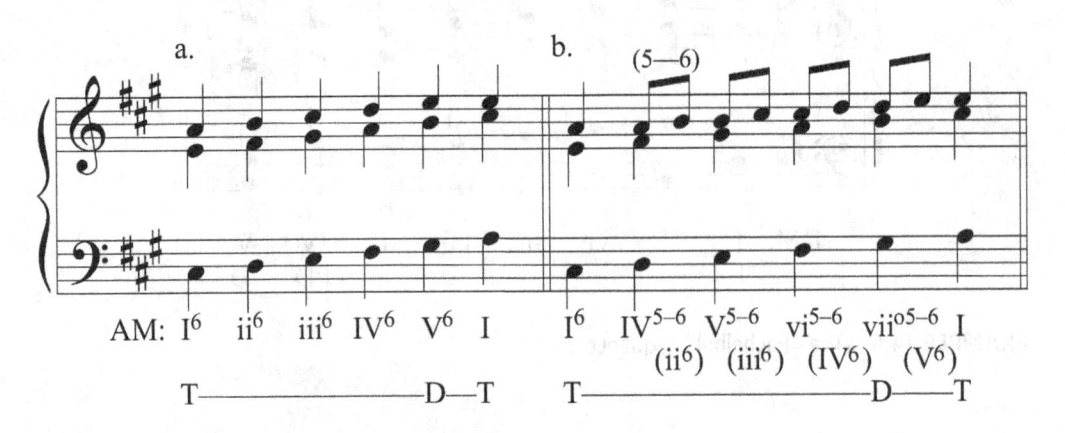

EXAMPLE 14.8 Ascending parallel $^6_3$ chords.

The last $^6_3$ chord in this ascending series, V^6, breaks the sequence to serve the Dominant function.

Applications

Exercises

1. Analyze the musical excerpts below and identify the type of sequence present in each.

EXAMPLE 14.9   G. F. Handel, Passacaglia in G Minor, HWV 432, mm. 1–4.

Type of Sequence: _____

EXAMPLE 14.10   Bach, Little Prelude in C Major, BWV 924, mm. 1–3.

Type of Sequence: _____

Exploring Music

1. Many musical works begin with the descending thirds sequence I–vi–IV. In popular music, the chord that most often follows IV is V, which breaks the sequence. I–vi–IV–V is known as the *doo-wop progression*. Can you identify songs that use this common progression?
2. The beginning of the "Pachelbel sequence," I–V–vi–iii, underlies many popular songs, including "Cryin'" by Aerosmith, "Holding Out For a Hero" by Bonnie Tyler, "Firework" by Katy Perry, and "Under the Bridge" by Red Hot Chili Peppers. Can you identify others?

Notes

1   See Example 18.4 for a descending fifths sequence in a popular song.
2   Ascending parallel $^6_3$ chords are less common than descending parallel $^6_3$ chords.

Part III

Chromatic Harmony

Part III explores *chromatic* chords—those *not* diatonic in a given key. Chromatic chords involve accidentals applied to one or more chord member. While chromatic chords expand the harmonic palette with an array of new colors, chromaticism is not a new or separate musical system—it may be viewed, and heard, as an elaboration of diatonic harmony. For the most part, chromatic chords either serve or prolong the same three tonal functions (T, PD, and D) studied in Part II. In many cases, chromatic alterations *enhance* tonal function by establishing more half-step resolutions to the next chord or function.

Chapter 15 describes how secondary dominants serve a Dominant function but on a *secondary* tonal level, making some chord *other than I* sound—briefly—like tonic. In Chapter 17, we discover that a chord "borrowed" from the parallel key, such as iv from C minor appearing in the key of C *major*, serves the same function as its diatonic counterpart (IV). Chapter 18 investigates two chromatic Predominant chords. Chapter 20 looks at extensions and alterations of V and V^7, as well as linear chords that embellish other chords and functions. In addition to these chromatic chords, the study of chromatic harmony examines the processes by which a musical work might change from one key to another, or *modulate* (Chapters 16 and 19).

15

Secondary Dominants and Tonicization

Dominant chords play the important musical role of defining the Tonic. Diatonic chords containing $\hat{7}$ have a strong attraction to chords containing $\hat{1}$, and these chords often include dissonant sevenths and tritones that intensify the pull toward Tonic. Certain chromatic chords behave like Dominants and cause triads *other than I* to briefly sound like Tonic.

Example 15.1a shows V^7 resolving to I in the key of D major. Identical chordal activity occurs in Example 15.1b—but in the key of G major. Here, a chromatic Mm7 chord built a perfect fifth above the root of V is applied to *tonicize* the dominant chord. This chord is labeled V^7/V (read: "V^7 of V") because it functions as the dominant *of* V. V^7/V is a **secondary dominant**—it tonicizes a chord other than I.

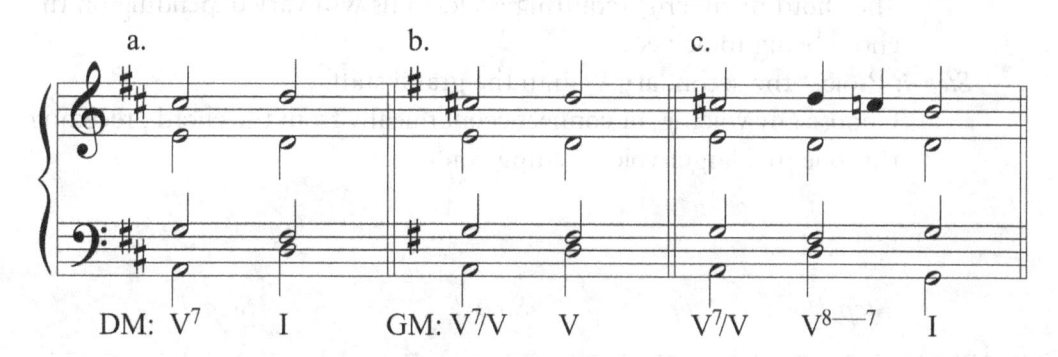

DM: V^7 I   GM: V^7/V V V^7/V V^{8-7} I

EXAMPLE 15.1 Tonicization of V.

Tonicization occurs when a chord other than I momentarily assumes the sound and character of the Tonic. Chromatic chords that resemble diatonic Dominant-functioning chords can tonicize any major or minor triad. Tonicization is a fleeting, surface-level phenomenon that does not change the underlying function of the tonicized chord. On the musical surface, V in Example 15.1b *sounds like* Tonic. However, on the primary level of tonal structure, V will serve the Dominant function in the key of D major, as heard in its resolution to I in Example 15.1c.

A major triad can tonicize a chord a perfect below (as V naturally tonicizes I), and a diminished triad can tonicize a chord a m2 above (as vii° tonicizes I). However, the most common secondary dominant chords are chromatic dominant sevenths (Mm7) and leading-tone sevenths (°7 and ⌀7).

Secondary Dominant Seventh Chords

Secondary V^7 Basics

- A chromatic Mm7 chord
- Tonicizes a chord a P5 below
- Can be built on any scale degree (including altered scale degrees)

Spelling Secondary V^7 Chords

The following steps outline the process for spelling secondary V^7 chords. Example 15.2 applies these steps to spell V^7/vi in B♭ major.

Step 1: Determine the root of the *target chord*—the triad to be tonicized by the secondary V^7.

Step 2: Identify the root of the secondary V^7 a P5 *above* the root of the target chord.

Step 3: Build a Mm7 chord on this root, using accidentals as needed.
  ○ Stack these intervals above the root: M3, m3, m3.
  ○ The chord member(s) requiring accidentals will vary depending on the chord being tonicized.

Step 4: Project the secondary V^7 into the grand staff.[1]
  ○ Choose any voicing, or connect economically from the chord preceding this one in a larger voice-leading context.

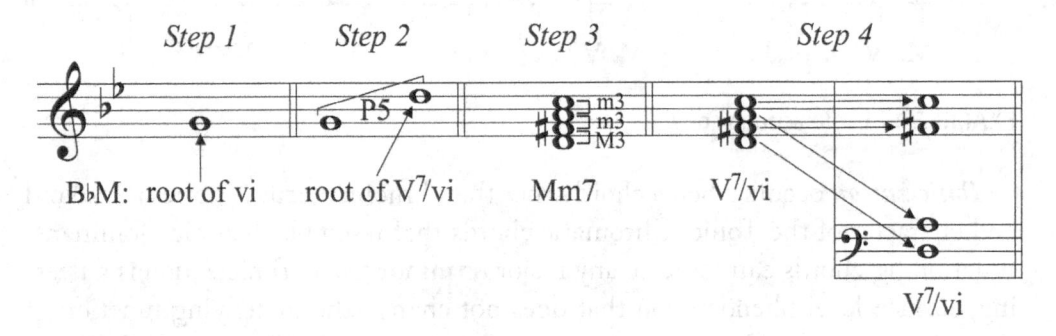

EXAMPLE 15.2 Spelling V^7/vi in B♭ major.

Resolving Secondary V⁷ Chords

Secondary V⁷ chords resolve to their target chord in the same manner that primary V⁷ chords resolve to I (see Chapter 12). Example 15.3 provides four different resolution scenarios. Observe the following resolution tendencies:

- The third and seventh form a tritone and resolve like tendency tones.
  - The third functions as a *secondary leading tone*, resolving *up* by a m2 to the root of the chord being tonicized.
    - In Example 15.3a, #4̂ (B♮) acts as the secondary leading tone to 5̂.
    - If located in an inner voice, the secondary leading tone may be frustrated (Example 15.3b).
  - The seventh resolves *down* by step.
  - When both chords are in root position, either the secondary V⁷ or its target chord may be incomplete.

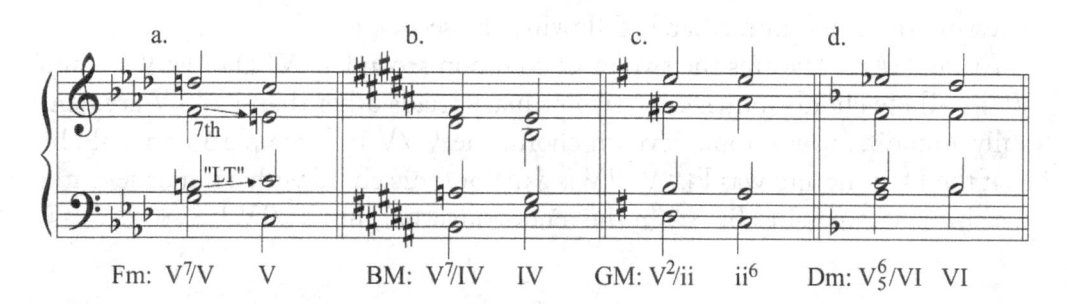

EXAMPLE 15.3 Resolving secondary V⁷ chords.

Identifying and Labeling Secondary V⁷ Chords

Any Mm7 chord other than the primary V⁷ should be labeled V⁷/__. The blank to the right of the slash is filled with the target of the secondary V⁷. A Mm7 chord built on 6̂, for example, is *not* labeled VI⁷—it should be labeled V⁷/ii. Example 15.4 illustrates the steps for labeling a secondary V⁷.

Step 1: Determine if the quality of a chromatic seventh chord is Mm7.
  - If helpful, arrange the chord members in stacked thirds on a single staff to assess the chord's quality.

Step 2: Think *down* a P5 from the root of the secondary V⁷. What scale degree is this note?

Step 3: The diatonic triad with this note as its root is the target chord. Determine its Roman numeral.

Step 4: Label the secondary V⁷. Check its positioning and apply any necessary inversion symbol.

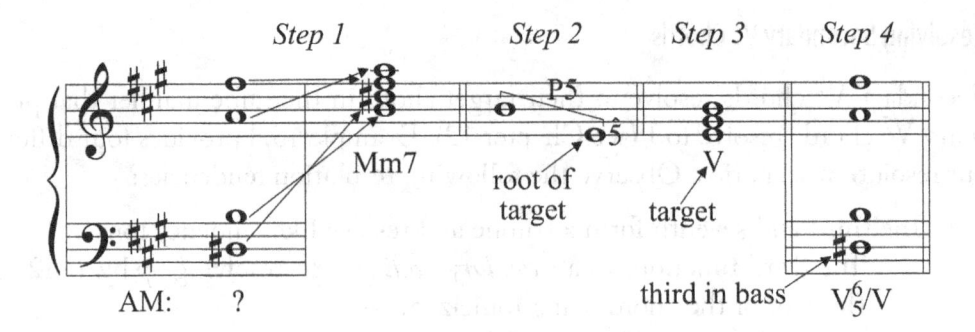

EXAMPLE 15.4 Labeling V^6_5/V in A major.

Secondary V^7 chords are labeled based on their *diatonic* target chords. This label reflects the chord's *expected* resolution. Secondary V^7 chords, however, do not always hit their targets—they can resolve deceptively, or to a chromatic chord. For this reason, we cannot determine the label for the target chord by simply assessing the chord immediately following the secondary V^7.

Example 15.5 features the two most common secondary V^7 chords: V^7/V and V^7/IV. These chords tonicize the two primary triads other than I. V^7/V is essentially a modified supertonic seventh chord: the V^7/V in Example 15.5 would be ii^7 if the F♯ in the alto was F♮.[2] V^7/IV is a major tonic chord with a minor seventh: the chromatic, passing B♭ (♭$\hat{7}$) in the tenor converts I into V^7/IV.[3]

EXAMPLE 15.5 J. S. Bach, Chorale 40, "Ach Gott und Herr," mm. 1–2.

In the analysis of Example 15.5, the function labels in parentheses (D–T) highlight the tonicizations occurring along the musical surface—on a secondary tonal level. These tonicizations are *embedded* in the syntax unfolding at the deeper, primary level of tonal structure.

In Example 15.6, ii is tonicized in the shift from T to PD. Several chromatic nonchord tones occur in this passage.

EXAMPLE 15.6 Chopin, Prelude in A Major, Op. 28, No. 7, mm. 11–14.

The Tonicized Half Cadence (THC)

In Example 15.7, the V at a half cadence is preceded by a tonicizing chord (V^7/V), forming a *tonicized half cadence (THC)*.[4] Revisit Example 12.7, mm. 3–4. How would you label the chord marked with an asterisk and the cadence closing this passage?

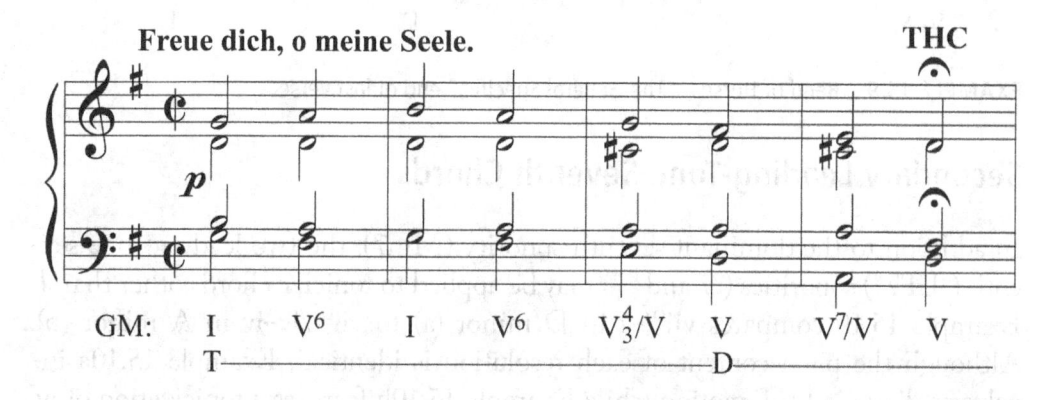

EXAMPLE 15.7 Robert Schumann, "A Chorale" from *Album for the Young*, Op. 68, No. 4, mm. 1–4.

Deceptive Resolution of Secondary V[7] Chords

Secondary V^7s can resolve deceptively. This effect is similar to the deceptive resolution V^7–vi, but playing out on a secondary tonal level. As Example 15.8a illustrates, when V^7 resolves deceptively to vi, it lands a *third* below its target, I. Similarly, when a secondary V^7 misses *its* target chord, it undershoots it by a third, as when V^7/IV resolves to ii (Example 15.8b).

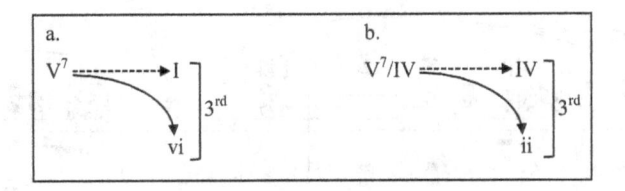

EXAMPLE 15.8 Primary and secondary deceptive resolutions.

In Example 15.9, V⁷/vi resolves deceptively to IV. IV then leads to V⁷/V, which hits its target chord, V.

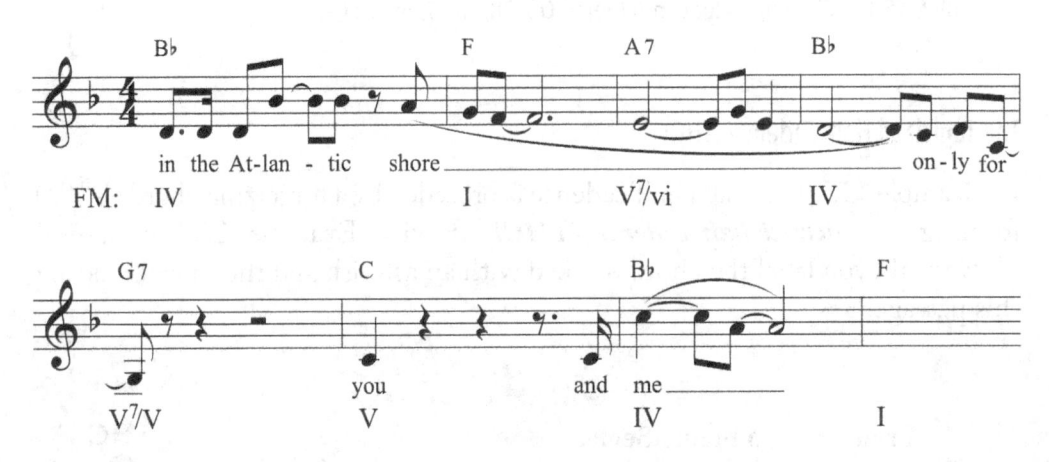

FM: IV — I — V⁷/vi — IV — V⁷/V — V — IV — I

"in the Atlantic shore ⸺ only for you and me"

EXAMPLE 15.9 Band of Horses, "The General Specific," end of last verse.

Secondary Leading-Tone Seventh Chords

In addition to the dominant seventh sonority (Mm7), the two leading-tone seventh ("LT7") sonorities (°7 and ⌀7) may be applied to tonicize chords other than I. Example 15.10 compares vii°7–i in D minor (a) to vii°7/iv–iv in A minor (b). Although the pitch content of each resolution is identical, Example 15.10a involves a diatonic D–T motion while Example 15.10b features a tonicization of iv.

Dm: vii°7 — i   Am: vii°7/iv — iv

EXAMPLE 15.10 Diatonic LT7 (a) and secondary LT7 tonicizing iv (b).

Secondary LT7 Basics

- A chromatic °7 or ⦰7 chord
    - °7 is most common
- Tonicizes a chord a m2 above
- Can be built on any scale degree (including altered scale degrees)

Spelling Secondary LT7 Chords

The following steps outline the process for spelling secondary LT7 chords. Example 15.11 applies these steps to spell vii°7/V in the key of E♭ major.

Step 1: Determine the root of the target chord.
Step 2: Identify the root of the secondary LT7 a m2 *below* the root of the target chord.
Step 3: Build the °7 or ⦰7 chord on this root, using accidentals as needed.
  - For °7, stack: m3, m3, m3.
  - For ⦰7, stack: m3, m3, M3.
Step 4: Project into the grand staff.

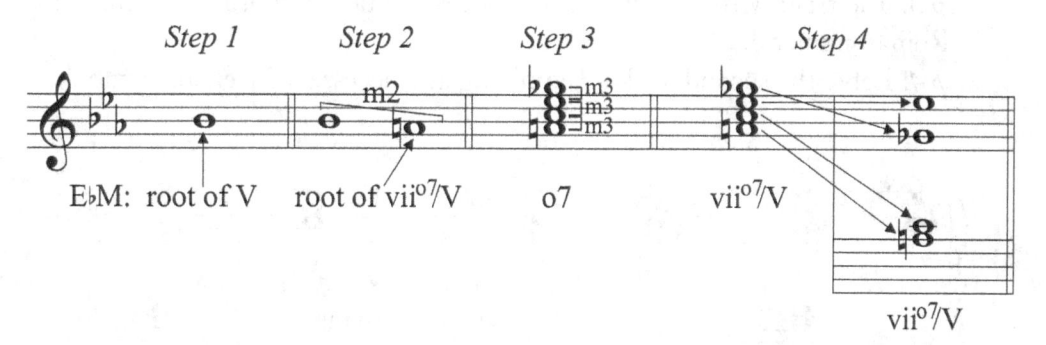

EXAMPLE 15.11   Spelling vii°7/V in E♭ major.

Resolving Secondary LT7 Chords

Secondary LT7 chords resolve to their target chords—they do not resolve deceptively. Their resolution is the same as the diatonic LT7 chords, as outlined in Chapter 12 and summarized below. Example 15.12 provides four resolution scenarios.

- All voices resolve by step:
    - Root steps up.
        - The root functions as a secondary leading tone to the root of the target chord.
    - Fifth and seventh step down.
    - Third steps up (option A) *or* down (option B).
        - In Example 15.12a, the third steps down to avoid doubling $\hat{7}$ in V.
        - In Example 15.12c, the third steps up to avoid //P5.

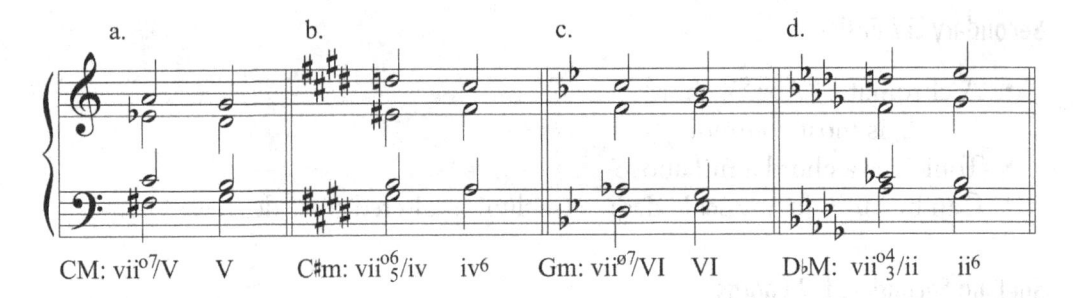

CM: vii°7/V   V   C#m: vii°6/5/iv   iv6   Gm: vii°7/VI   VI   D♭M: vii°4/3/ii   ii6

EXAMPLE 15.12 Resolving secondary LT7 chords.

Identifying and Labeling Secondary LT7 Chords

Label fully or half-diminished seventh chords other than vii°7, vii⌀7, and ii⌀7 (in minor) as secondary LT7 chords. Example 15.13 illustrates the steps for labeling secondary LT7s.

Step 1: Determine if a chromatic seventh chord is °7 or ⌀7.
Step 2: Think *up* a m2 from the root of the secondary LT7. What scale degree is this note?
Step 3: The triad with this note as its root is the target chord. Determine its Roman numeral.
Step 4: Label the secondary LT7, applying any necessary inversion symbol.

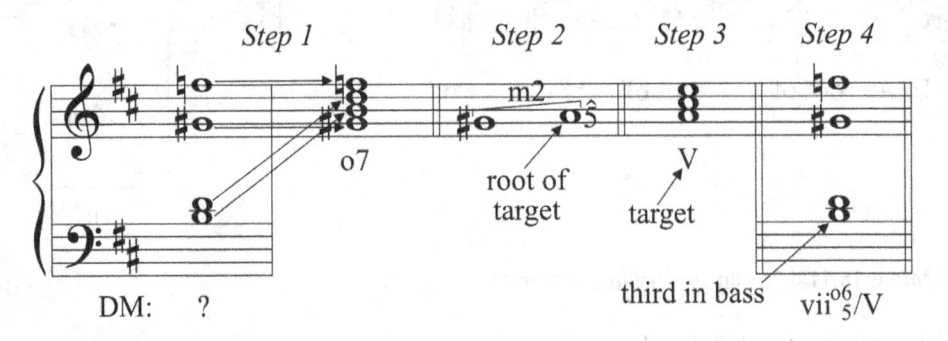

EXAMPLE 15.13 Labeling vii°6/5/V in D major.

In Example 15.14, vii°7/V tonicizes the dominant chord of a PAC ending the phrase.

B♭M: I   I6   V4/3   V7   I   vii°7/V   V7   I
      T————D————————T————————D————T

EXAMPLE 15.14 Schubert, Impromptu in B-flat Major, D. 935, No. 3, mm. 5–8.

In Example 15.15, three different chords are tonicized within the opening Tonic span—two of them by secondary LT7 chords. (Note the unusual P$^6_4$ chord connecting V to V$^6_5$ in m. 2.[5]) How do the two halves of this phrase relate to one another?[6] How many subsidiary expressions of the tonal syntax can you identify embedded in this prolongation of T?

AM: I I⁶ V vii°⁷/iii iii I⁵⁻⁶ V/V V P$^6_4$ V$^6_5$ I vii°⁷/vi vi ii⁶ V I
T——PD——D—T

EXAMPLE 15.15 Robert Schumann, "An Important Event" from *Scenes from Childhood*, Op. 15, No. 6, mm. 1–4.

Applications

Exercises

1. Spell and resolve secondary V⁷ chords in root position and inversion. Add any necessary inversion symbol to the target chord's Roman numeral.

1. DM: V⁷/V V   2. A♭M: V$^6_5$/IV IV   3. G♯m: V$^4_3$/V V   4. Cm: V$^6_5$/VI VI

5. Am: V⁷/iv iv   6. FM: V²/ii ii   7. GM: V$^4_3$/iii iii   8. F♯m: V²/V V

2. Spell and resolve secondary LT7 chords in root position and inversion. Add any necessary inversion symbol to the target chord's Roman numeral.

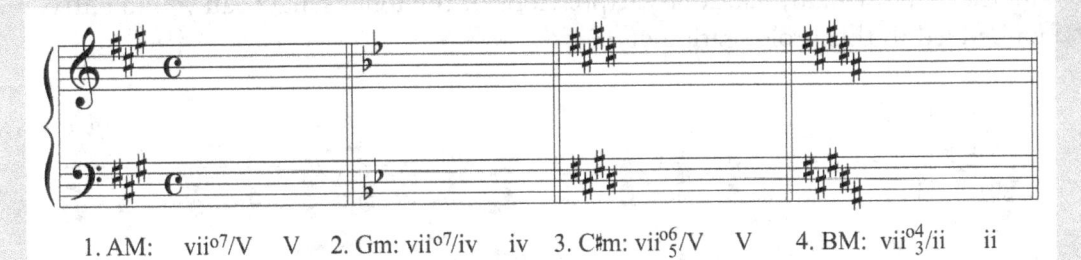

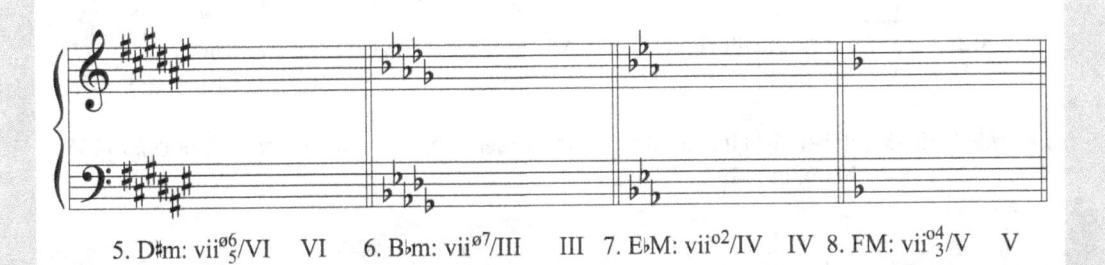

1. AM: vii°7/V   V   2. Gm: vii°7/iv   iv   3. C#m: vii°6/5/V   V   4. BM: vii°4/3/ii   ii

5. D#m: vii°6/5/VI   VI   6. B♭m: viiø7/III   III   7. E♭M: vii°2/IV   IV   8. FM: vii°4/3/V   V

3. Label secondary V^7 and secondary LT7 chords.

1. FM: ____   2. E♭M: ____   3. C#m: ____   4. A♭M: ____   5. Em: ____   6. G#m: ____

4. Provide a complete analysis of the chord progression below. Label chords with Roman numerals and inversion symbols, circle and label nonchord tones, indicate how the tonal syntax unfolds, and label the cadence.

B♭M:

Brain Teaser

Only one secondary V^7 chord, V^7/III in minor keys, does not require any accidentals. Why is this?

Thinking Critically

1. Return to Example 13.10 and determine a label for the chord marked with an asterisk. In this same example, the first bass note in m. 4 is labeled as a nonchord tone. Devise an alternative analysis for this beat that counts the A♮ as a chord tone. Which analysis, the original one given in Example 13.10 or this alternative version, do you find most convincing, and why?
2. When applying a secondary LT7 to tonicize a chord, what might motivate a composer to choose °7 over ⌀7? What advantage might the fully diminished sonority have over the half-diminished?

Notes

1. At some point you will no longer find it necessary to build a chord in a single staff before projecting it into SATB voicing. As soon as you feel comfortable eliminating this step (or as directed by your instructor), spell the chord directly in the grand staff.
2. In major, raising the third of ii^7 produces V^7/V; in minor, raising both the third and fifth of $ii^{ø7}$ yields V^7/V.
3. In major, adding a m7 ($♭\hat{7}$) to I creates V^7/IV; in minor, raising the third ($♮\hat{3}$) of the tonic chord and adding the subtonic scale degree produces V^7/iv.
4. The extended tonicization at the end of this passage (V is tonicized twice in close succession) borders on changing key, or *modulating*. Modulation is the topic of the next chapter.
5. This P^6_4 is literally ii^6_4—a rare passing six-four chord.
6. The two halves are related by sequence.

16

Modulation I
Phrase Modulation and Diatonic Pivot Chords

When a chord other than I is *tonicized*, it briefly sounds like Tonic but retains its identity and function in the original key. Sometimes, however, the tonal center will shift, and a new chord will function as Tonic for an extended period. A *modulation* is a change of key lasting for several measures or more and confirmed by functional progressions and cadences in the new key.

When a modulation occurs, scale degrees transfer to different notes. For example, a modulation from G major to D major shifts the tonal center, $\hat{1}$, from G to D, and other pitches are reorganized as scale degrees around this new tonic pitch. In the score, the key signature for D major might replace that of G major, especially when the modulation occurs between phrases or sections. Often, however, the composer will simply convert each C♮ ($\hat{4}$ in G major) to C♯ ($\hat{7}$ in D major) whenever this note appears in the music.

Closely and Distantly Related Keys

Modulations, and the relations among key areas, are defining features of a musical work's form. Any two keys are either *closely* or *distantly* related. The key signatures of two **closely related keys** differ by no more than one accidental, and these keys are adjacent on the circle of fifths. The rectangle on the circle of fifths in Example 16.1 shows the keys that are closely related to the keys of C major and A minor. A work in either C major or A minor could visit a closely related key by modulating to *any* of the other five keys in the rectangle. The rectangle could be rotated on the circle of fifths to identify all sets of closely related keys.

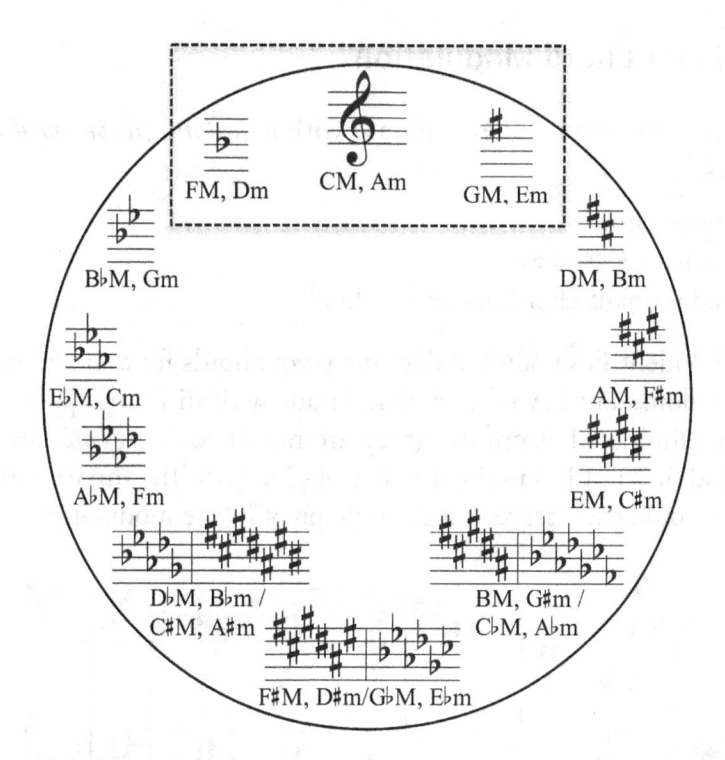

EXAMPLE 16.1 Closely related keys to C major or A minor.

The key signatures of **distantly related keys** differ by two or more accidentals. In Example 16.1, any key *not* contained in the rectangle is distantly related to both C major and A minor.

Music may modulate to any key. However, it is common for major-mode works to modulate to the dominant key (V), and for minor-mode works to modulate to the relative major (III) or the minor dominant (v)—all closely related keys.[1] Most works ultimately return to their original, "home" key before ending.

Phrase Modulation

A *phrase modulation* occurs *between* two phrases (or sections).[2] In Example 16.2, a PAC in E minor closes a phrase, and the next phrase begins in the closely related key of C major.[3]

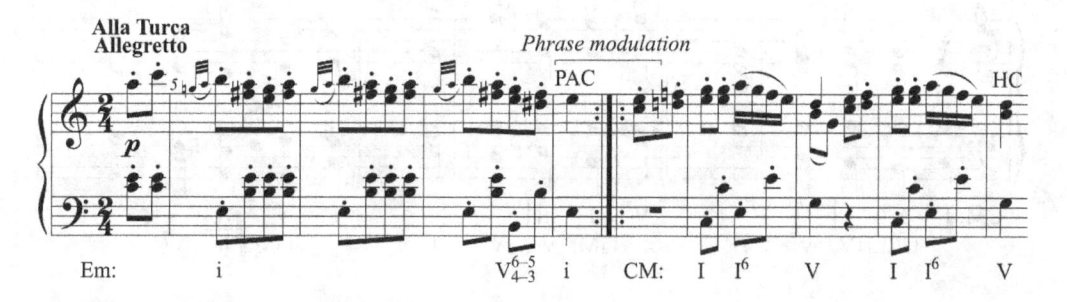

EXAMPLE 16.2 Mozart, Piano Sonata in A Major, K. 331, III, "Alla Turca," mm. 5–12.

Diatonic Pivot Chord Modulation

Modulations often occur *within* a phrase with a ***diatonic pivot chord*** connecting the two keys.[4]

A diatonic pivot chord:
- Is diatonic in *both* keys
- Is a Predominant chord in the *new* key[5]

Example 16.3 identifies potential diatonic pivot chords for a modulation from C major to the dominant key of G major. Triads with differing qualities between the keys are eliminated as options (they are not diatonic in *both* keys), as is the G-major triad (it is not PD in the *new* key of G major). The three chords enclosed in rectangles could each serve as a diatonic pivot in the modulation.

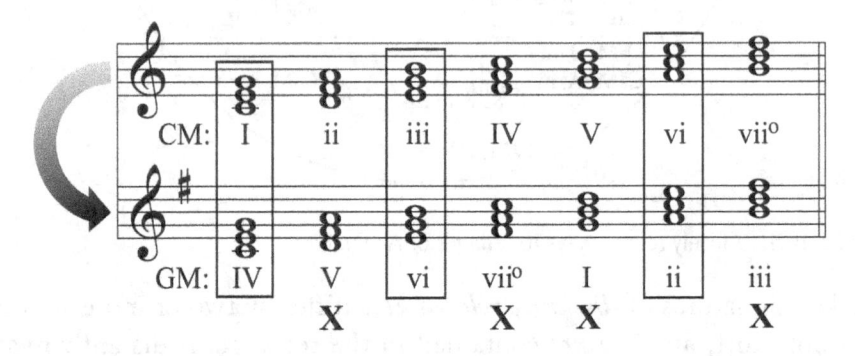

EXAMPLE 16.3 Potential diatonic pivot chords in a modulation from C major to G major.

Labeling Diatonic Pivot Chords

Example 16.4 finds the three diatonic pivot chords identified in Example 16.3 at work in short passages modulating from C major to G major (let us assume that each passage continues in G major). The pivot chords are labeled in both keys, and the new key (GM) is indicated where each pivot chord begins functioning as Predominant in that key. The diatonic pivot chord leads directly to the first Dominant chord in the new key.

EXAMPLE 16.4 Labeling diatonic pivot chords.

Modulation I

In Example 16.5, Mozart modulates from D major to the dominant key of A major via a diatonic pivot chord. The symbol "//" in the syntactic analysis marks the upheaval of tonal function as the B-minor chord is reinterpreted to function as ii in A major.

EXAMPLE 16.5 Mozart, String Quartet in D Major, K. 155, I, mm. 12–18.

The Chorale in Example 16.6 begins and ends in E minor. In the middle it establishes the relative key of G major with an IAC.

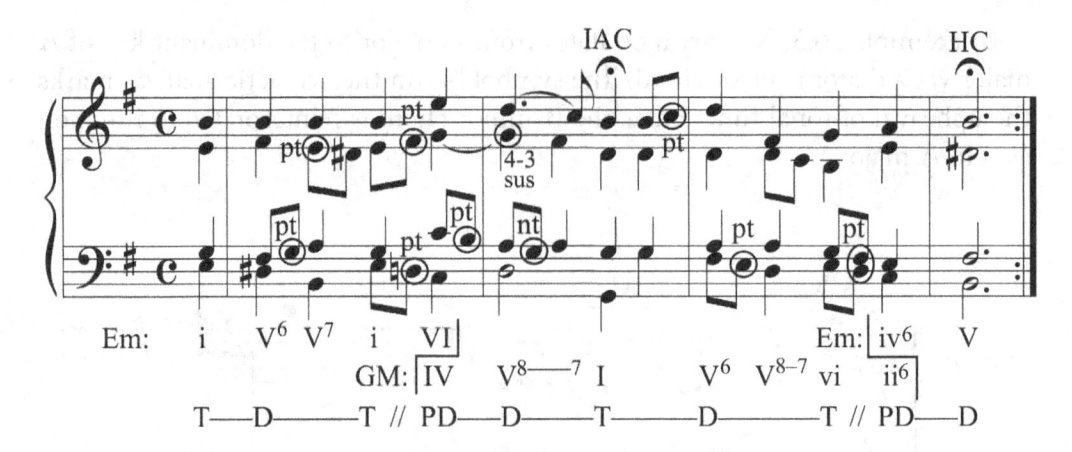

EXAMPLE 16.6 J. S. Bach, Chorale 129, "Keinen hat Gott verlassen," mm. 1–4.

Recognizing and Analyzing a Modulation

Modulations can be very obvious to the ear or somewhat subtle, and they are noticeable in the score. In the absence of a change of key signature, the following visual cues will alert the analyst that a modulation has taken place:

- Accidental(s) of the same kind will appear in the staff.
    - In Example 16.5, numerous G♯s appear after the diatonic pivot chord.
        - The more distant the key, the more accidentals appear in the score.
    - A notable exception is modulating from a minor key to the relative major, which typically involves a reduction of accidentals in the staff, as ♯$\hat{6}$ and ♯$\hat{7}$ are discontinued (Example 16.6).
- If the music is analyzed in the old key, past the point of modulation, the Roman numerals will be unusual and will not conform to tonal syntax.
- Functional progressions and clear cadences will be apparent in the new key.
    - In Example 16.5, numerous V^7–I motions following the modulation clarify the new key of A major. A PAC confirming the modulation appears in m. 28 (not shown).

Locating the Pivot Chord

The following steps for locating the point of modulation and labeling the diatonic pivot chord are applied to the modulating passage in Example 16.7.

Step 1: Identify the new key by taking an inventory of the accidentals appearing in the staff and locating cadences (especially PAC or IAC) in the new key.
Step 2: Find the *first* Dominant chord in the new key.
- This often involves working backward from a prominent cadence in the new key.

Step 3: Examine the chord immediately preceding the first D chord. If this chord is diatonic in both keys *and* functions as PD in the new key, label it as the diatonic pivot chord.

Step 1 – Many A♮s and PAC in B♭M

E♭M:

B♭M: ii⁶ vi⁶ V⁷ I

Step 2 – First D (V⁷) in B♭M

Step 3 – Diatonic pivot chord

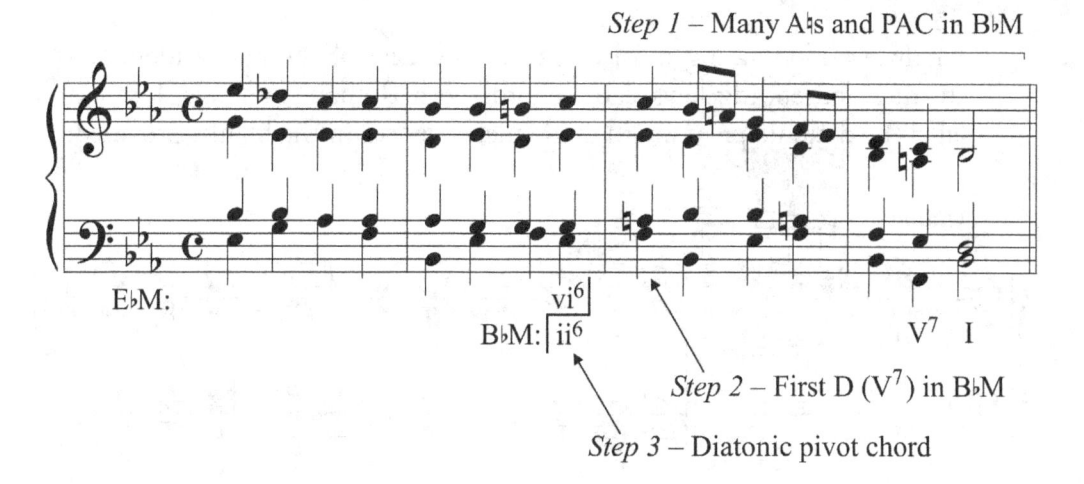

EXAMPLE 16.7 Locating the pivot chord in a modulation.

Not all pivot chords are diatonic. *Chromatic pivot chords* will be explored in Chapter 19.

Applications

Exercises

1. Analyze a modulating musical passage by Mozart. Identify the starting and ending keys, label chords with Roman numerals, locate and label the diatonic pivot chord, and label cadences in the blanks provided.

EXAMPLE 16.8 Mozart, Piano Sonata in D Major, K. 284, III, mm. 1–8.

2. Analyze a modulating musical passage by Clara Schumann. Identify the starting and ending keys, label chords with Roman numerals, locate and label the diatonic pivot chord, and label cadences in the blanks provided.

EXAMPLE 16.9   Clara Schumann, *Drei Romanzen*, Op. 21, No. 1, mm. 1–8.

Brain Teaser

In Example 16.9, identifying the chord on the downbeat of m. 8 is complicated by the absence of a chord member and the presence of a nonchord tone. What kind of nonchord tone is it?

Exploring Music

Listen to "Five Feet High and Rising" by Johnny Cash. How do the phrase modulations correspond to the narrative of the lyrics?

Thinking Critically

Why might modulations between closely related keys sound more smooth, or subtle, than those between distantly related keys?

Notes

1 This is particularly true of Classical works written prior to the early nineteenth century. Throughout the Romantic period (*c.* 1820–1900), composers explored many different key relationships—often modulating to distantly related keys.
2 Phrase modulations are also called *direct* or *abrupt modulations*. Phrase modulations up a step are heard toward the end of many popular songs—Broadway showtunes in particular (these modulations are sometimes referred to as the "truck driver's gear change").
3 The first eight measures of this work modulate from A minor to E minor, which explains the key signature for this excerpt. In the span of ten measures, this minor-mode work modulates to the minor dominant (v) and then to the relative major (III)—all closely related keys.
4 Diatonic pivot chords are sometimes referred to as *common chords*.
5 In tonal syntax, the Predominant function provides for a smooth transition from T to D. In the context of a modulation, the PD function helps to transition from one key to another—often from the tonic key to the dominant key.

17
Modal Mixture

Modal mixture involves changing the quality of a chord by applying accidentals to one or more of its chord members. A common example is the *minor* subdominant (iv) appearing in a *major* key (see Example 17.1). Modal mixture expands the palette of harmonic colors available to composers. There are two forms of mixture: *modal borrowing* and *quality conversion*.[1]

CM: I   iv   V   I

EXAMPLE 17.1 iv in a major key.

Modal Borrowing

The most common form of modal mixture is **modal borrowing**, where a major- or minor-mode work "borrows" chords from the parallel key. In Example 17.1, iv is borrowed from C minor. Which scale degree has been altered in this chord?[2]

In Major Keys

A major-mode work may borrow *any* chord from the parallel minor key. Example 17.2 compares the diatonic triads of F major (a) to those in F minor (b), excluding the chords in minor containing #$\hat{6}$ and #$\hat{7}$.[3] Example 17.2c shows how the triads from F minor are labeled when they appear in F major. The Roman numerals capture chord quality, and the ♭ in front of several labels (♭III, ♭VI, and ♭VII) indicates that the *roots* of these chords are lowered.

All chords borrowed from minor feature a lowered $\hat{3}$, $\hat{6}$, and/or $\hat{7}$, as these are the scale degrees that differ between parallel major and (natural) minor scales.

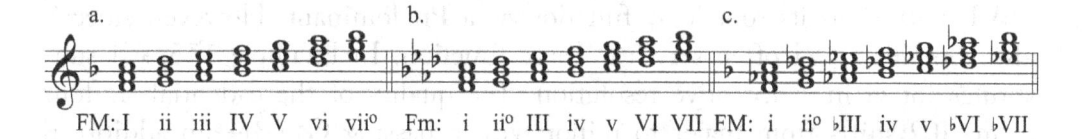

EXAMPLE 17.2 Diatonic triads in F major (a) and F minor (b); borrowed chords in F major (c).

A borrowed chord serves the same function as its diatonic counterpart, but its functionality may be strengthened or weakened by chromatic alterations. Among the more common borrowed chords are those containing ♭$\hat{6}$: iv, ii°, and ii°⁷. The Predominant function of these borrowed chords is enhanced, with ♭$\hat{6}$ acting as a tendency tone that resolves *down* by m2 to $\hat{5}$. In Example 17.3, a prolonged PD is strengthened as diatonic IV⁶ moves to a borrowed iv⁶. The positioning of these chords emphasizes the half-step resolution from ♭$\hat{6}$ to $\hat{5}$ in the bass.

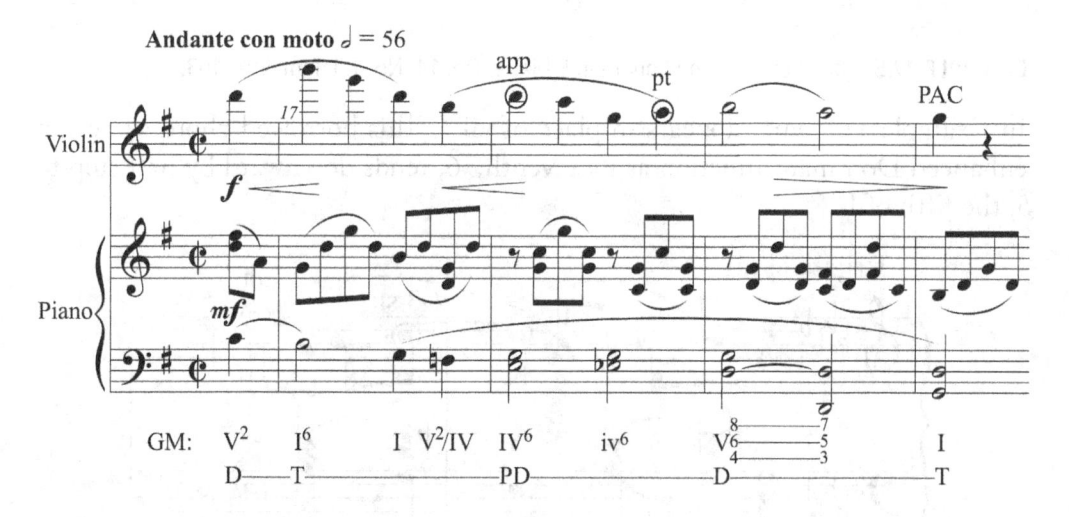

EXAMPLE 17.3 Luise Adolpha Le Beau, *Romanze*, Op. 35, mm. 17–20.

In Example 17.4, ♭$\hat{6}$–$\hat{5}$ plays out in the tenor as a borrowed supertonic seventh chord intensifies the Predominant.

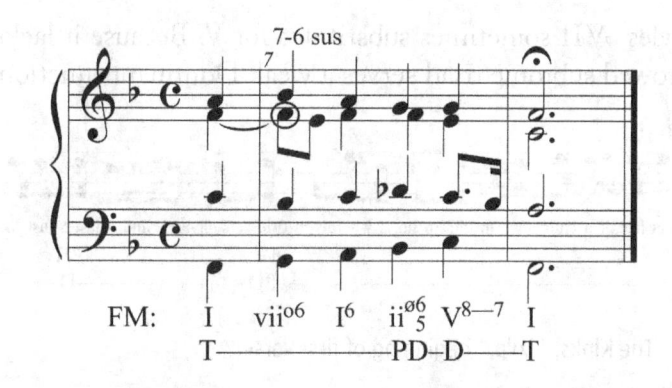

EXAMPLE 17.4 J. S. Bach, Chorale 6, "Christus, der ist mein Leben," mm. 7–8.

♭VI, with ♭$\hat{6}$ as its root, may function as a Predominant. However, since it also contains $\hat{1}$, ♭VI often serves a Tonic function. In Example 17.5, ♭VI substitutes for vi in a deceptive resolution. The quality of the cadential six-four in m. 102 shifts from major to minor with a passing G♮ (♭$\hat{3}$)—an additional instance of modal borrowing anticipating the ♭VI that follows.

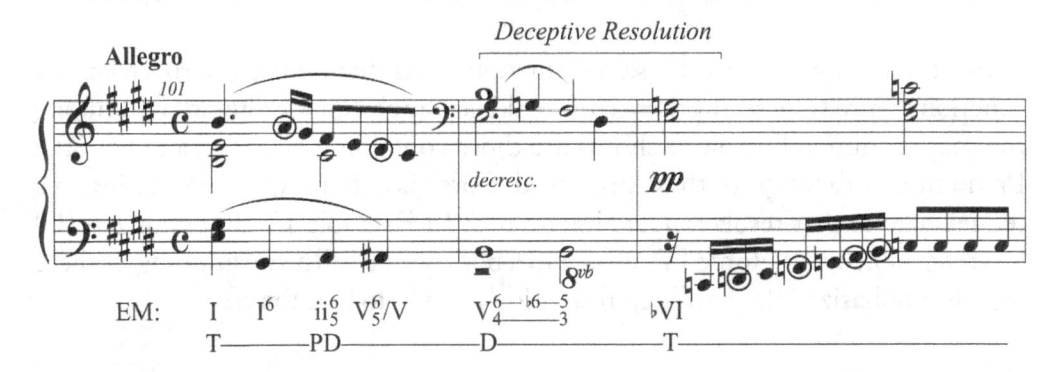

EXAMPLE 17.5 Beethoven, Piano Sonata in E Major, Op. 14, No. 1, I, mm. 101–103.

In Example 17.6, vii°7 appears in place of vii⌀7. This borrowed chord serves an enhanced Dominant function as its seventh, ♭$\hat{6}$, tends downward by half step to $\hat{5}$, the fifth of I.

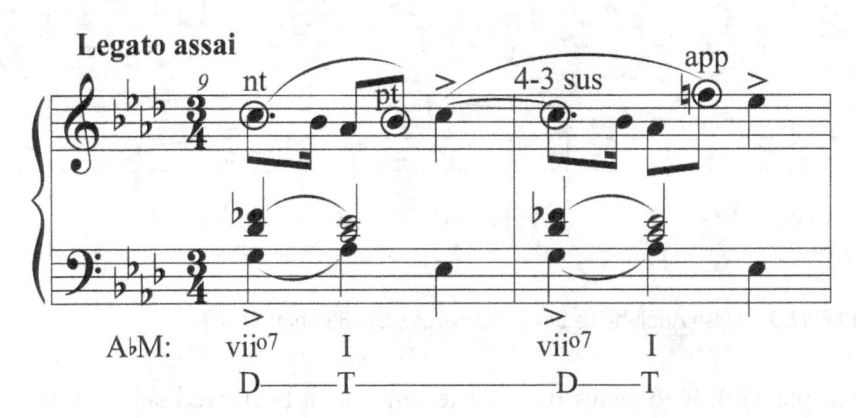

EXAMPLE 17.6 Chopin, Mazurka, Op. 17, No. 3, mm. 9–10.

In popular styles, ♭VII sometimes substitutes for V. Because it lacks the leading tone, the borrowed subtonic triad serves a weak Dominant function.

EXAMPLE 17.7 The Kinks, "Lola," beginning of first verse.

In Minor Keys

In minor, chords with #$\hat{6}$ or #$\hat{7}$ as chord members are considered diatonic rather than borrowed from the parallel major. In fact, only one chord is borrowed regularly from the parallel major: I. Many minor-mode works conclude with a major tonic chord. This effect is known as the **Picardy third**—it entails raising the third, $\hat{3}$, of the tonic chord. Examples 9.6 and 12.14 both conclude with the Picardy third. Within a phrase, a chord that looks like I may function as V/iv.

Quality Conversion

Quality conversion involves changing the quality of a diatonic chord in a manner that does not constitute modal borrowing. Under quality conversion, the chord contains at least one altered scale degree *other than* $\hat{3}$, $\hat{6}$, or $\hat{7}$. Example 17.8 features a *major* supertonic triad, II, with #$\hat{4}$ as its third.

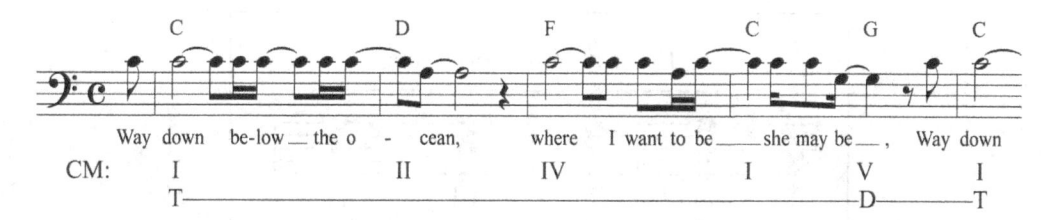

EXAMPLE 17.8 Donovan, "Atlantis," chorus.

A minor triad converted to major will often function as a secondary dominant. If the II in Example 17.8 resolved to V, it would be V/V. Since it moves to IV, this II is a converted triad.

The harmony of Radiohead's "Creep" involves a repeating, four-chord progression. As shown in Example 17.9, a B-major chord that appears to be III in fact functions as V/vi resolving deceptively to IV—an interpretation supported when the pitch A, emphasized in the vocal melody, is counted as a chord tone to form V^7/vi. This progression also features a borrowed iv.

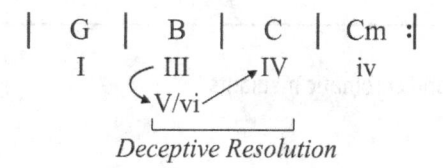

EXAMPLE 17.9 Deceptive resolution in "Creep" by Radiohead.

Spelling Mixture Chords

To spell a modal mixture chord, simply apply the accidental(s) necessary to produce the chord quality specified by the Roman numeral. When a ♭ appears in front of the Roman numeral, lower the root by a half step.[4]

Chromatic Mediants

Example 17.10 diagrams the eight triads related by third to I in G major. These include all major and minor triads lying a M3 and m3 above and below I. Two of these chords are diatonic (iii and vi); the other six are *chromatic mediants* resulting from modal borrowing (♭III and ♭VI), quality conversion (III and VI), or a combination of both (♭iii and ♭vi).[5]

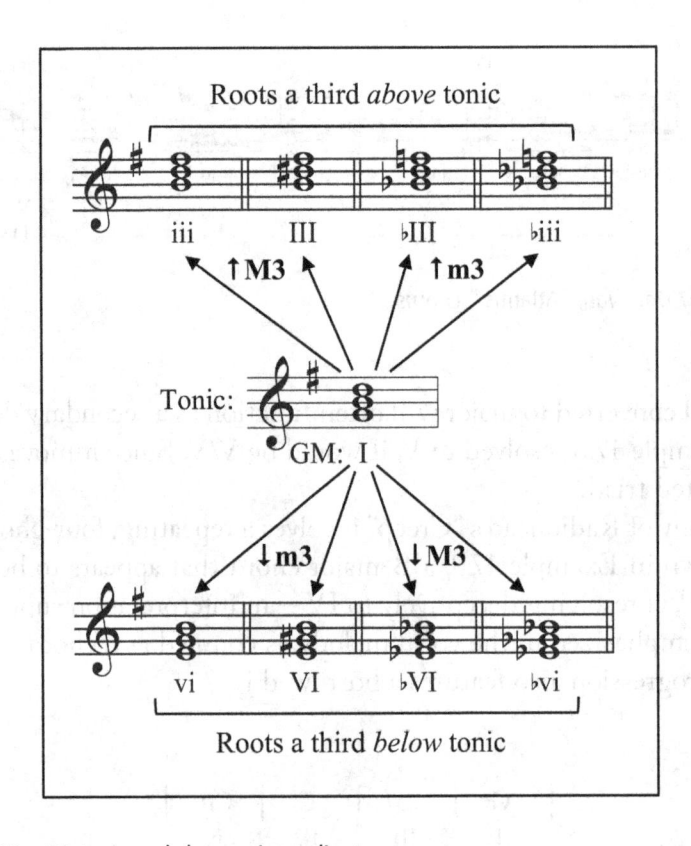

EXAMPLE 17.10 Diatonic and chromatic mediants.

Modal Mixture

Franz Schubert employs several chromatic mediants in his song "Die Sterne," lending harmonic color to the musical surface. As summarized in Example 17.11, the music moves from I to VI to begin the second verse (m. 31), from I to ♭VI for the fourth verse (m. 76), and from I to III for the sixth verse (m. 121). All three chromatic mediants shift back to the tonic chord (I⁶) before cadential passages close each verse with a PAC in E♭ major (not shown). How do the melodic beginnings of these three verses compare?

EXAMPLE 17.11 Schubert, "Die Sterne," Op. 96, No. 1, mm. 30–33 (a), 76–78 (b), 121–23 (c).

Chromatic mediants not only surface as colorful chords in musical passages—they also become key areas, such as when a piece modulates from A major to F major (I→♭VI).[6] Some processes for visiting these distantly related keys are explored in Chapter 19.

Applications

Exercises

1. Spell modal mixture chords in four voices. In the blanks below each Roman numeral, indicate whether the chord results from modal borrowing (MB) or quality conversion (QC).

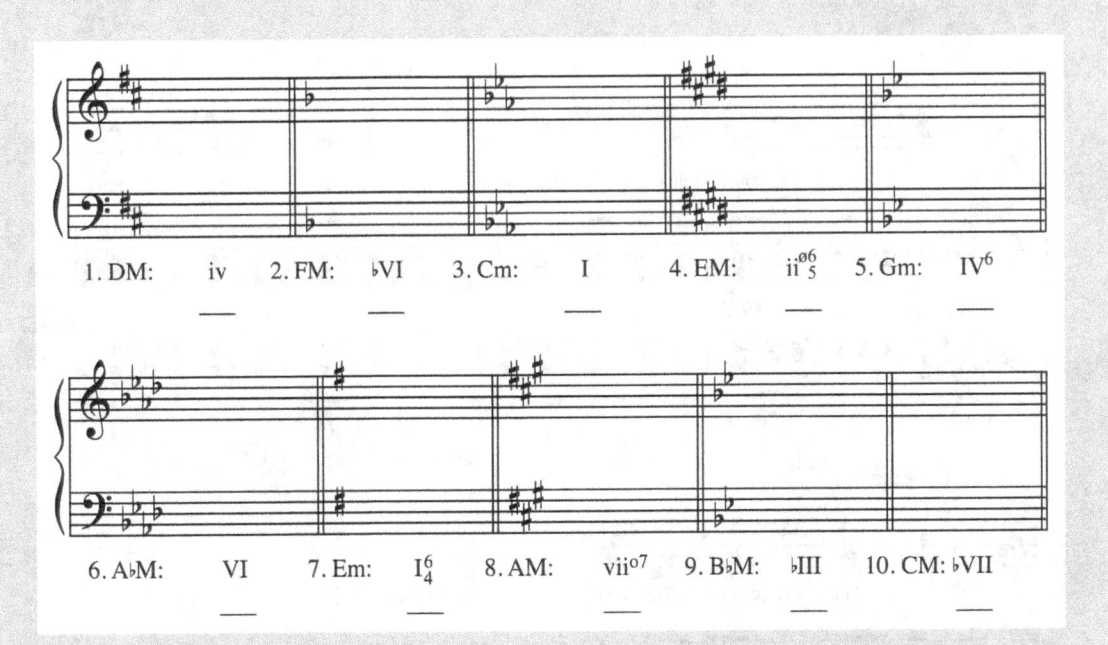

   1. DM: iv   2. FM: ♭VI   3. Cm: I   4. EM: ii⌀⁶₅   5. Gm: IV⁶

   6. A♭M: VI   7. Em: I⁶₄   8. AM: vii°⁷   9. B♭M: ♭III   10. CM: ♭VII

2. Label each modal mixture chord with a Roman numeral that clearly indicates its root (diatonic or altered), quality, and position. In the blanks below each Roman numeral, specify whether the chord results from modal borrowing (MB) or quality conversion (QC).

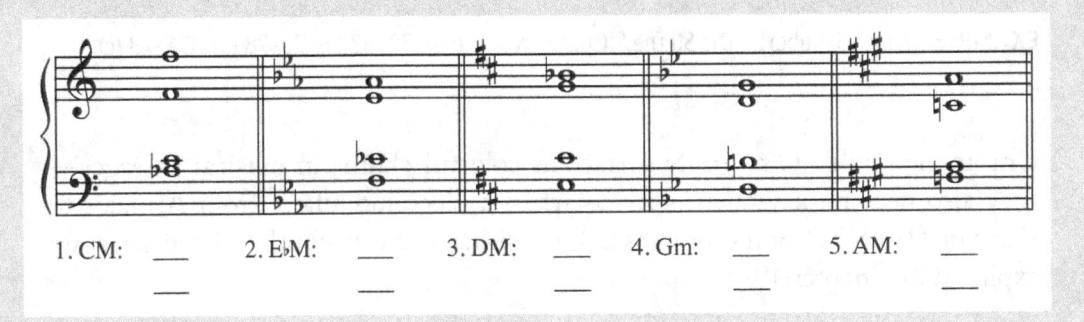

   1. CM: ___   2. E♭M: ___   3. DM: ___   4. Gm: ___   5. AM: ___

6. C♯m: ___ ___
7. FM: ___ ___
8. G♭M: ___ ___
9. F♯m: ___ ___
10. B♭M: ___ ___

Brain Teaser

What Roman numeral would apply to the chord below? Why are we unlikely to encounter this chord in a minor key?

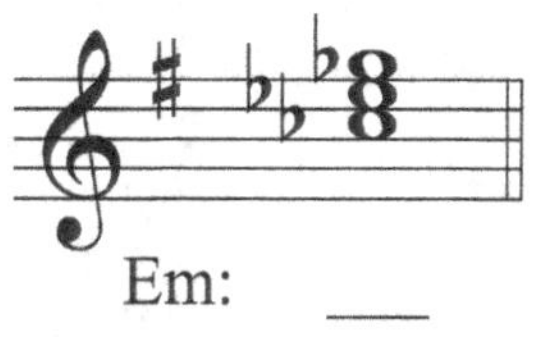
Em: ___

Exploring Music

Listen for borrowed chords in various styles of popular music. In particular, listen out for iv (in a major key).

Thinking Critically

Example 17.12 provides a piano reduction of the end of the second movement from Symphony No. 3 by Brahms. The tonic chord in m. 128 is part of a PAC. Provide a harmonic and syntactic analysis of the remainder of the excerpt. How do you describe the harmonic activity of these final seven bars?

(PAC)
128
CM: I
Syntax:

EXAMPLE 17.12 Brahms, Symphony No. 3, II, mm. 128–134 (orchestral reduction).

Notes

1 Some sources refer to modal borrowing as *primary mixture*, and quality conversion as *secondary mixture*.
2 $\hat{6}$.
3 Chords with #$\hat{6}$ and #$\hat{7}$ are considered diatonic in minor keys. These are identical to their major counterparts (IV = IV, V = V, vii° = vii°, etc.).
4 A ♭ is always used in front of the Roman numeral to indicate a lowered root, even when lowering the root entails using a ♮ to cancel a # in the key signature (e.g., ♭VI in E major).
5 ♭VI is borrowed from the parallel minor and then converted to ♭vi (some sources refer to this as *double mixture*). Both ♭vi and ♭iii do not contain *any* diatonic pitches and are rare compared to the other four chromatic mediants. The most common chromatic mediants in Classical music (Romantic works in particular) are ♭VI and ♭III.
6 Modulations to mediant keys grow increasingly common in the nineteenth century.

18

The Neapolitan and Augmented Sixth Chords

In minor keys, iv, ii°, and ii^{ø7} are diatonic chords. As we learned in Chapter 17, these chords may appear in major keys as mixture chords borrowed from the parallel minor. In either mode, they are typically Predominant chords, with ♭$\hat{6}$ tending downward to $\hat{5}$ as the syntax shifts to D. The ***Neapolitan*** and ***augmented sixth chords*** are chromatic Predominant chords containing ♭$\hat{6}$ as well as other altered scale degrees.

The Neapolitan Chord (♭II⁶)[1]

♭II⁶ Basics

- Major triad built on ♭$\hat{2}$
  - $\hat{2}$ must be lowered with an accidental in both major and minor keys.
  - ♭$\hat{2}$ is characteristically found in the main melody.
- Usually in first inversion, with $\hat{4}$ in the bass
- Third ($\hat{4}$) is doubled
- PD function
- Occurs in minor and major keys (more common in minor)
  - Requires *one* accidental in minor: ♭$\hat{2}$ (see Example 18.1a)
  - Requires *two* accidentals in major: ♭$\hat{2}$ and ♭$\hat{6}$ (see Example 18.1b)

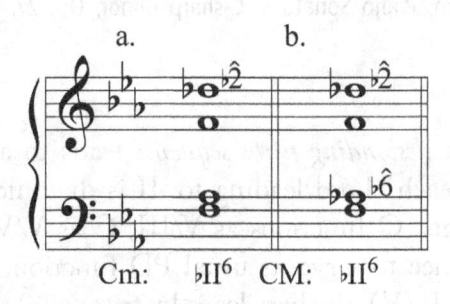

EXAMPLE 18.1 ♭II⁶ in C minor and C major.

Resolutions

- Resolves to V, V^7, or the cadential six-four chord.
- ♭$\hat{2}$ skips down to $\hat{7}$ (Example 18.2a–c).
  - Although it seems more economical, ♭$\hat{2}$ does not normally resolve to ♮$\hat{2}$.
  - When the cadential six-four is involved, ♭$\hat{2}$ passes through $\hat{1}$ on its way to $\hat{7}$ (Example 18.2d).
- When resolving to V^7, the smoothest voice leading results in an incomplete V^7 (Examples 18.2c and 18.3).

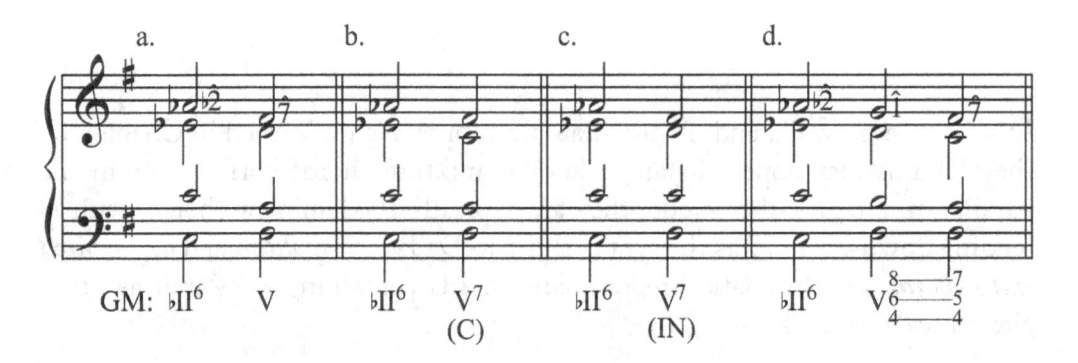

EXAMPLE 18.2 Resolving ♭II^6.

EXAMPLE 18.3 Beethoven, Piano Sonata in C-sharp Minor, Op. 27, No. 2, *Moonlight*, I, mm. 49–51.

In Example 18.4, a *descending fifths sequence* leads to a Neapolitan chord in root position. While each chord leading to ♭II is diatonic, some may be heard as secondary dominants: G functions as V/III, C as V/VI, and F as V/♭II. B♭ (♭II) breaks the sequence to serve its usual PD function. As this root-position Neapolitan resolves to E (V), the bass leaps by tritone (♭$\hat{2}$–5).

The Neapolitan and Augmented Sixth Chords

```
Am       Dm          G           C           F
Tell me how to win your heart, for I have-n't got  a clue.     But
i        iv          VII         III         VI

Bb              E                  Am
let me start  by  say - ing     I love you.
bII             V                  i
```

EXAMPLE 18.4 Lionel Richie, "Hello," end of chorus.[2]

Augmented Sixth Chords (+6)

+6 Basics

- Three different "nationalities" that share a common, three-note *frame*
- A collection of scale degrees rather than a traditional chord with a root, third, and fifth
- PD function
- Occur in major and minor keys

The +6 Frame

- Consists of ♭$\hat{6}$, ♯$\hat{4}$, and $\hat{1}$. See Example 18.5.
  - In minor keys, ♭$\hat{6}$ is diatonic; in major, $\hat{6}$ must be lowered.
    - ♭$\hat{6}$ almost always appears in the bass.
  - An accidental is *always* required to produce ♯$\hat{4}$.
    - ♯$\hat{4}$ often appears in the soprano.
    - What is the interval from ♭$\hat{6}$ up to ♯$\hat{4}$?[3]

GM: +6
      Frame

EXAMPLE 18.5 The +6 frame in G major.

Three Nationalities of +6 Chord

An +6 chord's "nationality" is determined by a variable fourth note added to the common frame—a pitch we might think of as the chord's "passport." Example 18.6 indicates the nationality, label, and "passport pitch" for the three +6 chords.

Nationality	Label	Passport Pitch
Italian	It+6	$\hat{1}$
French	Fr+6	$\hat{2}$
German	Gr+6	$\flat\hat{3}$

EXAMPLE 18.6 +6 chord nationalities, labels, and passport pitches.

In Example 18.7, the passport pitches are added to the tenor voice of the +6 frame (effectively conferring citizenship on the chords).

- When building Gr+6 in minor, $\flat\hat{3}$ is diatonic; in major, $\hat{3}$ must be lowered (Example 18.7c).

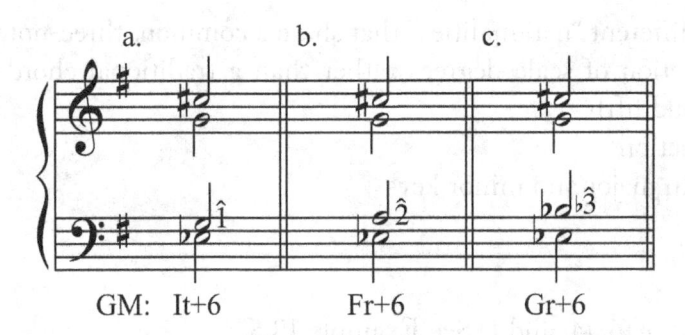

EXAMPLE 18.7 The three +6 "citizens."

Resolutions

The resolution of +6 chords (in minor) is summarized in the *quick peek* of Example 18.8 and shown in four voices (in major) in Example 18.9.

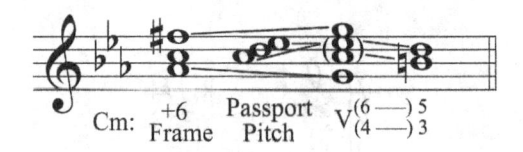

EXAMPLE 18.8 Resolution quick peek for +6 chords.

- $\flat\hat{6}$ and $\sharp\hat{4}$ both resolve *outward* to $\hat{5}$. Other tones follow the smoothest voice leading.
    - When resolving directly to V^7, $\sharp\hat{4}$ is lowered to $\natural\hat{4}$, the seventh of V^7 (Examples 18.9d–e).

The Neapolitan and Augmented Sixth Chords

- Any +6 chord can pass through the cadential six-four (in parentheses in the *quick peek*) prior to reaching V.
  - To avoid the parallel fifths that occur if Gr+6 moves directly to V (Example 18.9c), it typically goes through the cadential six-four (Example 18.9f).[4]

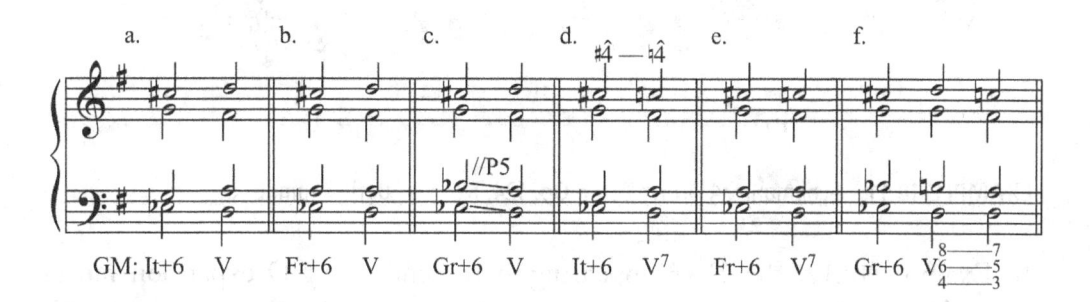

GM: It+6 V   Fr+6 V   Gr+6 V   It+6 V^7 Fr+6 V^7 Gr+6 V$^{8-7}_{6-5}_{4-3}$

EXAMPLE 18.9   Resolving +6 chords.

As the bass line in Example 18.10 descends chromatically from $\hat{1}$ to $\hat{5}$, it supports two chromatic chords: V^2/IV tonicizing IV^6 and It+6 prolonging PD. The rests preceding it, a fortepiano dynamic marking, and its relatively longer note values accentuate the dissonant It+6.

CM: I   V$^6_5$ V^2/IV   IV^6 It+6   V   V^7/V   V
T————————————PD————————D————————

EXAMPLE 18.10   Beethoven, String Quartet in G Major, Op. 18, No. 2, III, mm. 44–51.

The Fr+6 in Example 18.11 is last in a series of chords prolonging PD. After iv initiates PD, a filled-in bass arpeggiation ends with ii$^{ø4}_3$, a substitute for iv^6 (note the voice exchange between the outer voices). The ii$^{ø4}_3$ easily converts to Fr+6 as $\hat{4}$ (B♭) shifts up by semitone to ♯$\hat{4}$ (B♮).

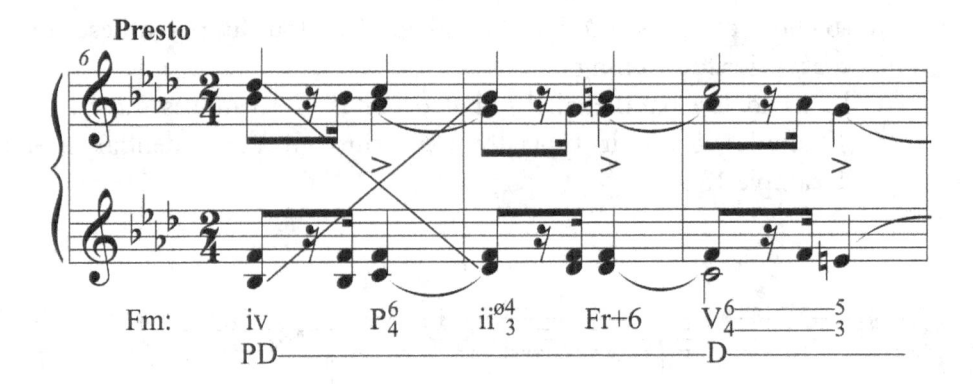

EXAMPLE 18.11 Schumann, *Albumblätter*, Op. 124, No. 12, "Burla," mm. 6–8.

In Example 18.12, the Gr+6 appearing at the end of a PD expansion moves through the cadential six-four on its way to V. $\sharp\hat{4}$ appears in an inner voice in this example.

EXAMPLE 18.12 Beethoven, Piano Sonata in C Minor, Op. 13, No. 8, *Pathétique*, III, mm. 184–186.

Chromatic Predominant Chords and Prolongation

In the previous three musical examples, +6 chords appear at the end of Predominant spans. In each case, the +6 chord is the only chromatic PD chord in the passage (the secondary dominants in Examples 18.10 and 18.12 are tonicizing chords embedded in prolongational spans). Chromatic chords tend to occur toward the *end* of a prolongational span, rather than the beginning. As mentioned in the Introduction to Part III, chromatic alterations often serve as "function enhancers" by establishing more half-step resolutions to the next chord or function—thereby functioning, and resolving, as chromatic tendency tones. The progression in Example 18.13 involves a systematic strengthening of the PD function as the outer voices slip chromatically closer to $\hat{5}$.

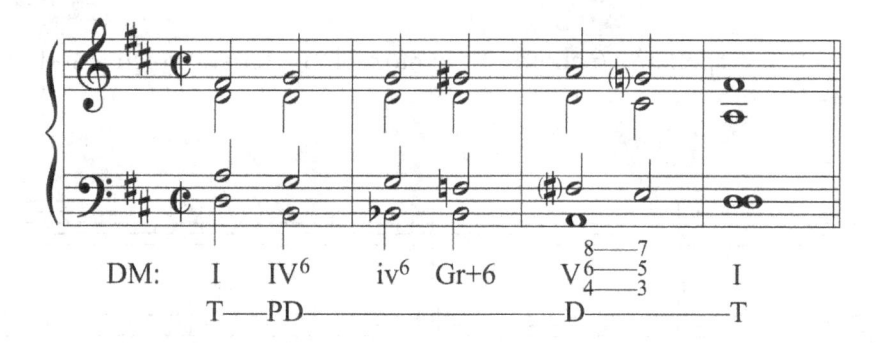

EXAMPLE 18.13 Predominant span prolonged with chromatic chords.

Applications

Exercises

1. In each key, spell a Neapolitan chord in the most characteristic voicing and resolve as specified. V^7 chords should be either complete (C) or incomplete (IN).

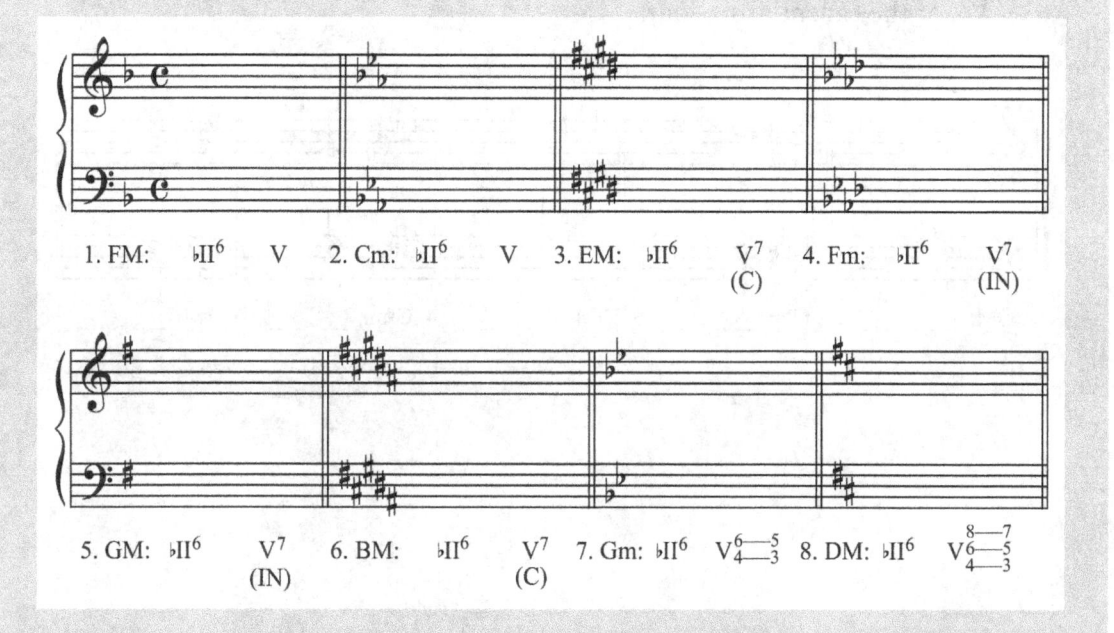

1. FM: ♭II⁶ V 2. Cm: ♭II⁶ V 3. EM: ♭II⁶ V⁷ (C) 4. Fm: ♭II⁶ V⁷ (IN)

5. GM: ♭II⁶ V⁷ (IN) 6. BM: ♭II⁶ V⁷ (C) 7. Gm: ♭II⁶ V⁶₄—⁵₃ 8. DM: ♭II⁶ V⁶⁸—⁷₄—⁵₃

2. In each key, spell an +6 chord in the most characteristic voicing and resolve as specified.

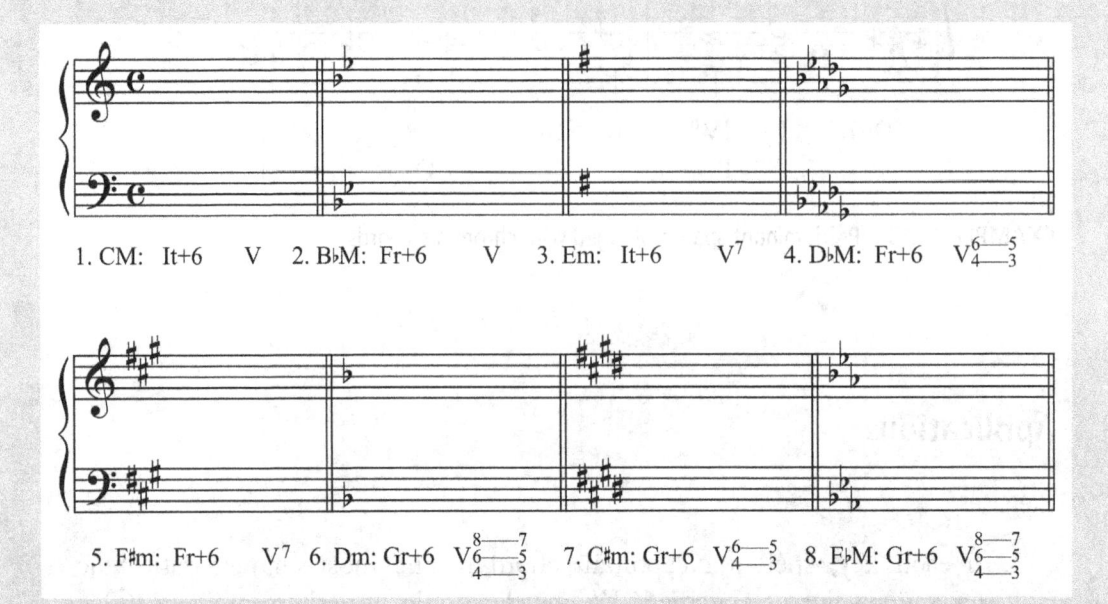

1. CM: It+6   V   2. B♭M: Fr+6   V   3. Em: It+6   V⁷   4. D♭M: Fr+6   V⁶⁻⁵₄₋₃

5. F♯m: Fr+6   V⁷   6. Dm: Gr+6   V⁸⁻⁷₆⁻⁵₄₋₃   7. C♯m: Gr+6   V⁶⁻⁵₄₋₃   8. E♭M: Gr+6   V⁸⁻⁷₆⁻⁵₄₋₃

3. Label each chromatic Predominant chord and resolve to your choice of V, V⁷, or the cadential six-four.

1. GM: ___   2. C♯m: ___   3. B♭M: ___   4. G♯m: ___   5. AM: ___

The Neapolitan and Augmented Sixth Chords

4. Provide a complete analysis of a chromatic progression. Label chords, the tonal syntax, nonchord tones, and cadences.

B♭M:

Brain Teasers

1. In the passage below, what nationality of +6 chord is enclosed in the box? Analyze the entire passage.

Gm:

EXAMPLE 18.14 Mozart, Piano Sonata in B-flat Major, K. 333, I, mm. 80–81.

2. In the following excerpt, the enclosed +6 chord is voiced such that ♭6̂ does not appear in the bass. Is this technically an +6 chord? How would you label it? Analyze the entire passage.

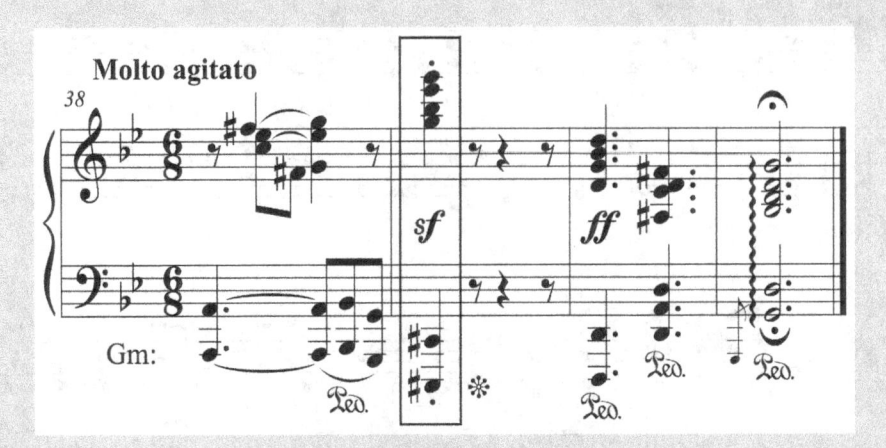

EXAMPLE 18.15 Chopin, Prelude in G Minor, Op. 28, No. 22, mm. 38–41.

Exploring Music

Locate at least one example of each +6 chord in music provided by your instructor or music of your choosing. You might explore music you are currently learning or that you select from an anthology. A useful strategy is to scan the lowest voice for ♭6̂, and then see if ♯4̂ appears somewhere above it. Once you locate an +6 chord, investigate how it is approached and resolved.

Thinking Critically

1. Example 18.16 provides a short tune with chord symbols placed above the melody. In the blanks below, provide a Roman-numeral "translation" of the chord symbols.

EXAMPLE 18.16 Excerpt for analysis.

2. The Gr+6 chord is enharmonically equivalent to another familiar chord. Although the two chords sound the same, their different spellings and Roman-numeral labels reflect their varying functions. Determine the enharmonic chord by listening to a Gr+6 (what else does it sound like?) and then respelling one of its notes as a different altered scale degree.
3. Refer back to the Roman numerals you provided in Question 1. Using the knowledge you gained from answering Question 2, challenge your initial assumptions about the labels and functions of the chords involved in Question 1. In particular, think carefully about the D♭7 chord. How is this chord, which appears to be a dominant seventh chord, truly functioning relative to the other chords?

Notes

1 The Neapolitan chord is so named due to its popularity among opera composers in eighteenth-century Naples, Italy. The chord is labeled N^6 in some sources.
2 The clef in this musical example is the *octave treble clef*, also known as the *vocal tenor clef*. The "8" beneath the treble clef indicates that the notes sound one octave lower than notated. This clef is used to avoid the many ledger lines that would be necessary if the part were notated in bass or (regular) treble clef.
3 +6.
4 When Gr+6 resolves to the cadential six-four in a major key, ♭$\hat{3}$ is often spelled enharmonically as ♯$\hat{2}$. The interval from ♭$\hat{6}$ in the bass up to ♯$\hat{2}$ is a ++4 (doubly augmented fourth). In Example 18.9f, the B♭ in the tenor could be respelled as A♯ to clarify the voice leading to the next pitch, B♮.

19

Modulation II

Chromatic Pivot Chords, Enharmonic Reinterpretation, and Common-Tone Modulation

Music modulates in a variety of ways. Chapter 16 explored diatonic pivot chords, which usually lead to a closely related key. Composers also use chromatic pivot chords and common tones to move between closely *or* distantly related keys.

Chromatic Pivot Chords

Searching for a *diatonic* pivot chord is an important first step when analyzing a modulation. In Chapter 16 we learned to do this by examining the chord right before the first Dominant chord in the new key. But at times we will be unable to locate a diatonic pivot—perhaps the chord is not diatonic in *both* keys or is not a Predominant in the *new* key. A **chromatic pivot chord** is chromatic in one or both keys, and may function as PD or D in the new key.

There are *three types* of chromatic pivot chord:

1. C–D: chromatic in the first key; diatonic in the new key.
2. D–C: diatonic in the first key; chromatic in the new key.
3. C–C: chromatic in both keys.[1]

Sometimes the chord preceding the first Dominant in the new key is not diatonic in both keys but *is* PD in the new key. In Example 19.1, the pivot chord is chromatic in the first key—♭VI⁶ is borrowed from the parallel key. However, it resolves as diatonic IV⁶ to function as PD in the new key. This ***C–D pivot*** moves to the distant, chromatic-mediant key of A♭ major (I→♭III).

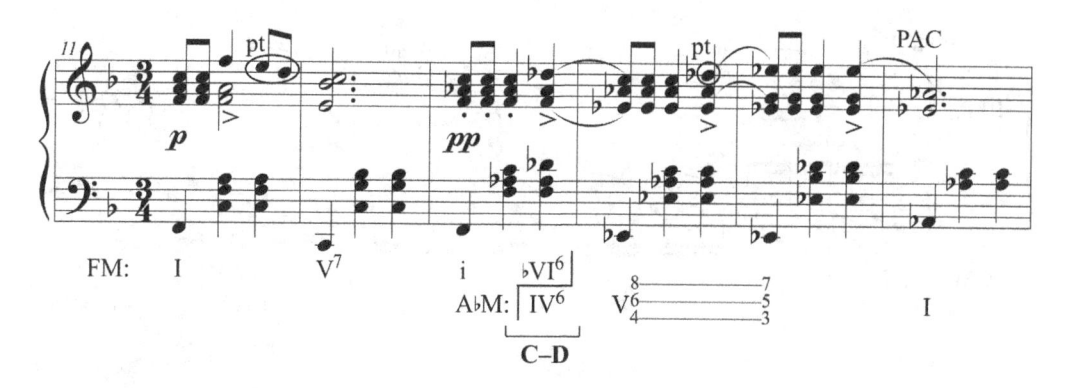

EXAMPLE 19.1 Schubert, Waltz No. 33, D. 365, mm. 11–16.

The ***D–C pivot*** in Example 19.2 is diatonic in the initial key and a chromatic Predominant chord (♭II) in the new key. Because this Neapolitan chord is in root position (rather than first inversion), the bass leaps by tritone as it resolves to V^7.[2]

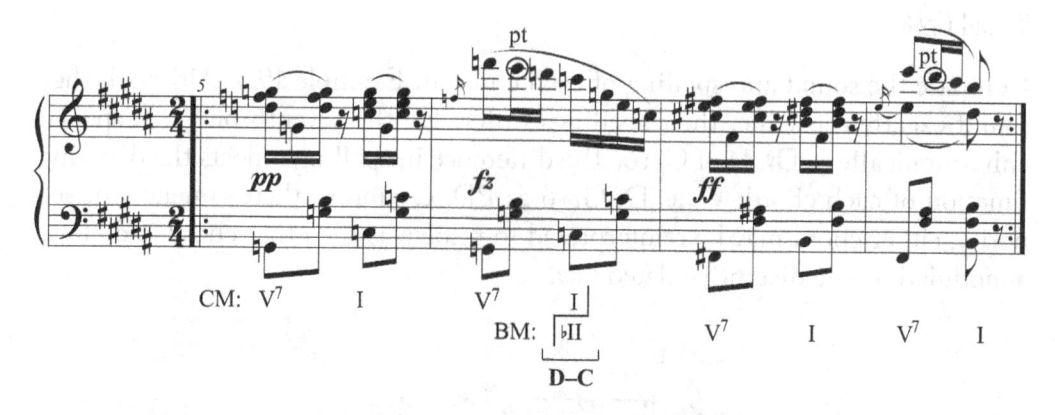

EXAMPLE 19.2 Schubert, Ecossaise No. 7, D. 145, mm. 5–8.

Example 19.3 features a modulation from G major to D major (I→V). Although these are closely related keys, the first Dominant chord in the new key, V$^6_5$, is *not* preceded by a diatonic pivot chord—the chord immediate before V$^6_5$ is v^6 in D major, which is neither diatonic *nor* PD in the new key. Therefore, V$^6_5$ *is* the pivot chord; it is labeled as a secondary dominant in G major and as the new, primary dominant in D major.

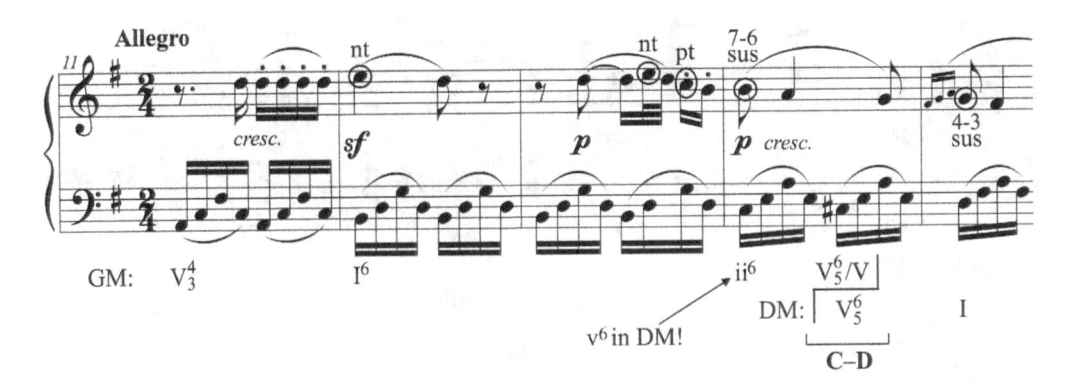

EXAMPLE 19.3 Beethoven, Piano Sonata in G Major, Op. 14, No. 2, I, mm. 11–15.

Enharmonic Reinterpretation

Enharmonic reinterpretation involves resolving a chord as if it were a different chord in order to modulate.

V⁷ and Gr+6

Compare the sound and spelling of each chord in Example 19.4. Although they sound exactly the same, their spellings differ: E♭, the seventh of V⁷, is spelled enharmonically as D♯, ♯$\hat{4}$ of Gr+6. The difference in spelling reflects the differing function of each chord: V⁷ as D; Gr+6 as PD. Owing to their sameness of sonority, either chord may be reinterpreted to resolve as the other chord and effect a modulation to a distantly related key.

EXAMPLE 19.4 Comparing V⁷ and Gr+6.

The chords in Example 19.4 are reinterpreted in Examples 19.5 and 19.6. Example 19.5 begins in B♭ major and approaches V⁷. Instead of leading to I, V⁷ resolves as Gr+6. This **D–C pivot** causes the music to modulate *down* a m2 to A major. The chord is not respelled in the score, but E♭ resolves up by chromatic semitone as if it were D♯ (♯$\hat{4}$ in A major).

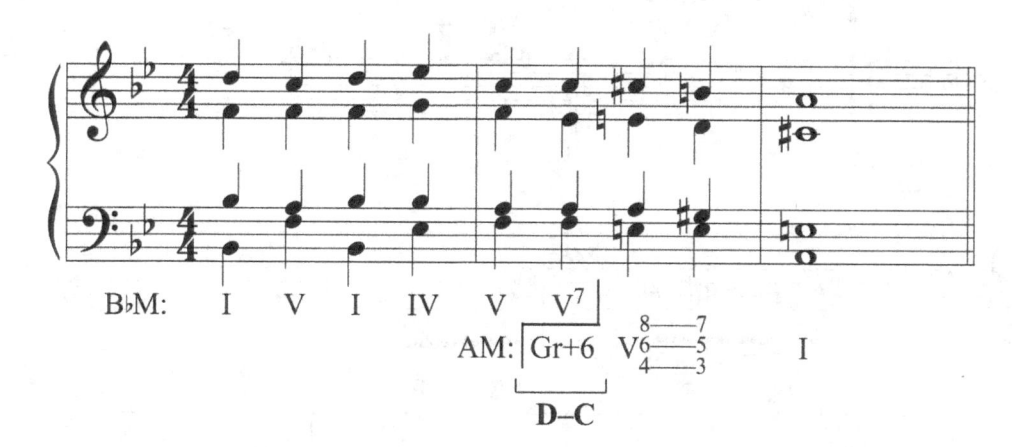

EXAMPLE 19.5 Reinterpretation of V^7 as Gr+6.

Example 19.6 modulates *up* a half step to the Neapolitan key (I→♭II), as Gr+6 in A major resolves as V^7 in B♭ major.

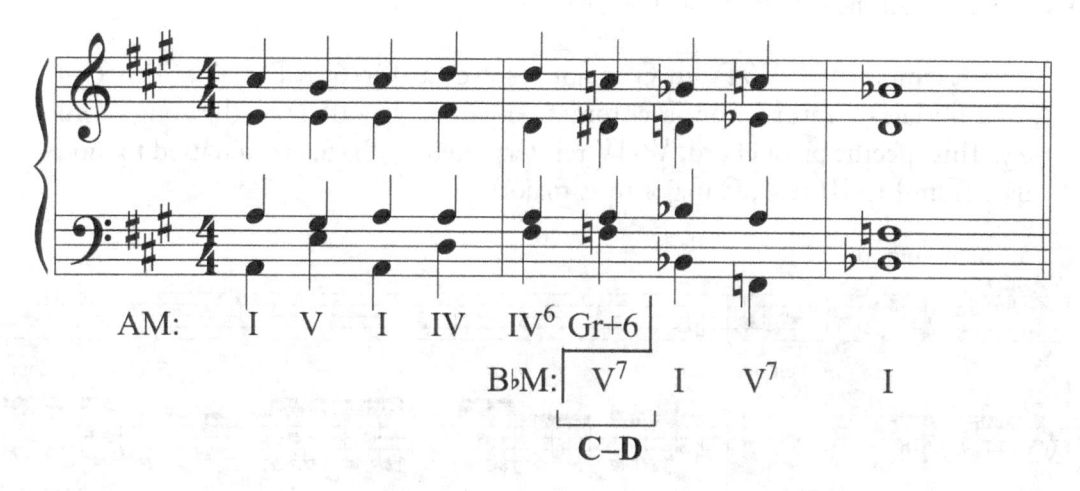

EXAMPLE 19.6 Reinterpretation of Gr+6 as V^7.

Example 19.7 features a modulation from the (enharmonic) Neapolitan key of D major to the tonic key, D♭ major. The **D–C pivot** is spelled as V^7 in D major but resolves as Gr+6 in D♭ major.

EXAMPLE 19.7 Schubert, Waltz No. 14, D. 365, mm. 17–24.

In Example 19.8, V^7/IV in G major resolves as Gr+6 in B major. This ***C–C pivot*** initiates a return from a chromatic-mediant key (♭VI) to the song's tonic key. This specific pivot chord, V^7/IV reinterpreted as Gr+6, is often used to modulate from I to III (e.g., C major to E major).

EXAMPLE 19.8 Schubert, "Der Neugierige" from *Die schöne Müllerin*, Op. 25, mm. 40–43.

vii^{o7}

Example 19.9 shows vii^{o7} in the key of E minor.

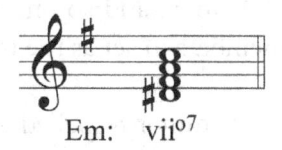

Em: vii^{o7}

EXAMPLE 19.9 vii^{o7} in E minor.

Example 19.10 plots vii^{o7} in E minor on a *pitch-class wheel*, or *"pc wheel."*

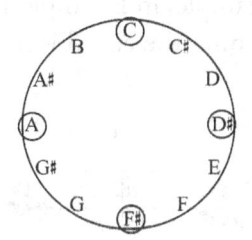

EXAMPLE 19.10 vii^{o7} on the pc wheel.

Introduction to the Pitch-Class Wheel (Pc Wheel)

The pc wheel provides an abstract view of pitch relationships, such as the intervallic content of a chord. The letter names represent pitch *classes* rather than specific pitches. Recall from Chapter 1 that a pitch class includes all notes with the same letter name in any octave (e.g., C3, C4, C5, and C6 all belong to pitch-class C, whereas C4 denotes a specific pitch). Imagine the pc wheel as a clock face with letters replacing the twelve numbers. Beginning with C at the twelve o'clock (12:00) position, the pitch classes are ordered as a chromatic scale going clockwise.[3]

Features of the pc wheel include:

- *Octave Equivalence*: C♯ appearing in any octave on the staff is plotted at the 1:00 position.
- *Enharmonic Equivalence*: C♯ and D♭ are both at 1:00; F♯ and G♭ at 6:00; and so on.
  - Similarly, the m3 C–E♭ and the +2 C–D♯ look identical on the pc wheel.
- *Inversional Equivalence*: the m3 C–E♭ and its inversion, the M6 E♭–C, look identical on the pc wheel.

The pc wheel is used throughout the remainder of this textbook, especially in Part IV. We will now use the pc wheel to learn how vii^{o7} can be reinterpreted to modulate to remote keys.

Viewing vii^{o7} on the pc wheel in Example 19.10, we see that it is a *symmetrical sonority*—it divides the octave evenly into four minor-third segments. Normally, the root of this sonority resolves up by half step to the chord it is tonicizing: $\hat{7}$–$\hat{1}$ with vii^{o7} to I, #$\hat{4}$–$\hat{5}$ with vii^{o7}/V to V, and so on. The perfect symmetry of this chord allows *any* of its chord members to act as the root and resolve up by half step to a different chord.

Example 19.11 shows vii^{o7} in E minor respelled and reinterpreted in three different keys. It continues to serve a Dominant function, but this function is transferred to different keys. Each pitch class circled on the pc wheel in Example 19.10 is reinterpreted as the root, and the roots appear as filled-in noteheads in Example 19.11. Pitch classes are held in their original positions on the staff, so the position of the °7 chord changes. For example, in Example 19.11b, D♯ is respelled as E♭, but it remains the lowest note, meaning the chord is in third inversion.

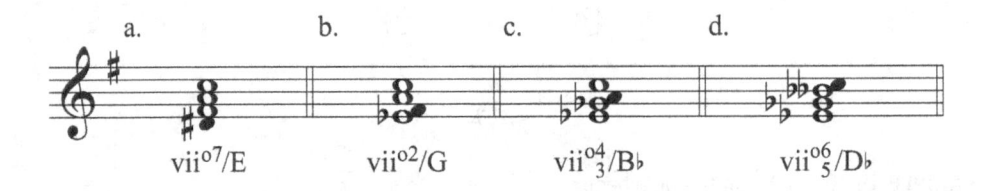

EXAMPLE 19.11 vii^{o7} in E minor reinterpreted in three different keys.

When vii^{o7} is reinterpreted, $\hat{1}$ of the new key lies a m3 above, a m3 below, or a tritone away from the initial tonic.[4] The new key may be major or minor. The reinterpreted chord in Example 19.11b, for instance, may pivot into G major *or* G minor. Enharmonic keys are also possible: the chord in Example 19.11d may modulate to D♭ major, C♯ major, or C♯ minor. (Why would it *not* go to D♭ minor?[5])

Example 19.12 modulates from G♭ major to C minor. The **C–D *pivot*** is a fully diminished seventh chord spelled to reflect its function and resolution in the new key.

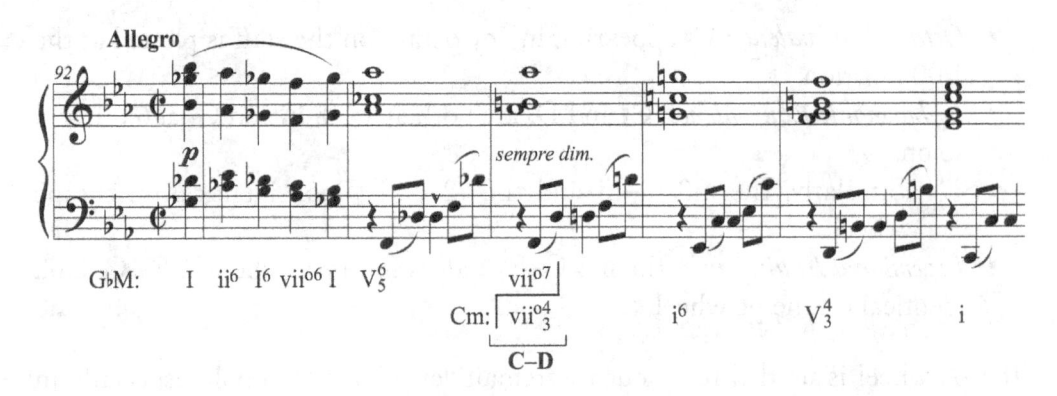

EXAMPLE 19.12 Beethoven, Piano Sonata in E-flat Major, Op. 81a, No. 26, I, mm. 92–98.

Common-Tone Modulation

In a *common-tone modulation*, a single pitch links two keys. This note is typically shared by a chord in the first key and another chord in the new key, and composers often emphasize this common tone at the point of modulation.

Example 19.13 shows a passage ending with a HC in B minor (mm. 24–25). F♯ ($\hat{5}$) is then highlighted through repetition, articulation, and a solo setting. When the next phrase begins, F♯ is suddenly recast as $\hat{3}$ in the relative key of D major.

EXAMPLE 19.13 Mozart, Fantasia in C Minor, K. 475, mm. 24–28.

Common-tone modulation is most often applied to connect two distantly related keys, especially chromatic-mediant keys. In Example 19.14, Schubert modulates from D major to B♭ major (I→♭VI) via the common-tone D, which is shared by the tonic chords of both keys.

EXAMPLE 19.14 Schubert, String Quartet No. 3 in B-flat Major, D. 36, III, mm. 77–87.

Applications

Exercises

1. The example below modulates via a chromatic pivot chord. Identify the starting and ending keys, locate and label the pivot chord, and provide a complete harmonic analysis, including the cadence and nonchord tones.

2. The passage below begins in C minor and modulates to a remote key via a chromatic pivot chord. Identify the new key, locate and label the pivot chord, and provide a complete harmonic analysis.

EXAMPLE 19.15 Beethoven, Piano Sonata in E Minor, Op. 90, No. 27, II, mm. 118–126.

Brain Teasers

1. How would the pivot chord in Example 19.7 be spelled if it looked like Gr+6 in D♭ major?
2. Example 19.7 starts in the *enharmonic* Neapolitan key of D major. What is the literal Neapolitan key in relation to D♭ major? What likely motivated Schubert to use D major instead of the literal Neapolitan key?

Exploring Music

Listen to and compare modulations that use diatonic pivot chords with those that use chromatic pivot chords. Describe the effects of these modulation types—do they differ?

Thinking Critically

Analyze the passage in Example 19.16. Identify and describe the type of modulation. How are the two keys related?

EXAMPLE 19.16 Robert Schumann, "Widmung" from *Myrthen*, Op. 25, No. 1, mm. 12–14.[6]

Notes

1. A diatonic pivot chord is a D–D pivot; there are four types of pivot chord in total (one diatonic and three chromatic).
2. This is similar to the resolution of ♭II in Example 18.4.
3. Although it bears some similarity to the circle of fifths, the pitch-class wheel is ordered in semitones rather than fifths and is therefore very different.
4. A tritone is the equivalent of two minor thirds.
5. This key is not used in practice, as it requires B♭♭.
6. "Innig" is an expressive indication that Schumann used often. It may be translated as "inward," "intimate," "heartfelt," or "tender." "Lebhaft" means "lively."

20

Dominant Ninth Chords, Altered Dominants, and Embellishing Chords

This chapter explores several chord types that are less common to tonal music in general, but that appear with some frequency in late Romantic and popular music.

Dominant Ninth Chords (V⁹)

Dominant ninth chords are created by stacking an additional third on top of V⁷. The new chord member is a *ninth* above the root. See Example 20.1.

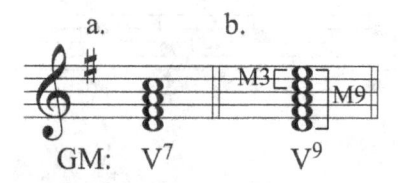

EXAMPLE 20.1 Forming a dominant ninth chord.

V⁹ Basics

- Dominant function
- The ninth, $\hat{6}$, is a tendency tone that resolves *down by step* to the fifth of I: $\hat{6} \searrow \hat{5}$.
    - The other two tendency tones resolve as usual: $\hat{7} \nearrow \hat{1}$; $\hat{4} \searrow \hat{3}$.
- Typically in root position
- In four voices, the fifth is omitted[1]
- Occur in major and minor keys
    - In major, the ninth is a M9 above the root (Example 20.2a).
    - In minor, the ninth is a m9 above the root (Example 20.2b).
    - In major, the ninth is sometimes lowered (♭$\hat{6}$); this is a form of modal borrowing (Example 20.2c).
        - The label for this borrowed chord is V♭⁹.

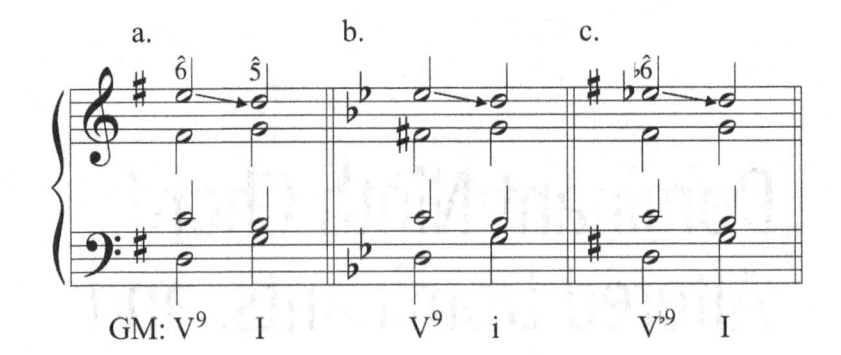

EXAMPLE 20.2 V⁹ resolving to I.

The work by Robert Schumann in Example 20.3 opens with a complete V⁹ in A minor. The ninth (F) is the first note of the melody, which is doubled in two inner voices. The ninth is emphasized with a longer note value relative to the other chord tones sounded at the same time.[2]

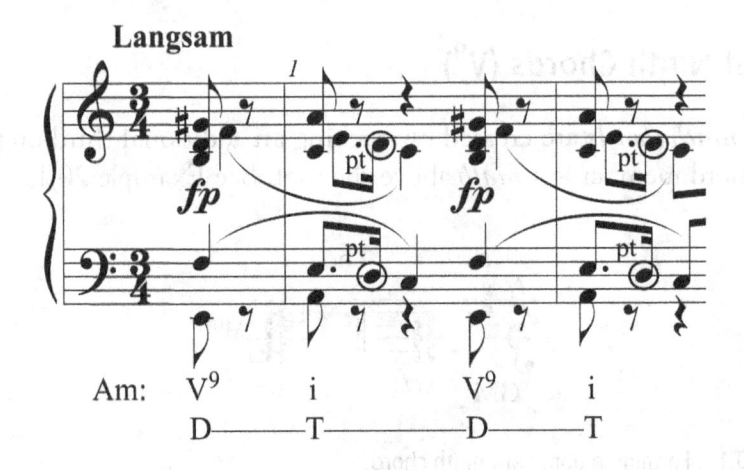

EXAMPLE 20.3 R. Schumann, "Leides Ahnung" from *Albumblätter*, Op. 124, No. 2, mm. 1–2.

Altered Dominant Chords (V+, V⁷₊, V°⁷)

In an altered dominant chord, the *fifth* is either raised or lowered by a half step. Both V and V⁷ may include an altered fifth. Adjusting this chord member in either direction destabilizes the harmony—increasing its dissonance and intensifying its pull toward Tonic.

V+ and V⁷₊

Raising the fifth of V makes the chord augmented (V+). This alteration may appear as a chromatic passing tone (Example 20.4a), or it may replace the diatonic fifth altogether (Example 20.4b). The raised fifth, #$\hat{2}$, is a chromatic tendency tone resolving *up by half step* to $\hat{3}$, the third of I. V+ and V⁷₊ typically occur in major keys; they are less effective in minor keys.

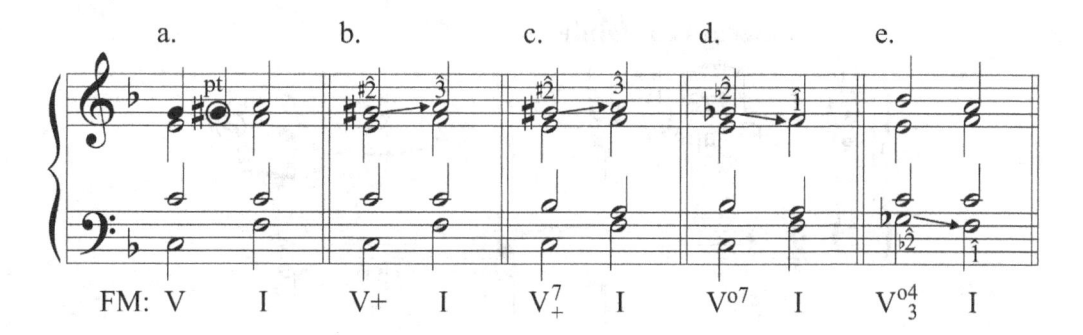

Dominant Ninth Chords, Altered Dominants, and Embellishing Chords

EXAMPLE 20.4 Altered dominant chords.

Whereas V^7 includes two tendency tones ($\hat{7}$ and $\hat{4}$), V^7_+ contains *three* tendency tones, all of which resolve by step. Root-position V^7_+ leads to an incomplete tonic chord (Example 20.4c).

Example 20.5 features three altered dominant chords—each resolving to I. The V^7/IV in m. 18 does not resolve to IV and may be heard as I with an E♭ embellishing E♮ in the framing dominant chords. In m. 21, a ninth is added to V^7_+, and all *four* tendency tones resolve by step to members of I. V+ in m. 23 forms a dissonant HC.

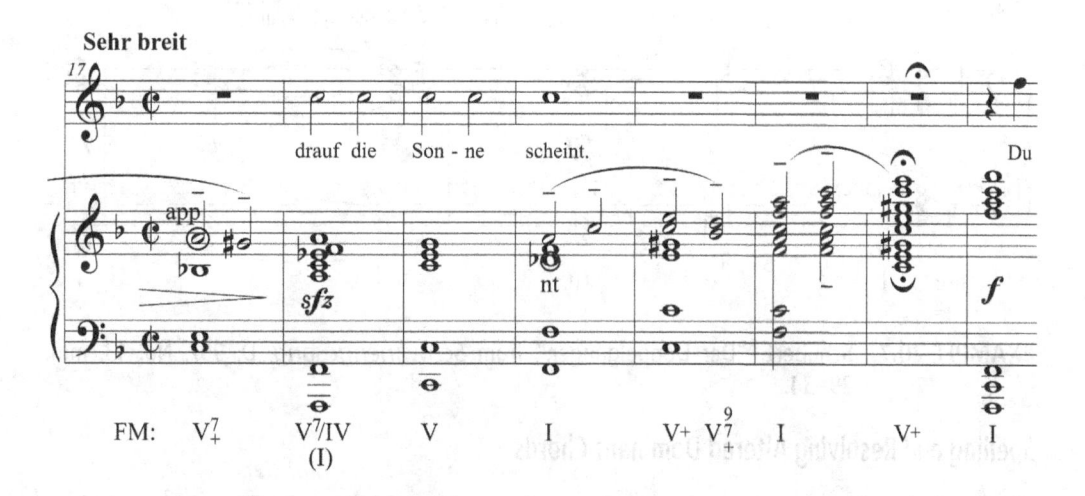

EXAMPLE 20.5 Alma Mahler, "Ekstase," from *Five Songs*, No. 2, mm. 17–24.

Like primary dominants, secondary dominants may be altered. In Example 20.6, both IV and V are tonicized by secondary $V+^6$ chords that arise from chromatic linear motion in the melody. Both V+ and V^7_+ often appear in first inversion, making the resolution to I quite economical (stepwise with one common tone).

[Musical example: Moderato cantabile]

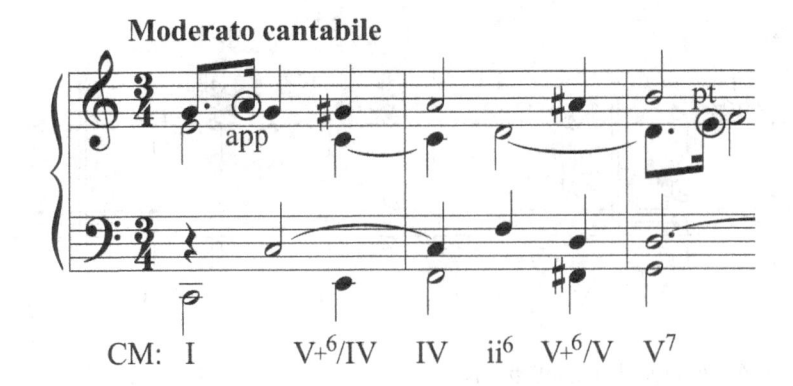

CM: I   V+6/IV   IV   ii6   V+6/V   V7

EXAMPLE 20.6   Beethoven, Bagatelle in C Major, Op. 119, No. 8, mm. 1–3.

V°7

In Example 20.4d, the fifth of V7 is *lowered*.[3] This chromatic alteration, ♭$\hat{2}$, tends *downward* to $\hat{1}$ as the chord resolves to tonic. This altered dominant is most often found in second inversion (V°$^4_3$), which emphasizes the lowered fifth and its descending stepwise resolution in the bass. See Examples 20.4e and 20.7.

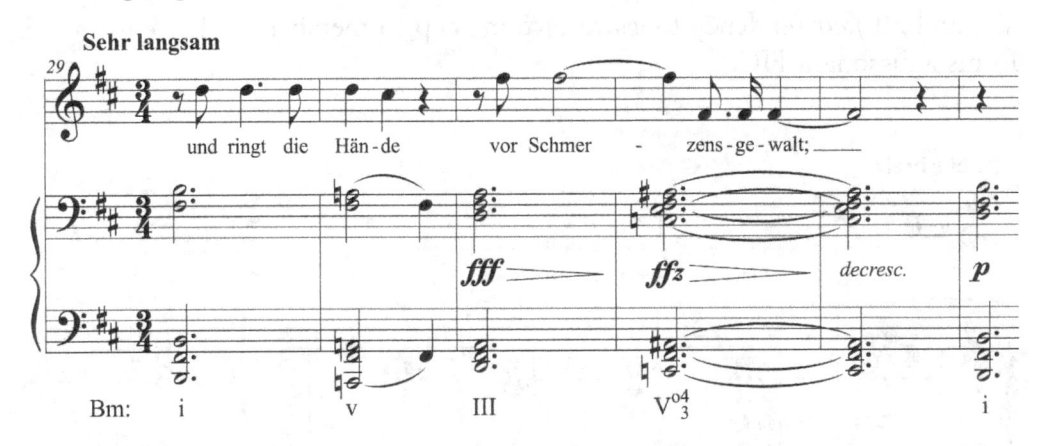

[Musical example: Sehr langsam — "und ringt die Hän-de vor Schmer-zens-ge-walt;"]

Bm: i   v   III   V°$^4_3$ i

EXAMPLE 20.7   Schubert, "Der Doppelgänger," from *Schwanengesang*, D. 957, No. 13, mm. 29–34.

Spelling and Resolving Altered Dominant Chords

To spell altered dominant chords, begin by spelling a diatonic V or V7 and then either raise or lower the fifth by half step. Resolve all tendency tones properly, as in the examples above.

Embellishing Chords (CT°7 and CT+6)

Embellishing chords sound and look like the familiar chords vii°7 and Gr+6. However, instead of functioning as these chords *normally* do (as D and PD, respectively), embellishing chords prolong a chord and function. The embellishing

Dominant Ninth Chords, Altered Dominants, and Embellishing Chords

chords CT°7 and CT+6 share at least one *common tone* ("CT") with the chords they expand—most often tonic harmonies.

CT°7

Example 20.8 shows CT°7 chords (*common-tone diminished seventh chords*) embellishing tonic harmonies in both major and minor. These °7 chords do *not* function as either primary or secondary dominants. While the bass holds on $\hat{1}$, other voices shift away—to both diatonic and chromatic tones—and then return. When the root of I is doubled, one voice leaps by a third (Examples 20.8a and c). When the fifth of I is doubled, all voices move by step (Example 20.8b). When embellishing a minor triad, there are *two* common tones (Example 20.8c).

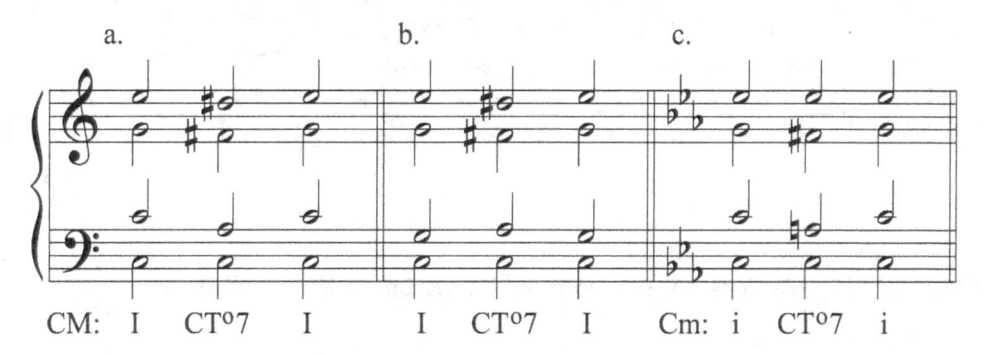

EXAMPLE 20.8 CT°7 embellishing tonic in major and minor.

Applying CT°7

Follow these steps to embellish a *major* triad:

Step 1: Locate the *third*.
Step 2: Think down a m2—this is the "root" of the CT°7.
Step 3: Build a °7 chord on the root.
Step 4: Distribute the members of CT°7 in the voices that make the most sense, and return to the original notes (of I).
  ○ Maximize economy of motion (common tones and conjunct motion).

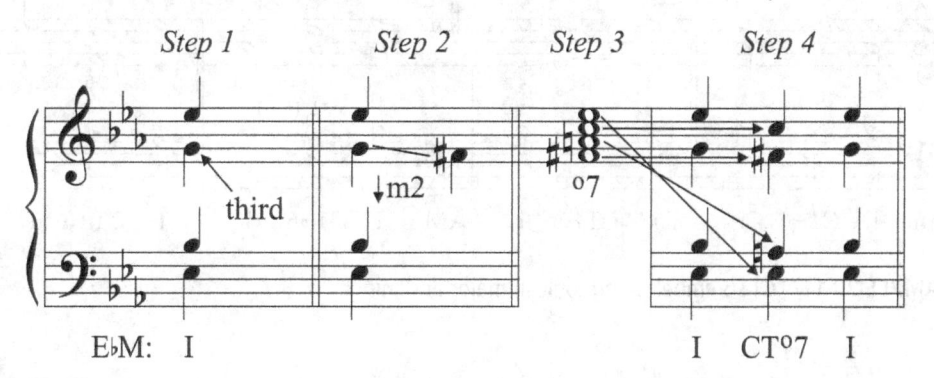

EXAMPLE 20.9 Building CT°7 to embellish a major chord.

To embellish a *minor* triad, locate the *fifth*—then apply steps 2–4 above. There will be two common tones.

In Example 20.10, CT°7 embellishes I in A♭ major. As the common-tone A♭ ($\hat{1}$) sustains in the bass and figures prominently in the melody, two inner voices visit chromatic lower neighbors: E♭ ↘ D♮ ↗ E♭ and C ↘ B♮ ↗ C. In analysis, our inclination might be to label this chord vii°$^4_3$/iii. This *would* be the proper label *if* the chord functioned as a secondary LT7 and progressed to iii^6. Context determines that this embellishing chord is labeled CT°7.

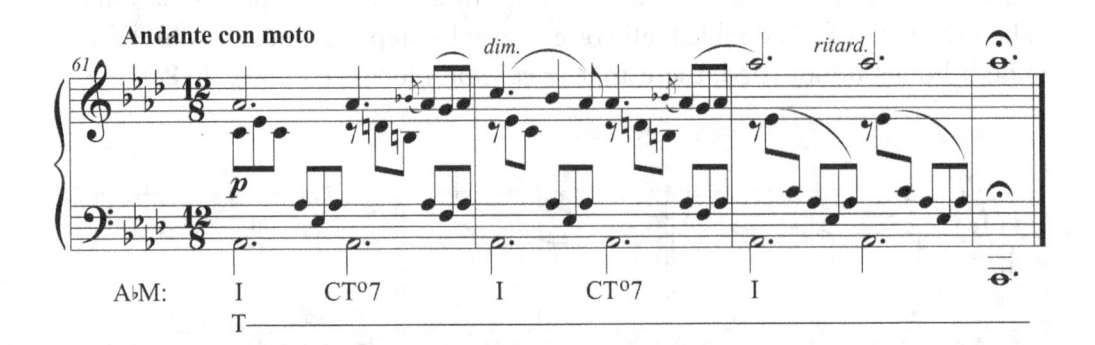

EXAMPLE 20.10 Mendelssohn, *Song Without Words*, Op. 53, No. 1, mm. 61–64.

CT+6

The Gr+6 sonority can be used to expand tonic harmony, in which case it does *not* serve a Predominant function. This linear embellishment, labeled CT+6, plays out in several different ways, as shown in Example 20.11.[4] The bass may either leap $\hat{1}$–(♭)$\hat{6}$–$\hat{1}$ or sustain on $\hat{1}$. When it sustains on $\hat{1}$, the fifth of I is typically doubled in the upper voices, allowing for half-step neighboring motions in contrary directions: $\hat{5}$–♯$\hat{4}$–$\hat{5}$ and $\hat{5}$–(♭)$\hat{6}$–$\hat{5}$ (Examples 20.11b and d).

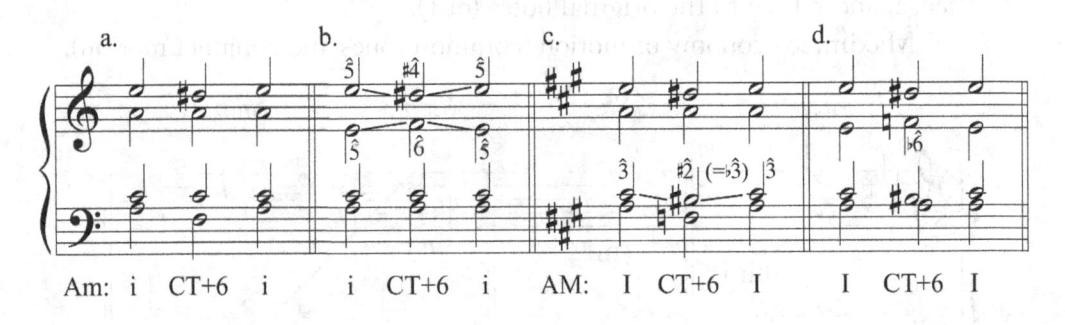

EXAMPLE 20.11 CT+6 embellishing tonic in major and minor.

When CT+6 embellishes i in minor, $\hat{3}$ (the "passport" pitch for Gr+6) holds as a common tone (Examples 20.11a–b). In major, this scale degree is lowered with an accidental (♭$\hat{3}$). When CT+6 expands I, ♭$\hat{3}$ acts as a chromatic lower neighbor to $\hat{3}$. In this context, it is often spelled enharmonically as ♯$\hat{2}$ to capture its embellishing role (Examples 20.11c–d).

In Example 20.12, Schubert prolongs the final T of his song "Sehnsucht" with two CT+6 chords. $\hat{1}$ sustains in the bass, and the passport pitch is spelled as ♭$\hat{3}$ (A♭).

EXAMPLE 20.12   Schubert, "Sehnsucht," D. 310b, mm. 38–39.

Example 20.13 highlights various chromatic phenomena addressed throughout Part III of this text:

- The passage begins with V^9 resolving to I.
  - The ninth sustains (in both the violin and piano parts), forming I^{6-5}, a reversal of 5-6 technique.[5]
- In mm. 9–10, I is embellished by *both* CT°7 and CT+6.
  - The "root" of CT°7, B♯, is spelled as C♮ (the passport pitch of CT+6).
- Measure 10 is an exact repeat of m. 9. However, instead of returning to I, the +6 at the end of m. 10 resolves to V^7. The same +6 chord plays two different roles: first as CT+6 (m. 9), and then as Gr+6 (m. 10).
- The music modulates to the chromatic-mediant key of C♯ major (I→III) via enharmonic reinterpretation (mm. 11–13).
  - V^6_5/IV resolves as Gr+6 in C♯ major (a C–C pivot).
    - The Gr+6 is "inverted," with $\hat{1}$ in the bass.
  - The embellishment of I with CT°7 and CT+6 recurs at this new tonal level (mm. 13–14).

EXAMPLE 20.13 César Frank, Sonata in A Major for Violin and Piano, I, mm. 7–14.

Applications

Exercises

1. Spell and resolve dominant ninth chords in four voices.

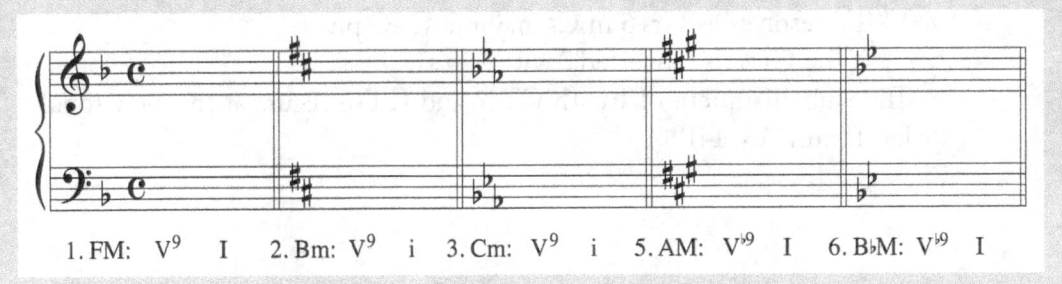

1. FM: V^9 I 2. Bm: V^9 i 3. Cm: V^9 i 5. AM: $V^{\flat 9}$ I 6. B♭M: $V^{\flat 9}$ I

2. Spell and resolve altered dominants in four voices.

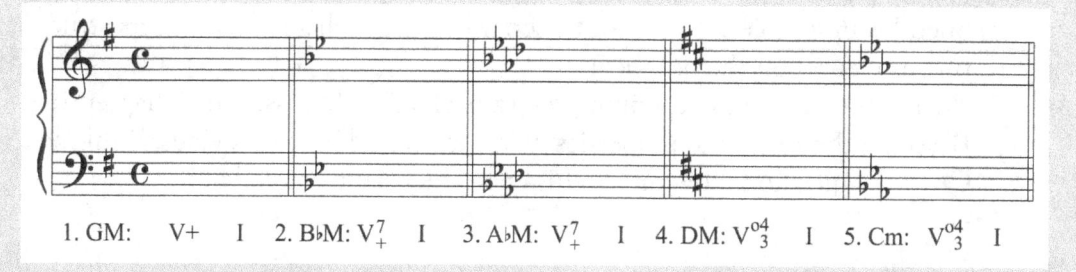

1. GM: V+ I   2. B♭M: V^7_+ I   3. A♭M: V^7_+ I   4. DM: V^{o4}_3 I   5. Cm: V^{o4}_3 I

3. Embellish the given tonic chords with either CT°7 or CT+6. Observe the chord member that is doubled in the provided chords.

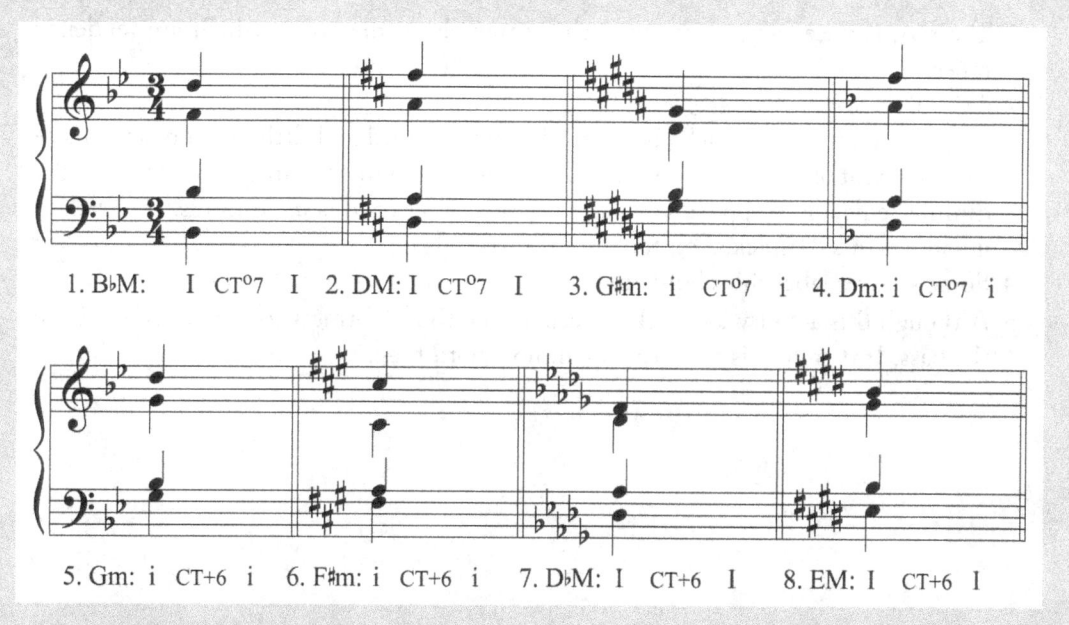

1. B♭M: I CT°7 I   2. DM: I CT°7 I   3. G♯m: i CT°7 i   4. Dm: i CT°7 i

5. Gm: i CT+6 i   6. F♯m: i CT+6 i   7. D♭M: I CT+6 I   8. EM: I CT+6 I

Brain Teasers

1. Unlike V^7, which may be complete or incomplete, why should altered dominants (V^7_+ and V^{o4}_3) be complete?
2. Why is V+ much more effective, and common, in major keys (rather than minor keys)?
3. What is the relationship between V^{o4}_3 in C major and Fr+6 in F major? Might this relationship enable a certain modulatory process? Why or why not?
4. Two chords in Example 16.9 are analyzable as dominant ninth chords. Which ones?

Thinking Critically

1. Spell V+ in F major. Then plot the chord on a pc wheel. Describe its structure as viewed on the pc wheel.
2. Revisit the enharmonic reinterpretation of vii°7 discussed in Chapter 19. Based on the structural properties of V+ uncovered in the previous Thinking Critically question, how might this chord be used to modulate?

Notes

1. The root is necessary, as are the other three chord members, which are tendency tones.
2. This effect is called an *agogic accent*.
3. The lowered fifth forms a °3 between the chord's third and fifth. The unusual intervallic content of this chord is reflected in its Roman numeral: an *uppercase* V with the diminished symbol appended to it. The underlying triad is *not* diminished—rather, it consists of a °3 stacked on top of a M3.
4. Some sources label this chord emb+6.
5. Although this activity looks like a suspension, the F♯ forms a consonant sixth above the bass. It therefore is not a dissonant nonchord tone.

Part IV

Post-Tonal and Popular Materials

Part IV examines the extension, and eventual dissolution, of the tonal system, and describes some alternative means by which composers organize their musical materials. Chapter 21 surveys the systematic increase in chromaticism and dissonance that contributes to the tonal system being stretched to its limits. New scale types (Chapter 22) and novel chord structures (Chapter 23) forge unique musical soundscapes. Chapter 24 introduces an entirely new analytic methodology for post-tonal music—one necessary for a body of music not governed by tonal procedures. In Chapter 25, we look into how some composers order the twelve pitch classes into a *tone row* and then use various permutations of the row to build entire musical works. The final chapter (Chapter 26) reunites with triadic harmony to explore extensions of the tonal system in jazz and popular music.

21

The Dissolution of the Tonal System

Music becomes increasingly chromatic and dissonant in the latter half of the nineteenth century. This chapter explores some of the ways that composers systematically pushed the tonal system to its limits—paving the way for new compositional approaches explored in the twentieth and twenty-first centuries. The dissolution of the tonal system is a gradual process resulting from the continuous and progressive development of the system.

Progressive Tonality

Music from the common-practice period almost always begins and ends in the same key. Some late Romantic works modulate and end in a key other than the opening tonic—a procedure known as ***progressive tonality***.[1] This creates a kind of global dissonance, as the music never returns to the initial tonic key. Progressive tonality is often tied to some extra-musical association or narrative. Consider Schubert's song "Der Jüngling und der Tod," which opens in C♯ minor with a young person pleading for death to end his earthly torment. A modulation to B♭ major (I→♯VI, enharmonically) anticipates a change of speaker, and the song closes in this key with death consoling the youth and answering his call.[2]

Ambiguity

Highly chromatic musical sections or works can be modally or tonally ambiguous. A passage might feature so much modal borrowing that the listener is unable to distinguish whether the music is primarily major or minor. Such ***modal ambiguity*** is pronounced at the end of "Lied" by Johannes Brahms (Example 21.1), where it plays out in the following two ways:

1. Chords from E♭ minor and E♭ major are intermixed.
    - The primary triads from E♭ *major* appear in mm. 41–43.

- Bars 44–45 feature chords from E♭ *minor*, with the glaring exception of the I$^6_4$ in m. 45 that connects directly to i. The modal conflict of the tonic harmony is accentuated in the melodic G♮–G♭ over these two chords.
2. Many chords lack thirds, making their quality ambiguous.
    - The third is missing from the dominant seventh chords in bars 42 and 44. In addition to obscuring chord quality (is it Mm7 or mm7?), the absence of $\hat{7}$ defuses the Dominant pull toward Tonic.
    - The final two chords, a subdominant and then tonic triad, do not contain thirds. The conflict between minor and major is left unsettled at the close of the song.[3]

Observe these additional chromatic features of Example 21.1:

- The Gr+6 in m. 45 is missing $\hat{1}$ from its +6 frame; #$\hat{4}$ (A♮), is spelled enharmonically as ♭$\hat{5}$ (B♭♭).
- Chordal function is denied at several points.
    - The dominant seventh chords in bars 42 and 44 resolve to chords that typically serve the PD function (IV and ii°). Since they lack $\hat{7}$, these dominant sevenths are weakened considerably.
    - The Gr+6 in m. 45 appears to serve PD by resolving to a cadential six-four. But I$^6_4$ moves to a root-position i prior to finding V. This activity is best described as an arpeggiating (tonic) six-four chord.
    - V in m. 46 resolves deceptively to VI, but the fifth of this chord is altered to form an + triad. Is the G♮ a chromatic lower neighbor to A♭, or does it form a secondary V+—perhaps V+/iv spelled enharmonically?
- The tonic pitch, E♭, is obscured by several instances of E♮ as a nonchord tone (circled throughout Example 21.1). What kind of nonchord tone is it?[4]

Some musical passages involve competing tonal centers. ***Tonal ambiguity*** emerges from a conflict between two or more different keys. Example 21.2 shows the opening of Wagner's Prelude to *Tristan und Isolde*. From the outset, A minor and C major compete for prominence—an effect known as the *double-tonic complex*.[5] The entire Prelude oscillates between A (major and minor), C, and several other tonal centers. Often, keys are suggested rather than firmly established by functional progressions and cadences.

Unresolved Dissonance and Implied Tonality

The opening phrase of the Prelude in Example 21.2 ends on V^7 in A minor. Although this dissonant chord does not resolve, it *implies* A as the tonal center. The next phrase ends with a different dominant seventh suggesting C as the center.

The Dissolution of the Tonal System

EXAMPLE 21.1 Brahms, "Lied," from *Sechs Gesänge*, Op. 3, No. 4, mm. 41–48.

EXAMPLE 21.2 Wagner, Prelude from *Tristan und Isolde*, mm. 1–7 (orchestral reduction).

Because the listener anticipates—and perhaps mentally "projects"—the resolution of certain chords, an unresolved dissonance can imply a specific tonal center.

Example 21.3 features a series of dissonant Mm7 chords, *none* of which resolve as expected: they do not function as either primary or secondary dominants, nor are they reinterpreted as Gr+6 chords, nor do they constitute a sequence of seventh chords.[6] Instead, one Mm7 chord *transforms* into the next. Roman-numeral labels do not apply to this passage because the harmony is operating outside the context of functional tonality, with no clear tonal center emerging.

How does each seventh chord transform into the next? Are the transformations economical? The notion of chordal *transformation* is distinct from that of *resolution* or *progression*, and is explored in greater detail below.

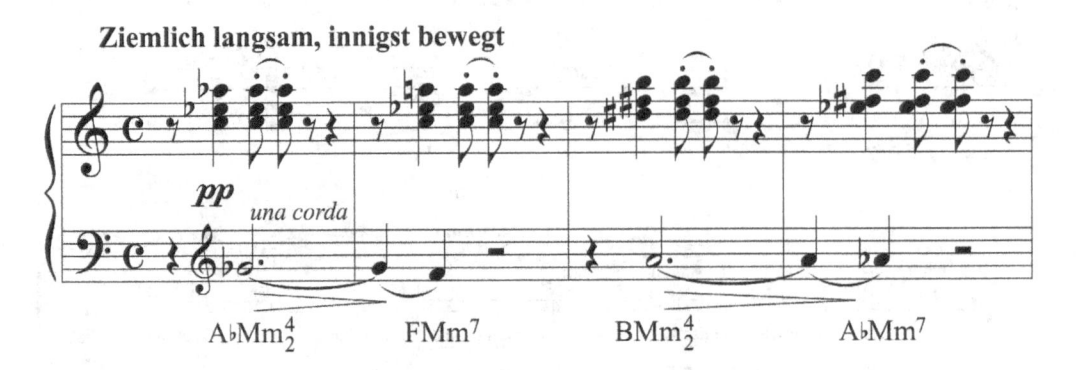

EXAMPLE 21.3 Liszt, "Blume und Duft," S. 324, mm. 1–4 (piano introduction).

Dissonant Prolongation

Most tonal music is overwhelmingly consonant, with dissonance providing points of instability that ultimately resolve. In many late nineteenth-century works, the proportion of consonance to dissonance changes in favor of the latter, and dissonant harmonies might be prolonged for extended passages before resolving—if they resolve at all. In Example 21.3, the dominant seventh sonority is expanded. In this short passage, A♭Mm7 serves as the point of both departure (m. 1) and return (m. 4); this specific dominant seventh chord is *prolonged* by the two different seventh chords in mm. 2–3.

Functional tonality is completely suppressed in Liszt's "Bagatelle Without Tonality," where a fully diminished seventh sonority built on G♯ is prolonged throughout the entire three-minute work. This "referential sonority," or "tonic seventh," emerges gradually, is expanded by other seventh chords (both diminished and dominant sevenths), and is embellished by nonchord tones.[7] Example 21.4 shows the coda, where a final G♯°7 is prolonged through repetition, bass arpeggiation, and parallel, passing °7 chords.[8]

Highly chromatic music like Liszt's *Bagatelle* demands a reconceptualization of *consonance* and *dissonance*. In such music, dissonance is defined on a purely contextual basis. A certain dissonant sonority may function as the more stable chord in a predominantly or exclusively dissonant setting. This "tonic dissonance" may be prolonged by other dissonant chords and even embellished by nonchord tones that are presumably heard (or conceived) as being more dissonant than the dissonant chord tones they embellish.

EXAMPLE 21.4 Liszt, *Bagatelle sans tonalité*, S. 216a, mm. 177–83 (coda).

Suspended Tonality

Certain musical passages contain tertian harmonies (triads and seventh chords) that do not progress in a functional manner. In phases of **suspended tonality**, Roman numerals are difficult or impossible to apply to a succession of chords. In Liszt's *Bagatelle sans tonalité* (Example 21.4), we encounter familiar sonorities, but traditional tonal relations and progressions are completely absent from the entire work. Suspended tonality is often more fleeting: the unfolding of the tonal syntax is put on pause, but it eventually resumes to close a phrase with a cadence.

Triadic Transformations (P, R, and L)

Above we encountered the concept of chordal transformation. Each Mm7 chord in Example 21.3 *transforms* into the next in a highly economical manner—two common tones are maintained while two notes shift by half step.[9] Example 21.5 models this series of transformations on pitch-class wheels.[10] These kinds of chordal transformations are often abstract—occurring in pitch-*class* space, but not necessarily in *pitch* space. Of the transformations modeled in Example 21.5, which ones also play out literally in pitch space?[11] (Refer to the score in Example 21.3.)

There are numerous ways that a triad may transform into another triad.[12] The three most common *triadic transformations* are highly economical, involving two common tones—or, a common interval—and one tone shifting by step. The names, abbreviations, and descriptions of these transformations are given

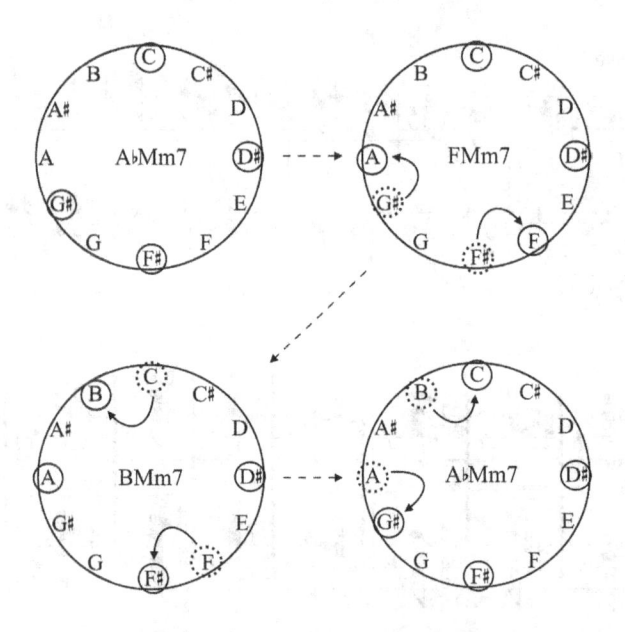

EXAMPLE 21.5 The chordal transformations from "Blume und Duft" (mm. 1–4) on pc wheels.

below and notated in Example 21.6. Each transformation connects a major triad to a minor triad, or vice versa.

- *Parallel* (P)
    - Common interval: P5
    - Other tone moves up or down by *half* step
    - Quality of triad changes (M→m *or* m→M)
        - Like going from tonic to tonic of *parallel* keys
- *Relative* (R)
    - Common interval: M3
    - Other tone moves away from M3 by *whole* step
    - Chord roots are m3 apart
        - Like going from tonic to tonic of *relative* keys
- *Leading-Tone Exchange* (L)
    - Common interval: m3
    - Other tone moves away from m3 by *half* step
    - Chord roots are M3 apart
        - The root of the major chord is exchanged for its leading tone

Cycles of Transformations (PL, PR, and LR)

Some works feature *cycles* of alternating transformations. These cycles are similar to harmonic sequences and will eventually lead back to the starting chord. Although tonal function is suspended during these cycles, the pattern of alternating

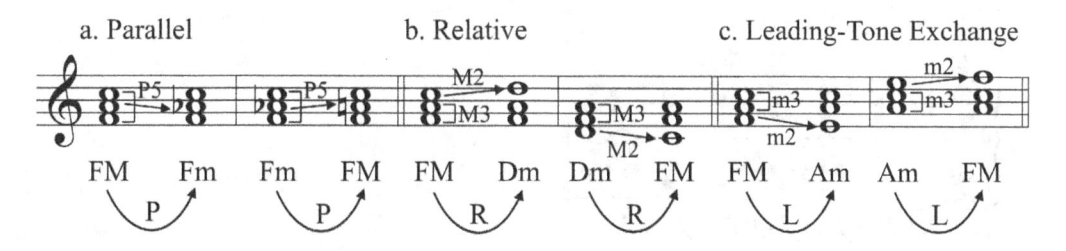

EXAMPLE 21.6 The P, R, and L triadic transformations.

transformations establishes a *process* that helps unify the passage. The three cycles involving pairs of P, R, and L transformations are described below and notated in their complete forms in Example 21.7.

- PL Cycle
    - 6 chords in total (before returning to starting chord)
    - Chord roots move by M3
        - Roots outline an + triad, dividing the octave equally into M3 units.
    - May begin with either P or L
        - If starting with L, the progression in Example 21.7a would be reversed.
- PR Cycle
    - 8 chords in total[13]
    - Roots move by m3
        - Roots outline a °7 chord, dividing the octave equally into m3 units.
- LR Cycle
    - 24 chords in total
        - Visits *every* M and m triad before returning to initial harmony
    - Roots alternate by M3 and m3

Enharmonic spellings are typically applied at some point during these cycles to minimize the use of accidentals. In Example 21.7a, for instance, the bass leaps down by °4 from A♭ to E—an enharmonic M3.

The Tonnetz

Example 21.8 shows a *Tonnetz*, or "tone network." This alternative means of modeling relationships and processes in pitch-class space is useful for plotting triadic transformations and tracking cycles of transformations. The letters at each node represent pitch classes (G♯ = A♭). Horizontal rows are organized by m3; vertical columns by M3. Triangles group the chord members of triads (find the C-major triad in the upper-left region), and these triangles "flip" on the Tonnetz as P, R, and L transformations are applied to change one triad into another: P flips the triangle across a diagonal axis; R across a vertical axis; and L across a horizontal axis.

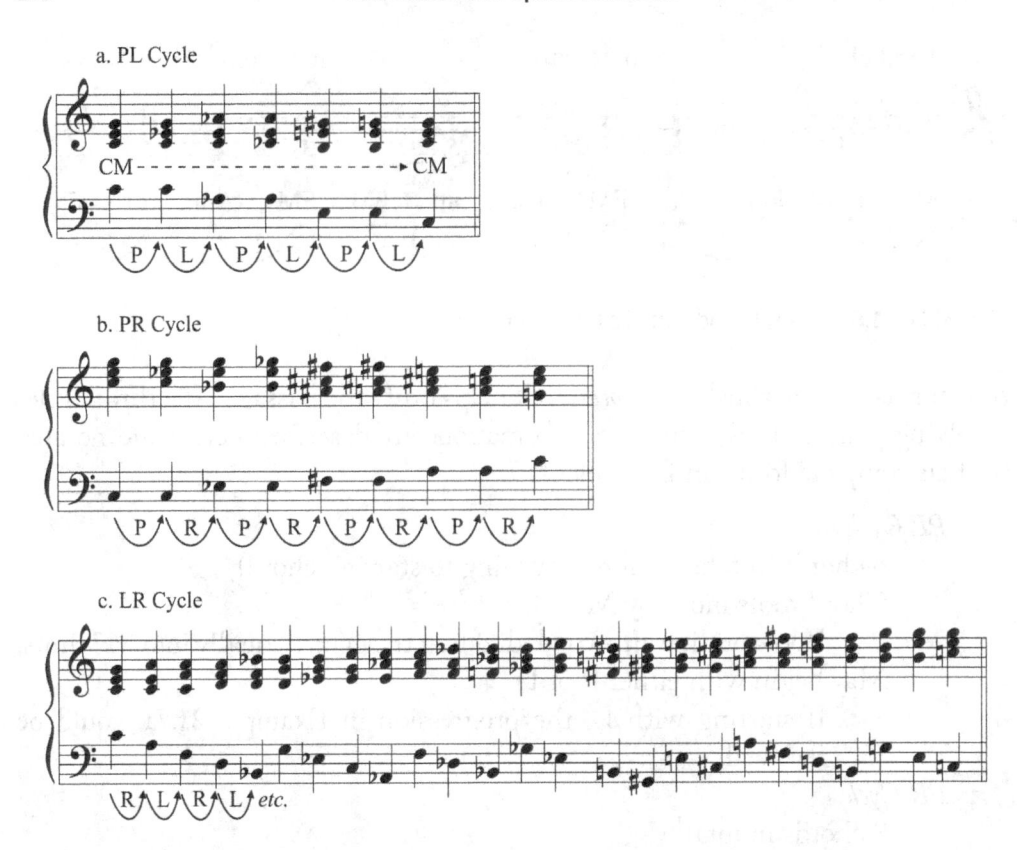

EXAMPLE 21.7 Complete transformation cycles: PL, PR, and LR. (Accidentals remain in effect until cancelled.)

The three cycles from Example 21.7 are shown weaving directional paths along the Tonnetz: the PL cycle travels *vertically* (upward or downward), the PR cycle *horizontally* (leftward or rightward), and the LR cycle *diagonally* (only a portion of this cycle is shown).

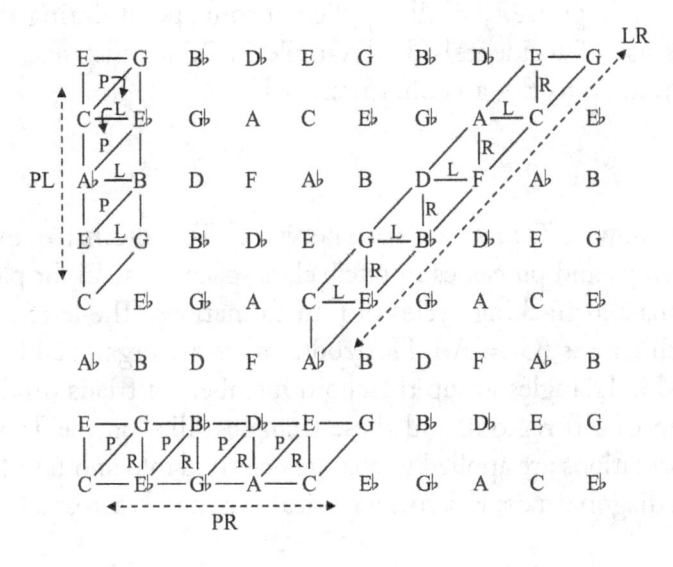

EXAMPLE 21.8 The Tonnetz with PL, PR, and LR cycles.

The Dissolution of the Tonal System

In Example 21.9, Schubert applies a portion of the LR cycle in a transition modulating from D major to F major. Tonality is suspended in this nonfunctional passage linking two fully functional passages. The LR cycle is disturbed by a single P operation (m. 123), which bumps the music to a lower diagonal path in the Tonnetz (can you visualize or trace the path of this cycle using Example 21.8?).

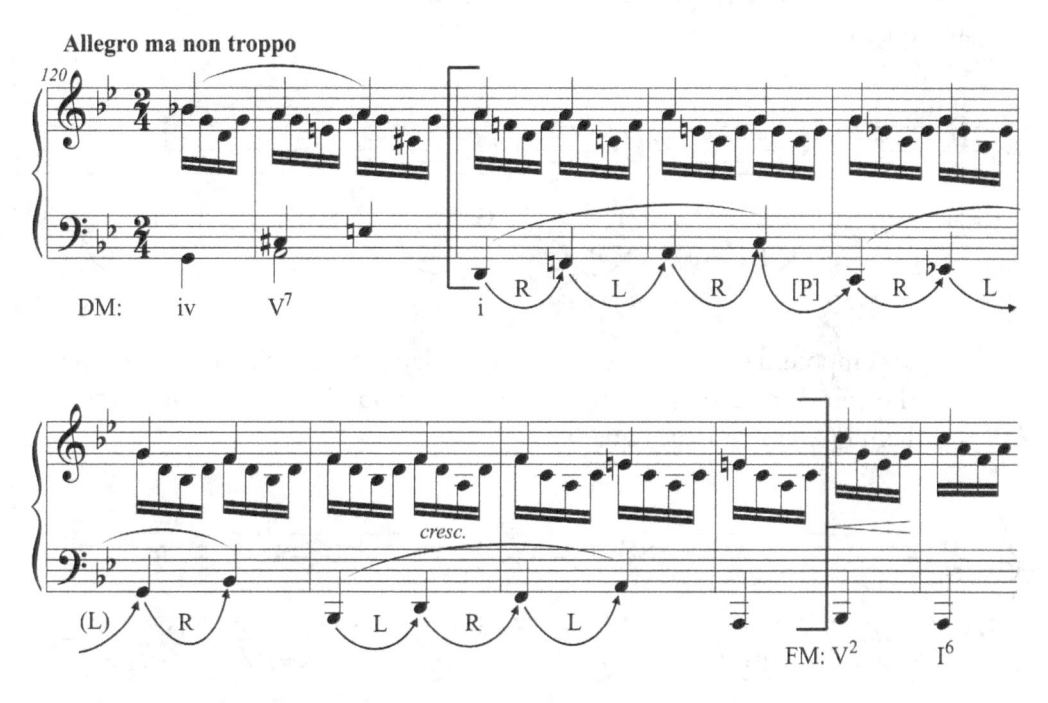

EXAMPLE 21.9 Schubert, Sonata No. 21 in B-Flat Major, D. 960, IV, mm. 120–129.

The P, R, and L transformations may be combined to form *compound operations*. Example 21.10 shows the compound PL operation connecting a G-major triad to an E♭-major triad (the G-minor chord in parentheses shows the intermediate step in this compound transformation). Binary operations like this one transform a triad into another triad of the same quality; these chords are connected by a single common tone, with two tones shifting by step. What would this compound transformation look like on the Tonnetz?[14]

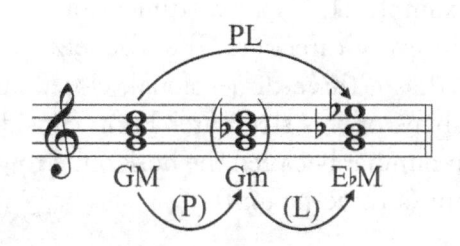

EXAMPLE 21.10 The compound PL operation applied to a G major triad.

Applications

Exercises

1. Apply P, R, and L transformations to the triads below, using accidentals as needed. Label the chords resulting from each transformation by their root and quality.

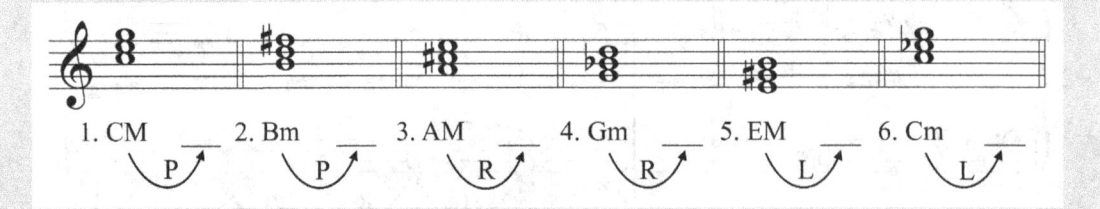

   1. CM __ P __   2. Bm __ P __   3. AM __ R __   4. Gm __ R __   5. EM __ L __   6. Cm __ L __

2. Apply compound operations to a G major triad, using accidentals as needed. Put the chords resulting from each transformation in root position, and label them by their root and quality.

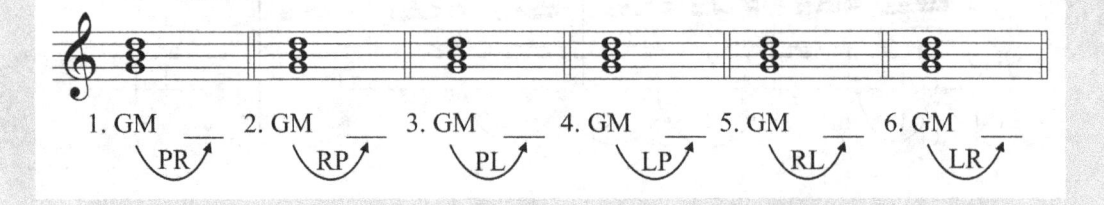

   1. GM __ PR __   2. GM __ RP __   3. GM __ PL __   4. GM __ LP __   5. GM __ RL __   6. GM __ LR __

3. Analyze the triads and transformations in an excerpt by Rachmaninoff (Example 21.11). In the blanks provided, label each chord by its root and quality. Above the arrows connecting blanks, label the operations (P, R, or L) that transform one chord into the next. (There is one compound operation.) Identify the cycle of transformation that prevails for most of this passage.

Brain Teasers

1. In Example 21.1, what might have motivated Brahms to omit $\hat{1}$ from the Gr+6 in m. 45?
2. The Tonnetz in Example 21.8 is a two-dimensional network that could extend indefinitely in every direction. The Tonnetz is more accurately conceived and depicted as a three-dimensional, closed structure. How would you describe the shape of this structure? Hint: consider that the repeating units of pcs vary in number between the horizontal rows (a four-pc unit) and the vertical columns (a three-pc unit).

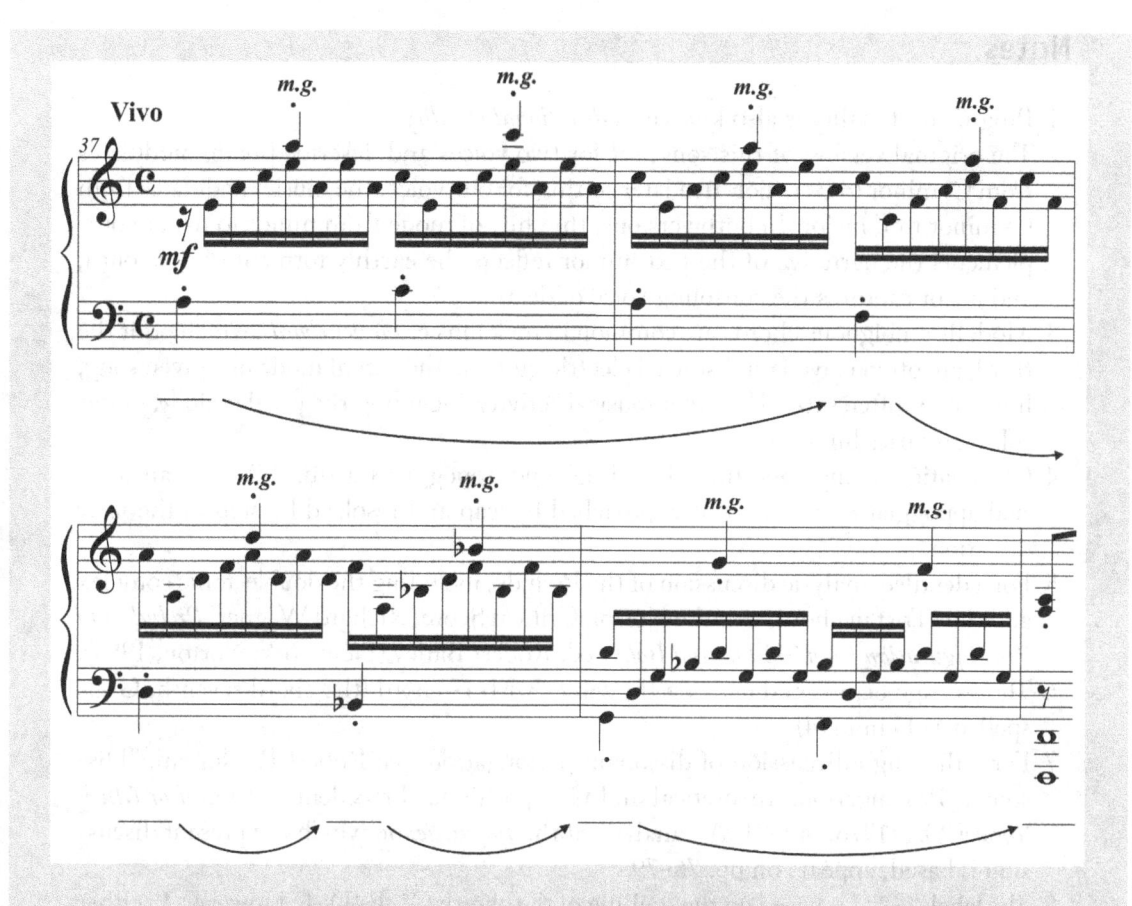

EXAMPLE 21.11 Rachmaninoff, Prelude in A Minor, Op. 32, No. 8, mm. 37–41.

Exploring Music

1. Analyze "Nuages Gris" by Liszt. Does this piece have a clear tonal center? If so, how is a tonal center established? What sonority prevails throughout?
2. Analyze Prelude No. 4 in E Minor by Chopin. Are Roman numerals applicable? How might we account for the chord-to-chord motions?

Thinking Critically

1. The first chord in Example 21.2 (m. 2) is known as the "Tristan chord." How would you label this chord? How would you describe its resolution?
2. The theme song of the sitcom *The Office* is based on the following chord progression: GM–Bm–Em–CM. This short progression repeats for the entirety of the song. Is this progression functional? Could triadic transformations (P, R, L)—including compound operations—be applied to account for the harmonic activity of this progression?

Notes

1. Progressive tonality is also known as *directional tonality*.
2. The original version of this song, set for two voices and described here, modulates from C♯ minor to B♭ major. In a later setting for one voice, the music modulates from C♯ minor to F major. In both versions, the shift of mode from minor to major complements the narrative of the text: minor reflects the earthly torment of the youth, and major captures the consoling voice of death.
3. Modally ambiguous chords are common in rock music. *Power chords*, which omit the third, are often played on distorted electric guitars. The actual mode of a given song, however, is often settled by other musical activity, including the vocal melody, guitar solos, and bass lines.
4. Chromatic passing tone (m. 41 and 43) and appoggiatura (m. 44). It is an unusual appoggiatura in that it is approached by leap and resolved by step in the *same* direction.
5. For a detailed analytic discussion of the Prelude, including the double-tonic complex and the "Tristan chord," see the Norton Critical Score, Richard Wagner, *Prelude and Transfiguration from Tristan and Isolde*, ed. Robert Bailey (New York: Norton, 1985).
6. The passage begins and ends on the same A♭Mm7 chord (the chord seventh, G♭, is spelled as F♯ in m. 4).
7. For a thorough discussion of dissonant prolongation, see Robert P. Morgan, "Dissonant Prolongation: Theoretical and Compositional Precedents," *Journal of Music Theory* 20.1 (1976): 49–91. An analysis of the *Bagatelle*, on which the present discussion is based, appears on pp. 76–79.
8. The label "G♯^{o7}" is based on the spelling of the chord: G♯–B–D–F. However, F, rather than G♯, is the principal bass note of the chord—hence the label "G♯^{o2}" bookending this passage. Since the fully diminished seventh chord is a symmetrical sonority, any chord member may sound like the root; inversion symbols are applied here to track the position of the chord during the bass arpeggiation.
9. Such economical chordal transformation is commonly referred to as *parsimonious voice leading*, or *semitonal voice leading*.
10. Pitch-class wheels are introduced in Chapter 19.
11. The first and third transformations play out literally in pitch space. The second occurs only in pitch-class space.
12. Hugo Riemann (1849–1919) and other early nineteenth-century music theorists developed sophisticated theories of chord transformation. More recently, "neo-Riemannian" theorists have expanded these theories and applied them in analyses of highly chromatic and atonal music. In particular, see the work of David Lewin, Richard Cohn, Henry Klumpenhouwer, Bryan Hyer, and Clifton Callender. Additionally, Adrian Childs (1998) applies transformational theory to seventh chords, and Guy Capuzzo (2004) applies it to pop-rock music.
13. The PL cycle is known as the *hexatonic system*; the PR cycle as the *octatonic system*.
14. The triangle flips downward (vertically), pivoting on the pc-G node.

22

New Pitch Collections

Throughout this book, chromaticism has been approached as an elaboration of diatonicism. Chromatic music is based fundamentally on the diatonic major and minor scales, with altered scale degrees and chromatic embellishments resulting from tonicization, modal mixture, chromatic nonchord tones, and other chromatic procedures. Even as tonal function begins to dissolve and the tonal system is stretched to its limits (as described in Chapter 21), tertian sonorities like triads and seventh chords continue to prevail. In efforts to break away from functional tonality completely, composers in the twentieth century explored different ways of using diatonic scales; they also began using entirely *new* scales, or pitch collections, as source material for their music. These collections of notes, known as the *referential collections*, include the diatonic, pentatonic, octatonic, whole-tone, and hexatonic collections.

The Diatonic Collection

The *diatonic collection (DIA)* is the set of pitch classes with the same intervallic structure as a major scale. Example 22.1 shows the "1-sharp collection" on a pc wheel. This specific diatonic collection, which is identical to the G-major scale, is labeled $DIA_{1\sharp}$.[1] This label applies to musical passages using $DIA_{1\sharp}$ that either do not define G as the tonic (1) in a traditional, tonal manner, or that emphasize some note other than G as a pitch center.

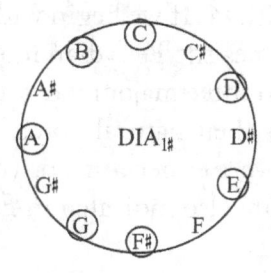

EXAMPLE 22.1 $DIA_{1\sharp}$ on the pitch-class wheel.

The 12 (total) transpositions of the diatonic collection are labeled accordingly: $DIA_{2\sharp}$ (the 2-sharp collection), $DIA_{4\flat}$ (the 4-flat collection), and so on.

Pandiatonicism

Pandiatonicism describes the nonfunctional and sometimes dissonant use of the diatonic collection. A pandiatonic work or passage lacks an obvious pitch center. The excerpt in Example 22.2 draws from $DIA_{0\sharp}$ but avoids tonicizing C or emphasizing any other pitch of the collection.

EXAMPLE 22.2 Stravinsky, *Serenade in A*, I ("Hymne"), mm. 52–55.

The Diatonic Modes

Any pitch of a diatonic collection may be defined as a musical focal point through certain compositional procedures. (Nonfunctional pitch *centricity* is addressed in Chapter 23.) When a pitch center is present, the diatonic collection may be identified as a certain *mode*. The **diatonic modes** are specific *orderings* of a diatonic collection—or, *rotations* of a major scale.[2]

The seven different modes are shown in Example 22.3. Each mode in this example is a different ordering of $DIA_{0\sharp}$—or, a different rotation of the C-major scale. The first rotation (R1), the Ionian mode, is identical to the C-major scale. When the collection is rotated to begin and end on D (R2), it is the Dorian mode, and so on. R6, the Aeolian mode, is identical to the natural minor scale (m).

Because the modes can be transposed to begin on any pitch, it is helpful to think of them as altered forms of the major and (natural) minor scales. For example, Lydian is a major scale with $\sharp\hat{4}$. If we begin with an F-major scale and *raise* $\hat{4}$ (B♭ ↗ B♮), the collection becomes the F-Lydian mode (M, ↑$\hat{4}$).

The seven modes divide into three major modes and four minor modes. Example 22.4 sorts the modes, lists their natural-note, "white-key" forms, and shows the alterations needed to convert either a major (M) or a minor (m) scale into each mode (these alterations are also indicated in Example 22.3).

R1. **Ionian** (M)

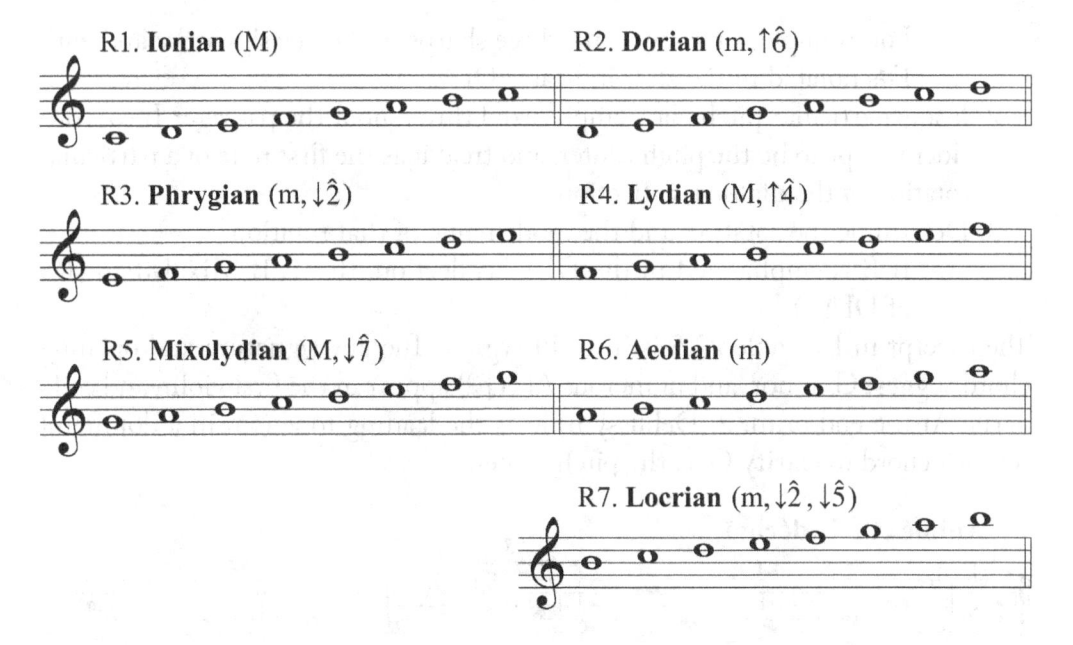

R2. **Dorian** (m, ↑6̂)

R3. **Phrygian** (m, ↓2̂)

R4. **Lydian** (M, ↑4̂)

R5. **Mixolydian** (M, ↓7̂)

R6. **Aeolian** (m)

R7. **Locrian** (m, ↓2̂, ↓5̂)

EXAMPLE 22.3 The diatonic modes (as rotations of DIA₀♯).

Major Modes	Natural Notes	Like
Ionian	C–C	M (major scale)
Lydian	F–F	M with ↑4̂
Mixolydian	G–G	M with ↓7̂

Minor Modes	Natural Notes	Like
Aeolian	A–A	m (minor scale)
Dorian	D–D	m with ↑6̂
Phrygian	E–E	m with ↓2̂
Locrian	B–B	m with ↓2̂, ↓5̂

EXAMPLE 22.4 The major and minor diatonic modes.

Spelling Diatonic Modes

1. When spelling a major mode, begin by spelling a major scale (with or without a key signature); if spelling a minor mode, begin with a natural minor scale.
   - For example, to spell F Phrygian, begin by writing the F-minor scale.
2. Apply the alteration needed to convert the scale into the mode.
   - Lower 2̂ (G ↘ G♭) to turn the F-minor scale into F Phrygian.

Identifying Modes

1. Identify the diatonic collection by taking an inventory of *all* accidentals—including any key signature that might be present.

- For example, a passage with three sharps in the key signature and with D♯s notated in the staff indicates DIA$_{4\sharp}$.
2. Is any particular pitch class emphasized throughout the passage? If so, consider this pc to be the pitch center, and treat it as the first note of a particular rotation of the diatonic collection.
3. Determine the rotation and the mode name of that rotation.
    - If B is emphasized in the DIA$_{4\sharp}$ collection, this is B Mixolydian (R5 of DIA$_{4\sharp}$).

The excerpt in Example 22.5 is in G Phrygian. The key signature and opening chord suggest G minor, and numerous A♭s (↓$\hat{2}$) appear in the first violin and cello parts. At the end of m. 2, Debussy inflects the leading tone (F♯) in a dominant seventh chord to clarify G as the pitch center.

EXAMPLE 22.5 Debussy, String Quartet in G Minor, Op. 10, I, mm. 1–3.

The Pentatonic Collection

The *pentatonic collection (PENT)* is a five-note *subset* of the diatonic collection. The collection may be rotated to begin on any of its five notes, but the two most common rotations are the major and minor pentatonic scales.

Example 22.6 forms pentatonic scales by deleting certain scale degrees from major or natural minor scales. Omitting these scale degrees also removes certain intervals from the collection—namely, m2s and the tritone.

- The *major pentatonic scale* is a major scale *without* $\hat{4}$ and $\hat{7}$ (Example 22.6a).
- The *minor pentatonic scale* is a natural minor scale *without* $\hat{2}$ and $\hat{6}$ (Example 22.6b).

- The major and minor pentatonic scales in Example 22.6 contain the same five notes and are related by rotation. They are *relative* pentatonic scales.

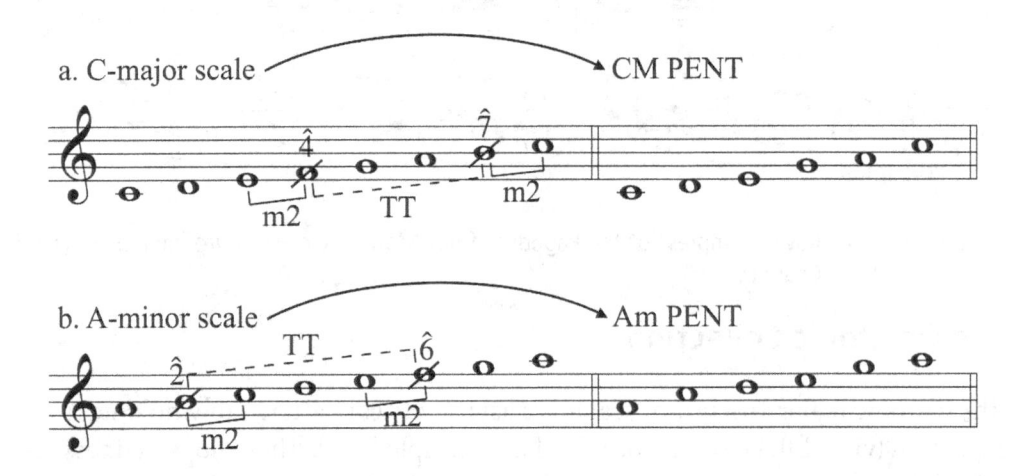

EXAMPLE 22.6 Pentatonic major and minor scales.

The pentatonic collection is common to non-Western music as well as to folk and popular styles of Western music. Because it lacks a leading tone, half steps, and the tritone (the "key-defining interval"), the pentatonic collection does not have the same tonal strength as a complete diatonic scale. Its simplicity makes the pentatonic collection both ambiguous and versatile; it is quite easy to compose or improvise pentatonic melodies over simple chord progressions. In rock music, for example, many electric guitar solos utilize pentatonic scales. The traditional song "Amazing Grace" (Example 22.7) is based on the major pentatonic scale.

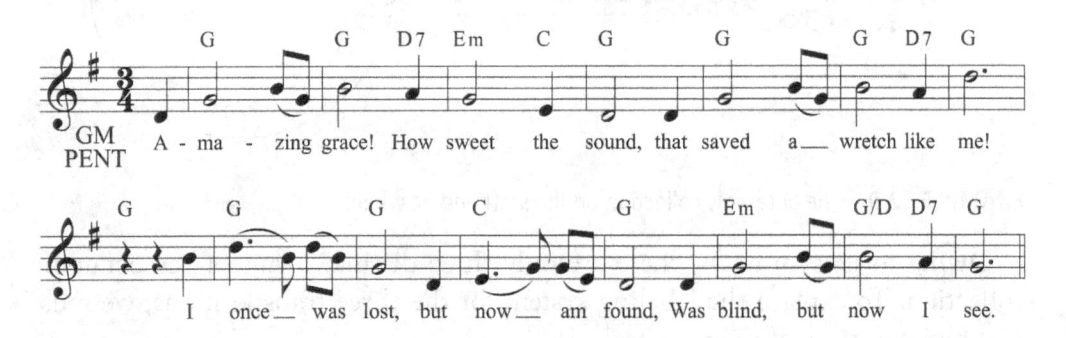

EXAMPLE 22.7 "Amazing Grace," first verse (traditional American melody, arr. J. Solomon).

Composers sometimes use this collection to evoke a folk-like or Eastern sound. In Example 22.8, Maurice Ravel paints a musical picture of the Orient with a lively figure based on the notes of F♯M PENT. Ravel uses the key signature for F♯M and avoids the notes B ($\hat{4}$) and E♯ ($\hat{7}$).

EXAMPLE 22.8 Ravel, "Empress of the Pagodas" from *Mother Goose Suite*, mm. 9–13 (arr. J. Charlot).

The Octatonic Collection

The diatonic major and minor scales are asymmetrical patterns of whole steps and half steps (view $DIA_{1\sharp}$ on the pc wheel in Example 22.1). Their "lopsidedness" establishes a hierarchy among the scale degrees with $\hat{1}$ as the inherent pitch center. To avoid a predetermined pitch center, some composers turn to *symmetrical* pitch collections. The **octatonic collection (OCT)**, also known as the *diminished scale* (particularly in jazz), consists of alternating half steps and whole steps. In Example 22.9, this eight-note collection is notated on the staff (a) and also plotted on a pc wheel (b), where its symmetry is more visibly apparent.

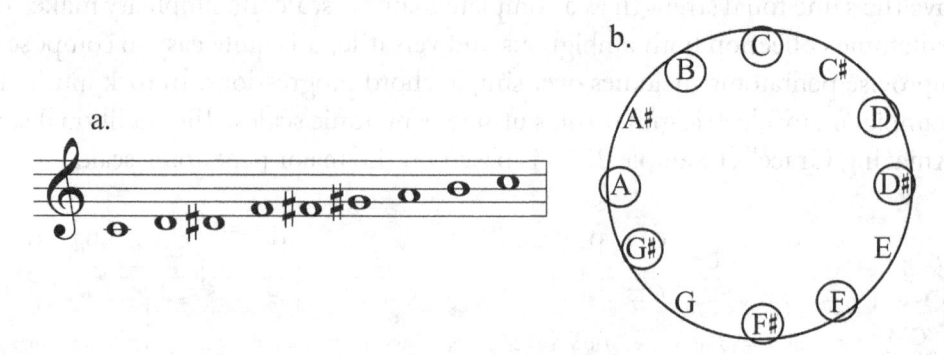

EXAMPLE 22.9 The octatonic collection on the staff and pc wheel.

Owing to its symmetry, there are only three distinct forms of the octatonic collection. To explain the labeling system for the three transpositions, we must first revise our use of the pc wheel.

The Pitch-Class Wheel with Integers

Example 22.10 replaces the letter names for pitch classes with integers. The pc wheel now resembles the face of an analog clock, with 0 in place of 12 at the twelve o'clock position. The application of integers to pitch-class letter names is consistent: 0 always represents pc C, 1 = C♯ (or D♭), 2 = D, 6 = F♯ (or G♭), and so on. (The advantage of using integers instead of letter names will become more clear in Chapters 24 and 25.)

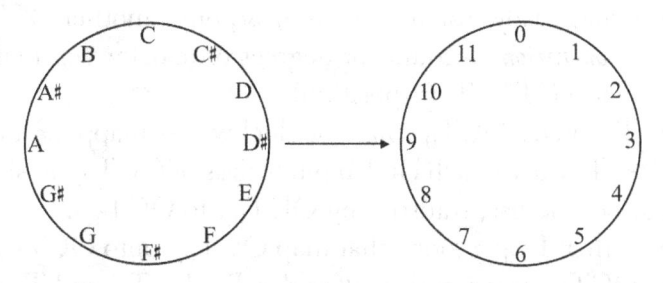

EXAMPLE 22.10 Replacing letters with integers on the pc wheel.

The three transpositions of the octatonic collection are plotted and labeled in Example 22.11.

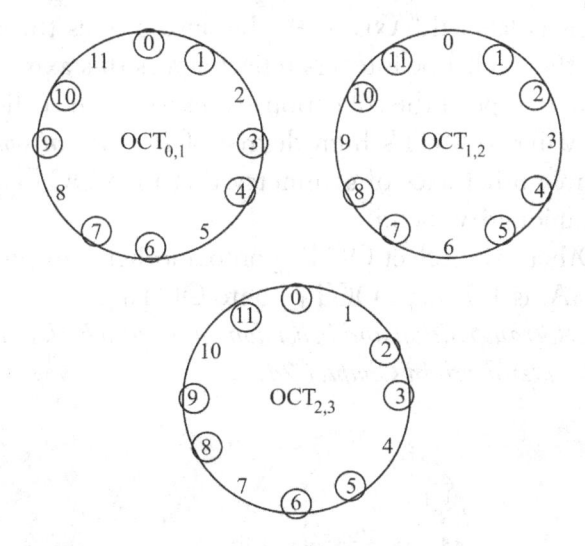

EXAMPLE 22.11 The three transpositions of the octatonic collection.

The numeric subscripts in the OCT labels indicate the first half step in each collection going clockwise from 0 (in other words, the lowest-integer pc semitone). For example, in $OCT_{0,1}$ the first m2 falls between 0 and 1 (C and C♯).

Each OCT transposition may be spelled on the staff as a scale beginning with any pitch class. Choose the simplest enharmonic spelling for each pc (e.g., pc 3 = D♯ or E♭). It is often necessary to mix sharps and flats when writing an octatonic scale.

Following are additional observations pertaining to the octatonic collection (refer to Example 22.11). These specific observations model ways to assess pitch-class collections in general.

- Each OCT contains major, minor, and diminished triads.
- Each OCT contains two °7 chords.
    - In $OCT_{0,1}$, the *pitch-class sets* {0, 3, 6, 9} and {1, 4, 7, 10} form °7 chords.

- Any two OCT transpositions share one °7 chord (four common tones).
  - $OCT_{0,1}$ and $OCT_{2,3}$ both contain {0, 3, 6, 9}.
- One OCT may easily "rotate," or *transpose*, onto another OCT.
  - *T-operations* account for degrees of (clockwise) rotation on the pc wheel ("T" = Transposition).
  - T_1 rotates $OCT_{0,1}$ *one* slot clockwise—mapping it onto $OCT_{1,2}$.
    - T_1 causes each circled pitch class of $OCT_{0,1}$ to shift one integer clockwise, transposing $OCT_{0,1}$ to $OCT_{1,2}$.
  - Other T-operations that map $OCT_{0,1}$ onto $OCT_{1,2}$: T_4, T_7, T_{10}.
  - $OCT_{0,1}$ maps onto *itself* under T_0, T_3, T_6, and T_9. This indicates a high degree of *transpositional symmetry*.
- One OCT may "reflect," or *invert*, onto itself or another transposition of OCT.
  - Example 22.12 shows an *axis of symmetry* dividing the pc wheel in half. The axis is labeled "Axis 3—9" because it goes through pcs 3 and 9. When the circled pc integers reflect across this axis, they map directly onto another pc of the collection—preserving the collection as a whole.
    - Owing to OCT's high degree of *inversional symmetry*, there are three other axes of symmetry that map $OCT_{1,2}$ onto itself. Can you identify them?[3]
  - Other axes reflect $OCT_{1,2}$ onto another transposition of OCT.
    - Axis 1–7 maps $OCT_{1,2}$ onto $OCT_{0,1}$.
- *Pitch-class sets, transposition and inversion on the pc wheel, and symmetry will be explored in greater depth in Chapter 24.*

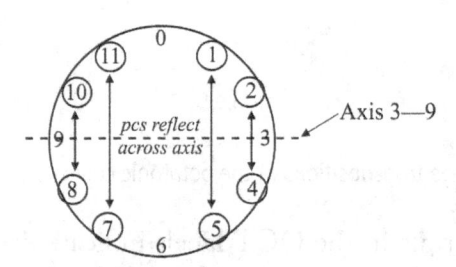

EXAMPLE 22.12 Inversional symmetry across Axis 3—9 for $OCT_{1,2}$.

OCT can transpose ("rotate") and invert ("reflect") onto itself in numerous ways (eight total). It is highly symmetrical, and, while it lacks a natural pitch center, any note may be emphasized and contextually defined as a center.

In "Diminished Fifth," Béla Bartók "modulates" among the three transpositions of the octatonic collection. The excerpt in Example 22.13 begins with $OCT_{0,1}$ and shifts to $OCT_{2,3}$ in m. 20. Bartók links these two transpositions with pc 9 (A), occurring on the downbeat of m. 20. This shared note serves as a "pivot tone" in the transition from $OCT_{0,1}$ to $OCT_{2,3}$ (a process similar to common-tone modulation). In m. 26, pc 5 (F) serves as the pivot tone linking $OCT_{2,3}$ to $OCT_{1,2}$.

EXAMPLE 22.13 Bartók, "Diminished Fifth," No. 101 from *Mikrokosmos*, Book 4, mm. 12–28.

The Whole-Tone Collection

The *whole-tone collection (WT)* consists exclusively of whole steps. This six-note collection is highly symmetrical and can transpose and invert onto itself in multiple ways. The two transpositions of the whole-tone collection, shown on pc wheels in Example 22.14, are WT_0 (the "even" collection) and WT_1 (the "odd" collection). The labels are based on the lowest pc integer of each transposition. In addition:

- WT contains two augmented triads—the only quality of triad in the collection (in WT_0, pc sets {0, 4, 8} and {2, 6, 10} form + triads).
- WT_0 and WT_1 do not share any pcs.
- Combining WT_0 and WT_1 forms the *aggregate*, or the complete chromatic scale.

Every pc of WT_0 appears in Example 22.15. In addition, the left hand articulates the + triads of the collection. Does any pc stand out as a pitch center?[4]

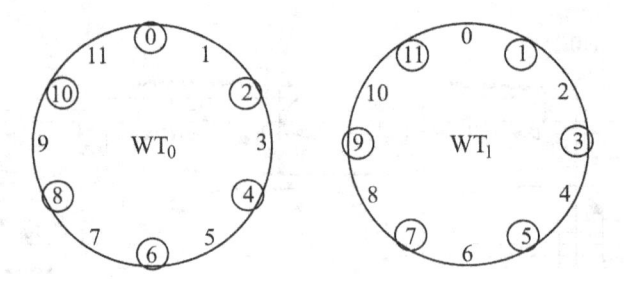

EXAMPLE 22.14 The two transpositions of the whole-tone collection.

EXAMPLE 22.15 Debussy, "Voiles," from *Preludes*, Book 1, mm. 15–22.

The Hexatonic Collection

The **hexatonic collection (HEX)**, sometimes called the *augmented scale*, alternates m2s and m3s. Like the whole-tone collection, it features six pcs and two + triads. Unlike the WT collection, HEX does not contain *any* whole steps. The four transpositions of the hexatonic collection are shown in Example 22.16. As with the octatonic collection, the labels are based on the lowest pc-integer half step in each transposition.

Viewing $HEX_{0,1}$ on the pc wheel, what collection is formed by the pcs that are *not* circled?[5]

In Example 22.17, a rapidly descending, angular figure articulates every pc of $HEX_{0,1}$.

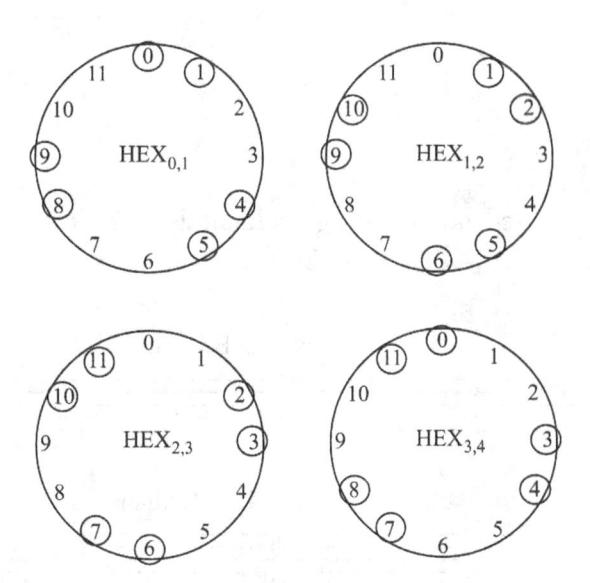

EXAMPLE 22.16 The four transpositions of the hexatonic collection.

EXAMPLE 22.17 Ellen Taaffe Zwilich, *Trio for Violin, Cello, and Piano*, III, mm. 3–5 (solo piano introduction).

Sometimes a note not belonging to the prevailing collection appears. An **outlier**, or "noncollectional tone," is similar to a nonchord tone in tonal practice. The difference is that, while it might be perceived as embellishing, or "other," it might not sound dissonant—especially if emerging in a predominantly dissonant passage. The melodic fragment in Example 22.18 is taken from the same work as the preceding example (22.17). It comprises notes of $HEX_{0,1}$ with a single outlier, E♭ (pc 3).

EXAMPLE 22.18 Zwilich, *Trio for Violin, Cello, and Piano*, III, mm. 11–12 (violin only).

Applications

Exercises

1. Spell the requested modes using accidentals as necessary (do not use key signatures).

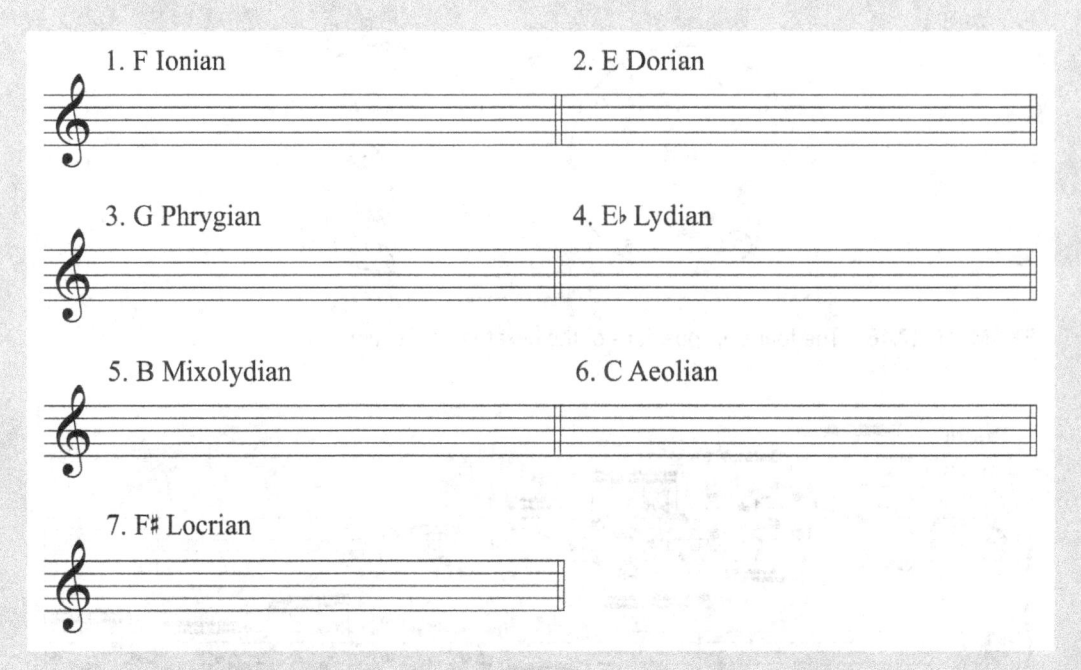

   1. F Ionian
   2. E Dorian
   3. G Phrygian
   4. E♭ Lydian
   5. B Mixolydian
   6. C Aeolian
   7. F♯ Locrian

2. Spell the requested pentatonic scales using accidentals as necessary (do not use key signatures).

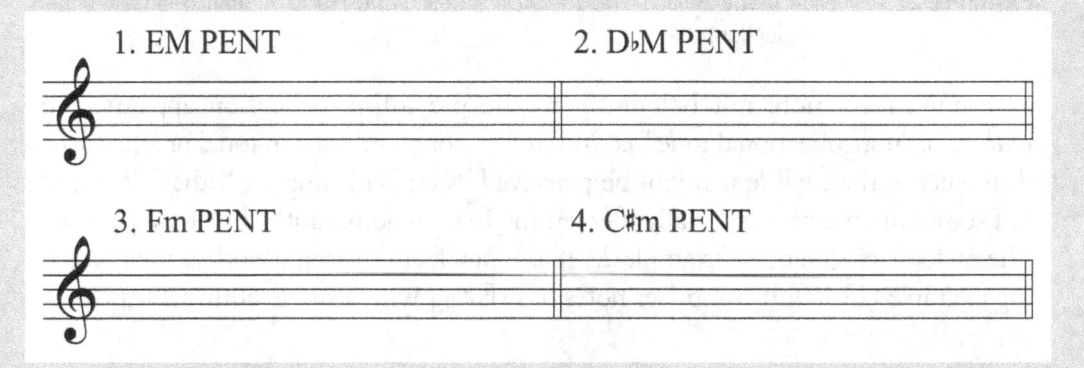

   1. EM PENT
   2. D♭M PENT
   3. Fm PENT
   4. C♯m PENT

3. Plot each collection on the pc wheel, and then spell it in the staff as a one-octave ascending scale beginning on the pitch-class specified.

1. OCT$_{0,1}$ beginning on F♯

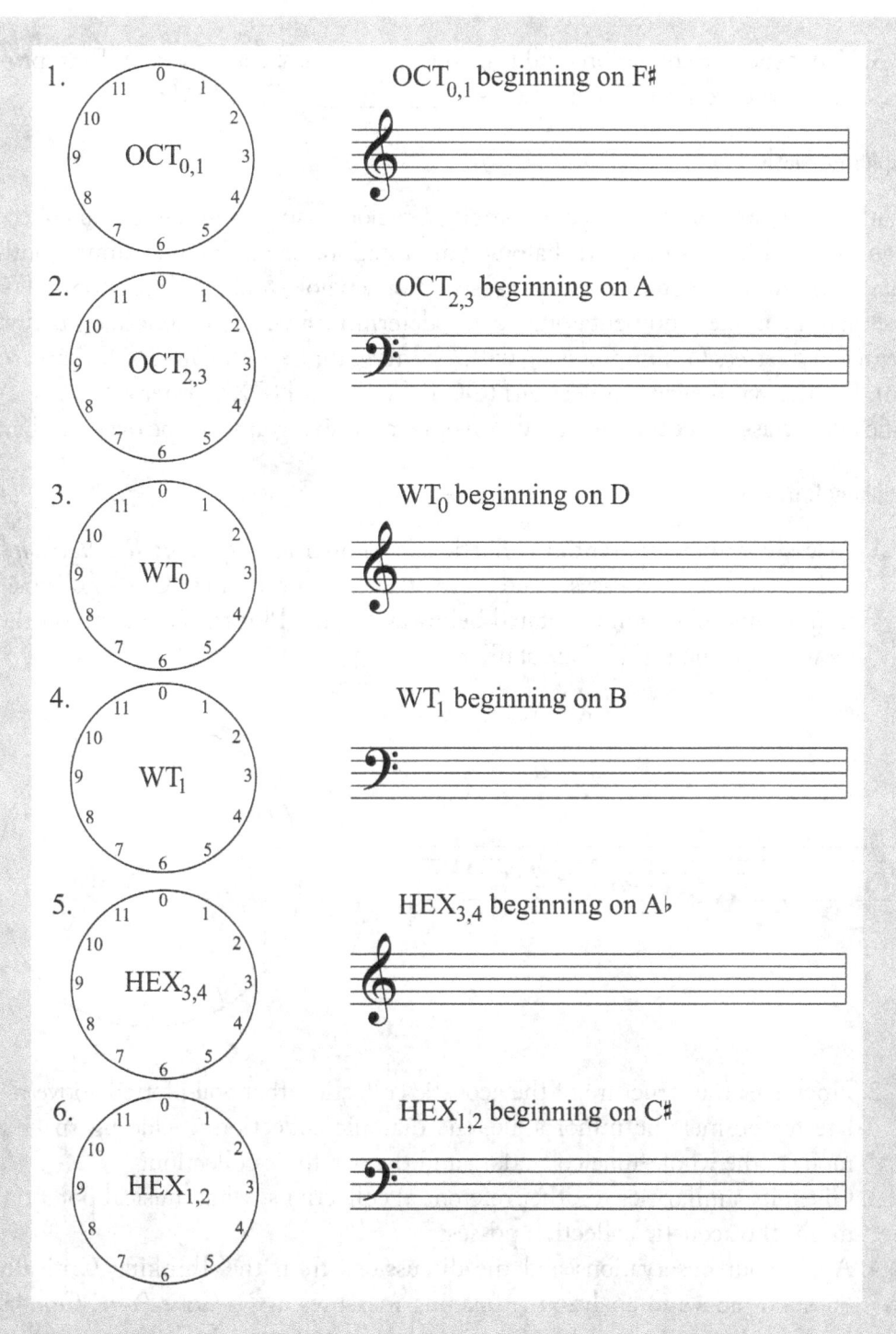

2. OCT$_{2,3}$ beginning on A

3. WT$_0$ beginning on D

4. WT$_1$ beginning on B

5. HEX$_{3,4}$ beginning on A♭

6. HEX$_{1,2}$ beginning on C♯

Brain Teasers

1. What is left over when a pentatonic collection is subtracted from the chromatic scale: CHROM − PENT = _____?
2. What remains when any octatonic collection is subtracted from the chromatic scale: CHROM − OCT = _____?

3. What specific collection (and transposition) could be added to WT_1 to produce the chromatic scale: $WT_1 +$ _____ = CHROM?

Exploring Music

With your instrument or voice, improvise a melody using each referential collection explored in this chapter: diatonic (any rotation, or mode), pentatonic (both major and minor), octatonic (any transposition), whole-tone, and hexatonic. For the diatonic modes and pentatonic scales, determine a way to emphasize the first degree (e.g., stress G if improvising with G Phrygian; E♭ with E♭M PENT, and so on). For the symmetrical collections (OCT, WT, and HEX), either select a specific pitch-class to accentuate or try to avoid emphasizing any one pc over another.

Thinking Critically

1. A less common referential collection is known as the *acoustic collection*.[6] This collection possesses interesting structural properties. One transposition of this collection is notated below as a scale. Plot the collection on the pc wheel to the right of the staff.

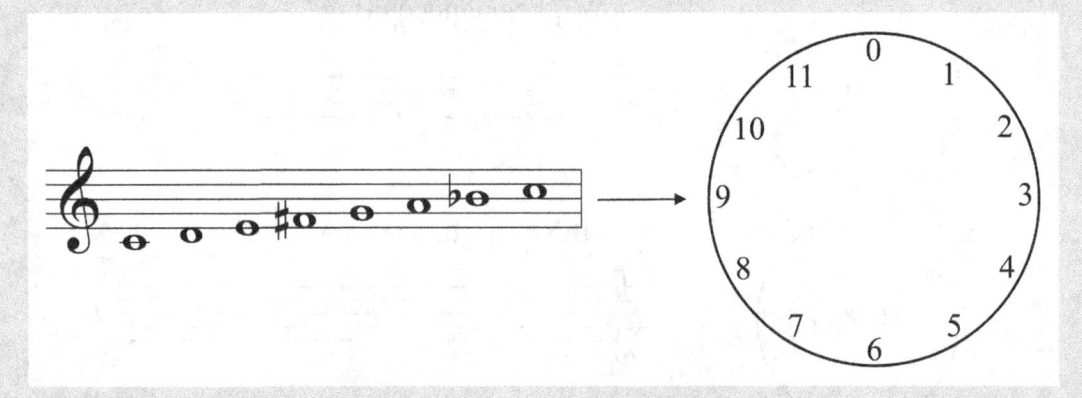

2. How does the structure of the acoustic collection that you plotted above relate to the melodic minor scale, the diatonic collection (including specific modes), the whole-tone collection, and the octatonic collection?
3. Given its similarities to other referential collections, what musical potential might the acoustic collection possess?
4. Apply your observations and the discussions from the Thinking Critically questions above to analyze the opening measures of *Fantastic Poem*, Op. 45, No. 2 by Alexander Scriabin. Identify the larger referential collections at work, and consider the relation of one to the next—including the process of transformation connecting one to another. Specifically, focus on the collectional shift that occurs from m. 1 to m. 2, and also the shift from m. 3 to m. 4. Use pc wheels to illustrate the transformation from one collection to another. In the score, circle any outliers (some of which look like chromatic passing tones).

EXAMPLE 22.19 Scriabin, *Fantastic Poem*, Op. 45, No. 2, mm. 1–5.

5. Apply your observations and the discussions from the Thinking Critically questions above to analyze the pitch content of *L'isle joyeuse* by Debussy. Specifically, focus on how the collection in mm. 145–148 changes (in m. 148) to the collection in mm. 148–159, and also how the collection in mm. 160–166 shifts (in m. 166) to that in mm. 166–185. Use pc wheels to illustrate the transformation from one collection to another. In the score, circle any outliers.

Notes

1 The labeling schemes for the referential collections applied here are taken from Joseph N. Straus, *Introduction to Post-Tonal Theory*, 4th ed. (New York and London: Norton, 2016).
2 Music before the common-practice tonal period (i.e., before *c.* 1600) is based largely on modes. Modes are often referred to as the *diatonic church modes* owing to their early liturgical applications.
3 Axis 0–6, Axis 1/2–7/8, Axis 4/5–10/11 (the latter two axes go *between* pc integers rather than *through* them).
4 B♭ (pc 10), a pedal tone, functions as the pitch center. It receives emphasis through repetition, by being the lowest pitch in the texture, and by serving as a melodic goal in m. 16.
5 $HEX_{2,3}$.
6 The collection is so named because it comprises the upper portion of the overtone series (partials 7–13). It is also referred to as the *acoustic scale*, the *overtone scale*, and (in jazz) the *Lydian-dominant scale*.

23

Centricity and Harmony

This chapter examines nonfunctional pitch centricity and post-tonal approaches to harmony.

Centricity

As suggested in the previous chapter, composers may designate a given note as a *pitch center* in a number of ways without tonicizing it in a traditional, functional manner. **Nonfunctional pitch centricity** occurs when a certain pitch class is emphasized over others through one or more of the following procedures:

1. *Repetition*
   - A note occurring more frequently than others easily assumes prominence. Repetition may be immediate, as when one pitch is stated two or more times in succession, or it may be intermittent, as when a melodic line continually returns to a note so that it recurs multiple times throughout a passage.
2. *Melodic placement* (points of arrival and departure)
   - A pitch is emphasized when placed as the first and/or last note of a melodic line.
3. *Voicing* (placement at registral extremes)
   - Notes sounding in the lowest and highest registers are generally more obvious. Pedal points and melodic zeniths often emerge as pitch centers.
4. *Accent*
   - A pitch may be accented in several ways: *metric accent*, when a note appears on a strong beat; *dynamic accent*, when a note is louder than surrounding notes—marked either at a higher dynamic level or with an accent mark (>); and *agogic accent*, when a note lasts longer than other notes.

The notes in Example 23.1 belong to $DIA_{1\flat}$. G emerges as the pitch center through *repetition* (it is heard six times), *melodic placement* (it serves as the melodic starting and ending points), *voicing* (it is the lowest note), and *metric accent* (it falls on the downbeat of m. 1 and on beat 2 of m. 4). With G as the focal point of this $DIA_{1\flat}$ collection, which mode is at work?[1]

EXAMPLE 23.1   Bartók, "Little Study," No. 77 from *Mikrokosmos*, Book 3, mm. 1–4.

5. *Doubling*
   ○ Unison or octave doublings reinforce a pitch class. Doublings are a kind of "vertical repetition," with one pc appearing in two or more voices simultaneously.

Example 23.2 is in E Lydian—$DIA_{5\sharp}$ with E established as the pitch center through *doubling* and *repetition*, as a three-octave pedal point on E is articulated at irregular intervals.

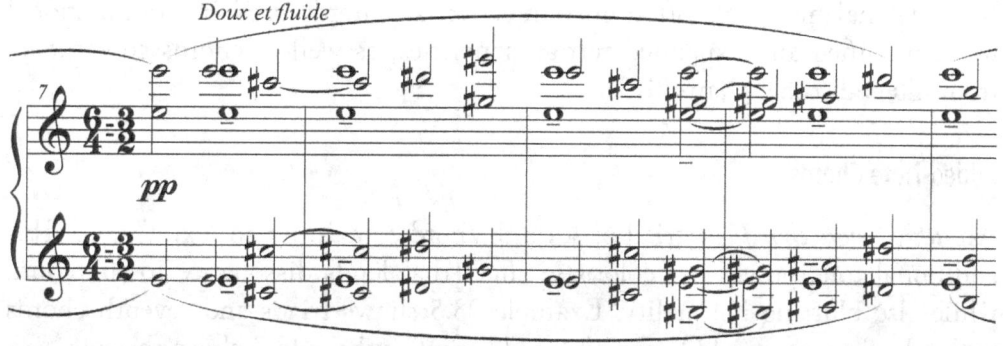

EXAMPLE 23.2   Debussy, "La Cathédrale engloutie," No. 10 from *Preludes*, Book 1, mm. 7–11.

6. *Symmetry*
   ○ Composers might specify a pitch center on or around an axis of symmetry.

In Example 23.3, a melody in the lower staff unfolds against a reiterated "pedal interval" in the upper staff. In pitch space, the melody straddles the pedal interval—forming an expanding *wedge* from B♮4 to E♭5.[2] In pitch-*class* space, the pcs are balanced around Axis 3—9. Example 23.4 shows Axis 3—9 dividing the pc wheel, a bracket marking the pedal interval, and arrows tracing the melodic path from pc 11 to pc 3—a centric pc lying *on* the axis.

Allegro giocoso
= 84
p

EXAMPLE 23.3 Bartók, *Bagatelle*, Op. 6, No. 2, mm. 1–4.

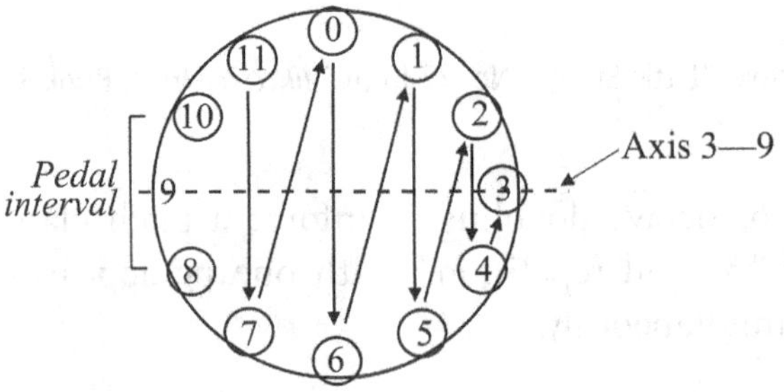
Pedal interval
Axis 3—9
0
1
2
3
4
5
6
7
8
9
10
11

EXAMPLE 23.4 Melodic path in Bartók's *Bagatelle*.

Harmony

In post-tonal music we often encounter tertian chords used in nonfunctional ways, modified and expanded tertian sonorities, as well as chords constructed from intervals other than thirds.

Added-Note Chords

An ***added-note chord*** is a triad or seventh chord containing an "extra" note. This additional tone provides a coloristic effect that lends dissonance to the chord while also blurring its quality. Example 23.5 shows triads and seventh chords with added seconds (add2), fourths (add4), and sixths (add6) above the root.

a.
b.
c.
d.
e.
f.
CMadd2
CMadd4
CMadd6
Dm7add2
Dm7add4
Dm7add6

EXAMPLE 23.5 Added-note chords.

Example 23.6 is based entirely on the Dm7^{add4} chord from Example 23.5e. Although the circled tones *do* form an added sixth (B) and added second (E) with Dm7^{add4}, their melodic nature makes them stand out as embellishing tones rather than actual chord members.

EXAMPLE 23.6 Debussy, "La Cathédrale engloutie," No. 10 from *Preludes*, Book 1, mm. 23–25.

Split-Third Chords

A *split-third chord* is a triad or seventh chord with a M3 *and* m3 above the root—the third is "split" between major and minor. The split third charges the chord with both dissonance and modal conflict. Example 23.7 shows several voicings for a C triad with split third.[3]

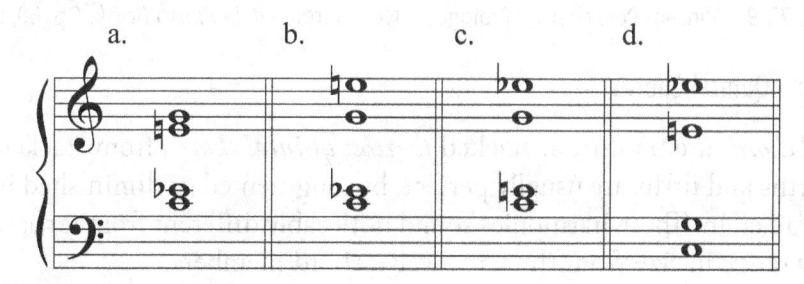

EXAMPLE 23.7 C triad with split third.

Polychords

A *polychord* is a combination of two or more distinct chords. In Example 23.8a, a B♭-major triad is stacked on top of a C-major triad. This chord could be considered a complete *eleventh chord*—that is, a C-major triad with a seventh, ninth, and eleventh all added above the root (or, a dominant ninth chord with an extra third stacked on top of the ninth). Such extended tertian sonorities are very common in jazz—where they are typically *in*complete—and will be considered in Chapter 26. True polychords are usually complete; moreover, the individual chords are often separated by register or timbre to differentiate them from one another.

In a polychord label, the symbols for the component chords are arranged vertically and separated by a horizontal line, with the upper chord placed above the line and the lower chord beneath. The polychord label for the chord in Example 23.8a is provided in Example 23.8b.

EXAMPLE 23.8 Polychord (a) and polychord label (b).

Example 23.9 features a series of complete polychords. The component triads of each polychord are spaced fairly close together—one notable exception being B♭/E, where the chords are separated by nearly an octave.

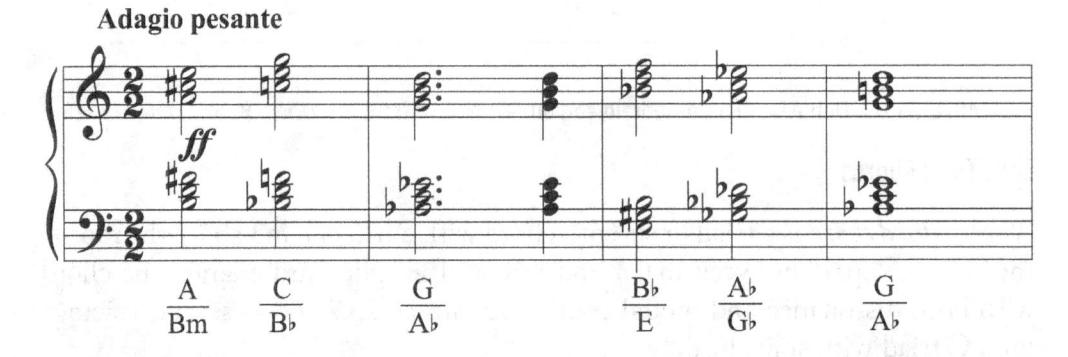

Adagio pesante

$\frac{A}{Bm}$ $\frac{C}{B♭}$ $\frac{G}{A♭}$ $\frac{B♭}{E}$ $\frac{A♭}{G♭}$ $\frac{G}{A♭}$

EXAMPLE 23.9 Vincent Persichetti, "Prologue," No. 10 from *Little Piano Book*, Op. 60, mm. 1–4.

Quartal and Quintal Chords

Quartal chords are built from stacked *fourths*; ***quintal chords*** from stacked *fifths*.[4] The fourths and fifths are usually perfect, but augmented or diminished intervals may be mixed in. These harmonies sound noticeably different from tertian chords and may range in size from three to twelve chord members.

In "The Cage," a song by Charles Ives, quartal and quintal harmonies figure prominently in the piano accompaniment. Example 23.10 shows a quartal chord (a) and a quintal chord (b) from the song. All fourths and fifths are perfect in both harmonies.

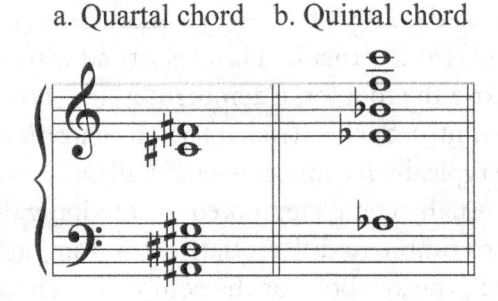

a. Quartal chord   b. Quintal chord

EXAMPLE 23.10 Quartal and quintal harmonies (from "The Cage" by Charles Ives).

Tone Clusters (Secundal Chords)

Chords built from seconds create *tone clusters*. Clusters form a dissonant "blur" of sound that is primarily a textural, coloristic device. The tone clusters in Example 23.11 are *diatonic clusters*, or "white-key clusters"—they use only the white keys of the piano ($DIA_{0\sharp}$). Clusters may also be pentatonic ("black-key") or fully chromatic. Clusters may be notated in a variety of ways, and composers often provide instructions in the score on how to execute them. For instance, Ives indicates that the clusters in Example 23.11 are "better played by using the palm of the hand or the clenched fist."

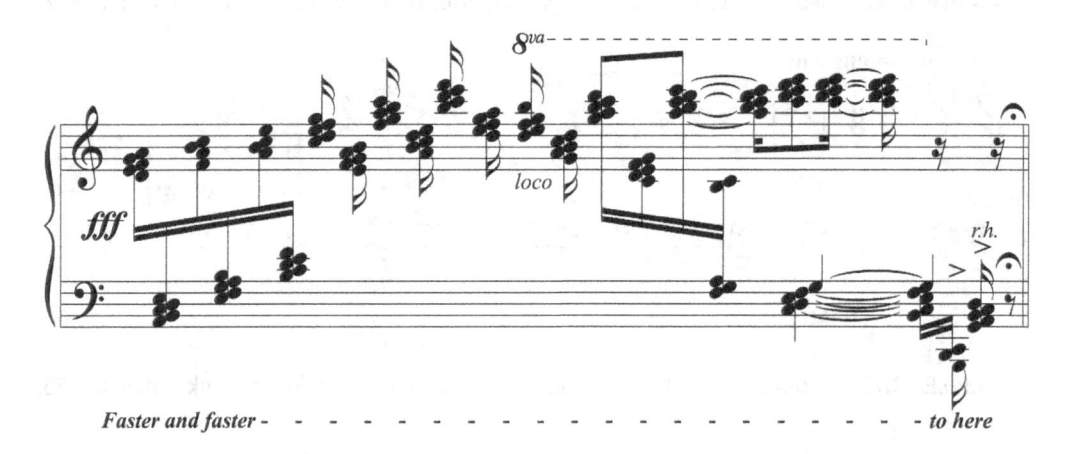

EXAMPLE 23.11   Ives, Piano Sonata No. 2 (*Concord*), II. "Hawthorne," select passage.

Planing

Planing is parallel motion from one chord to another. *All* voices move in parallel by the same interval. Traditional voice-leading practices are abandoned in favor of parallel fifths and octaves. Planing may be applied to any chord type but often occurs with tertian harmonies. The two types of planing are:

1. *Diatonic planing*
    - Chord quality varies as a single diatonic collection is preserved.
    - All voices move by the same size, but not necessarily same quality, of interval.
    - In Example 23.12, diatonic triads of $DIA_{0\sharp}$ are planed. Chord root and quality—which varies between major and minor—is listed beneath the first six triads. (Roman numerals do not apply in this nonfunctional context.)
2. *Chromatic planing*
    - Chord quality remains the same; no single collection is preserved.
    - All voices move by the same size *and* quality of interval.
    - Mm7 chords are planed in Example 23.13.

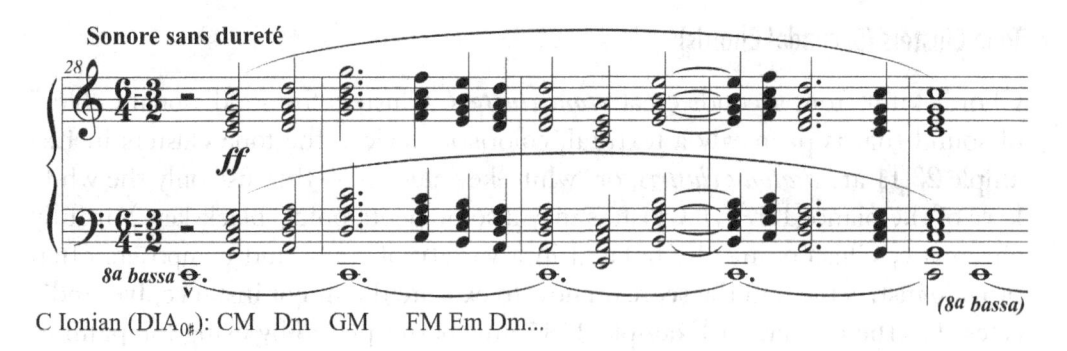

EXAMPLE 23.12 Debussy, "La Cathédrale engloutie," No. 10 from *Preludes*, Book 1, mm. 28–32.

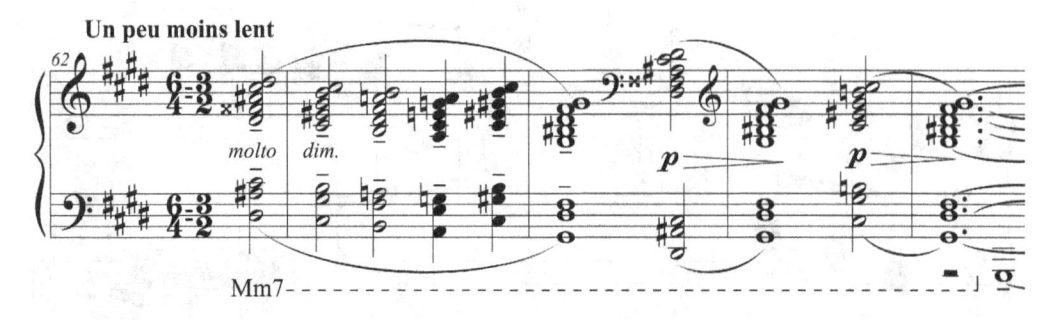

C Ionian (DIA$_{0\#}$): CM Dm GM FM Em Dm...

EXAMPLE 23.13 Debussy, "La Cathédrale engloutie," No. 10 from *Preludes*, Book 1, mm. 62–66.

Mm7

Applications

Exercises

1. Which referential collection is found in Example 23.14? What is the pitch center, and how is this center defined?

EXAMPLE 23.14 Debussy, "La Cathédrale engloutie," No. 10 from *Preludes*, Book 1, mm. 47–53.

2. Determine the pitch center in Example 23.15. List the way(s) in which this center is delineated. Identify the referential collection(s) in this passage, and describe the type of harmonic motion present.

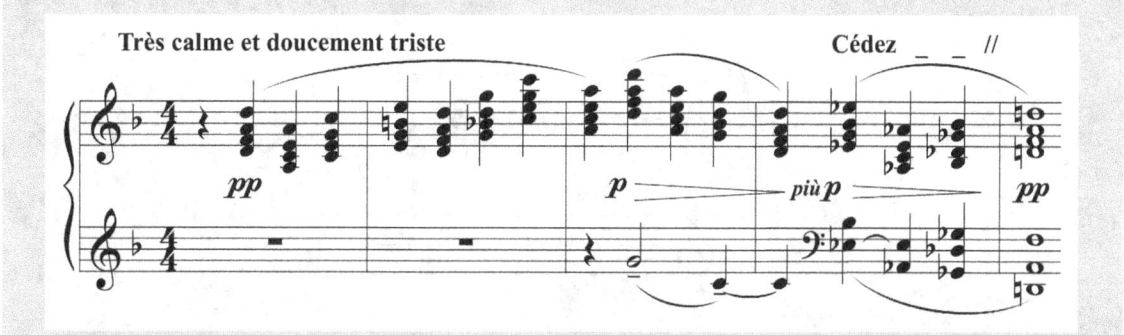

EXAMPLE 23.15 Debussy, "Canope," No. 10 from *Preludes*, Book 2, mm. 1–5.

3. Identify the chord types below, and label each chord as described in this chapter. Label split-third chords by their root and "split" (e.g., "C split"); label quartal and quintal chords as "quartal" or "quintal."

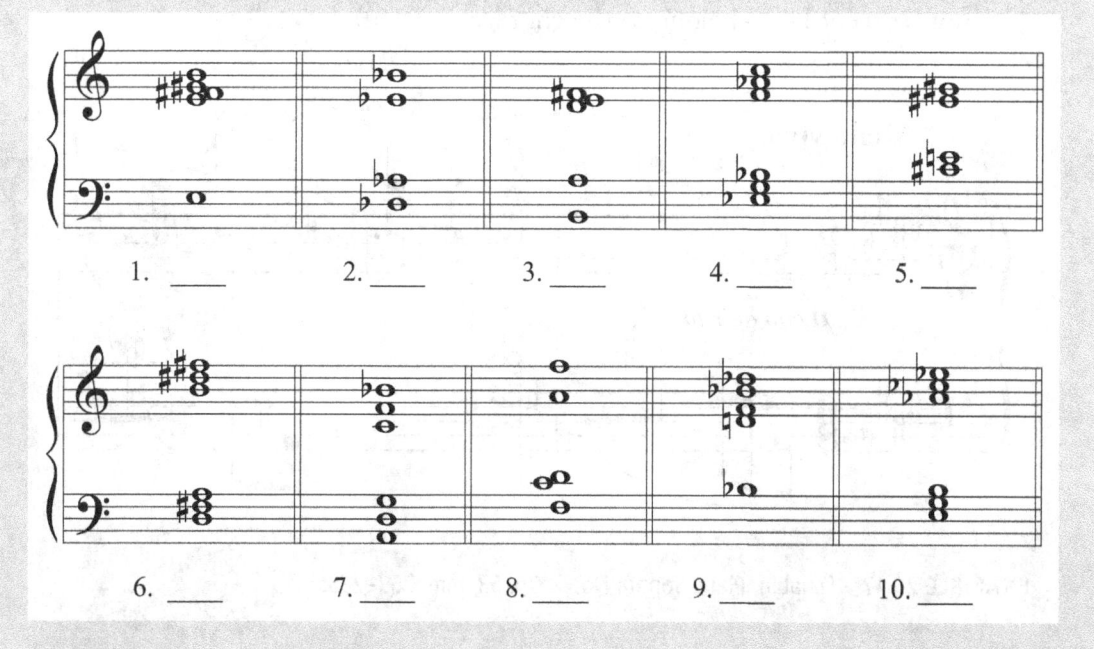

1. ____   2. ____   3. ____   4. ____   5. ____

6. ____   7. ____   8. ____   9. ____   10. ____

Brain Teasers

1. How else might one analyze and label the added-note chord in Example 23.5c?
2. How might the chords in Example 22.8 (bottom staff) be explained in terms of quartal/quintal harmony?

Thinking Critically

1. Example 23.16 shows the "Petrushka chord" that figures prominently throughout Stravinsky's *Petrushka*. Determine a label for the chord. Does it belong to a particular referential collection?

EXAMPLE 23.16 The Petrushka chord.

2. Example 23.17 features an instance of Alexander Scriabin's "mystic chord." How do you account for this chord? How is it voiced (particularly in the lower staff)? From what larger referential collection does it derive? (All notes except F♮/E♯ belong to the chord/collection).

EXAMPLE 23.17 Scriabin, Piano Sonata No. 5, Op. 53, mm. 263–265.

Notes

1 G Dorian (R2 of $DIA_{1♭}$).
2 In performance, the pianist's left hand must "straddle" the right hand.
3 Split-root and split-fifth chords are possible but much less common than split-third chords.
4 A quartal chord inverts as a quintal chord, and vice versa.

24

Set Theory

The preceding chapters outline the late nineteenth-century breakdown of the tonal system and introduce some of the new ways that composers began organizing musical sound in the early twentieth century. Alternative pitch collections (scales) and chord types give rise to new sound worlds, and pitch centers—when present—are established on a contextual basis. During this time, no single compositional style or aesthetic emerges as a wholesale replacement of the tonal system, and numerous schools of composition coexist and impact one another.[1] Some composers continue writing tonal music, and the tonal tradition is further extended through various styles of popular music as well as film scores.

As we have seen, Roman-numeral and syntactic analyses simply do not apply to non-tonal music. And while identifying octatonic collections or added-note chords is interesting, this alone tells us very little about the *structure* of a musical work—about how the *parts* are arranged to form a coherent musical *whole*. **Set theory** provides a way to uncover the organization of post-tonal music by identifying interrelated and recurring groups, or *sets*, of pitch classes.[2]

Set theory relies on the concepts of *pitch class* and *pitch-class space*. Integers represent pitch classes, and the *pitch-class wheel* (pc wheel) is used to model and analyze relationships among pitch classes and sets of pitch classes. These concepts have been introduced and described in previous chapters; the reader is encouraged to review the relevant sections of Chapters 19 and 22.

Pitch-Class Sets

A ***pitch-class set (pc set)*** is an unordered group of pitch classes. In essence, a pc set is an abstract motive that may unfold musically in numerous ways. Example 24.1a shows pc-set {1, 3, 6, 7} on a pc wheel. (For now, pc-set labels are ordered from lowest pc integer to highest.) A four-pc set like this one is called a *tetrachord*. The pc set {1, 3, 6, 7} is shown projected into two different musical settings: as a melodic fragment (Example 24.1b), and as a chord (Example 24.1c).

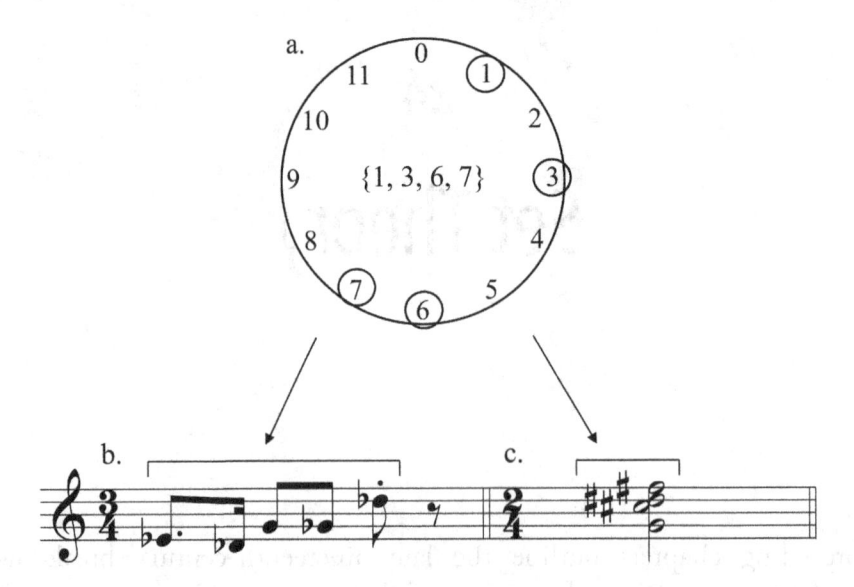

EXAMPLE 24.1 Pc-set {1, 3, 6, 7} on the pc wheel (a) and in two musical settings (b–c).

A pc set derives its sonic identity, or character, from its intervallic content rather than from its specific pitch-class content. ***Interval class (ic)*** is a calculation of the total number of pitch-class semitones separating two pcs. In pitch-class space, there are only six interval classes, numbered 1 through 6. Interval-class 1, or ic 1, is one pc semitone, ic 2 is two pc semitones, and so on. Two intervals related by inversion, like M2 and m7, belong to the *same* interval class. The smallest interval of the pair (i.e., the *shortest* distance between two pcs on the pc wheel) is used to determine interval class. M2 and m7 both belong to ic 2, because the smaller of the two intervals, M2, is a total of two semitones. Example 24.2 lists the six interval classes.

> ic 1 = 1 pc semitone (m2/M7)
> ic 2 = 2 pc semitones (M2/m7)
> ic 3 = 3 pc semitones (m3/M6)
> ic 4 = 4 pc semitones (M3/m6)
> ic 5 = 5 pc semitones (P4/P5)
> ic 6 = 6 pc semitones (+4/°5)

EXAMPLE 24.2 The six interval classes.

Example 24.3a traces every interval class of pc-set {1, 3, 6, 7} on a pc wheel. Interval classes exist between adjacent pcs (linked with solid lines), and also between nonadjacent pcs (connected with dashed lines), accounting for every pair of pitch classes. Example 24.3b tallies the number of occurrences of interval classes 1–6 and lists the specific pcs forming each ic.

There are two ways to calculate interval class. One way is simply to count the pc semitones separating the pcs on the pc wheel. Another way is to subtract the lowest-integer pc from the highest. For example, pcs 3 and 7 form ic 4: 7 – 3 = 4.

a.

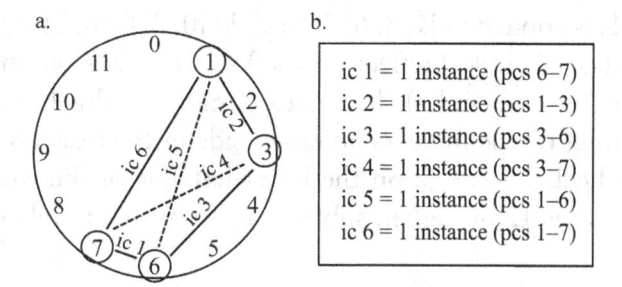

b.
ic 1 = 1 instance (pcs 6–7)
ic 2 = 1 instance (pcs 1–3)
ic 3 = 1 instance (pcs 3–6)
ic 4 = 1 instance (pcs 3–7)
ic 5 = 1 instance (pcs 1–6)
ic 6 = 1 instance (pcs 1–7)

EXAMPLE 24.3 Interval classes in set {1, 3, 6, 7}.

The interval-class content of a pc set is represented by its *interval-class vector (ic vector)*, which is a string of integers listing the total number of instances of each interval class. The first number in the vector indicates the occurrences of ic 1, the second number the instances of ic 2, and so on. The ic vector for pc-set {1, 3, 6, 7} is <111111>—it contains one instance of each ic.

Transposition and Inversion of Pitch-Class Sets

A pitch-class set may be transposed and inverted in pitch-class space. Applying either of these operations maps the original pitch classes of the set onto new pitch classes but preserves the interval-class content of the set. *Transposition* in pc space is equivalent to (clockwise) *rotation* on the pc wheel. A *T-operation* rotates every pitch class of a pc set by a certain number of pc semitones. T-operations are abbreviated T_x, where the subscript index number (x) indicates the number of semitones: T_1 rotates the set by one pc semitone, T_2 by two pc semitones, and so on. In Example 24.4, {1, 3, 6, 7} is rotated by T_3 to produce {4, 6, 9, 10}. T_3 maps pc 1 onto 4 (1 + 3 = 4), 3 onto 6, 6 onto 9, and 7 onto 10.

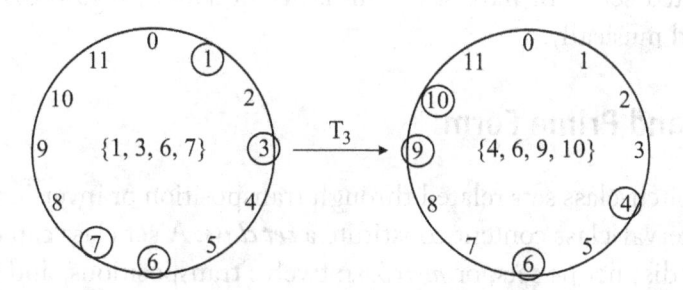

EXAMPLE 24.4 T_3 applied to pc-set {1, 3, 6, 7}.

Inversion in pc space is equivalent to *reflection* across the pc wheel. An *I-operation* (I_x) reflects every pitch-class of a pc set across an axis of symmetry. An axis of symmetry divides the pc wheel into two equal halves and may be drawn either *through* pc integers or *between* them. The index number (x) for an I-operation is calculated by summing the two pc integers on either side of the axis. In

Example 24.5, I_3 is applied to {1, 3, 6, 7} to yield {0, 2, 8, 9}. The pcs of {1, 3, 6, 7} (enclosed with dashed circles) reflect across Axis 1/2—7/8 and map onto the pcs of {0, 2, 8, 9} (set in solid circles). The index number for this I-operation is determined by summing the pc integers on either side of the axis: on the upper-right side of the pc wheel, 1 + 2 = 3; on the lower-left side of the wheel, 7 + 8 = 15. Whenever the sum is 12 or higher, subtract 12 from that number: 15 − 12 = 3.[3]

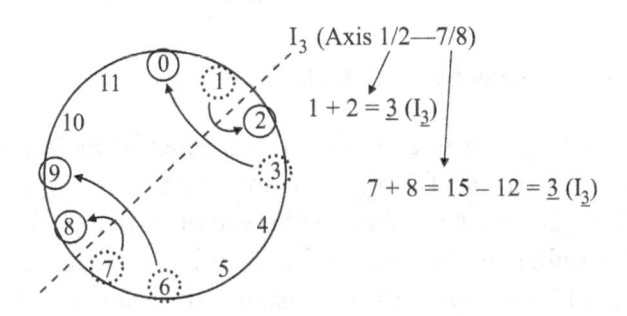

EXAMPLE 24.5 I_3 applied to {1, 3, 6, 7}.

Although their pitch-class contents differ, tetrachords {1, 3, 6, 7}, {4, 6, 9, 10}, and {0, 2, 8, 9} share the same interval-class content, represented by ic vector <111111>. These sets map onto one another through *some* T- or I-operation. T_3 rotates {1, 3, 6, 7} onto {4, 6, 9, 10} (Example 24.4). Conversely, T_9 would map {4, 6, 9, 10} back onto {1, 3, 6, 7}. I_3 reflects {1, 3, 6, 7} onto {0, 2, 8, 9} (Example 24.5). I-operations are reciprocal: the same I-operation, I_3, would map {0, 2, 8, 9} back onto {1, 3, 6, 7}. What operation would map {4, 6, 9, 10} onto {0, 2, 8, 9}?[4]

Different T- and I-operations map these sets onto other pc sets with the *same* interval-class content. This is an important point—it means all of these distinct yet interrelated sets will have *some* similarity of sound, regardless of how they might unfold musically.

Set Class and Prime Form

A group of pitch-class sets related through transposition or inversion and sharing the same interval-class content constitute a ***set class***. A set class can contain up to twenty-four distinct pc sets, or *members*: twelve transpositions, and twelve inversions.[5] Each member of a set class can map onto every other member at *some* level of transposition or inversion. If a pc set exhibits transpositional or inversional symmetry, meaning it can rotate or reflect *onto itself*, there will be fewer than twenty-four distinct members in the set class.

To simplify analysis, one member from each set class is chosen to represent the entire class. This member, called the ***prime form***, is the most compressed member of the set class beginning from pc-integer 0. The Appendix toward the end of this book lists every set class by its prime form. In musical analysis, pc sets are circled and labeled with the prime form.

Determining the Prime Form of a Pitch-Class Set

The following steps outline one procedure for determining the prime form of a pc set. Example 24.6 applies these steps to pc-set {1, 3, 6, 7}.

Step 1: Plot the pitch-class set on a pc wheel. Count the number of pc semitones between adjacent pcs and write these numbers outside the pc wheel.
- These numbers always add up to 12.
  - In Example 24.6, 2 + 3 + 1 + 6 = 12.

Step 2: Compare the clockwise and counterclockwise orderings of these numbers, and choose the one with the *highest number last* and the *smallest number first* (or with smaller numbers appearing as early in the ordering as possible). This ordering is called the *interval normal form (INF)*.[6]
- The numbers must be kept in order, both clockwise and counterclockwise.
- In Example 24.6, clockwise ordering (2316) and counterclockwise ordering (1326) both place the highest number (6) last. Since (1326) has a smaller integer first, *it* is the INF.

Step 3: On a new pc wheel, circle pc-integer 0.

Step 4: Going clockwise from 0, apply the integers of the INF to plot a new pc set. *This* is the prime form of the set class to which the original pc set belongs.
- The prime form of pc-set {1, 3, 6, 7} is [0146].
  - Consult the Appendix to confirm that [0146] is listed as a tetrachord.
    - If you are unable to locate a prime form on the List of Set Classes, an error must have been made when calculating it (perhaps the wrong ordering was selected as the INF).

The above procedure is one of several methods for determining prime form. As you become increasingly fluent with this process, you might discover (or invent) timesaving shortcuts. For example, it is possible to view a pc set on the pc wheel and visualize the set in its most compressed ordering (with smaller intervals toward the front of the ordering, and larger ones toward the rear). Viewing pc-set {1, 3, 6, 7} on the pc wheel (see Example 24.7), it is clear that the most compressed ordering of the set begins at pc 7 and proceeds counterclockwise. Assign "0" to pc 7 and then move counterclockwise, counting pc semitones and assigning integers to each circled pitch class. These numbers (underlined in Example 24.7) spell the prime form.

The prime form [0146] represents *all* twenty-four members of this set class; any member of set-class [0146] reduces to the *same* prime-form label.

Step 1

0
11 (1) 2
10   2
9 {1, 3, 6, 7} (3)
8   4
(7)   5   3
   (6)
1

Step 2

Clockwise: (**2316**)
Counterclockwise: (**1326**)

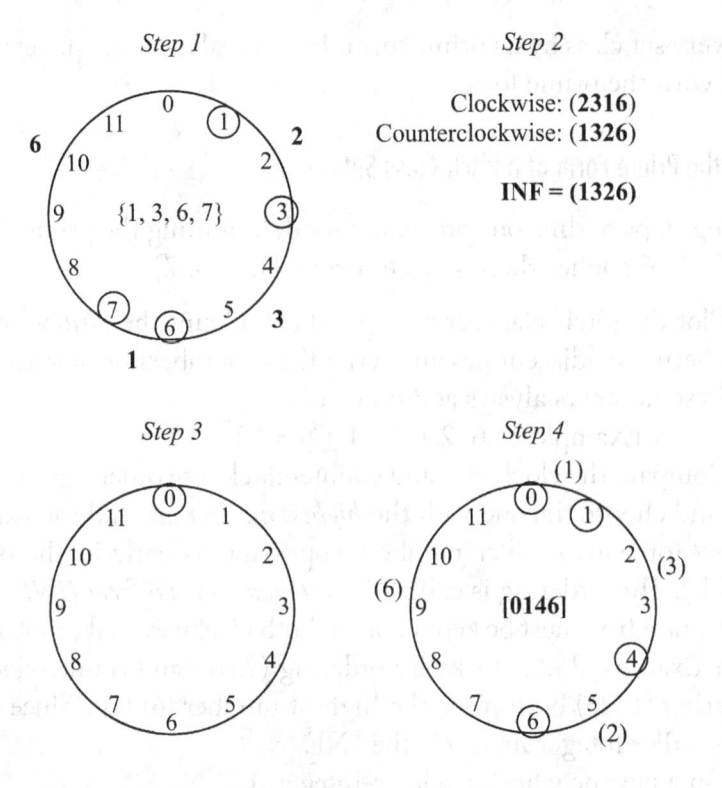

INF = (**1326**)

Step 3

0
(0)
11   1
10   2
9   3
8   4
 7   5
   6

Step 4

(1)
0
11 (0) (1)
10   2 (3)
9   [0146] 3
8   (4)
 7   5
   (6)
    (2)

EXAMPLE 24.6 Finding the prime form of a pc set.

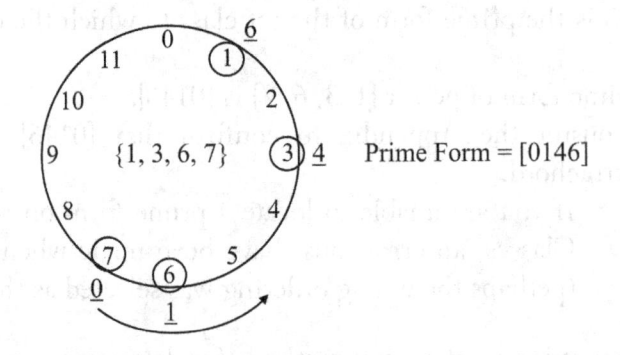

6
0 (1)
11   2
10
9 {1, 3, 6, 7} (3) 4   Prime Form = [0146]
8   4
 (7)   5
  0 (6)
     1

EXAMPLE 24.7 Shortcut to determine prime form.

Segmentation

Perhaps the biggest challenge to pitch-class set analysis is deciding how to *segment* the music into small and meaningful units that are analyzable as pc sets. The primary objective is to locate recurring pc sets (members from the same set class) and assess the transpositional and inversional relations among those sets. This process, a "treasure hunt" of sorts, typically involves a degree of trial and error, and there is no single correct way to segment a musical work. *Listening* should always inform analysis: the music will often suggest certain segmentations. In turn, an effective analysis should inform, and challenge, our listening.

Following are some tips for segmenting a musical work:

1. Focus on *small* pc sets: trichords (3 pcs), tetrachords (4 pcs), and/or pentachords (5 pcs).
2. You might identify recurring members of more than one set class.
    - For example, a work might contain numerous [024] trichords *and* [0134] tetrachords.
3. Recurring sets are often characteristics *subsets* of the larger referential collections (diatonic, octatonic, whole-tone, and hexatonic). These subsets might interact in interesting ways.
    - [024] is a subset of the whole-tone collection, and [0134] is a subset of the octatonic collection. A profusion of these two set classes in a musical work puts the larger referential collections in dialogue with one another.
4. A pc set may be a vertical simultaneity (chord) or a linear string of pitch classes (melodic segment). It may also be a combination of the two.
5. Adjacent notes make the most sense to include in a linear set, but also consider nonadjacent pitches. Intervening notes may be considered outliers.
6. A set may span multiple voices or parts.
7. Sets may overlap one another in the score—a pc may belong to more than one set.
8. The pcs constituting a set may be associated with a certain register, timbre, dynamic, articulation, duration, or metric placement.

Analysis

When conducting a pitch-class set analysis, circle or bracket the sets you are analyzing so that they stand out from surrounding pitches and other sets. When applying the prime-form label to a set, place it as close to the circled set as possible—it should be clear that the label applies to a specific set.

Pitch-class sets are circled and labeled in the analyses that follow. For practice, select some of the sets and apply the steps for determining their prime form.

Example 24.8a shows the closing chords of Bartók's "From the Island of Bali." The two chords are both members of set-class [0358], a subset of the octatonic collection. In pitch space (in the staff), the first chord connects to the second through semitonal voice leading, as a °6 in each staff collapses to a P4. In pitch-*class* space, the first chord maps onto the second under T_6.[7] The two chords *together* complete $OCT_{2,3}$. This process of *transpositional combination*, where a set is combined with a transposition of itself to produce a larger set (like a referential collection), is shown in Example 24.8b, with the first chord set in solid circles and the second in dashed circles.

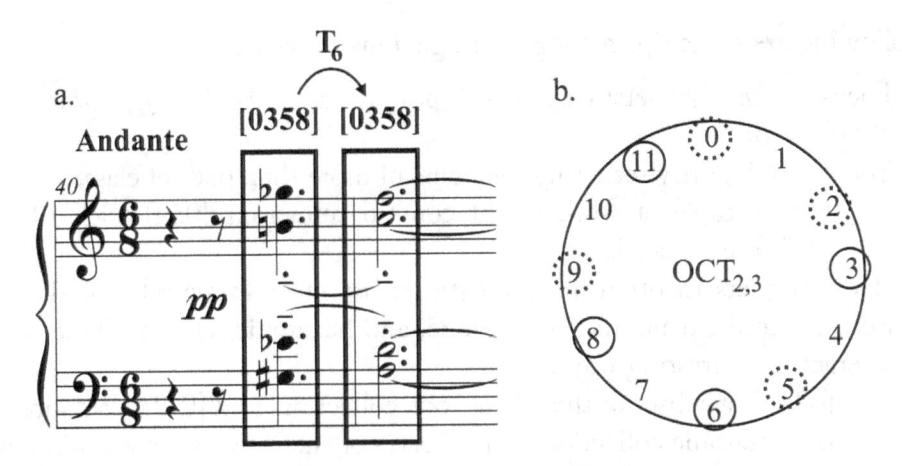

EXAMPLE 24.8 Bartók, "From the Island of Bali," No. 109 from *Mikrokosmos*, Book 4, mm. 40–41 (a); transpositional combination (b).

Example 24.9 provides a detailed analysis of the first eight measures of a string quartet by Anton Webern. Study the segmentation choices, and observe the following:

- Every note is grouped in at least one pc set *except* for the pedal C♯ in the cello.
- [014] and [015] trichords dominate the excerpt, and their recurrence unifies the musical structure.
  - Both trichords are subsets of HEX.
  - [014] unfolds both horizontally (linearly) and vertically.
  - [015] is exclusively linear.
- Horizontal and vertical sets overlap in mm. 2–3 and m. 6.
- The melodic lines in mm. 7–8 (first violin and cello) feature overlapping [015] trichords. While only three [015] trichords are identified in the analysis, *every* set of three contiguous notes belongs to set-class [015].
- The melodies in m. 4 (first violin and viola) are members of set-class [012468]. This is a large WT subset, with one pitch-class outlier.
  - [014] and [015] are both subsets of [012468].

The song excerpt in Example 24.10 is based entirely on pc-set [0268], a tetrachordal subset of the whole-tone collection. This set is highly symmetrical: it can rotate onto itself under two different levels of transposition, *and* it can reflect onto itself under two different levels of inversion. In other words, a total of four different operations replicate the set. Owing to this symmetry, there are only six unique members of set-class [0268], rather than twenty-four. To determine the total number of distinct members within any set class, divide 24 by the total number of T- and I-operations that map the set onto itself (always include T_0). In the case of [0268], 24 ÷ 4 = 6.

All six members of set-class [0268] appear in the first four measures of the song. In Example 24.10, the sets are numbered in order of appearance and labeled with prime-form [0268]. The two melodic notes not included in a set (C♭ and B♭), as well as the circled C♮ in m. 4, are outliers.

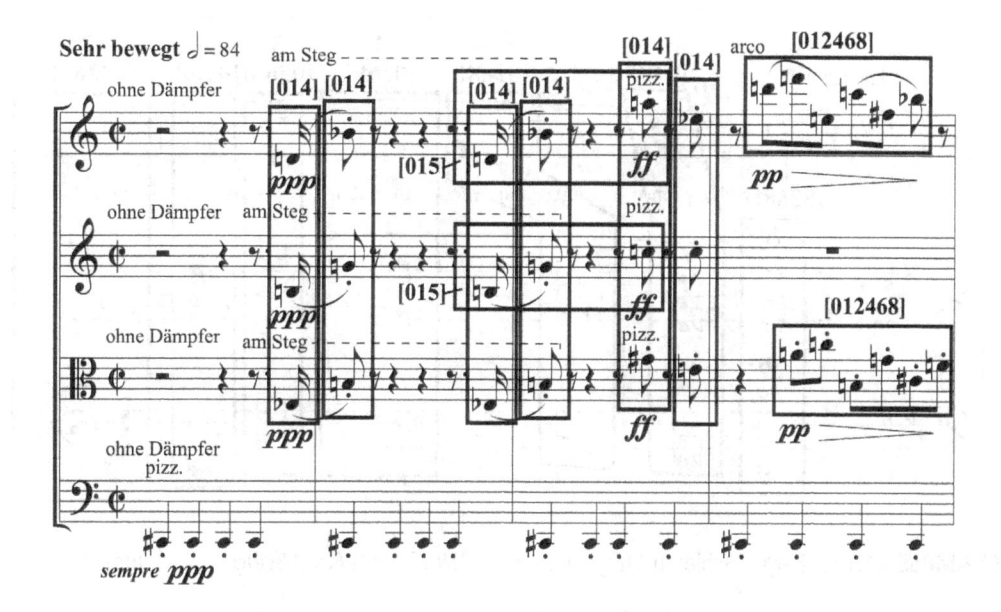

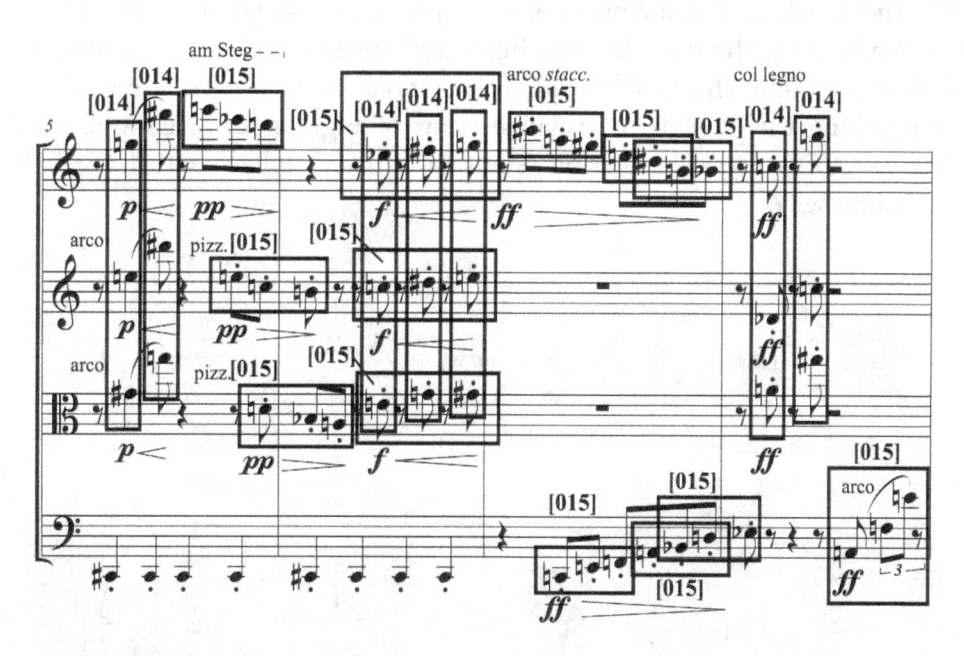

EXAMPLE 24.9 Webern, *Five Movements for String Quartet*, Op. 5, III, mm. 1–8.

All seven sets from Example 24.10 are plotted on pc wheels in Example 24.11. This diagram shows the series of transformations mapping each set onto the next set. The *same* operation, T$_5$, connects each set to the set that follows it. (T$_{11}$ also maps each set onto the next, as do two different I-operations.) The recurrence of this specific T-operation (T$_5$) helps unify the music by serving as a kind of *syntax* structuring the underlying musical motion. This phrase also exhibits a process of *departure and return*: after visiting all six members of set-class [0268], the phrase returns to, and closes with, the same member that opened the song (sets 1 and 7 are both {2, 4, 8, 10}).

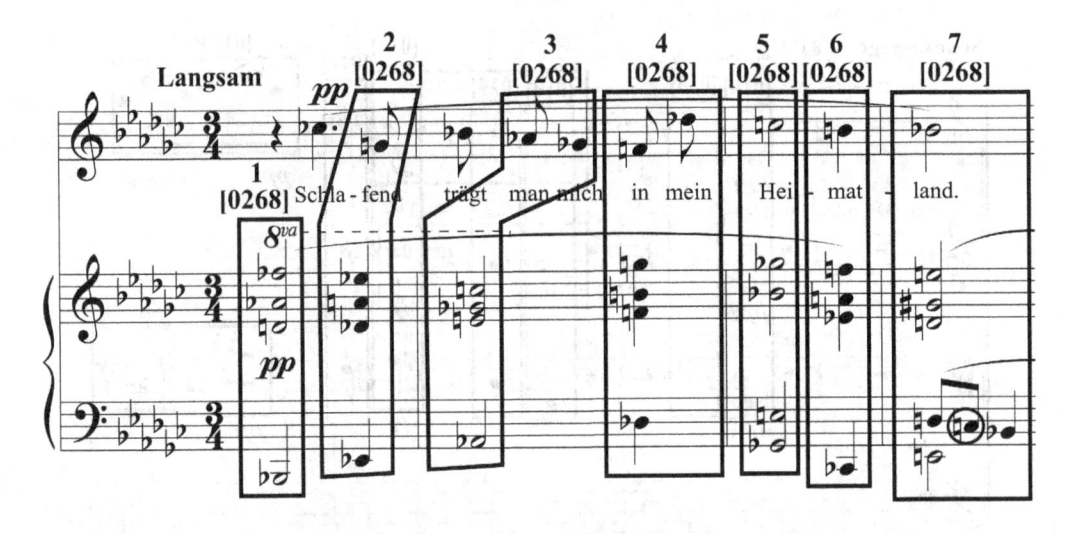

EXAMPLE 24.10 Berg, "Schlafend trägt man mich," No. 2 from *Four Songs*, Op. 2, mm. 1–4.

On the pc wheel, the members of [0268] form the shape of a rectangle (imagine "connecting the dots" by drawing lines between circled pitch classes that are adjacent on the wheel). While all T-operations are labeled in terms of clockwise rotation, it is possible to visualize each rectangular set in Example 24.11 tilting *counter*clockwise by one pc semitone until set 1 has rotated a full 180 degrees into set 7.[8]

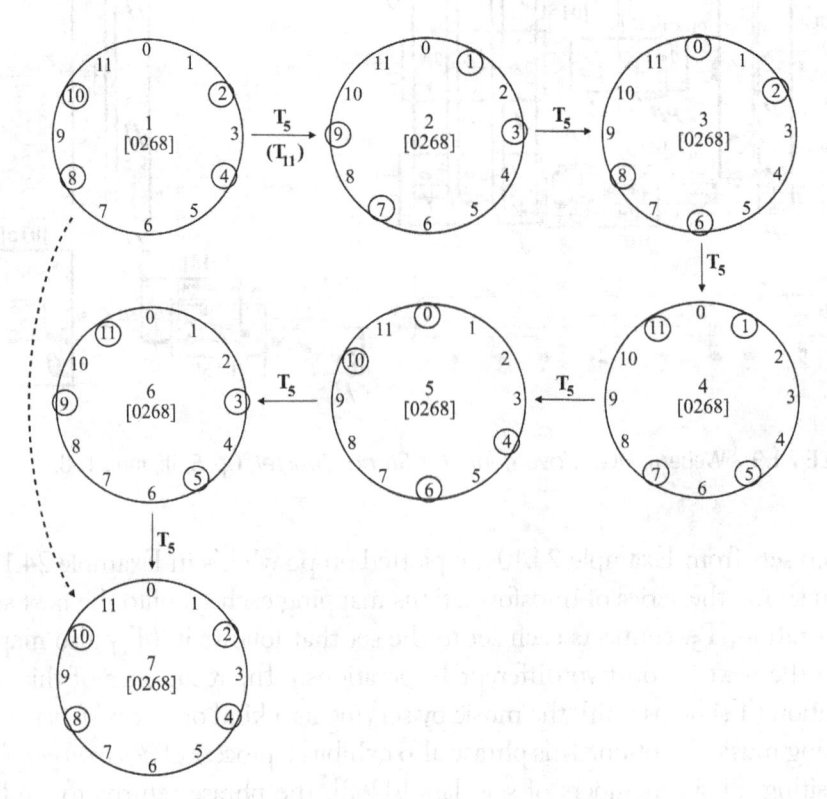

EXAMPLE 24.11 The process of pc-set transformation in "Schlafend trägt man mich."

Applications

Exercises

1. Determine the *interval normal form* (INF) and *prime form* (PF) for each pc set below. (A sheet of pc wheels is available on the online companion to this textbook.) After determining each prime form, confirm that it appears on the List of Set Classes (Appendix).

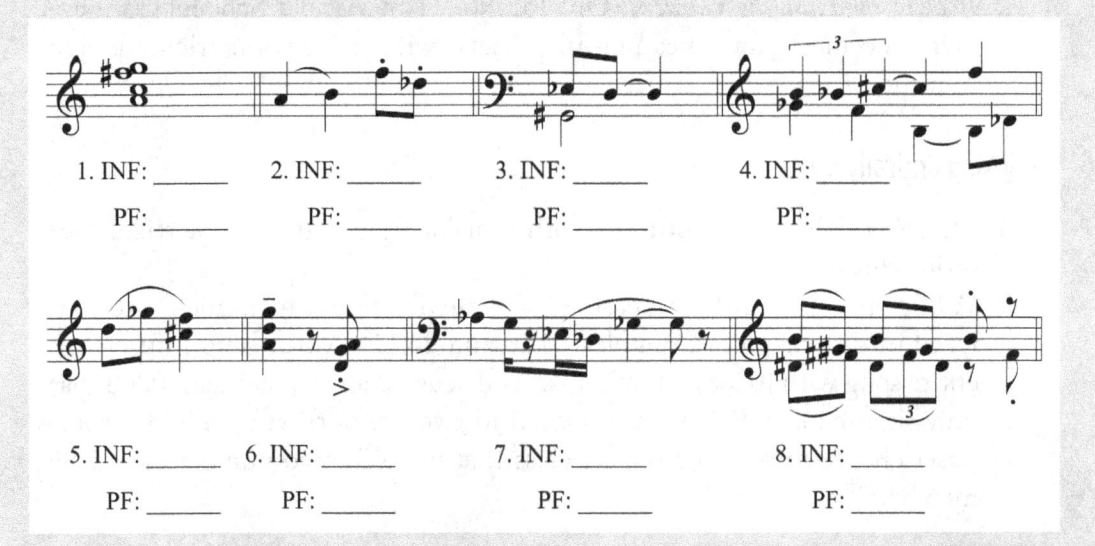

1. INF: _____	2. INF: _____	3. INF: _____	4. INF: _____
PF: _____	PF: _____	PF: _____	PF: _____

5. INF: _____	6. INF: _____	7. INF: _____	8. INF: _____
PF: _____	PF: _____	PF: _____	PF: _____

2. Describe how *transpositional combination* could be applied to an augmented triad to produce the whole-tone collection. Show this process on a pc wheel using pc set {1, 5, 9} (an + triad).
3. Determine the prime form for the referential collections: diatonic, octatonic, whole-tone, and hexatonic. How many unique members are found in each set class?

Brain Teasers

1. [0146] is used throughout this chapter. How does it relate to [0137]? Plot both tetrachords on separate pc wheels, and compare their interval-class contents.
2. [0268] (from Examples 24.10 and 24.11) can be spelled as a certain chromatic chord. Which one?

Exploring Music

Analyze the works listed below. Segment the music into meaningful pc sets, with a focus on trichords and tetrachords. Circle the sets in the score and label them with the prime form of the set class to which they belong. Sets might overlap one another, and smaller sets might be embedded in larger ones. Some sets will be horizontal (melodic fragments) and others will be vertical (chords). A single set may span multiple staves.

1. Bagatelles Nos. 4 and 5 from *Sechs Bagatellen für Streichquartett*, Op. 9 by Anton Webern. Although they come from the same collection, analyze each bagatelle separately. *Be mindful of clef changes.*
2. *Book of the Hanging Gardens*, Op. 15, No. 11 by Arnold Schoenberg. Segment the music into meaningful pc sets, with a focus on trichords and tetrachords.

Thinking Critically

1. Determine the prime form for both a major triad and a minor triad. Describe this relationship.
2. While only the first four measures of "Schlafend trägt man mich" are analyzed in this chapter (Examples 24.10 and 24.11), Alban Berg infuses this entire song with [0268] tetrachords. As discussed above, set-class [0268] has only six unique members (as opposed to twenty-four). Why might a composer choose to work with a set class that has a limited number of unique members?

Notes

1 Some of the major compositional schools and aesthetics (or, "-isms") include: neo-Classicism, neo-Romanticism, impressionism, futurism, serialism, minimalism, and maximalism. Twentieth-century composers also begin experimenting with tape music (*musique concrète*) and electronic music (*elektronische Musik*).
2 Music theorist Allen Forte is credited with the first large-scale application of set theory to musical analysis. See Allen Forte, *The Structure of Atonal Music* (New Haven: Yale University Press, 1973).
3 The application of set theory to pitch-class set analysis uses **arithmetic modulo 12 (mod 12)**, where any number larger than 11 is equivalent to a number between 0 and 11, and this number is determined by subtracting 12 (or any multiple of 12) until a number between 0 and 11 is reached.
4 I_6. This operation reflects pcs across Axis 3—9. Since it lies *on* the axis of symmetry, pc 9 maps onto itself.
5 The twelve inversions are related to one another through transposition.
6 The concept of *interval normal form* seems to originate in Eric Regener, "On Allen Forte's Theory of Chords," *Perspectives of New Music* 13.1 (Autumn–Winter 1974): 191–212.

7 The two chords also map onto one another under I_8 (inversion across Axis 4—10).
8 Although not common in practice, a counterclockwise T-operation could be indicated with a negative subscript index number: T_{-x}. Counterclockwise rotation by one semitone, T_{-1}, is equivalent to T_{11}. The index numbers for equivalent clockwise and counterclockwise T-operations always equate to 12 (0 mod 12): $T_{10} = T_{-2}$ (10 + 2 = 12), $T_9 = T_{-3}$ (9 + 3 = 12), and so on. The main advantage to thinking of T-operations in terms of counterclockwise rotation is that they might allow a transformation, or process of transformation, to be better depicted and visualized on the pc wheel (as is the case in Example 24.11).

25

Serialism

In an effort to systematically avoid a pitch center, some twentieth-century composers turned to *serialism*, a method in which all twelve pitch classes are arranged in a row that serves as the basis for a work of music. Composers use not only the original row but also transformations of that row, including transposed and inverted forms. Serialism is arguably the closest that twentieth-century composers came to establishing a new common practice. Accordingly, it is a very complex subject. This chapter explores the basics of serialism.

Twelve-Tone Rows

A *twelve-tone row* is an ordering of the twelve pitch classes with each pc occurring once and only once. A row represented by pc integers is provided as Example 25.1a.[1] Since it is pitch *classes* that are ordered, octave designations are not fixed, so pc 6 could be set as F♯ (or G♭) in any octave. Examples 25.1b and c show two musical renderings of the row, each exploring different registers and exhibiting unique rhythmic profiles.

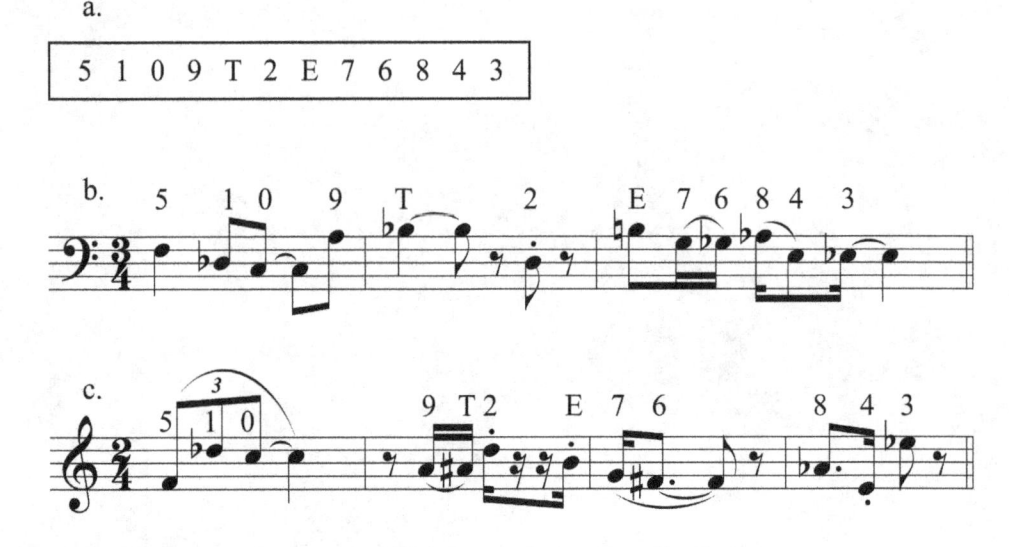

a.

5 1 0 9 T 2 E 7 6 8 4 3

EXAMPLE 25.1 A twelve-tone row (a) in two musical settings (b–c).

Example 25.2 presents an analysis of the row's discrete (non-overlapping) segments—its four trichords, three tetrachords, and two hexachords. You will notice that all four trichords belong to set-class [015], and the two hexachords are members of [013458]. Composers often design rows with recurring sets and then exploit those sets musically. In Example 25.1c, the rhythmic partitioning of the row emphasizes its trichords.

```
Trichords:    [015]   [015]   [015]   [015]
              5 1 0   9 T 2   E 7 6   8 4 3
Tetrachords: [0148]      [0347]     [0135]
Hexachords:    [013458]         [013458]
```

EXAMPLE 25.2 Analysis of row segments.

Portions of rows can "bunch up" to create chords. When adjacent pcs of a row occur simultaneously, there is no set rule guiding the vertical distribution of those notes relative to one another. In Example 25.3, the discrete [015] trichords from the row in Example 25.1a are set as chords.

EXAMPLE 25.3 Chords built from row segments (trichords).

Row Transformations

Some composers use a single row form for an entire work, but most use the initial row along with any number of transformations of that row.[2] The original row is called the *prime form (P)*. The prime form can be transposed eleven times, for a total of twelve P-forms (including the original). Each P-form can be read backwards for twelve *retrograde (R)* forms. Each of the twelve P-forms can also be inverted in pitch-class space, so there are twelve *inversions (I)*. Finally, each I-form can be read backwards for twelve *retrograde-inversion (RI)* forms. This makes for a total of forty-eight related row forms (12 P-forms + 12 R-forms + 12 I-forms + 12 RI-forms).

While each one of the forty-eight related rows exhibits a unique ordering of pitch classes, they all share the same series of *interval* classes: all P- and I-forms exhibit the same sequence of ics, and this series is reversed in the R- and RI-forms. Example 25.4 shows the interval-class series for the P-, I-, R-, and RI-forms of the row from Example 25.1a. In twelve-tone music, the recurring series of interval classes functions as an abstract theme that structures and unifies the music. What is more, the discrete segments of all forty-eight related row forms have the *same* set-class memberships. For example, the four trichords of *every* row related to the one in Example 25.1a belong to set-class [015]. In addition to the proliferation of related row forms, recurring pc sets further unify twelve-tone compositions.

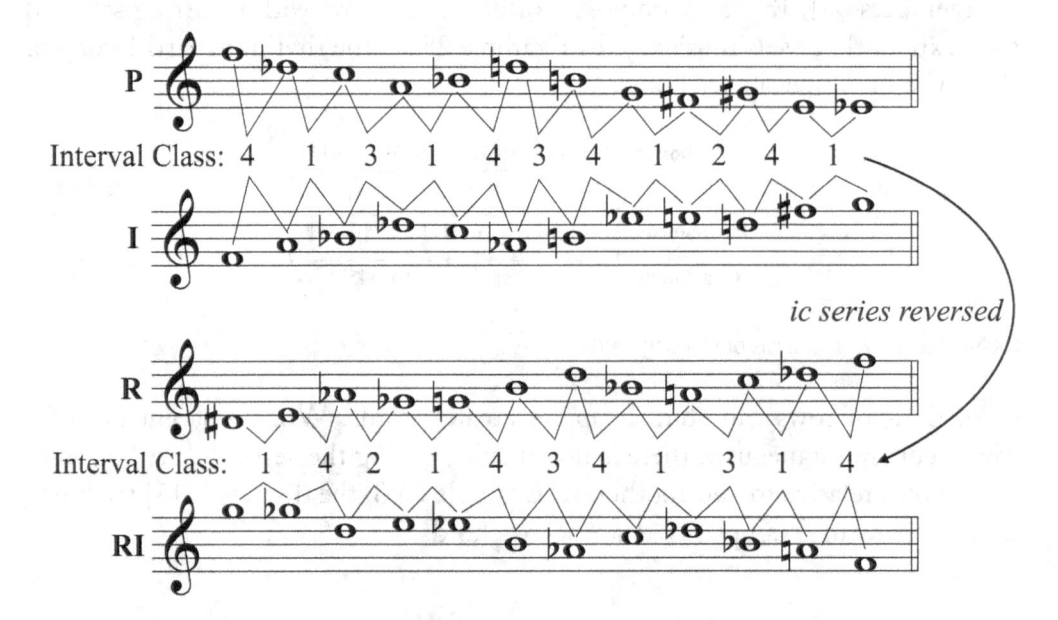

EXAMPLE 25.4 Recurring interval-class series in related row forms.

The Twelve-Tone Matrix

The *twelve-tone matrix* is a succinct listing of all forty-eight related row forms. It is a square comprising twelve columns and twelve rows of pc integers.

Building a Twelve-Tone Matrix

The following steps outline one of several ways to construct a matrix. Examples 25.5a–e apply these steps to build a matrix from a row with prime form 4 5 7 1 6 3 8 2 E 0 9 T.

Step 1: Write out the prime form to serve as the top row of the matrix. See Example 25.5a.

4 5 7 1 6 3 8 2 E 0 9 T

EXAMPLE 25.5A Prime form as top row of matrix.

Step 2: Use a pc wheel to invert the prime form. Draw an axis of symmetry through the first integer of the row (four in this case). Make sure the axis divides the wheel into two equal halves: it should go through an integer on the opposite side of the wheel (10 in this case). See Example 25.5b.

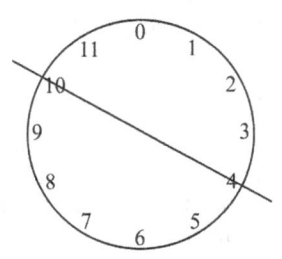

EXAMPLE 25.5B Axis of symmetry (Axis 4—10) drawn through first pc integer of row (4).

Step 3: Proceeding downward from the first pc of the prime form, write the reflection of each pc from the prime form. Since it lies on the axis, pc 4 reflects onto itself. Pc 5 reflects across the axis onto pc 3. Write pc 3 directly under pc 4. Continue this process to build the left column of the matrix (Example 25.5c).

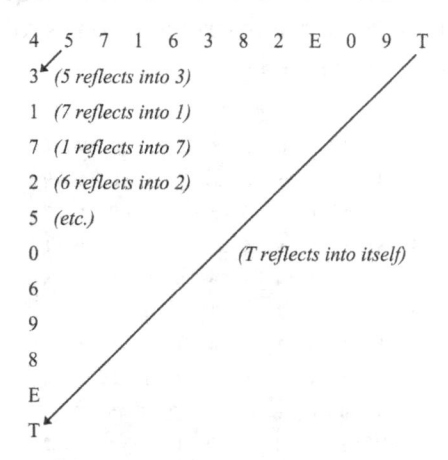

```
4   5   7   1   6   3   8   2   E   0   9   T
3   (5 reflects into 3)
1   (7 reflects into 1)
7   (1 reflects into 7)
2   (6 reflects into 2)
5   (etc.)
0               (T reflects into itself)
6
9
8
E
T
```

EXAMPLE 25.5C Inversion of prime form as left column.

Step 4: With the inversion of the prime form in place, the matrix can be completed using simple math. In the inversion column, locate the pc integer that is one number higher than the first integer of the prime form. The prime form begins with pc 4, so locate pc 5 in the inversion column. Add 1 to each pc integer of the prime form to complete a new row beginning from pc 5. This new row, set in bold in Example 25.5d, is a transposition (T_1) of the original prime form.

After finishing the row beginning on pc 5, locate pc 6 in the inversion column and fill out this row by adding 1 to each integer of the row starting with pc 5. The beginning of this process is shown in Example 25.5d. This results in yet another transposition of the prime form. Next, fill out the row beginning on pc 7, then pc 8, and so on until the matrix is complete.[3]

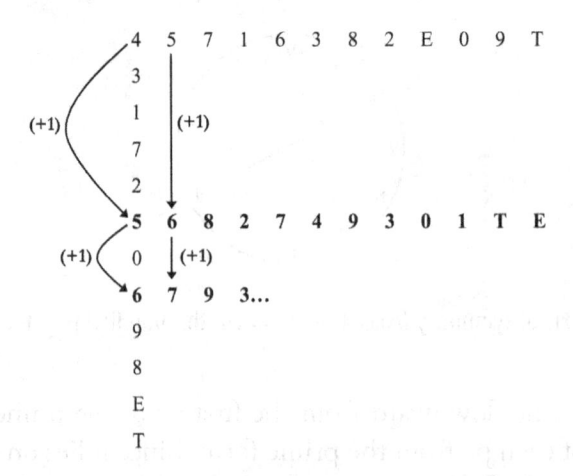

```
          4  5  7  1  6  3  8  2  E  0  9  T
          3
          1
  (+1) ⎧  1    ⎫(+1)
          7
          2
          ↓
          5  6  8  2  7  4  9  3  0  1  T  E
  (+1) ⎧  0    ⎫(+1)
          ↓
          6  7  9  3...
          9
          8
          E
          T
```

EXAMPLE 25.5D Filling out rows to complete the matrix.

If all numbers have been calculated correctly, the diagonal running from the top left to the bottom right (↘) of the matrix will consist of the *exact same number* (see the boldfaced 4s in Example 25.5e).

```
4  5  7  1  6  3  8  2  E  0  9  T
3  4  6  0  5  2  7  1  T  E  8  9
1  2  4  T  3  0  5  E  8  9  6  7
7  8  T  4  9  6  E  5  2  3  0  1
2  3  5  E  4  1  6  0  9  T  7  8
5  6  8  2  7  4  9  3  0  1  T  E
0  1  3  9  2  E  4  T  7  8  5  6
6  7  9  3  8  5  T  4  1  2  E  0
9  T  0  6  E  8  1  7  4  5  2  3
8  9  E  5  T  7  0  6  3  4  1  2
E  0  2  8  1  T  3  9  6  7  4  5
T  E  1  7  0  9  2  8  5  6  3  4
```

EXAMPLE 25.5E Completed matrix with uniform ↘ diagonal highlighted.

Reading and Labeling Row Forms

Rows are read left-to-right for the P-forms and right-to-left for R-forms. Columns are read top-to-bottom for I-forms and bottom-to-top for RI-forms. All P-forms are related to one another through transposition, as are all R-forms, I-forms, and RI-forms.

The labels P, R, I, and RI specify row *type*, and a subscript index number indicates a row's *level of transposition*. P-forms and I-forms are labeled based on the *first* pc integer of the row. R-forms and RI-forms are identified by the *last* integer of the row. In Example 25.6, three transpositions of each row type are labeled, and arrows show the direction that the P-, R-, I-, and RI-forms are read.

Serialism

```
            I₄  I₅  I₇
            ↓   ↓   ↓
    P₄ →  4  5  7  1  6  3  8  2  E  0  9  T  ← R₄ (retrograde of P₄)
    P₃ →  3  4  6  0  5  2  7  1  T  E  8  9  ← R₃ (retrograde of P₃)
    P₁ →  1  2  4  T  3  0  5  E  8  9  6  7  ← R₁ (retrograde of P₁)
          7  8  T  4  9  6  E  5  2  3  0  1
          2  3  5  E  4  1  6  0  9  T  7  8
          5  6  8  2  7  4  9  3  0  1  T  E
          0  1  3  9  2  E  4  T  7  8  5  6
          6  7  9  3  8  5  T  4  1  2  E  0
          9  T  0  6  E  8  1  7  4  5  2  3
          8  9  E  5  T  7  0  6  3  4  1  2
          E  0  2  8  1  T  3  9  6  7  4  5
          T  E  1  7  0  9  2  8  5  6  3  4
          ↑   ↑   ↑
         RI₄ RI₅ RI₇

         (retrograde of I₄)
```

EXAMPLE 25.6 Reading and labeling row forms in the matrix.

P₄ and R₄ are the *same row* read in *different directions*. Even though R₄ begins with pc 10, it is labeled R₄ to show that it is simply P₄ reversed. Similarly, I₄ and RI₄ are the same column read in different directions.

Analysis

The matrix we created above will be used to analyze a passage from the Minuet and Trio of Schoenberg's Piano Suite, Op. 25, provided as Example 25.7. The objective is to identify in the music specific row forms from the matrix. Begin by writing pc integers next to noteheads in the score. It is not necessary to do this for every pitch—just enough to uncover the rows being used. The first six notes are labeled with pc integers. The row in the matrix beginning with the same six pitch classes is P₄. In the score, this row and two other rows are enclosed in rectangles and labeled, and a fourth row is enclosed but not labeled. (P₄ begins again at the first ending and continues through the repeat.) Confirm the row forms I₁₀ and I₄ by labeling their starting notes with pc integers and locating the forms in the matrix. Then determine the label for the unidentified row.[4]

The layering and rhythmic treatment of these four row forms weaves an intricate counterpoint. The rows are divided into two recurring rhythmic patterns: a clustering of six longer values (five eighths + one dotted quarter) followed by a rapid burst of six sixteenth notes. An analysis of discrete row segments reveals that the two hexachords belong to set-class [012346]. Schoenberg's rhythmic partitioning of each row form highlights the uniform hexachords.

EXAMPLE 25.7 Schoenberg, Minuet and Trio from *Suite für Klavier*, Op. 25, mm. 34–38.

Serialism: Beyond Pitch

In the latter half of the twentieth century, some composers began serializing musical elements other than pitch, including duration, rhythm, dynamics, articulation, and timbre. **Integral serialism** (also known as *total serialism* or *multiserialism*) is an attempt to serialize all musical parameters in a work, often using rows from a single matrix. While an in-depth study of integral serialism lies beyond the scope of this chapter, we will briefly consider how the row from Example 25.1 could be used to serialize duration and generate the rhythm for a musical line. Each integer in the row can be interpreted as a total number of beat units. If the beat unit is set as the sixteenth note, then the first integer in the row, 5, represents a total of five sixteenths, or one quarter tied to a sixteenth. Example 25.8 shows the highly syncopated line that emerges from this process. Rests are occasionally interspersed with note values, summing to a total duration. In this example, integer 0 is interpreted as twelve sixteenths (three quarter notes), and an eighth rest (m. 2) completes this duration. In Example 25.8, the same row is used to set both pitch and duration, but composers often use different row forms in combination to set various musical elements.

EXAMPLE 25.8 Pitch and duration serialized with the same row form.

Advanced Topics for Further Exploration

- Hexachordal combinatoriality and twelve-tone areas (Schoenberg)
- Serialism blended with tonal elements (Berg)
- Invariance, derived rows, and row symmetry (Webern)
- Rotational arrays and rows with fewer than twelve pitch classes (Stravinsky)
- Trichordal arrays and durational rows (Babbitt)
- The time-point system (Babbitt and Wuorinen)
- Multiplication (Boulez)
- Twelve-tone themes (Shostakovich)
- Twelve-tone techniques in jazz (Bill Evans, "Twelve Tone Tune")

Applications

Exercises

1. Complete the following for each twelve-tone row provided below:
   - Analyze the discrete row segments (trichords, tetrachords, and hexachords).
   - Construct a matrix, treating the given row as the prime form (top row of the matrix).

   A. 6 5 2 4 3 0 9 1 8 E T 7

   B. T 9 5 2 0 6 7 3 1 8 E 4

Brain Teaser

Build a matrix from row 0 9 T E 7 8 2 1 5 4 3 6 (from Symphony, Op. 21 by Anton Webern). You will discover that row forms are replicated throughout the matrix. For example, P_0 and R_6 are identical. How many unique row forms exist in total? What is it about the structure of the row itself that results in fewer than forty-eight related row forms?

Exploring Music

1. Using the row analyses and matrices you completed in Exercise 1 above, analyze two serial compositions. Complete the following for each work:
   - Use the matrix to identify the specific row forms in the music.
   - Circle (or bracket) and label all row forms in the score.
   - Answer the following questions:
     - Does the composer emphasize any row segments? If so, how?
     - Are there any repeated row forms?
     - Is there any pattern or logic to the row forms present in the work?
   A. Anton Webern, "Wie bin ich froh" from *Drei Lieder nach Gedichten von Hildegard Jone*
      - Prime form: 6 5 2 4 3 0 9 1 8 E T 7 (from Exercise 1A)
      - Tips:
        - All row forms are complete.
        - For the majority of the piece, two row forms occur simultaneously: one in the voice part, and another in the piano part.
        - Rows overlap on a couple of occasions, with the last note of one row serving as the first note of a new row.
   B. Luigi Dallapiccola, "Quartina," No. 11 from *Quaderno musicale di Annalibera*
      - Prime form: T 9 5 2 0 6 7 3 1 8 E 4 (from Exercise 1B)
      - Tips:
        - All row forms are complete.
        - There are always two distinct row forms unfolding at the same time.
        - In m. 6, pc 11 belongs to both of the row forms occurring at that time.
        - In m. 16, a single pc from the row in the bottom two staves is superposed above the row form in the upper staff.
2. Explore the other two songs in Webern's *Drei Lieder*, or some of the other pieces in Dallapiccola's *Quaderno musicale di Annalibera*. Are the rows in these works from the same matrices that you built in the exercises above? If so, do any row forms recur between pieces? If a piece seems to contain different row forms, create a matrix from the first row that you encounter and use it to analyze the music. Note any similarities or differences among the selections in each collection.
3. Create an original twelve-tone row. Design one with recurring set classes among either the trichords or tetrachords. Build a matrix from your row. Optional: compose a short work using the rows from your matrix (your instructor might give you additional guidelines).

Thinking Critically

1. What are some significant differences between a pitch-class set and a twelve-tone row?
2. Based on the examples in this chapter, it might be easy to assume that serial composers always set their tone rows in an obvious, transparent manner. To challenge this assumption, analyze the following brief passage, which comes from the Minuet and Trio by Schoenberg analyzed above. In it, a single row form from the matrix in Example 25.5e is set in an unconventional and nontransparent manner. Determine the row being used and describe how it is set. (You might find it helpful to label every pitch with its corresponding pitch-class integer.)

EXAMPLE 25.9 Schoenberg, Minuet and Trio from *Suite für Klavier*, Op. 25, mm. 39–40 (left hand only).

Notes

1. T is used for pc 10 to avoid misreading it as pc 1 followed by pc 0. Similarly, E is used for pc 11.
2. The first movement of the *Suite for Solo Cello*, Op. 84 by Ernst Krenek is composed with a single row form.
3. Subtraction can also be used to complete row forms. For example, the row directly beneath the prime form begins with pc 3. Subtract 1 from each integer of the prime form to fill out this row.
4. P_{10}.

26

Introduction to Jazz and Pop Harmony

Jazz began developing out of blues and ragtime in the early twentieth century. The jazz genre breaks down into numerous styles, including swing, bebop, Dixieland, cool jazz, free jazz, smooth jazz, and various fusion styles. Jazz exhibits many of the same harmonic and functional trends present in common-practice tonality, and therefore may be viewed as an extension of the tonal system developing in parallel with the post-tonal practices of the twentieth and twenty-first centuries. This chapter explores basic elements of jazz harmony, with a focus on the unique features that distinguish it from other tonal styles.

Jazz tunes are notated on *lead sheets*. Jazz chords, which are for the most part tertian, are indicated by *chord symbols*. (Readers are encouraged to review the end of Chapter 5, where chord symbols and lead sheets are introduced.) While a chord symbol provides all the information necessary to realize a given chord, voicings and doublings are variable. The symbol G7/B specifies a dominant seventh chord built on G with B in the bass. The precise distribution of the chord tones G, D, and F above B is left to the performer's discretion. What is more, the player may omit, add, or alter chord tones. Finally, chord symbols do not necessarily indicate diatonic chords within a given key. In C major, G7/B specifies the diatonic V$^6_5$. What Roman numeral would apply to the same chord (and symbol) in F major? In A major?[1]

Sus Chords

A **sus chord**, or *suspended chord*, contains a fourth above the root in place of the third. This note might be suspended from the previous chord and will sometimes resolve down by step before the harmony changes, as with the motion Csus–C. Often, however, the fourth is neither prepared nor resolved. Example 26.1 shows a major triad (a) and dominant seventh chord (b) with a suspended fourth.

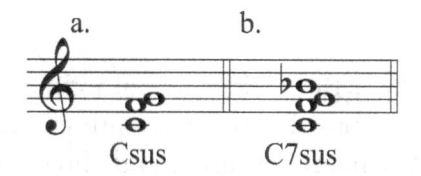

EXAMPLE 26.1   Csus (a) and C7sus (b).

Sixth Chords

Added-note chords, described in Chapter 23, include a second, fourth, or sixth above the root. In jazz, triads with a *major* sixth added above the root are known as **sixth chords**. The chord symbol C6 indicates a C-major triad with a major sixth, A, added above the root. The "6" in the chord symbol does *not* specify inversion—a C-major chord in first inversion is represented by the symbol C/E. Example 26.2 shows C6 (a) and Cm6 (b).

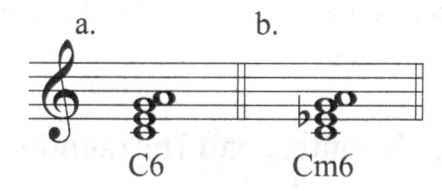

EXAMPLE 26.2   C6 (a) and Cm6 (b).

Seventh Chords

Most chords heard in jazz are "taller" than the triad. In fact, the seventh chord—rather than the triad—is the principal sonority in jazz. All five qualities of seventh chord are common, including the major seventh chord (MM7), which is rare in Classical music.[2] The table in Example 26.3 names the five qualities of seventh chord (using jazz terms) and includes the abbreviations for these qualities. The table also shows the chord symbols for seventh chords (built on C) and lists the function(s) associated with each quality.[3]

Seventh Chord Name	Quality	Symbol	Function(s)
Major seventh	MM7	Cmaj7	T, PD
Dominant seventh	Mm7	C7	D
Minor seventh	mm7	Cm7	T, PD
Half-diminished seventh	ø7	Cm7♭5	PD, D
Diminished seventh	°7	C°7	D

EXAMPLE 26.3   Seventh chord terms, symbols, and functions.

Quality and Function

As shown in Example 26.3, the various seventh chord qualities are associated with the three tonal functions. The major seventh chord, for example, typically functions as T or PD. For many seventh chords (major sevenths in particular), the chord seventh is a *coloristic dissonance* rather than a tendency tone that resolves in a specific manner.

In general, *diatonic* seventh chords in jazz serve the same function as diatonic triads and seventh chords in common-practice works. For example, in major keys, the diatonic seventh chord built on $\hat{1}$ is a major seventh. This chord serves the Tonic function in jazz. The seventh chord built on $\hat{4}$ is also a major seventh—this chord serves the Predominant function. The familiar dominant seventh built on $\hat{5}$ continues to function as D. The dominant seventh is also used to modulate or tonicize other chords and qualities (major and minor sevenths in particular).

As jazz is highly chromatic and often involves rapidly shifting tonal centers, the *quality* of a seventh chord can be more helpful in determining its function than its scale-degree contents.

Extensions: Ninths, Elevenths, and Thirteenths

A number of **extensions** may be added to seventh chords. These include ninths, elevenths, and thirteenths. Extensions provide coloristic dissonance and may enhance chord function.

Ninths

Chapter 20 described two qualities of dominant ninth chord heard in some Classical works: V9 and V♭9. These chords, with ninths added to V^7 chords to strengthen Dominant function, are also found in jazz. Ninths are often added to other qualities of seventh chord, including those not serving a Dominant function.

- In chord symbols, "9" always indicates a *major* ninth (M9); "♭9" specifies a m9.
    - A M9 is a compound M2; a m9 is a compound m2.
    - A M9, D, appears in both C9 and Cm9 (Examples 26.4a–b). C(♭9) contains a m9, D♭ (Example 26.4c).
- Chord symbols are usually abbreviated, with certain details implied. For example, sevenths are to be included in ninth chords, even though "7" is sometimes absent from the symbol.
    - C9, Cm9, and C(♭9) all include a m7 (Examples 26.4a–c); Cmaj9 includes a M7 (Example 26.4d).
    - The symbol Cadd9 indicates that a ninth is added to a C-major triad—*without* any seventh (Example 26.4e).

a.   b.   c.   d.   e.

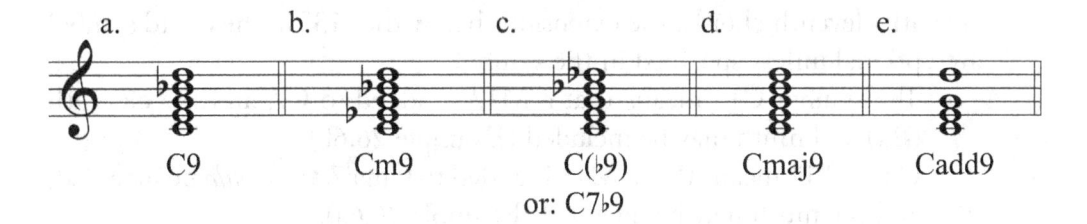

C9   Cm9   C(♭9)   Cmaj9   Cadd9
             or: C7♭9

CHAPTER 26.4 Ninth chords.

Eleventhh

An eleventh is a compound fourth above the chord root. It also results from stacking an additional third on top of a ninth chord.

- The eleventh is typically *raised* (♯11; a compound +4) when added to major seventh and dominant seventh chords (Examples 26.5a–b).
    - ♯11 avoids a clash between the eleventh and the third of the chord.
- The eleventh is usually *not* raised (a compound P4) when added to minor seventh and half-diminished seventh chords (Examples 26.5c–d).
- Extensions below the highest one indicated in the chord symbol are assumed and may or may not be included by the performer realizing the chord.
    - Although not specified by the chord symbols, ninths are included in each eleventh chord in Example 26.5.
    - The symbol Cm11 (Example 26.5c) assumes both the ninth and seventh to be included in the chord.

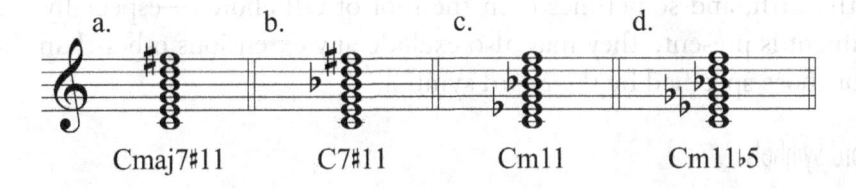

a.   b.   c.   d.

Cmaj7♯11   C7♯11   Cm11   Cm11♭5

EXAMPLE 26.5 Eleventh chords.

Thirteenths

A thirteenth is a compound sixth above the chord root, or an extra third stacked on an eleventh.

- The thirteenth is typically M13 (compound *major* sixth), regardless of the quality of the underlying seventh chord (Example 26.6a–c).
- m13 may be used to form a ♭13 chord.
    - ♭13 is most often added to the dominant seventh chord in conjunction with ♭9 (Example 26.6d).

- As with eleventh chords, the extensions below the "13" in the chord symbol are optional unless specified in the symbol.
  - The symbol C13 means that a M13 is added to C7, and the eleventh (♯11) and ninth may be included (Example 26.6b).
  - Cmaj13♯11 means that a M13 is added to Cmaj7, ♯11 *should* be included, and the ninth may be included (Example 26.6a).
  - Because it is not required by the chord symbol C7♭13♭9, the eleventh is omitted from Example 26.6d (but ♯11 would be necessary since the underlying seventh chord is a dominant seventh).
  - Although not required by the chord symbol Cm♭13♭9♭5, the eleventh is included in Example 26.6e (P11 is used because the underlying seventh chord is half-diminished).

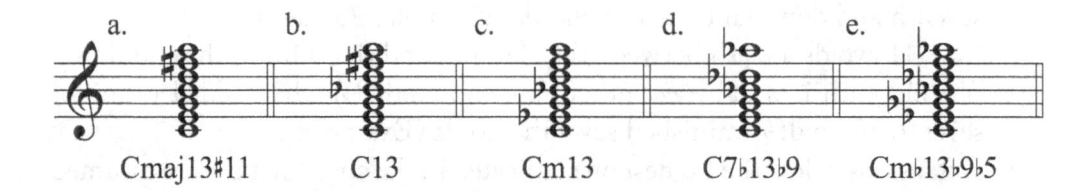

EXAMPLE 26.6 Thirteenth chords.

Fully voiced thirteenth chords are relatively rare. In general, the taller the chord, the less likely it is to be fully voiced in performance. Jazz musicians might drop the fifth, and sometimes even the root of tall chords—especially if a bass instrument is present. They may also exclude any extensions other than the seventh or those specified by the chord symbol.

Polychord Symbols

Thirteenth chords are often indicated with polychord symbols. As described in Chapter 23, a *polychord* is a combination of two or more distinct chords. Each thirteenth chord in Example 26.6 can be analyzed as a triad stacked on top of a seventh chord (the triad comprises the upper extensions—the ninth, eleventh, and thirteenth). The polychord symbol for thirteenth chords places the triad symbol above the seventh chord symbol. The chord in Example 26.6a is a D-major triad on top of Cmaj7, or D/Cmaj7.

Example 26.7 compares thirteenth-chord symbols with equivalent polychord symbols. All chords in this example are built on roots other than C. Study the symbols and the notes making up each chord.

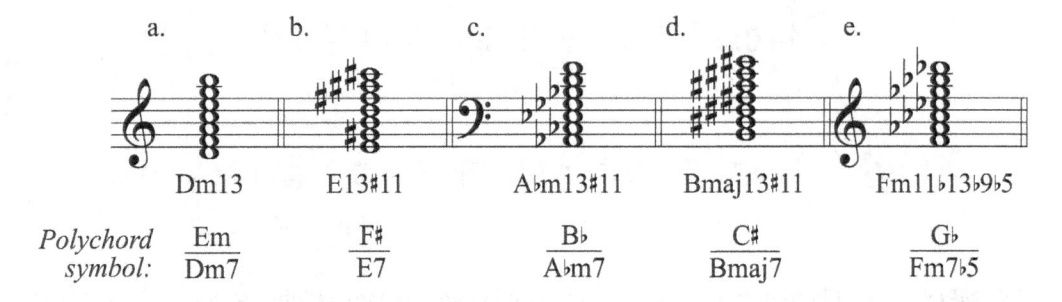

	a.	b.	c.	d.	e.
	Dm13	E13#11	A♭m13#11	Bmaj13#11	Fm11♭13♭9♭5
Polychord symbol:	Em/Dm7	F#/E7	B♭/A♭m7	C#/Bmaj7	G♭/Fm7♭5

EXAMPLE 26.7 Thirteenth chords with polychord symbols.

ii–V–I

The fundamental chord progression in jazz is ***ii–V–I***. Sevenths are almost always attached to chords, and upper extensions and alterations may be applied in a variety of ways. There are two diatonic forms of the progression:

- *Major diatonic form*: iim7–V7–Imaj7
- *Minor diatonic form*: iim7♭5–V7–im7

The ubiquitous ii–V–I progression often occurs at multiple tonal levels in a single jazz tune. Recognizing the qualities of underlying seventh chords and the root relationships among chords is critical to assessing and understanding chord function.

Example 26.8 shows the chord progression structuring the refrain, or *head*, of "Afternoon in Paris" by John Lewis.[4] The simplified Roman numerals beneath the staff indicate chord function and highlight the *major* diatonic form of the ii–V–I progression that unfolds four different times at various tonal levels. Observe the following features:

- C–[7] is an alternative symbol for Cm7.
- As the *quality* of the opening tonic chord converts from major seventh to minor seventh (Cmaj7–Cm7), its *function* changes from Tonic (I) to Predominant (ii).
  - This conversion of quality and function recurs in mm. 3–4 (B♭maj7–B♭m7).
- The last bar (m. 8), involves a *turnaround progression* (ii–V) to set up a repeat of the head.[5]

```
‖: Cmaj7  | C-7  F7  | B♭maj7 | B♭-7  E♭7 |
    I]      [ii   V     I]      [ii   V
  | A♭maj7 | D-7  G7  | Cmaj7  | D-7   G7 :‖
    I]      [ii   V     I]      [ii   V
```

EXAMPLE 26.8 Chord progression for "Afternoon in Paris" (head) by John Lewis.

In the opening bars of "Black Orpheus" (Example 26.9), two statements of the minor ii–V–I progression establish the key of A minor. A shift to the relative major key in mm. 6–7 is confirmed by ii–V–I in C major.

EXAMPLE 26.9 Luiz Bonfa, "Black Orpheus," mm. 1–7.

Chord Substitution

Chord substitution, or *reharmonization*, allows for tremendous harmonic variety and plays out in a number of ways. In general, diatonic seventh chords may substitute for one another in the same manner as diatonic triads and seventh chords do in common-practice music. For example, in a major key, vim7 and iiim7 may both substitute for Imaj7; IVmaj7 or vim7 may replace iim7 in the Predominant position; and viim7♭5 or iiim7 may substitute for V7. The various extensions that may be added to chords provide different colors without changing chord function. For example, V♭9 may substitute for V9 in certain contexts. Some additional forms of substitution are detailed below.

Modal Borrowing

Composers often borrow seventh chords from the parallel minor key—particularly those with ♭$\hat{6}$. For example, the basic ii–V–I progression may appear as iim7♭5–V7–Imaj7, with iim7♭5 borrowed from the parallel minor. Although less common, minor-mode tunes may borrow chords from the parallel major key. Composers might also change the quality of a seventh chord in a manner that does not constitute modal borrowing (this procedure is referred to as *quality conversion* in Chapter 17). Such a change of quality often involves converting a chord to a dominant seventh to modulate or tonicize another chord.

Tonicization

Any diatonic seventh chord may be converted to a dominant seventh in order to tonicize a chord a P5 below. A common example is iim7 moving to II7 (V7/V) before progressing to V7: Cmaj7–Dm7–D7–G7–Cmaj7. The secondary dominant may also replace the diatonic chord altogether: Cmaj7–D7–G7–Cmaj7.

Passing °7 Chords

Diminished seventh chords sometimes "pass" between chords a whole step apart, where they act as linear embellishments but also tonicize the chord to which they resolve. In Example 26.10, C♯°7 arises from chromatic passing motion in the bass (C–C♯–D) and functions as vii°7/ii, expanding the motion from T to PD.

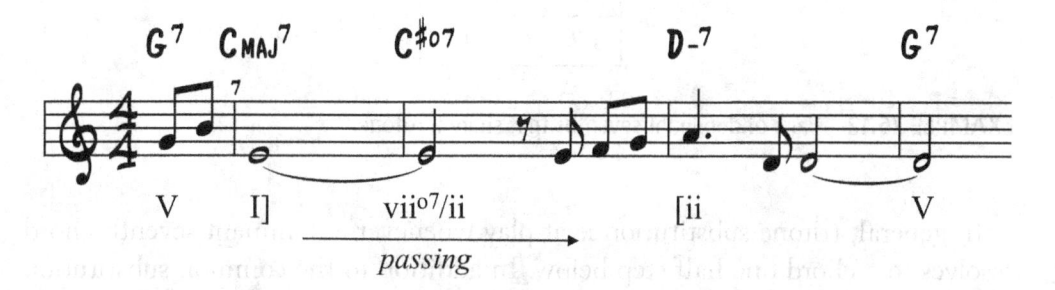

EXAMPLE 26.10 Bonfa, "Black Orpheus," mm. 7–10.

Tritone Substitution

Compare the two dominant seventh chords in Example 26.11. These chords share the same tritone (enharmonically)—the third of one is the seventh of the other, and vice versa. The shared tritone makes these chords interchangeable, meaning that either may substitute for the other. This technique, known as *tritone substitution*, is very common in jazz.[6]

EXAMPLE 26.11 Two dominant seventh chords that share the same (enharmonic) tritone.

Consider the standard progression Dm7–G7–Cmaj7 (ii7–V7–Imaj7) in C major. D♭7 may substitute for G7: Dm7–D♭7–Cmaj7 (ii7–♭II7–Imaj7). When this occurs, the tendency tones forming the tritone in D♭7 resolve in the same directions as they would in G7: C♭ (=B) ↗ C; F ↘ E. Conversely, G7 may substitute for D♭7 in the key of G♭ major: A♭m7–G7–G♭maj7 (ii7–♭II7–Imaj7).

With twelve dominant seventh chords in total, there are six pairs of dominant sevenths that share a tritone and may substitute for one another. These pairs are listed in Example 26.12. The roots of the chords in each pair are a tritone apart.

C7	↔	F♯7
C♯7	↔	G7
D7	↔	A♭7
E♭7	↔	A7
E7	↔	B♭7
F7	↔	B7

EXAMPLE 26.12 Pairs of dominant sevenths that share a tritone.[7]

In general, tritone substitution is at play whenever a dominant seventh chord resolves to a chord one half step below. In addition to the common substitution of ♭II7 for V7, tritone substitution may occur on a secondary tonal level as a tonicization, or be part of a modulation. For example, with the motion ♭III7–ii7, ♭III7 is the tritone substitute for VI7, or V7/ii; ii7 is either tonicized momentarily, or it assumes tonic status (i7) for a longer period.

Example 26.13 diagrams chords from the verse of "The Girl From Ipanema" by Antonio Carlos Jobim. This progression features several of the substitution techniques described above. In m. 3, II7 appears in place of iim7—a result of quality conversion. While this dominant seventh *could* resolve as V7/V, it instead changes to the diatonic form (iim7) in m. 5. In m. 6, ♭II7 serves as the tritone substitute for V7. After a return to Imaj7 in m. 7, the tritone substitute reappears in the turnaround at m. 8—this time with ♭5 to vary its color.

F Maj7		G7	
--------		----	
Imaj7		II7	

| G-7 | G♭7 | F Maj7 | G♭7(♭5) :‖
| iim7 | ♭II7 | Imaj7 | ♭II7(♭5) |

EXAMPLE 26.13 Chord progression for "The Girl From Ipanema" (verse) by Antonio Carlos Jobim.

One final note regarding chord substitution in general: while options for chord substitution are numerous, any substitution must support the melody of a tune and not clash with it.

Form and Progression in Pop and Jazz

Jazz standards and popular songs exhibit a variety of forms. Two common designs, AABA and strophic form, are described in this section. Several prominent chord progressions are explored as well. For specific examples of these forms and progressions, see the List of Supplemental Musical Examples (online).

AABA Form

AABA form is also known as *standard song form*, or *32-bar form*. This form strikes an effective balance between repetition and contrast. Features of AABA form include:

- An eight-measure A section known as the **refrain**, or *head*
  - The refrain presents the main melody and chord progressions in the tonic key.
  - The refrain often consists of two four-measure phrases, in which case it is either a period structure or a phrase group (see Chapter 13).
  - After its initial presentation, the refrain repeats—often with new lyrics and some degree of melodic variation, and perhaps with altered chord progressions (resulting from reharmonization or a different cadential ending).
- An eight-measure B section called the **bridge**[8]
  - The bridge provides contrast to the refrain. It generally features a new melody, a new chord progression (often in a different key), and new lyrics (often expressing a sentiment either amplifying or contrasting that of the refrain lyrics).
- A return of the refrain to close the form
  - This final statement of the A material is often extended and varied.
- To summarize AABA form and its typical proportions: A (8 bars) + A (8 bars) + B (8 bars) + A (8 bars) = 32 bars.

- In addition:
  - Some sections may be more or less than eight bars.
  - Part or all of the AABA structure may repeat. For example, AABABA is a common expansion of the basic 32-bar design.
    - Portions of the structure might repeat numerous times to support instrumental solos and improvisation.
  - The AABA structure might be preceded by an introduction, and it might close with an outro, or *coda*.

Strophic Form

Strophic form is a simple structure consisting of a series of verses: V–V–V–V. The number of verses is variable. All verses are usually in the same key, set to the same chord progression, and feature the same basic melody. The element that changes from verse to verse is the lyrics. The main melody remains fundamentally unchanged from one verse to the next, but it is typically varied or elaborated to a certain extent. Strophic form is common to folk- and blues-based styles of popular music.

The 12-Bar Blues Progression

In many strophic blues songs, each verse is structured by the ***12-bar blues progression***. This chord progression unfolds over twelve measures partitioned into three lines of four bars each. See Example 26.14.

$$\|: \text{I} \quad | \quad (\text{IV} \quad | \quad \text{I}) \quad | \quad \quad |$$

$$| \text{IV} \quad | \quad \quad | \quad \text{I} \quad | \quad \quad |$$

$$| \text{V} \quad | \quad (\text{IV}) \quad | \quad \text{I} \quad | \quad (\text{V}) :\|$$

EXAMPLE 26.14 The 12-bar blues progression.

The 12-bar blues progression is a pattern of the primary chords I, IV, and V, with chord changes occurring at specific points in the structure. The chords enclosed in parentheses in Example 26.14 depict optional chord changes. For example, the tonic chord might occupy the entire first line (bars 1–4), or IV might appear in bar 2 (in which case I returns in bar 3). The (V) at the end of bar 12 is an optional turnaround figure that helps set up a repeat of the entire progression—and the start of a new verse.

The 12-bar blues progression is the most ubiquitous chord progression in popular music—occurring in blues, rock, and many other styles.

Other Forms

Verse-Chorus Strophic Form

In *verse-chorus strophic form* (V-C strophic), a series of verses alternate with a chorus: V–C–V–C–V–C. The relationship among verses is the same as in simple strophic form, with new lyrics set to the same music. The recurring chorus is invariant, with the same lyrics set to the same music. The melodic and harmonic material of the chorus typically differs from that of the verses. Instrumental solos may unfold at any point in the form and usually occur over either the V or C material. The chorus often repeats several times at the end of the song.

Hybrid Form

Hybrid forms, common to pop and rock songs, add a bridge (B) to the verse-chorus strophic design: V–C–V–C–B–V–C. The bridge can appear at any point in the form, and the precise sequence of V, C, and B is variable. As in AABA form, the bridge might provide contrast on multiple levels. The bridge often features lyrics but may also serve as a section for instrumental solos.

Other Chord Progressions

The Doo-Wop Progression (I–vi–IV–V)

The **doo-wop progression**, also known as the *'50s progression*, is the short harmonic pattern I–vi–IV–V. Repetitions of the doo-wop progression might lay the harmonic foundation for an entire song or a substantial song section (such as the A section of AABA form). The doo-wop progression often occurs in conjunction with a compound duple meter. It appears extensively in the "doo-wop" music of the 1950s and 1960s but is found in many other styles as well. The progression conforms to tonal syntax, with vi either prolonging T or initiating PD.

The Axis Progression (I–V–vi–IV)

The *axis progression* underlies many pop and rock songs from the 1970s through the present day. There are four *rotations* of this progression that each begin on a different chord but preserve the ordering of chords.[9] The two most common rotations are I–V–vi–IV and vi–IV–I–V. The other two rotations, encountered less frequently, are IV–I–V–vi and V–vi–IV–I. Regardless of the rotation, a degree of tonal ambiguity is built into the axis progression, as V never resolves directly to I. In the two rotations beginning on vi and IV, a conflict between the major and Aeolian modes can arise. For example, vi–IV–I–V might be heard as i–VI–III–VII, with the initial chord heard as tonic and the final subtonic chord serving a weak Dominant function.

Applications

Exercises

1. Spell the following chords using accidentals as needed. Include all extensions below the highest one indicated (assume the typical qualities of extensions unless alterations are specified).

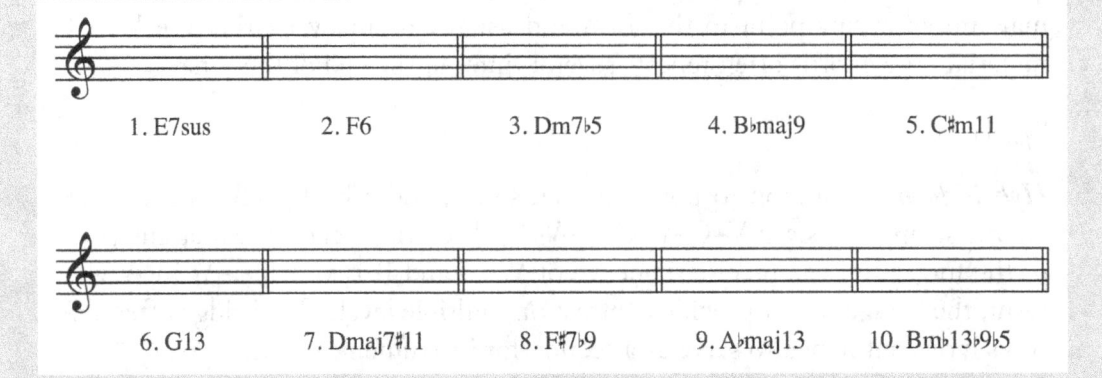

   1. E7sus 2. F6 3. Dm7♭5 4. B♭maj9 5. C♯m11

   6. G13 7. Dmaj7♯11 8. F♯7♭9 9. A♭maj13 10. B♭m13♭9♭5

2. Apply symbols to the chords below. For thirteenth chords, provide both the full label (showing all extensions and alterations) and the polychord symbol.

Brain Teaser

Consider the pitch content of an F6 chord. What Roman numeral would apply to this chord in the key of C major?

Exploring Music

Examine various lead sheets. Study the chord symbols, and consider how the harmonies support the notated melody. Select several chord symbols, and spell the chords in the staff (as in Exercise 1 above). Search for and mark any instances of the fundamental ii–V–I progression.

Thinking Critically

1. Apply Roman numerals to the following progressions:

    A. Dmaj7–Bm7–B♭7–B♭7/A♭–E♭maj7/G–A7–Dmaj7

    B. Dmaj7–Bm7–B♭7–A7–Dmaj7

2. Consider the G♭7♭5 chord from Example 26.13 (m. 8). If this same chord occurred in the key of B♭ major, and it progressed to an F7 chord, what Roman numeral would apply to it? (You might find it helpful to think enharmonically.)

Notes

1 G7/B is V$^6_5$/V in F major; it is V$^6_5$/♭III in A major.
2 In addition to the five qualities of seventh chord described in Chapter 5, a major seventh is sometimes added to a minor triad, forming a mM7 chord.
3 In practice, different chord symbols are used for the same chord. For example, Cm7 may be indicated by the symbols Cmin7 or C–7. The symbols used in this chapter are some of the more commonly encountered ones. To become familiar and fluent with alternative chord symbols, the reader is encouraged to explore lead sheets, comprehensive books on jazz theory, and online resources.
4 The chord progression diagrams and jazz excerpts in this chapter are set in the "handwritten" font commonly found in jazz notation (particularly in *fake books*, which are collections of lead sheets).
5 Turnaround progressions often involve the submediant seventh chord: vi7–ii7–V7.
6 Tritone substitution is also referred to as "flat-five substitution."
7 Enharmonic equivalence applies: F♯7 = G♭7, C♯7 = D♭7, and so on.
8 The bridge is also known as the "release," or the "middle eight."
9 The axis progression is so named for two reasons. An "axis" is a line about which a body rotates, and there are four different *rotations* of the progression. Its name also derives from the song "4 Chords" by comedic musical group The Axis of Awesome (viewable on YouTube). This song is a parodic medley of numerous pop songs that employ various rotations of the progression. For a detailed discussion of the axis progression, see Mark Richards, "Tonal Ambiguity in Popular Music's Axis Progressions," *Music Theory Online* 23.3 (2017).

Appendix
List of Set Classes

This list shows all set classes that contain between three and nine pitch classes. The outer columns show the prime form for each set class, and complementary set classes are organized on the same row. For example, trichord [012] and nonachord [012345678], found on the top row of the list, are complementary set classes. Interval-class vectors are shown in the columns closest to the prime-form columns. (Complementary hexachords share the same ic vector, and unpaired hexachords are self-complementary.)

The middle column, "T/I Symmetry," describes the transpositional and inversional symmetry of each set class by indicating the number of T- and I-operations that map the set onto itself. This property is the same for complementary set classes. For example, "2/2" specifies that two different T-operations and two different I-operations map tetrachord [0167] onto itself. (The minimum number of T-operations is always 1, to account for T_0). Dividing 24 by the total number of T- and I-operations reveals the number of unique members in a set class. For example, there are 24 unique members of set-class [0157]: 24 ÷ 1 (1 T-operation + 0 I-operations) = 24; there are six unique members of set-class [0167]: 24 ÷ 4 (2 T-operations + 2 I-operations) = 6.

Trichords	ic vector	T/I Symmetry	ic vector	Nonachords
[012]	<210000>	1/1	<876663>	[012345678]
[013]	<111000>	1/0	<777663>	[012345679]
[014]	<101100>	1/0	<767763>	[012345689]
[015]	<100110>	1/0	<766773>	[012345789]
[016]	<100011>	1/0	<766674>	[012346789]
[024]	<020100>	1/1	<686763>	[01234568T]
[025]	<011010>	1/0	<677673>	[01234578T]
[026]	<010101>	1/0	<676764>	[01234678T]

(Continued)

Appendix

Trichords	ic vector	T/I Symmetry	ic vector	Nonachords
[027]	<010020>	1/1	<676683>	[01235678T]
[036]	<002001>	1/1	<668664>	[01234679T]
[037]	<001110>	1/0	<667773>	[01235679T]
[048]	<000300>	3/3	<666963>	[01245689T]

Tetrachords	ic vector	T/I Symmetry	ic vector	Octachords
[0123]	<321000>	1/1	<765442>	[01234567]
[0124]	<221100>	1/0	<665542>	[01234568]
[0125]	<211110>	1/0	<655552>	[01234578]
[0126]	<210111>	1/0	<654553>	[01234678]
[0127]	<210021>	1/1	<654463>	[01235678]
[0134]	<212100>	1/1	<656542>	[01234569]
[0135]	<121110>	1/0	<565552>	[01234579]
[0136]	<112011>	1/0	<556453>	[01234679]
[0137]	<111111>	1/0	<555553>	[01235679]
[0145]	<201210>	1/1	<645652>	[01234589]
[0146]	<111111>	1/0	<555553>	[01234689]
[0147]	<102111>	1/0	<546553>	[01235689]
[0148]	<101310>	1/0	<545752>	[01245689]
[0156]	<200121>	1/1	<644563>	[01234789]
[0157]	<110121>	1/0	<554563>	[01235789]
[0158]	<101220>	1/1	<545662>	[01245789]
[0167]	<200022>	2/2	<644464>	[01236789]
[0235]	<122010>	1/1	<566452>	[02345679]
[0236]	<112101>	1/0	<556543>	[01345679]
[0237]	<111120>	1/0	<555562>	[01245679]
[0246]	<030201>	1/1	<474643>	[0123468T]
[0247]	<021120>	1/0	<465562>	[0123568T]
[0248]	<020301>	1/1	<464743>	[0124568T]
[0257]	<021030>	1/1	<465472>	[0123578T]
[0258]	<012111>	1/0	<456553>	[0124578T]
[0268]	<020202>	2/2	<464644>	[0124678T]
[0347]	<102210>	1/1	<546652>	[01345689]
[0358]	<012120>	1/1	<456562>	[0134578T]
[0369]	<004002>	4/4	<448444>	[0134679T]

Appendix

Pentachords	ic vector	T/I Symmetry	ic vector	Septachords
[01234]	<432100>	1/1	<654321>	[0123456]
[01235]	<332110>	1/0	<554331>	[0123457]
[01236]	<322111>	1/0	<544332>	[0123467]
[01237]	<321121>	1/0	<543342>	[0123567]
[01245]	<322210>	1/0	<544431>	[0123458]
[01246]	<231211>	1/0	<453432>	[0123468]
[01247]	<222121>	1/0	<444342>	[0123568]
[01248]	<221311>	1/0	<443532>	[0124568]
[01256]	<311221>	1/0	<533442>	[0123478]
[01257]	<221131>	1/0	<443352>	[0123578]
[01258]	<212221>	1/0	<434442>	[0124578]
[01267]	<310132>	1/0	<532353>	[0123678]
[01268]	<220222>	1/1	<442443>	[0124678]
[01346]	<223111>	1/0	<445332>	[0123469]
[01347]	<213211>	1/0	<435432>	[0123569]
[01348]	<212320>	1/1	<434541>	[0124569]
[01356]	<222121>	1/1	<444342>	[0123479]
[01357]	<131221>	1/0	<353442>	[0123579]
[01358]	<122230>	1/0	<344451>	[0124579]
[01367]	<212122>	1/0	<434343>	[0123679]
[01368]	<122131>	1/0	<344352>	[0124679]
[01369]	<114112>	1/0	<336333>	[0134679]
[01457]	<212221>	1/0	<434442>	[0145679]
[01458]	<202420>	1/0	<424641>	[0124589]
[01468]	<121321>	1/0	<343542>	[0124689]
[01469]	<113221>	1/0	<335442>	[0134689]
[01478]	<202321>	1/1	<424542>	[0125689]
[01568]	<211231>	1/0	<433452>	[0125679]
[02346]	<232201>	1/1	<454422>	[0234568]
[02347]	<222220>	1/0	<444441>	[0134568]
[02357]	<132130>	1/0	<354351>	[0234579]
[02358]	<123121>	1/0	<345342>	[0234679]
[02368]	<122212>	1/0	<344433>	[0135679]
[02458]	<122311>	1/0	<344532>	[0134579]
[02468]	<040402>	1/1	<262623>	[012468T]
[02469]	<032221>	1/1	<254442>	[013468T]
[02479]	<032140>	1/1	<254361>	[013568T]
[03458]	<212320>	1/1	<434541>	[0134578]

Appendix

Hexachords	ic vector	T/I Symmetry	Hexachords
[012345]	<543210>	1/1	–
[012346]	<443211>	1/0	–
[012347]	<433221>	1/0	[012356]
[012348]	<432321>	1/1	[012456]
[012357]	<342231>	1/0	–
[012358]	<333231>	1/0	[012457]
[012367]	<422232>	1/0	–
[012368]	<332232>	1/0	[012467]
[012369]	<324222>	1/1	[013467]
[012378]	<421242>	1/1	[012567]
[012458]	<323421>	1/0	–
[012468]	<241422>	1/0	–
[012469]	<233331>	1/0	[013468]
[012478]	<322332>	1/0	[012568]
[012479]	<233241>	1/0	[013568]
[012569]	<313431>	1/0	[013478]
[012578]	<322242>	1/0	–
[012579]	<232341>	1/1	[013578]
[012678]	<420243>	2/2	–
[013457]	<333321>	1/0	[023458]
[013458]	<323430>	1/0	–
[013469]	<225222>	1/0	–
[013479]	<224322>	1/1	[013569]
[013579]	<142422>	1/0	–
[013679]	<224223>	2/0	–
[014568]	<322431>	1/0	–
[014579]	<223431>	1/0	–
[014589]	<303630>	3/3	–
[014679]	<224232>	1/1	[023679]
[023457]	<343230>	1/1	–
[023468]	<242412>	1/0	–
[023469]	<234222>	1/1	[023568]
[023579]	<143241>	1/0	–
[024579]	<143250>	1/1	–
[02468T]	<060603>	6/6	–

Credits

"Black Orpheus" a/k/a "Manha de Carnaval"
  By Luiz Bonfa and Antonio Carlos Jobim
  Copyright © 1959 (Renewed) Les Nouvelles Editions Meridian
  All rights administered by Chappell & Co., Inc. All rights reserved
  Used by permission of Alfred Music

"Diminished Fifth" from *Mikrokosmos*, Sz.107 by Béla Bartók
  © Copyright 1940 by Hawkes & Son (London) Ltd.
  Reprinted by permission of Boosey & Hawkes, Inc.

Excerpt from "Ekstase" by Alma Mahler
  © 1924 Josef Weinberger, Vienna
  Reprinted by permission of the copyright holder

"From the Island of Bali" from *Mikrokosmos*, Sz.107 by Béla Bartók
  © Copyright 1940 by Hawkes & Son (London) Ltd.
  Reprinted by permission of Boosey & Hawkes, Inc.

"Little Study" from *Mikrokosmos*, Sz.107 by Béla Bartók
  © Copyright 1940 by Hawkes & Son (London) Ltd.
  Reprinted by permission of Boosey & Hawkes, Inc.

"Lola"
  Words and Music by Ray Davies
  Copyright © 1970 (Renewed) Abkco Music Inc. and Davray Music Ltd.
  All rights for Davray Music Ltd. Administered by Unichappell Music Inc.
  All rights reserved
  Used by permission of Alfred Music

Minuet and Trio from *Suite für Klavier*, Op. 25 by Arnold Schoenberg
   Used by permission of Belmont Music Publishers, Los Angeles

"Prologue," No. 10 from *Little Piano Book*
   By Vincent Persichetti
   Copyright © 1954 by Elkan-Vogel, Inc. Copyright renewed
   Theodore Presser Company authorized representative
   All rights reserved. Used with permission

Serenade en A by Igor Stravinsky
   © Copyright 1926 by Hawkes & Son (London) Ltd.
   Reprinted by permission of Boosey & Hawkes, Inc.

Trio for Violin Cello and Piano
   By Ellen Taaffe Zwilich
   Copyright © 1990 by Merion Music, Inc.
   Theodore Presser Company authorized representative
   All rights reserved. Used with permission

"You Don't Own Me"
   Words and Music by John Madara and Dave White
   Copyright © 1963 (Renewed) Unichappell Music Inc.
   All rights reserved
   Used by permission of Alfred Music

Notes on the Text

Chapter 12

The passage by J. S. Bach in Example 12.15 appears also in Miguel A. Roig-Francolí, *Harmony in Context*, 2nd ed. (New York: McGraw-Hill, 2011), 367 (Example 15.15b). There, the author labels the chord under scrutiny as IV^7. Some sources indeed label such chords as subdominant sevenths.

Chapter 17

A similar reduction of the excerpt by Brahms on p. 175 (Example 17.12) can be found in *Harmony in Context*, 2nd ed., by Miguel A. Roig-Francolí (Example 23.10, p. 548). My exposure to this passage as a prime example of modal mixture was through *Harmony in Context*. The orchestral reductions appearing in both books are literal transcriptions of the original score.

Chapter 20

The excerpt from "Ekstase" by Alma Mahler on p. 201 (Example 20.5) appears also in *Harmony in Context*, 2nd ed., by Miguel A. Roig-Francolí (Example 27.10, p. 635). I am grateful to the author and his text for introducing me to this striking example of altered dominants and also to *Five Songs* as a whole.

I adopt the same passage from "Der Doppelgänger" (Example 20.7, p. 202) to exemplify an altered dominant chord as appears in *Harmony in Context*, 2nd ed., by Miguel A. Roig-Francolí (Example 27.13, p. 638).

Chapter 21

The scope of Chapter 21 is inspired in large part by Chapter 31 from *Harmony in Context*, 2nd ed., by Miguel A. Roig-Francolí (pp. 717–45). In particular, I adopt the same version of the Tonnetz as Roig-Francolí—the "parsimonious Tonnetz" organized by minor thirds (horizontal rows) and major thirds (vertical columns). This particular Tonnetz is described extensively by Richard Cohn in "Neo-Riemannian Operations, Parsimonious Trichords, and Their *Tonnetz* Representations," *Journal of Music Theory* 41.1 (1997): 1–66. (Roig-Francolí cites Cohn's article on p. 729n3.)

The analysis presented as Example 21.9 (p. 219) derives from Guy Capuzzo, "Neo-Riemannian Theory and the Analysis of Pop-Rock Music," *Music Theory Spectrum* 26.2 (2004), 181–2. Specifically, the transformational section of the analysis in mm. 122–27 is by Capuzzo; the framing portions highlighting functional and cadential activity in the keys of D and F major are my own.

Chapter 23

A similar assessment (in the context of centricity) of the passage from Bartok's "Little Study" (Example 23.1, pp. 238–39) appears in Miguel A. Roig-Francolí, *Understanding Post-Tonal Music*, 5–6.

The passage from Bartok's *Bagatelle*, Op. 6, No. 2 on pp. 239–40 (Example 23.3) is discussed in the same context of centricity and symmetry in Joseph N. Straus, *Introduction to Post-Tonal Theory*, 4th ed. (New York and London: Norton, 2016), 237–38; and also in Jane Piper Clendinning and Elizabeth West Marvin, *The Musician's Guide to Theory and Analysis*, 3rd ed. (New York and London: Norton, 2016), 742–45.

My initial exposure to several of the excerpts in Chapters 22 and 23 was through Stefan Kostka, *Materials and Techniques of Twentieth-Century Music*, 3rd ed. (New Jersey: Pearson Prentice Hall, 2006). I adopt related or overlapping versions of these passages as Examples 22.2, 22.17, 23.9, and 23.11 (all analytic annotations are my own). I thank the author for introducing me to these crystal-clear examples of scalar and harmonic trends in post-tonal music. (The 5th edition of this book, featuring coauthor Matthew Santa, was published by Routledge in 2018).

Chapter 24

Anton Webern's *Five Movements for String Quartet*, Op. 5, III has been analyzed extensively. My own discussion of an excerpt from this movement appears on pp. 254–55 (Example 24.9). A similar and more comprehensive analysis of the entire movement appears in Miguel A. Roig-Francolí, *Understanding Post-Tonal Music*, 111–20.

The analysis and discussion of Alban Berg's "Schlafend trägt man mich" on pp. 254–56 (Examples 24.10–24.11) is based on Joseph Straus's lucid analysis of the same passage in *Introduction to Post-Tonal Theory*, 4th ed., 143–48. Straus cites other texts referencing this song on p. 158.

Index of Musical Examples

Common-practice and post-tonal works are arranged by composer name; popular songs and jazz tunes by song title. Pages listed include references to an example.

"Afternoon in Paris (John Lewis) 275–6
"Amazing Grace" (Traditional) 227
"Atlantis" (Donovan) 171

Bach, Johann Sebastian: Chorale 6, "Christus, der ist mein Leben" 169; Chorale 14, "O Herre Gott, dein göttlich Wort" 102; Chorale 22, "Schmücke dich, o liebe Seele" 94; Chorale 25, "Wo soll ich fliehen hin" 125–6, 171; Chorale 40, "Ach Gott und Herr" 152; Chorale 58, "Herzlich lieb hab' ich dich, o Herr" 103; Chorale 117, "Nun ruhen alle Wälder" 126; Chorale 129, "Keinen hat Gott verlassen" 163–4; Chorale 146, "Werr nur den lieben Gott läßt walten" 102; Chorale 196, "Da der Herr Christ zu Tische sass" 106, 117n3; Fugue No. 2 in C minor, BWV 847 92, 95, 171; Little Prelude in C Major, BWV 924 145; "Soll den der Pales Opfer" (Recitative) from Cantata No. 208 112–13

Bartók, Béla: *Bagatelle*, Op. 6, No. 2 239–40; "Diminished Fifth," No. 101 from *Mikrokosmos*, Book 4 230–1; "From the Island of Bali," No. 109 from *Mikrokosmos*, Book 4 253–4; "Little Study," No. 77 from *Mikrokosmos*, Book 3 238–9

Beethoven, Ludwig van: Bagatelle in C Major, Op. 119, No. 8 201–2; Piano Sonata in C Minor, Op. 13, No. 8, *Pathétique*, II 121–2, 132, 153; Piano Sonata in C Minor, Op. 13, No. 8, *Pathétique*, III 182; Piano Sonata in C-sharp Minor, Op. 27, No. 2, *Moonlight*, I 178; Piano Sonata in E Major, Op. 14, No. 1, I 170; Piano Sonata in E Minor, Op. 90, No. 27, II 197; Piano Sonata in E-flat Major, Op. 81a, No. 26, I 194; Piano Sonata in G Major, Op. 14, No. 2, I 189–90; String Quartet in G Major, Op. 18, No. 2, III 181–2; Symphony No. 5 in C Minor, Op. 67, I 130–1; Symphony No. 9, IV 24–5

Berg, Alban: "Schlafend trägt man mich," No. 2 from *Four Songs*, Op. 2 254–6, 258, 259n8

"Black Orpheus" (Luiz Bonfa) 276–7

Brahms, Johannes: "Lied" from *Sechs Gesänge*, Op. 3, No. 4 211–13; Symphony No. 3, II 175

Chopin, Frédéric: Mazurka, Op. 17, No. 3 170; Prelude in A Major, Op. 28, No. 7 152–3; Prelude in G Minor, Op. 28, No. 22 186

"Come, Thou Fount of Every Blessing" (Hymn) 134

"Creep" (Radiohead) 171

Debussy, Claude: "Canope," No. 10 from *Preludes*, Book 2 244–5; *L'isle joyeuse*, L. 109 237; "La Cathédrale engloutie," No. 10 from *Preludes*, Book 1 239–41, 243–4; String Quartet in G Minor, Op. 10, I 226; "Voiles," from *Preludes*, Book 1 231–2

Frank, César: Sonata in A Major for Violin and Piano, I 205–6

"The General Specific" (Band of Horses) 154
"The Girl From Ipanema" (Antonio Carlos Jobim) 278–9

Handel, George Frideric: Passacaglia in G Minor, HWV 432 145

Haydn, Joseph: Piano Sonata in F Major, Hob. XVI/9, III 106; String Quartet in G Major, Op. 17, No. 5, III 124, 132

"Hello" (Lionel Richie) 178–9, 198n2

Ives, Charles: "The Cage" from *114 Songs*, No. 64 242; Piano Sonata No. 2 (*Concord*), II. "Hawthorne" 243

Le Beau, Luise Adolpha: *Romanze*, Op. 35 169

Liszt, Franz: *Bagatelle sans tonalité*, S. 216a 214–15, 222n7, n8; "Blume und Duft," S. 324 213–16, 222n6; Grand Étude No. 10 in F Minor, S. 137 105

"Lola" (The Kinks) 170

Mahler, Alma: "Ekstase" from *Five Songs*, No. 2 201
Mendelssohn, Felix: *Song Without Words*, Op. 53, No. 1 204
Mozart, Wolfgang Amadeus: "Der Hölle Rache kocht in meinem Herzen" from *The Magic Flute*, K. 620 412; Fantasia in C Minor, K. 475 195; Piano Sonata in A Major, K. 331, I 134–5; Piano Sonata in A Major, K. 331, III 161; Piano Sonata in B-flat Major, K. 333, I 185; Piano Sonata in B-flat Major, K. 333, II 135–6, 159; Piano Sonata in B-flat Major, K. 333, III 138; Piano Sonata in C Major, K. 545, I 121, 132; Piano Sonata in D Major, K. 284, III 124, 132, 165; Piano Sonata in G Major, K. 283, I 113; String Quartet in D Major, K. 155, I 163–4
"My Country, 'Tis of Thee" 133

"Ode to Joy" 24–5, 28n6
"The Office" (theme song) 221

Persichetti, Vincent: "Prologue," No. 10 from *Little Piano Book*, Op. 60 242

Rachmaninoff, Sergei: Prelude in A Minor, Op. 32, No. 8 220–1
Ravel, Maurice: "Empress of the Pagodas" from *Mother Goose Suite* 227–8, 245

Scarlatti, Domenico: Sonata in D Major, K. 21 116
Schoenberg, Arnold: Minuet and Trio from *Suite für Klavier*, Op. 25 265–6, 269
Schubert, Franz: "Der Doppelgänger" from *Schwanengesang*, D. 957, No. 13 202; "Der Neugierige" from *Die schöne Müllerin*, Op. 25 192; "Die Sterne," Op. 96, No. 1 173; Ecossaise No. 7, D. 145 189; Impromptu in B-flat Major, D. 935, No. 3 156; "Sehnsucht," D. 310b 205; Sonata No. 21 in B-Flat Major, D. 960, IV 219; String Quartet No. 3 in B-flat Major, D. 36, III 195–6; Waltz No. 14, D. 365 191–2, 198; Waltz No. 33, D. 365 188–9
Schumann, Clara: *Drei Romanzen*, Op. 21, No. 1 166, 207; "Ich Hab' In Deinem Auge," Op. 13, No. 5 120
Schumann, Robert: "A Chorale" from *Album for the Young*, Op. 68, No. 4 153; "An Important Event" from *Scenes from Childhood*, Op. 15, No. 6 157; "Burla" from *Albumblätter*, Op. 124, No. 12 181–2; "Leides Ahnung" from *Albumblätter*, Op. 124, No. 2 200; "Little Folk Song" from *Album for the Young*, Op. 68, No. 9 109; Nord oder Süd from *Vier Gesänge*, Op. 59, No. 1 108, 116; "Widmung" from *Myrthen*, Op. 25, No. 1 198
Scriabin, Alexander: *Fantastic Poem*, Op. 45, No. 2 236–7; Piano Sonata No. 5, Op. 53 246
Stravinsky, Igor: *Petrushka* 245–6; *Serenade in A*, I ("Hymne") 224

Wagner, Richard: Prelude from *Tristan und Isolde* 212–13, 221, 222n5
"The Wanton Song" (Led Zeppelin) 130
Webern, Anton: *Five Movements for String Quartet*, Op. 5, III 254–5; Symphony, Op. 21 267

"You Don't Own Me" (Madara and White) 47–8, 50n9

Zwilich, Ellen Taaffe: *Trio for Violin, Cello, and Piano*, III 232–3

Index of Terms and Concepts

$\hat{1}$ *see* tonic scale degree
$\hat{2}$ *see* supertonic scale degree
$\hat{3}$ *see* mediant scale degree
$\hat{4}$ *see* subdominant scale degree
$\hat{5}$ *see* dominant scale degree
$\hat{6}$ *see* submediant scale degree
$\hat{7}$ *see* leading tone; *see* subtonic scale degree

I *see* tonic triad; in minor (Picardy third) 171
I^{5-6} *see* 5-6 technique
i *see* tonic triad
♭II^6 *see* the Neapolitan chord
II 171
ii *see* supertonic triad
ii^6 106
ii^7 *see* supertonic seventh chord
ii^o *see* supertonic triad; as borrowed chord 169
$ii^{\emptyset 7}$ *see* supertonic seventh chord; as borrowed chord 169
♭III 168, 172, 176n5
III *see* mediant triad
iii *see* mediant triad
iii^6 *see* 5-6 technique
IV *see* subdominant triad
iv *see* subdominant triad; as borrowed chord 168–9, 171
V *see* dominant triad
V+ *see* altered dominant chords
V^{5-6} *see* 5-6 technique
V^{6-5}_{4-3} *see* cadential six-four chord
V^7 *see* dominant seventh chord
V^7 inversions (V^6_5, V^4_3, V^2) *see* dominant seventh chord
V^7_+ *see* altered dominant chords
V^{o4}_3 *see* altered dominant chords
V^{o7} *see* altered dominant chords
V^{8-7} *see* the passing seventh
V^9 *see* dominant ninth chords
$V^{♭9}$ *see* dominant ninth chords
v *see* dominant triad
♭VI 168, 170, 172–3, 176n5
VI *see* submediant triad
vi *see* submediant triad
vi^6 *see* 5-6 technique

♭VII *see* subtonic triad; as borrowed chord 168–70
VII *see* subtonic triad
vii^o *see* leading-tone triad
vii^{o6} 106–8, 132
$vii^{\emptyset 7}$ *see* leading-tone seventh chord
vii^{o7} *see* leading-tone seventh chord; as borrowed chord 170

I–IV–V–I 85, 98
I–V–I *see* fundamental progression
I–V–vi–IV *see* axis progression
I–vi–IV–V *see* doo-wop progression
ii–V–I 275–6
IV–I–V–vi *see* axis progression
V–IV–I 99
V–vi–IV–I *see* axis progression
vi–IV–I–V *see* axis progression

AABA form 279–81
abrupt modulation *see* phrase modulation
abrupt shift 51
accelerando 51
accidentals 6–7; cancelation of 6–7, 15, 22, 50n6, 176n4; and interval quality 14–15; notation of 7
acoustic collection 236, 237n6
acoustic scale *see* acoustic collection
added-note chords 240–1, 271
additive meters *see* irregular meters
Aeolian 224–5, 281
aggregate 231
agogic accent 208n2, 238
alla breve 57
alterations 47, 147, 182, 200–2, 275
altered chord members *see* alterations
altered dominant chords 200–2, 207; and tonicization 201–2
alto clef 5–6, 10n2
ambiguity 140, 211–12, 222n3, 227, 281
antecedent 134–6
anticipation 91
appoggiatura 91, 222n4
arpeggiating six-four chord 109–10
asymmetrical meters *see* irregular meters
augmentation 131

augmented interval 11–13, 15
augmented scale *see* hexatonic collection
augmented sixth chords 177, 179–83
  the +6 frame 179
augmented triad 39–40, 200–2, 231
authentic cadence 132
axis of symmetry *see* symmetry
axis progression 281, 283n9

backbeat 62
bar 55
bar lines 54–5
bass arpeggiation 100; filled-in bass arpeggiation 111–12, 125–6, 181–2
bass clef 5–6
beams 52, 54–5
beat 51
beats per minute (bpm) 51
bridge 279, 281, 283n8

cadence 132–4; authentic cadence 132; deceptive cadence 133; half cadence 132–3; imperfect authentic cadence 132; perfect authentic cadence 132; Phrygian half cadence 132–3; plagal extension 134; tonicized half cadence 153
cadential six-four chord 112–14
cantus firmus 67
C clef 5–6; strategy for reading notes in 10n2
C–C pivot *see* chromatic pivot chord modulation
C–D pivot *see* chromatic pivot chord modulation
centricity 238–40; *see also* tonal center
change of position 80
change of voicing 80
chart of tonal functions 96–7
chord 39; basic inversions of 43–4; position of 43–4; seventh chords 40; triads 39–40; *see also* diatonic chords
chord inversions 43–4; *see also* inversion; prolongation
chord members 39
chord progression 80–1
chord substitution 99–100, 106, 117n3, 125, 132, 170, 181, 276–9
chord symbols (in lead-sheet notation) 47–8, 270–5, 283n3
chord voicing 78–80; change of voicing 80; change of position 80
chromatic mediants 172–3, 176n5; as key areas 188, 192, 195, 205
chromatic pivot chord modulation 188–94
chromatic planing 243–4
chromatic Predominant chords 177–83, 189
circle of fifths 35–6, 160–1, 198n3
clefs 4–6

closely related keys 160–1, 167n3
close spacing 78–9
common chord modulation *see* diatonic pivot chord modulation
common time 57–8
common-tone augmented sixth chords (CT+6) 204–6
common-tone diminished seventh chords (CT°7) 203–6
common-tone modulation 195–6
common tones 81
composite meters *see* irregular meters
compound intervals 16
compound meters 56–7
compound operations 219
conjunct motion 24, 81
consequent 134–6
consonance 11–12, 18, 39
contrary motion 66–7
contrasting period 135–6
counterpoint 67–70
CT+6 *see* common-tone augmented sixth chords
CT°7 *see* common-tone diminished seventh chords
cut time 57–8
cycles of transformations (PL, PR, and LR) 216–19

D *see* Dominant function
DC *see* deceptive cadence
D–C pivot *see* chromatic pivot chord modulation
deceptive cadence 133
deceptive resolution 99, 133, 170, 212; of secondary V^7 chords 152–4, 171
descending thirds sequence 142–3
developmental procedures 131
diatonic chords 41–3; diatonic seventh chords 42–3; diatonic triads 41–2; labeling of 44–6; names of 41; spelling 46–7
diatonic collection 223–6
diatonic modes 224–6, 237n2
diatonic pivot chord modulation 162–5
diatonic planing 243–4
diatonic scale 20; *see also* diatonic collection
diminished interval 11–12
diminished scale *see* octatonic collection
diminished seventh chord (in jazz) 271, 277
diminished triad 39–40
diminution 131
direct fifths and octaves 82, 88n5
directional tonality *see* progressive tonality
direct modulation *see* phrase modulation
disjunct motion 24, 81
dissonance 11–12, 39; perfect fourth as 68–9; *see also* dissonant prolongation; unresolved dissonance

dissonant prolongation 214–15, 222n7
distantly related keys 160–1, 167n1, 173, 188, 190–2, 195
Dominant function (D) 96–8
dominant ninth chords 199–200; *see also* extensions
dominant scale degree ($\hat{5}$) 23–4
dominant seventh chord 42–3, 118–22, 271–2; enharmonic reinterpretation of 190–2; inversions of 120–2; the passing seventh 119–20; secondary dominant seventh chords 149–54
dominant triad (V, v) 41–2, 96–7; in first inversion 100–1, 105–6
doo-wop progression 145, 281
Dorian 224–5
dot 51–3, 55
dotted value 56
double dot 52
double flat 6–7
double mixture 176n5
double neighbor *see* neighbor group
double sharp 6–7
double-tonic complex 212–13, 222n5
doubling 78; and centricity 239; with vii°6 106–7; with six-four chords 110–14; unison doubling 82–3
downbeat 55–6, 59, 62
duple meter 55–8
duplet 61
duration 51–3; notation of 54–5; and prolongation 99; serialization of 266–7
duration and repetition *see* prolongation
dynamic accent 238, 181

economy of motion 81, 104n4, 203; and triadic transformations 215–17, 222n9
elevenths 273
emb+6 *see* common-tone augmented sixth chords (CT+6)
embellishing chords 202–6; CT+6 204–6; CT°7 203–6
enharmonic equivalence 193
enharmonic intervals 16; and tritone substitution 277–9
enharmonic keys 35–6, 194
enharmonic pitches 7
enharmonic reinterpretation 190–4, 205–6
escape tone 91
extended chords *see* extensions
extensions 272–5; elevenths 273; ninths 272–3; thirteenths 273–4

F clef 5
fifth (chord member) 39; alterations of 47, 200–2, 271; and incomplete chords 107, 119, 129

fifths sequences 140–2, 178–9
filled-in bass arpeggiation 111–12, 125–6, 181–2
first inversion 43–4; triads in 100–1, 105–9, 143–3
5-6 technique 108–9; in harmonic sequences 144
flags 52, 54
flat 3, 6–7
flat-five substitution *see* tritone substitution
flat keys 30–1
Fr+6 179–82
French augmented sixth chord (Fr+6) 179–82
frustrating the leading tone 119
fully diminished seventh chord (°7) 40, 42–3, 47, 122–4, 154–7, 202–4, 214–15, 222n8, 229–30, 271, 277; enharmonic reinterpretation of 193–4
function *see* tonal function
fundamental progression (I–V–I) 85, 98

G clef 5
German augmented sixth chord (Gr+6) 179–82, 187n4, 202–3; enharmonic reinterpretation of 190–2, 205–6
grand staff 6; four voices in 77
Gr+6 179–82, 187n4, 202–3; enharmonic reinterpretation of 190–2, 205–6
grouplets 60–1

half cadence 132–3; tonicized half cadence 153
half-diminished seventh chord (ø7) 40, 47, 42–3, 47, 118, 122–6, 154–6, 169, 271
half step 6–7, 19n1
harmonic function *see* tonal function
harmonic minor scale 28n3
harmonic sequences 140–4; descending thirds sequence 142–3; fifths sequences 140–2, 178–9; the "Pachelbel" sequence 143; parallel $^6_3$ chords 143–4
harmony 39; and post-tonal music 240–4
HC *see* half cadence
head 275, 279
hexatonic collection 232–3
hexatonic scale *see* hexatonic collection
hexatonic system 222n13
hidden fifths and octaves *see* direct fifths and octaves
hybrid forms 281

IAC *see* imperfect authentic cadence
ic *see* interval class
ic vector *see* interval-class vector
I-forms *see* row transformations
imperfect authentic cadence 132
imperfect consonances 12–14; and parallel motion 67

implied tonality 212–13
incomplete neighbors 91
incomplete triads and seventh chords 107, 119, 125, 151, 178, 201
INF *see* interval normal form
integers *see* pitch-class integers
integral serialism 266–7
interval 11–16; and accidentals 14–15; augmented 11–12; classification of 11–12; compound intervals 16; consonant 11–12; diminished 11–12; dissonant 11–12; enharmonic intervals 16; harmonic interval 11; imperfect consonances 12; inversion of 12–14; large natural intervals 12–14; major 11–12; melodic interval 11; minor 11–12; perfect 11–12; perfect consonances 12; quality 11; recognizing and labeling 12–16; simple intervals 16; size 11; small natural intervals 12
interval class 248–50; series of (in twelve-tone rows) 261–2
interval-class vector 249, 285
interval normal form 251, 258n6
inversion: of chords 43–4; of intervals 12–14; of motives 131; of pc sets 230, 249–50; and prolongation 100–1, 106–14; of seventh chords 120–4; of triads 105–14; of twelve-tone rows 261–2, 264–5
inversional equivalence 193
inversional symmetry *see* symmetry
inversion symbols 43–4, 50n7
Ionian 224–5
I-operation 249–50
irregular meters 58–9
Italian augmented sixth chord (It+6) 179–81
It+6 179–81

key 29–36; closely related keys 160–1; distantly related keys 161; enharmonic keys 35–6; flat keys 30–1; key signature 29; major keys 30–2; minor keys 33–4; parallel keys 34–5; relative keys 33; sharp keys 30
key signature *see* key

large natural intervals 12–14
leading tone ($\hat{7}$) 23–5; frustration of 119; and melodic tendency 24–6; in minor melodies 25–6; in the minor scale 21–4; as tendency tone 25, 78, 119–24, 129n2
leading-tone seventh chord 42–3, 122–4; enharmonic reinterpretation of 193–4; secondary leading-tone seventh chords 154–7
leading-tone triad (vii°) 41–2, 96–7; in first inversion 106–8, 132
lead sheet 47–8, 270

ledger lines 4
lines (of staff) 4
link 135–6
Locrian 225
LR *see* cycles of transformations
Lydian 224–5, 239
Lydian-dominant scale *see* acoustic collection

major interval 11–12
major keys 30–2
major-major seventh chord (Mm7) 40, 47, 129n6, 271
major-minor seventh chord (Mm7) 40, 47, 118–22, 149–54, 271
major pentatonic scale 226–8
major scale 20–1, 23–4; *see also* diatonic collection
major seventh chord (in jazz) 47, 271–2
major triad 39–40
measure 55
mediant scale degree ($\hat{3}$) 23–4
mediant triad (iii, III) 41–2, 96–8, 100, 171; in first inversion 108–9
melodic minor scale 28n3
melody 24–6; minor melodies 25–6; and motion 24; and musical forces 25–6, 28; tendencies of 25–6
meter 55–9; aural identification of 59; compound meters 56–7; duple meter 55–8; irregular meters 58–9; quadruple meter 55–8; regular meters 55; simple meters 56; time signatures 56–8; triple meter 55–8
metric accent 55–6, 62, 238
middle C 3
minor interval 11–12
minor keys 33–4
minor melodies 25–6
minor-minor seventh chord (mm7) 40, 47, 271
minor pentatonic scale 226–7
minor scale 21–4, 28n3
minor seventh chord (in jazz) 47, 271
minor triad 39–40
Mixolydian 224–6
modal ambiguity 211–12, 222n3
modal borrowing 168–71, 176n1, 199–200, 277
modal mixture 168–73; modal borrowing 168–71, 176n1, 199–200, 277; quality conversion 171, 176n1, 277
modes *see* diatonic modes
mod 12 258n3
modulation 160–5, 188–96; diatonic pivot chord modulation 162–5; chromatic pivot chord modulation 188–94; common-tone modulation 195–6; enharmonic reinterpretation 190–4, 205–6; phrase modulation 161, 167n2

Index of Terms and Concepts

motion between two voices 66–7; contrary 66–7; oblique 66, 82–3; parallel 67, 81–2, 143–4, and planing 243; similar 67; static 66
motive 60, 130–1; developmental procedures of 131; pitch-class sets as 247–8
multiserialism *see* integral serialism
musical form 130
mystic chord 246

natural (accidental) 6–7; and cancelation 7, 15, 22, 26, 50n6, 176n4
natural minor scale 28n3
natural scale 5, 12, 20
the Neapolitan chord ($♭II^6$) 177–9, 187n1, 189
neighbor V^6 101, 106
neighbor group 92
neighbor motion in the bass 101
neighbor six-four chord (N^6_4) 110–11, 117n6
neighbor tone 69, 89–90
neo-Riemannian theory 222n12
ninths 272–3; dominant ninth chords 199–200; as tendency tones 199–200
nonchord tones 89–92; identification of 93
noncollectional tone *see* outlier
nonfunctional chords 101, 109; cycles of transformations 216–19; embellishing chords 202–6; harmonic sequences 140–4; planing 243–4; six-four chords 109–14; suspended tonality 215–19; triadic transformations 215–16
nonfunctional pitch centricity 238–40
notation: of accidentals 6–7, 19n4; of pitch 4–7; of rhythm 54–5
note 3
notehead 4
N^6 *see* the Neapolitan chord ($♭II^6$)
N^6_4 *see* neighbor six-four chord

oblique motion 66, 82–3
octatonic collection 228–31, 253–4
octatonic scale *see* octatonic collection
octatonic system 222n13
octave equivalence 193
octaves: as intervals 12; numeric designation of 3–4
octave treble clef 187n2
offbeats 56; and syncopation 62
open spacing 78–9
outlier 233
overtone scale *see* acoustic collection

PAC *see* perfect authentic cadence
the "Pachelbel" sequence 143
pandiatonicism 224
parallel fifths and octaves 82, 117n2; and economy of motion 81; and planing 243

parallel keys 34–6; borrowed chords from 168–71
parallel motion 67, 81–2, 143–4; and planing 243
parallel period 134–5
parallel $^6_3$ chords 143–4
parsimonious voice leading 222n9; *see also* triadic transformations
passing $°7$ chords 214–15, 277
passing vii^{o6} 108
the passing seventh 119–20
passing six-four chords (P^6_4) 111–12
passing tone 69, 89–90
passport pitch (of +6 chords) 180
pc *see* pitch class
pc integers *see* pitch-class integers
pc set *see* pitch-class set
pc wheel *see* pitch-class wheel
PD *see* Predominant function
pedal point *see* pedal tone
pedal six-four *see* neighbor six-four chord
pedal tone 92
pentatonic collection 226–8
pentatonic scale *see* pentatonic collection
perfect authentic cadence 132
perfect consonances 12–14
perfect fourth as dissonance 68–9; in 4–3 suspensions 90
perfect interval 11–14
period structure 134–6; contrasting period 135–6; parallel period 134–5; *see also* phrase group
Petrushka chord 245–6
PF *see* prime form (of a set class)
P-forms *see* row transformations
phrase 132; and period structure 134–6
phrase group 136
phrase modulation 161, 167n2
Phrygian 224–6
Phrygian half cadence 132–3
Picardy third 171
pitch 3–4; enharmonic pitches 7; and frequency 3–4; letter names of 3; natural notes 3; pitch continuum 3–4
pitch class 3–4, 193, 228–33, 247–56, 260–7
pitch-class integers 228–33, 247–56, 260–7
pitch-class set 229–32, 247–56, 261–2; and segmentation 252–4
pitch-class space 215, 217, 239–40, 247–56
pitch-class wheel: introduction to 193–4; with letters 193–4, 215–16, 223, 228–9; with pc integers 228–33, 247–56, 262–3
pivot chord: chromatic pivot chord 188–94; diatonic pivot chord 162–5
pivot tone 230–1
PL *see* cycles of transformations
plagal cadence *see* plagal extension

plagal extension 134
planing 243–4
polychords 241–2, 274–5
polyrhythm 62
power chords 222n3
PR *see* cycles of transformations
Predominant function (PD) 96–8
primary mixture *see* modal borrowing
primary triads 96; in first inversion 105–6
prime form: of a motive 131; of a set class 250–2; of a twelve-tone row 261–2, 264–5
P, R, L *see* triadic transformations
progressive tonality 211
prolongation 99–101, 105–14; and chromatic Predominant chords 182–3; and embellishing chords 202–5; and harmonic sequences 140, 142; and inverted V^7 chords 120–2; and the plagal extension 134; *see also* dissonant prolongation
prototype chords 96–7
P^6_4 *see* passing six-four chord
pulse 51

quadruple meter 55–8
quadruplet 61
quality conversion 171, 176n1, 277
quartal chords 242–3
quick peek *see* resolution quick peek
quintal chords 242–3

referential collections 223–33; diatonic collection 223–6; hexatonic collection 232–3; interaction among 253; octatonic collection 228–31, 253–4; pentatonic collection 226–8; whole-tone collection 231–2
reflection (as inversion on pc wheel) 230, 249–50
refrain 275, 279
regular meters 55
relative keys 33
repetition 34, 60, 99, 130–1, 237n4, 238–9, 279
resolution quick peek: for +6 chords 180–1; for V^7 119; introduction to 106–7; for vii^{o6} 106–7; for vii^{o7} 122–3
rests 53
retardations 90
retrograde: of motives 131; of twelve-tone rows 261–2, 264–5
retrograde-inversion: of motives 131; of twelve-tone rows 261–2, 264–5
R-forms *see* row transformations
rhythm 60–2, 130–1; notation of 54–5; serialization of 266–7
Riemann, H. 104n1, 222n12
riff 60, 130, 139n1

RI-forms *see* row transformations
ritardando 51
Roman numerals 41–4
root 39–40
root position 43–4
root-position progressions 83–4; root motion by fifth 83–4; root motion by second 84; root motion by third 83
rotation: of the axis progression 281, 283n9; of a scale 28n2, 224–6; as transposition on pc wheel 230, 249–50, 254, 256, 259n8
row forms *see* row transformations
row transformations 261–2; inversion 261–2; labeling row forms 264–5; prime form 261–2; retrograde 261–2; retrograde-inversion 261–2
rubato 51

SATB 77; labeling chords in 84–5; spacing of chords in 78–9; voice leading in 80–4; voicing chords in 78–9
scale degrees 20–3; names of 23–4; melodic tendencies of 25–6
scales 20–6; acoustic scale *see* acoustic collection; diatonic scales 20, *see also* diatonic collection; harmonic minor scale 28n3; hexatonic scale *see* hexatonic collection; major scale 20–1; melodic minor scale 28n3; minor scale 21–3; modes *see* diatonic modes; natural minor scale 28n3; natural scale 5, 12, 20; octatonic scale *see* octatonic collection; pentatonic scale *see* pentatonic collection; whole-tone scale *see* whole-tone collection
secondary beams 54–5
secondary dominant seventh chords 149–54
secondary dominants 149–57; altered secondary dominants 201–2; secondary dominant seventh chords 149–54; secondary leading-tone seventh chords 154–7
secondary leading tone 151; as tendency tone 151, 155–6
secondary leading-tone seventh chords 154–7
secondary mixture *see* quality conversion
second inversion 43–4; triads in 109–14
secundal chords 243
segmentation (in pc set analysis) 252–4
segments (of a twelve-tone row) 216
semitonal voice leading 222n9, 253; *see also* triadic transformations
semitone *see* half step
sequence: harmonic sequences 140–4; of motive 131
serialism 260–7
series *see* prolongation
set class 250–2

set theory 247–56
seventh (chord member) 40; as coloristic dissonance 272; as function enhancer 97, 118, 125, 170; the passing seventh 119–20; resolution of 118–21, 151, 170, 199, 201; as tendency tone 78, 118–21, 122–3, 125, 151, 155–6, 199, 201
seventh chords 39–40, 118–26; diatonic seventh chords 42–3, 95n5; in jazz 271–2, 275–9, 283n2; nonfunctional transformations of 213–16, 222n12; *see also* dominant seventh chord; embellishing chords; leading-tone seventh chord; secondary dominants; supertonic seventh chord
sextuplet 60–1
sharp 6–7
sharp keys 30
similar motion 67
simple intervals 16
simple meters 56
simple values 51–2
six-four chords 109–14; arpeggiating six-four chord 109–10; cadential six-four chord 112–14; neighbor six-four chord (N$_4^6$) 110–11, 117n6; passing six-four chord (P$_4^6$) 111–12; pedal six-four 117n6; second inversion triads 43–4, 109–14
sixth chords 271
small natural intervals 12
spaces (of staff) 4
spacing (of a chord) 78–9
species counterpoint 67, 73n1; first species 68; second species 68–9; third species 69–70; fourth species 70
split-third chords 241
staff 4; grand staff 6, 77
standard song form *see* AABA form
static motion 66
stems 52; notation of 54–5, 77
stepwise motion 24, 81
strophic form 280–1
subdominant scale degree (4̂) 23–4
subdominant triad (IV, iv) 41–2, 96–7; in first inversion 100–1, 105–6
submediant scale degree (6̂) 23–4; in minor melodies 25–6; in the minor scale 21–4
submediant triad (vi, VI) 41–2, 96–7; in deceptive cadences 133; in deceptive resolutions 98–9, 133, 170; in first inversion 108–9
subset (of referential collection) 226, 253–4
substitution 99–100, 106, 117n3, 125–6, 132, 170, 181–2, 276–9
subtonic scale degree 23–4; in minor melodies 25–6; in the minor scale 21–4

subtonic triad (VII, ♭VII) 42, 97, 140–1, 168–70, 281
supertonic scale degree (2̂) 23–4
supertonic seventh chord 42–3, 118, 125–6, 159n2, 169
supertonic triad (ii, ii°) 41–2, 96–7; in first inversion 106
sus chord 270–1
suspended chord *see* sus chord
suspended tonality 215–19
suspension 70, 90, 208n5; in harmonic sequences 143–4
symmetry: axis of symmetry 230, 237n3, 239–40, 249–50, 258n4, 262–3; and centricity 239–40; inversional symmetry 250, 254–5, 285; of the octatonic collection 228–30; and set-class membership 250; of vii^{o7} 193–4, 222n8; transpositional symmetry 250, 254–5, 285; of the whole-tone collection 231–2
syncopation 62
syntactic analysis 98–100, 104n3
syntax *see* tonal syntax

T *see* Tonic function
target chord (of secondary dominants) 150–6
T–D–T *see* tonal syntax
tempo 51; changes of 51
tendency tones 119; altered scale degrees and chord members as 159n2, 159n3, 169, 170, 177, 182–3, 199–202; and +6 chords 179–81; chord sevenths as 78, 118–21, 122–3, 125, 151, 155–6, 199, 201; leading tone as 25, 78, 119–24, 129n2; ninths as 199–200; notes of tritone as 107, 117n2, 118–19, 129n2, 151, 278; secondary leading tones as 151, 155–6
tenor clef 5–6, 10n2, 30
THC *see* tonicized half cadence
third (chord member) 39; absence of 212–13, 222n3, 270–1; of V in minor keys 42, 118; Picardy third 171; split-third chords 241
third inversion 43–4; V^2 120–2; vii^{o2} 123
thirteenths 272–5
32-bar form *see* AABA form
tie 52–3, 55; and suspensions 90; and syncopation 62
time signatures 56–8
tonal ambiguity 211–12, 281
tonal center 29, 34, 160, 212–14
tonal function 42, 96–101; and context 42, 96, 98–100, 105, 204, 214; and scale-degree contents 97–8, 105; and seventh chord quality 271–2
tonal motion (of a phrase) 132
tonal progress 132

tonal syntax (T–PD–D–T) 98–9; embedded statements of 124; and phrases 132; suspension of 140–1, 215–19; tonicizations embedded in 152–3, 181–2
tone clusters 243
tone network *see* Tonnetz
tone row *see* twelve-tone row
Tonic function (T) 96–8
tonicization 149–57, 277–8; with altered dominants 201–2; and modulation 160; and syntactic analysis 152–3
tonicized half cadence 153
tonic scale degree ($\hat{1}$) 23–4; and melodic tendency 24–5
tonic triad (I, i) 41–2, 96–7; in first inversion 100–1, 105–6
Tonnetz 217–19
T-operation 230, 249, 259n8
total serialism *see* integral serialism
T–PD–D–T *see* tonal syntax
transformation: of intervals 14–15; of pitch-class sets 249–50, 255–6; of seventh chords 213–15; of triads *see* triadic transformations; of a twelve-tone row 260–2
transposition: of motives 131; of pc sets 249–50, 255–6; of referential collections 223–33; of twelve-tone rows 260–5
transpositional combination 253–4
transpositional symmetry *see* symmetry
treble clef 5–6
triad 39–40; diatonic triads 41–2; in first inversion 43–4, 100–1, 105–9, 143–4; in second inversion 43–4, 109–14
triadic transformations (P, R, and L) 215–19
triple meter 55–8

triplet 60–1
Tristan chord 221, 222n5
tritone 12; notes as tendency tones 107, 117n2, 118–19, 129n2, 151, 278
tritone substitution 277–9
truck driver's gear change 167n2; *see also* phrase modulation
turnaround 275, 281, 283n5
12-bar blues progression 280
twelve-tone matrix 262; building a matrix 262–4; reading row forms in 264–5
twelve-tone row 260–1; transformations of 261–2
two-beat bass 109–10

unequal fifths 82, 107, 123
unison doubling 82–3, 239
unresolved dissonance 212–14
upbeat 55–6

value 51–2
verse-chorus strophic form 281
vocal tenor clef 187n2
voice crossing 82–3
voice exchange 111–12, 181–2
voice leading 66; counterpoint 67–70; economy of motion 81; four-part voice leading 77, 80–4; motion between two voices 66–7; root-position progressions 83–4
voice overlap 82–3, 88n6
voicing *see* chord voicing

whole step 7, 19n1
whole-tone collection 231–2
whole-tone scale *see* whole-tone collection